the Unofficial Guide® to Miami and the Keys

3rd Edition

Also available from Macmillan Travel:

Mini-Mickey: The Pocket-Sized Unofficial Guide to Walt Disney World, by Bob Sehlinger

The Unofficial Disney Companion: The Inside Story of Walt Disney World and the Man Behind the Mouse, by Eve Zibart

The Unofficial Guide to Atlanta, by Fred Brown and Bob Sehlinger

The Unofficial Guide to Branson, Missouri, by Bob Sehlinger and Eve Zibart

The Unofficial Guide to Chicago, by Joe Surkiewicz and Bob Sehlinger

The Unofficial Guide to Cruises, by Kay Showker and Bob Sehlinger

The Unofficial Guide to Disneyland, by Bob Sehlinger

The Unofficial Guide to the Great Smoky and Blue Ridge Mountains, by Bob Sehlinger and Joe Surkiewicz

The Unofficial Guide to Las Vegas, by Bob Sehlinger

The Unofficial Guide to New Orleans, by Eve Zibart with Bob Sehlinger

The Unofficial Guide to New York, by Eve Zibart and Bob Sehlinger with Jim Leff

The Unofficial Guide to San Francisco, by Joe Surkiewicz and Bob Sehlinger with Richard Sterling

The Unofficial Guide to Skiing in the West, by Lito Tejada-Flores, Peter Shelton, Seth Masia, and Bob Sehlinger

The Unofficial Guide to Walt Disney World, by Bob Sehlinger

The Unofficial Guide to Washington, D.C., by Bob Sehlinger and Joe Surkiewicz with Eve Zibart

the Unofficial Guide® to Miami and the Keys

3rd Edition

Bob Sehlinger
and
Joe Surkiewicz

Macmillan • USA

To Ann Lembo, Esquire—best friend . . . and counselor
—J. S.
For Cotton and Janice, Bon voyage
—B. S.

Every effort has been made to ensure the accuracy of information throughout this book. Bear in mind, however, that prices, schedules, etc., are constantly changing. Readers should always verify information before making final plans.

Macmillan Travel
A Simon & Schuster Macmillan Company
1633 Broadway
New York, New York 10019-6785

Copyright © 1998 by Bob Sehlinger

All rights reserved. No part of this book may be reproduced or transmitted in any form or by any means, electronic or mechanical, including photocopying, recording, or by any information storage and retrieval system, without permission in writing from the publisher.

Produced by Menasha Ridge Press
Design by Barbara E. Williams

MACMILLAN is a registered trademark of Macmillan, Inc.
UNOFFICIAL GUIDE is a registered trademark of Simon & Schuster, Inc.

ISBN 0-02-862765-2
ISSN 1089-9146

Manufactured in the United States of America
10 9 8 7 6 5 4 3 2 1

Third edition

Contents

List of Illustrations

Acknowledgments

People from Miami are crazy about their town: they use words like young, vibrant, spicy, and seductive to describe its fun-in-the-sun climate, vibrant multiethnic culture, and lush, tropical beauty. Because Miami is not a prim and proper place—in fact, a threat of danger defines its persona—it wasn't always easy to get a handle on this unconventional city. Luckily, we got some help along the way.

Thanks to Michelle Abram of the Miami Convention and Visitors Bureau, who was unstinting in her efforts—almost always requested at the last minute—to get us all kinds of arcane information (for example, the latest crime statistics) and a fix on a convenient, yet cheap, hotel.

Lucy Cooper, for 15 years the restaurant critic at the *Miami Herald* and author of the cookbook *Southern Entertaining—A New Taste of the South* (Seaside Publishers) and *The Unofficial Guide to Dining in Miami and Southeastern Florida,* drew on her vast experience of South Florida's diversified array of dining spots to write our section on restaurants and dining.

Tara Solomon, familiar to *Miami Herald* readers as "The Queen of the Night," the South Beach night life columnist, delivered the straight scoop on South Florida night clubs and Miami's unique shopping opportunities.

Captain Jeff Cardenas, owner of The Salt Water Angler in Key West, took the time to explain to a novice the ins and outs of deep-sea fishing. Captain Ed Sides shared 20 years of scuba diving expertise for our section on underwater exploration.

To fulfill their task, the hotel inspection team of Grace Walton and Diane Kuhr endured sore feet, a cramped South Beach hotel room, and perennial parking hassles in Miami Beach. (But the weather was great.)

Finally, many thanks to Molly Burns, Holly Brown, Laura Poole, Caroline Carr, Sarah Nawrocki, and Ann Cassar, the pros who managed to transform all this effort into a book.

—*Joe Surkiewicz*

the Unofficial Guide® to Miami and the Keys

3rd Edition

Introduction

The Capital of the Caribbean

Mention Miami and most folks are hit with a flood of impressions:

- Broad beaches, white sand, palm trees, and a stunning and intoxicatingly beautiful city by the sea.
- Candy-colored Art Deco palaces shimmering in the hot sun, and sidewalks jammed with slim-hipped Euro boys and girls, gorgeous fashion models with portfolios tucked under their arms, and Lycra-clad Rollerbladers.
- Guns and cocaine, Al Capone, and "Miami Vice": a city awash in illegal money that proudly wears its reputation for crime and violence like a cheap perfume.

Vivid impressions, all, and totally in sync with this chamber-of-commerce message: Miami is the sun-and-fun capital of the universe, a jet-setter's paradise with a bad-boy reputation, a sun-drenched escape from the winter cold.

All of which is true.

Yet Miami is something else.

It's a city of two million where more people speak Spanish than English; a multicultural collage and ethnic grab bag; the new capital of Latin America, full of banks and financial institutions; one of the premier convention sites in the United States; *the* place to go for millions of well-heeled Latin American and European tourists.

To put it another way: For Americans, Miami is an international destination that doesn't require a passport.

Yet, to unprepared travelers, Miami's Hispanic soul can come as a shock. From the moment they deplane at Miami International Airport, these unwary vacationers and business travelers are confronted with a confusing Babel of foreign languages, the pungent odors of cigars and *cafe Cubano,* the highly charged hustle and bustle that says "we're not in Kansas anymore."

For visitors like these, Miami isn't really a city—it's a discordant clash of cultures that's best ignored in the rush to safe harbor at a beach or convention hall.

These folks are missing a lot of what this city has to offer: the chance to luxuriate in a warm, vibrant, and gregarious Latin culture, and the opportunity to experience an exotic metropolis where news from Havana, Caracas, or Bogotá can overshadow the latest scandal in Washington.

The unfamiliarity of the Latin culture to most Americans *does* make Miami intimidating to many visitors—especially if you step off the plane expecting to find a "normal" U.S. city.

It doesn't have to be this way for you.

This book is the reason why.

Inside, you'll find suggestions for things to do that reveal the essence of this young, vibrant, and uninhibited city. With this guidebook in hand, you'll discover why Miami is described with words such as *sensual, spicy,* and *seductive.*

We give visitors explicit directions on how to visit Little Havana; where to sample the best in Cuban, Haitian, and Caribbean cuisine; where you can walk down streets and hear Spanish, Creole, Yiddish, Russian, and German spoken within a single block. This book will introduce you to a culture that's outspoken and unrestrained, offering visitors a taste of a vivid street life like no other city in North America.

That's not all. The *Unofficial Guide* offers a critical analysis of the traditional attractions that have made Miami a legendary vacation destination: the sparkling white beaches; great family places such as Parrot Jungle, the Historical Museum of South Florida, and Metrozoo; the cityscapes made famous in "Miami Vice"; and the hip Art Deco District on Miami Beach.

You'll also find explicit instructions for a night on the town in Little Havana, reviews of Miami's best restaurants, the latest on the nation's hottest nightclub scene, and a guide to South Florida's unique shopping opportunities. We've also included timely advice about how to avoid this beautiful city's worst hassles: crime and traffic.

We'll tell you the best times of year to visit, how to save a few bucks on a hotel room, and where to find Miami's best views. This guide also points out the best places to take a walk, ride a bike, and play golf and tennis. You'll find tons of information that will save your feet and your wallet, not to mention your temper.

This guide is designed both for folks planning a family trip to Miami to enjoy its famous beaches, exciting night life, and beautiful outdoor scenery, and for business travelers who want to avoid the city's worst hassles. You'll find plenty of information on the Florida Keys, a vacation destination that draws more than a million visitors a year, and the Everglades, a destination close to Miami that shouldn't be missed.

We give you the information it takes to really enjoy this fabulous international tourist destination that's set beside the cool, blue waters of Biscayne Bay—a city with a sharp contemporary style and a downtown skyline that glows in the warm night air.

And who knows? Armed with this book, you may discover that Miami is more than just a sun-and-fun beach destination. You'll discover, as we did while researching this guidebook, why Miami is called the Capital of the Caribbean, and an exciting city that represents the future.

About This Guide

How Come "Unofficial"?

Most "official" guides to Miami and South Florida tout the well-known sights, promote the local restaurants and hotels indiscriminately, and leave out a lot of good stuff. This one is different.

Instead of pandering to the tourist industry, we'll tell you if it's not worth the wait for the mediocre food served in a well-known restaurant, we'll complain loudly about overpriced hotel rooms that aren't convenient to the beach or the convention center, and we'll guide you away from the crowds and congestion for a break now and then.

With its ethnic mix and high energy level, Miami is a town that can bewilder first-time visitors. We've sent in a team of evaluators who toured its beaches and popular attractions, ate in the area's best restaurants, performed critical evaluations of its hotels, and visited South Florida's best nightclubs. If a museum is boring or stopping at a roadside tourist attraction is a waste of time and money, we say so—and, in the process, hopefully make your visit more fun, efficient, and economical.

Creating a Guidebook

We got into the guidebook business because we were unhappy with the way travel guides make the reader work to get any usable information. Wouldn't it be nice, we thought, if we made guides that were easy to use?

Most guidebooks are compilations of lists. This is true regardless of whether the information is presented in list form or artfully distributed within pages of prose. There is insufficient detail in a list, and with prose the presentation can be tedious and contain large helpings of nonessential or only marginally useful information. Not enough wheat, so to speak, for nourishment in one instance, too much chaff in the other. Either way, these guides provide little more than departure points from which readers initiate their own quests.

Many guides are readable and well researched, but they tend to be difficult to use. To select a hotel, for example, a reader must study several pages of descriptions with only the names of the hotels in bold type breaking up the text. Because each description essentially deals with the same variables, it is difficult to recall what was said concerning a particular hotel. Readers generally have no alternative but to work through all the write-ups before beginning to narrow their choices. The presentation of restaurants, clubs, and attractions is similar except that even more reading is usually required. To use such a guide is to undertake an exhaustive research process that requires examining nearly as many options and possibilities as starting from scratch. Recommendations, if any, lack depth and conviction. These guides compound rather than solve problems by failing to narrow travelers' choices down to a thoughtfully considered, well-distilled, and manageable few.

How *Unofficial Guides* Are Different

Readers care about the author's opinion. The author, after all, *is* supposed to know what he or she is talking about. This, coupled with the fact that the traveler wants quick answers (as opposed to endless alternatives), dictates that authors should be explicit, prescriptive and, above all, direct. The *Unofficial Guide* tries to do just that. It spells out alternatives and recommends specific courses of action. It simplifies complicated destinations and attractions and allows the traveler to feel in control in the most unfamiliar environments. The objective of the *Unofficial Guide* is not to have the most information or all of the information; it aims to have the most accessible, useful information, unbiased by affiliation with any organization or industry.

Our authors and research team are completely independent from the attractions, restaurants, and hotels we describe. *The Unofficial Guide to Miami and the Keys* is designed for individuals and families traveling for the fun of it, as well as for business travelers and convention-goers, especially those visiting the Miami area for the first time. The guide is directed at value-conscious, consumer-oriented adults who seek a cost-effective, though not spartan, travel style.

Special Features

The *Unofficial Guide* incorporates the following special features:

- Friendly introductions to Miami's most fascinating neighborhoods.

- "Best of" listings giving our well-qualified opinions on things ranging from bagels to baguettes, four-star hotels to the best views of Miami by night.
- Listings that are keyed to your interests, so you can pick and choose.
- Advice to sight-seers on how to avoid crowds, advice to business travelers on how to avoid traffic and excessive cost.
- A zone system and maps to make it easy to find places you want to go to and avoid places you don't.
- Expert advice on avoiding Miami's notorious street and highway crime.
- A hotel chart that helps narrow your choices fast, according to your needs.
- Shorter listings that include only those restaurants, clubs, and hotels we think are worth considering.
- A detailed index and table of contents to help you find things quickly.

What you *won't* get:

- Long, useless lists where everything looks the same.
- Information that gets you somewhere you want to go at the worst possible time.
- Information without advice on how to use it.

How This Guide Was Researched and Written

While a lot of guidebooks have been written about Miami and the Keys, very little has been evaluative. Some guides come close to regurgitating the hotels' and tourist offices' own promotional material. In preparing this work, nothing was taken for granted. Each museum, monument, art gallery, hotel, restaurant, shop, and attraction was visited by a team of trained observers who conducted detailed evaluations and rated each according to formal criteria. Interviews were conducted to determine what tourists of all ages enjoyed most and least during their Miami visit.

While our observers are independent and impartial, we do not claim to have special expertise. Like you, we visit Miami as tourists or business travelers, noting our satisfaction or dissatisfaction.

The primary difference between the average tourist and the trained evaluator is the evaluator's skills in organization, preparation, and observation. The trained evaluator is responsible for much more than simply observing and cataloging. While the average tourist is gazing in awe as a 10,000-pound killer whale is leaping into the air at the Seaquarium, for instance, the professional is rating the show in terms of pace, how quickly crowds move, the location of rest rooms, and how well children can see the exhibits. The evaluator also checks out things such as other nearby attractions, alternative places to go if the line at a main attraction is too long, and where to find the best local lunch options. Observer teams use detailed checklists to analyze hotel rooms, restaurants, nightclubs, and attractions. Finally, evaluator ratings and observations are integrated with tourist reactions and the opinions of patrons for a comprehensive quality profile of each feature and service.

In compiling this guide, we recognize that tourists' ages, backgrounds, and interests will strongly influence their taste in Miami's wide array of activities and attractions and will account for a preference of one over another. Our sole objective is to provide the reader with sufficient description, critical evaluation, and pertinent data to make knowledgeable decisions of their own.

Letters and Comments from Readers

We expect to learn from our mistakes, as well as from the input of our readers, and to improve with each book and edition. Many of those who use the *Unofficial Guides* write to us making comments or sharing their own discoveries and lessons learned in Miami. We appreciate all such input, both positive and critical, and encourage our readers to continue writing. Readers' comments and observations will be frequently incorporated in revised editions of the *Unofficial Guide,* and will contribute immeasurably to its improvement.

How to Write the Authors:

Bob and Joe
The Unofficial Guide to Miami
P.O. Box 43059
Birmingham, AL 35243

When you write, be sure to put your return address on your letter as well as on the envelope—sometimes envelopes and letters get separated. And remember, our work takes us out of the office for long periods of time, so forgive us if our response is delayed. Also, please keep in mind that the authors do not sell *Unofficial Guides.*

Reader Survey

At the back of the guide you will find a short questionnaire that you can use to express opinions concerning your Miami visit. Clip the questionnaire along the dotted line and mail it to the above address.

How Information Is Organized: By Subject and by Geographic Zones

To give you fast access to information about the best of Miami and South Florida, we've organized material in several formats.

Hotels Because most people visiting Miami stay in one hotel for the duration of their trip, we have summarized our coverage of hotels in charts, maps, ratings, and rankings that allow you to quickly focus your decision-making process. We do not go on page after page describing lobbies and rooms which, in the final analysis, sound much the same. Instead, we concentrate on the variables that differentiate one hotel from another: location, size, room quality, services, amenities, and cost.

Restaurants We provide a lot of detail when it comes to restaurants. Because you will probably eat a dozen or more restaurant meals during your stay, and because not even *you* can predict what you might be in the mood for on Saturday night, we provide detailed profiles of the best restaurants in and around Miami.

Entertainment and Night Life Visitors frequently try several different clubs or nightspots during their stay. Because clubs and nightspots, like restaurants, are usually selected spontaneously after arriving in Miami, we believe detailed descriptions are warranted. The best nightspots and lounges in Miami are profiled by category under night life in the same section (see pages 101–127).

Geographic Zones Once you've decided where you're going, getting there becomes the issue. To help you do that, we have divided the Miami area into geographic zones.

Zone 1.	Miami Beach
Zone 2.	Miami North
Zone 3.	Miami South
Zone 4.	Southern Dade County
Zone 5.	The Florida Keys

All profiles of hotels, restaurants, and nightspots include zone numbers. If you are staying at the Indian Creek Hotel, for example, and are interested in dinner at a Japanese restaurant, scanning the restaurant profiles for restaurants in Zone 1 (Miami Beach) will provide you with the best choices.

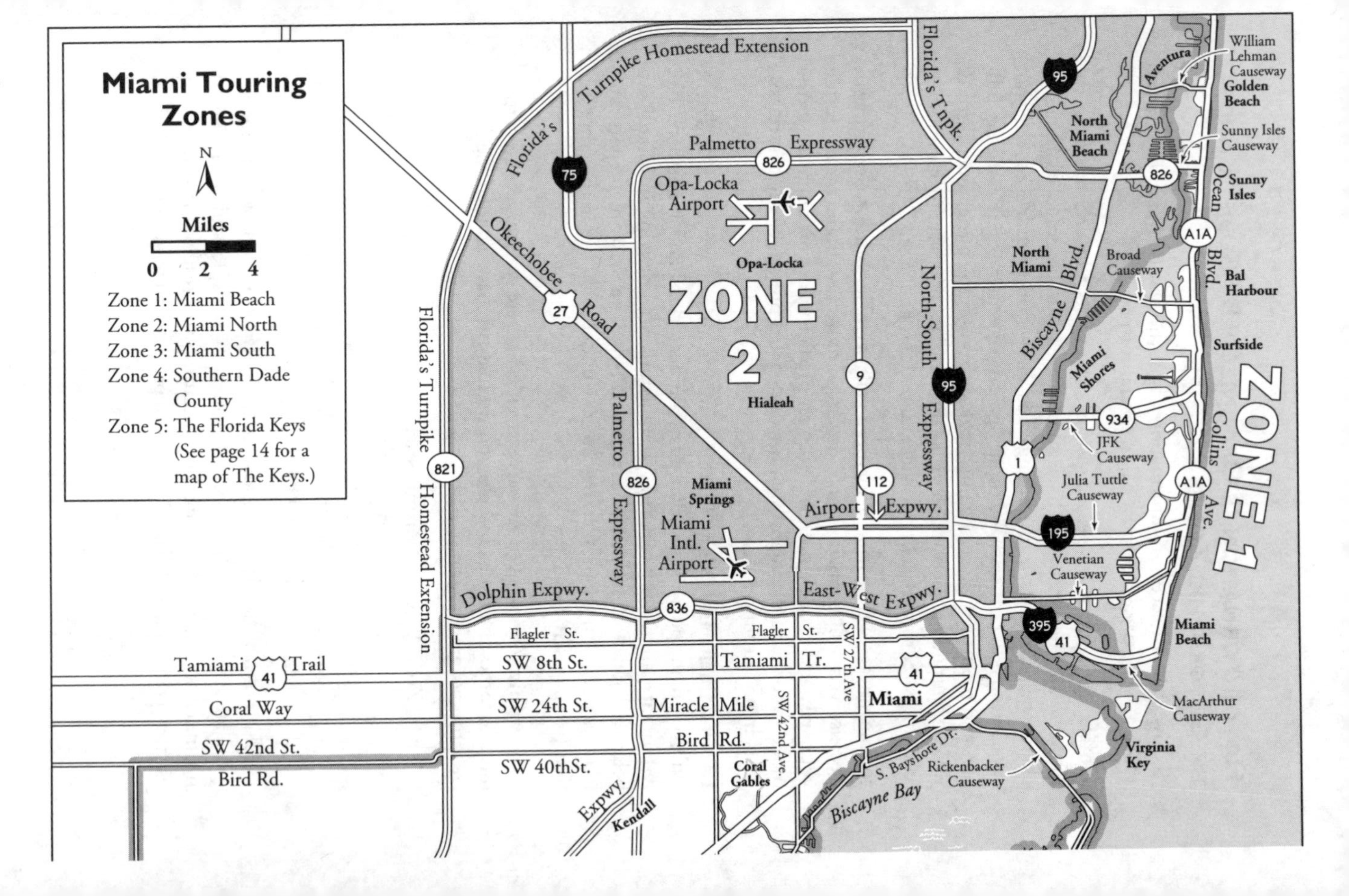

Miami Touring Zones
N
Miles
0 2 4
Zone 1: Miami Beach
Zone 2: Miami North
Zone 3: Miami South
Zone 4: Southern Dade County
Zone 5: The Florida Keys (See page 14 for a map of The Keys.)
ZONE 1
ZONE 2
William Lehman Causeway
Golden Beach
Aventura
Sunny Isles Causeway
Sunny Isles
Ocean Blvd.
A1A
Bal Harbour
Surfside
Collins Ave.
826
North Miami Beach
95
Florida's Tnpk.
Turnpike Homestead Extension
Florida's
75
Palmetto Expressway
Opa-Locka Airport
Opa-Locka
Okeechobee Road
27
Hialeah
9
North-South Expressway
North Miami
Biscayne Blvd.
Broad Causeway
Miami Shores
934
JFK Causeway
1
Julia Tuttle Causeway
195
Venetian Causeway
395
41
Miami Beach
MacArthur Causeway
Virginia Key
Rickenbacker Causeway
S. Bayshore Dr.
Biscayne Bay
Florida's Turnpike Homestead Extension
821
Miami Springs
112
Airport Expwy.
Miami Intl. Airport
East-West Expwy.
Dolphin Expwy.
836
Flagler St.
SW 27th Ave
Tamiami Trail
SW 8th St.
Tamiami Tr.
Miami
Coral Way
SW 24th St.
Miracle Mile
SW 42nd Ave.
SW 42nd St.
Bird Rd.
SW 40thSt.
Coral Gables
Kendall Expwy.

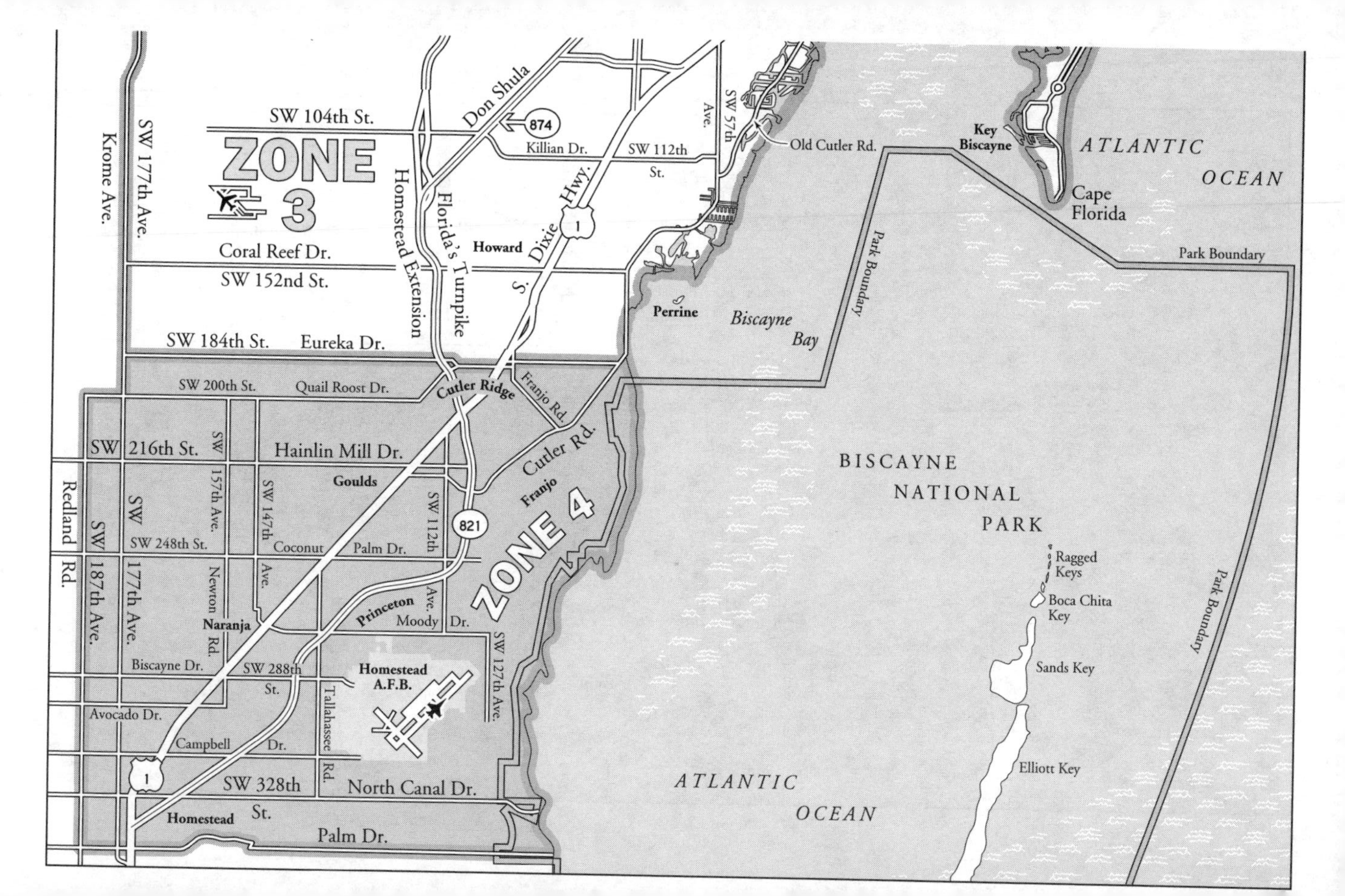
SW 104th St.
ZONE 3
Don Shula
874
Killian Dr.
SW 112th St.
SW 57th Ave.
Old Cutler Rd.
Key Biscayne
ATLANTIC OCEAN
Cape Florida
Park Boundary
Krome Ave.
SW 177th Ave.
Homestead Extension
Florida's Turnpike
S. Dixie Hwy.
1
Howard
Coral Reef Dr.
SW 152nd St.
Perrine
Biscayne Bay
Park Boundary
SW 184th St.
Eureka Dr.
SW 200th St.
Quail Roost Dr.
Cutler Ridge
Franjo Rd.
Cutler Rd.
SW 216th St.
Hainlin Mill Dr.
Goulds
Franjo
BISCAYNE NATIONAL PARK
SW 157th Ave.
SW 147th Ave.
SW 112th Ave.
821
ZONE 4
Redland Rd.
SW 187th Ave.
SW 177th Ave.
SW 248th St.
Coconut
Palm Dr.
Ragged Keys
Boca Chita Key
Newton Rd.
Naranja
Princeton
Moody Dr.
Park Boundary
Biscayne Dr.
SW 288th St.
Homestead A.F.B.
SW 127th Ave.
Sands Key
Avocado Dr.
Tallahassee Rd.
Campbell Dr.
SW 328th St.
North Canal Dr.
Elliott Key
ATLANTIC OCEAN
Homestead
Palm Dr.

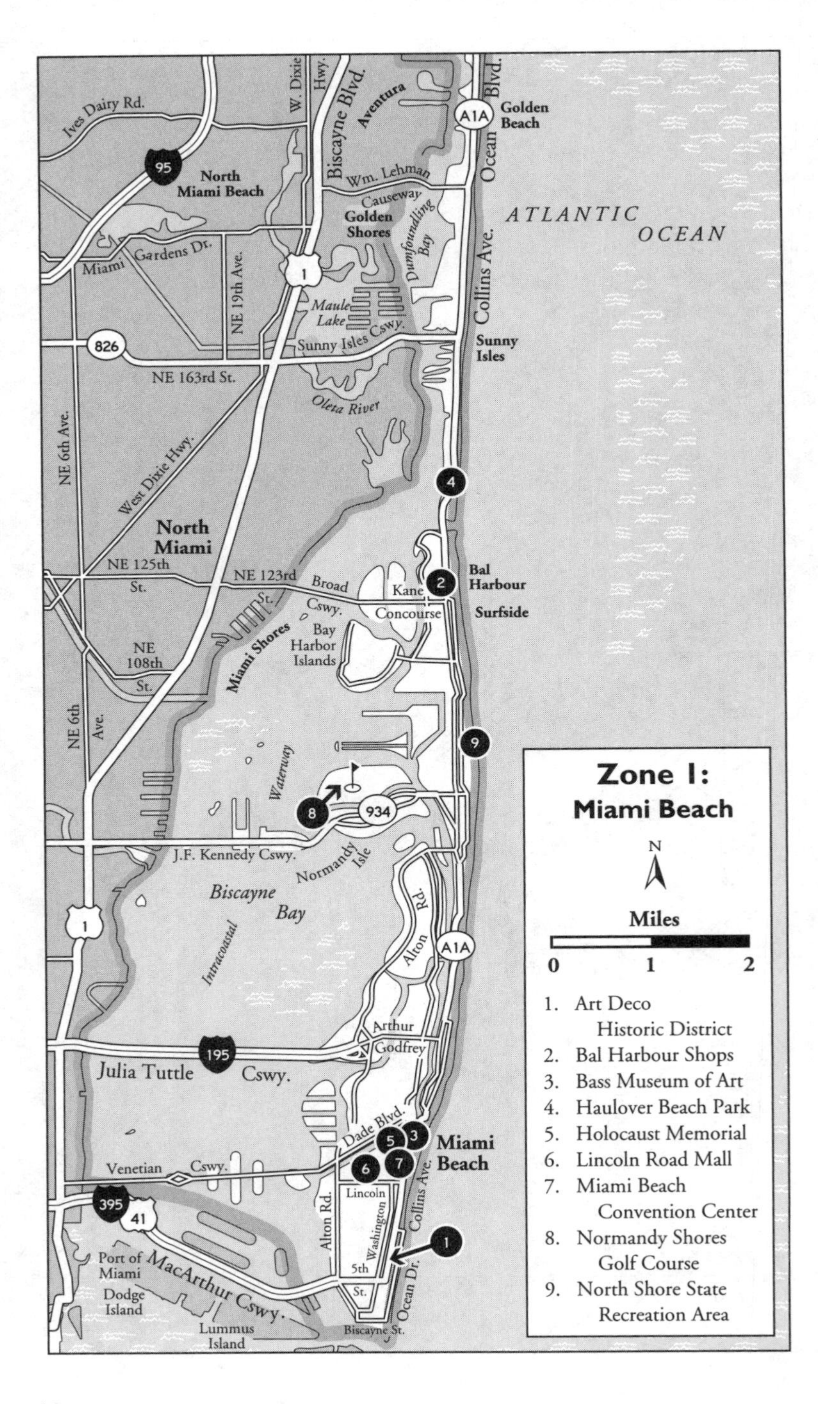

Zone I:
Miami Beach
N
Miles
0
1
2
1. Art Deco Historic District
2. Bal Harbour Shops
3. Bass Museum of Art
4. Haulover Beach Park
5. Holocaust Memorial
6. Lincoln Road Mall
7. Miami Beach Convention Center
8. Normandy Shores Golf Course
9. North Shore State Recreation Area
ATLANTIC OCEAN
Golden Beach
Aventura
North Miami Beach
Golden Shores
Sunny Isles
North Miami
Bal Harbour
Surfside
Miami Shores
Bay Harbor Islands
Biscayne Bay
Miami Beach
Ives Dairy Rd.
W. Dixie Hwy.
Biscayne Blvd.
Ocean Blvd.
Wm. Lehman Causeway
Dumfoundling Bay
Miami Gardens Dr.
NE 19th Ave.
Collins Ave.
Maule Lake
Sunny Isles Cswy.
NE 163rd St.
Oleta River
NE 6th Ave.
West Dixie Hwy.
NE 125th St.
NE 123rd St.
Broad Cswy.
Kane Concourse
NE 108th St.
Waterway
J.F. Kennedy Cswy.
Normandy Isle
Intracoastal
Alton Rd.
Arthur Godfrey
Julia Tuttle Cswy.
Dade Blvd.
Venetian Cswy.
Lincoln
Washington
5th St.
Port of Miami
MacArthur Cswy.
Dodge Island
Lummus Island
Biscayne St.
Ocean Dr.
A1A
95
1
826
934
195
395
41

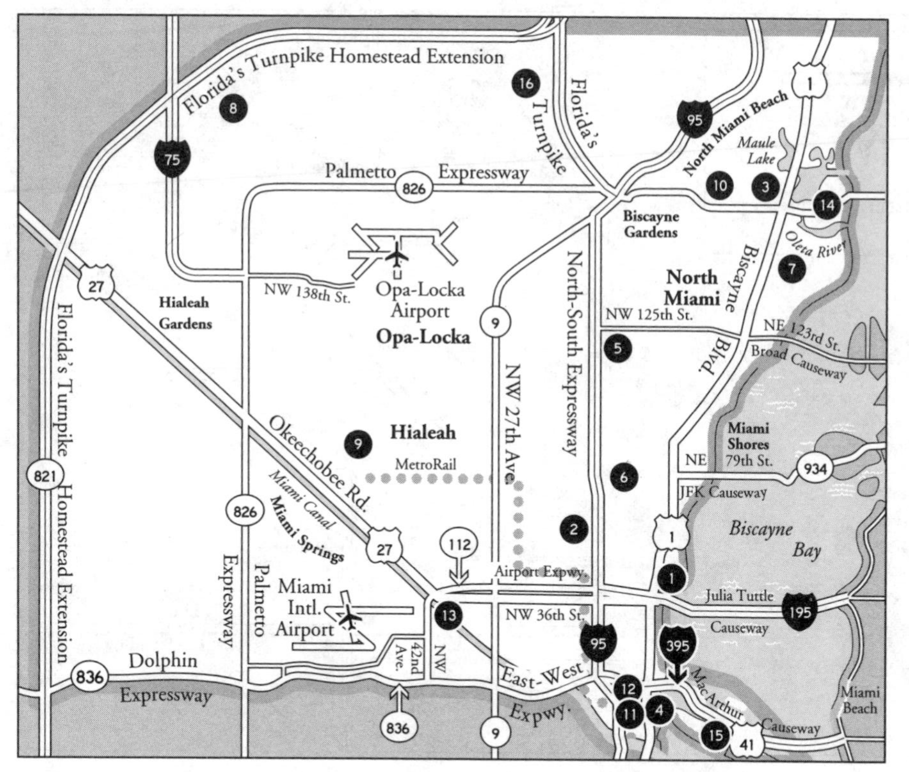

Zone 2: Miami North

N

Miles

0 1 2

1. American Police
   Hall of Fame and Museum
2. African Heritage
   Cultural Arts Center
3. Ancient Spanish Monastery
4. Bayside Marketplace
5. Biscayne Dog Track
6. Caribbean Marketplace
7. Florida International University
8. Golf Club of Miami
9. Hialeah Park
10. Mall at 163rd Street
11. Metro-Dade Cultural Center
12. Miami Arena
13. Miami Jai Alai
14. Oleta River State Recreation Area
15. Port of Miami
16. Pro Player Stadium

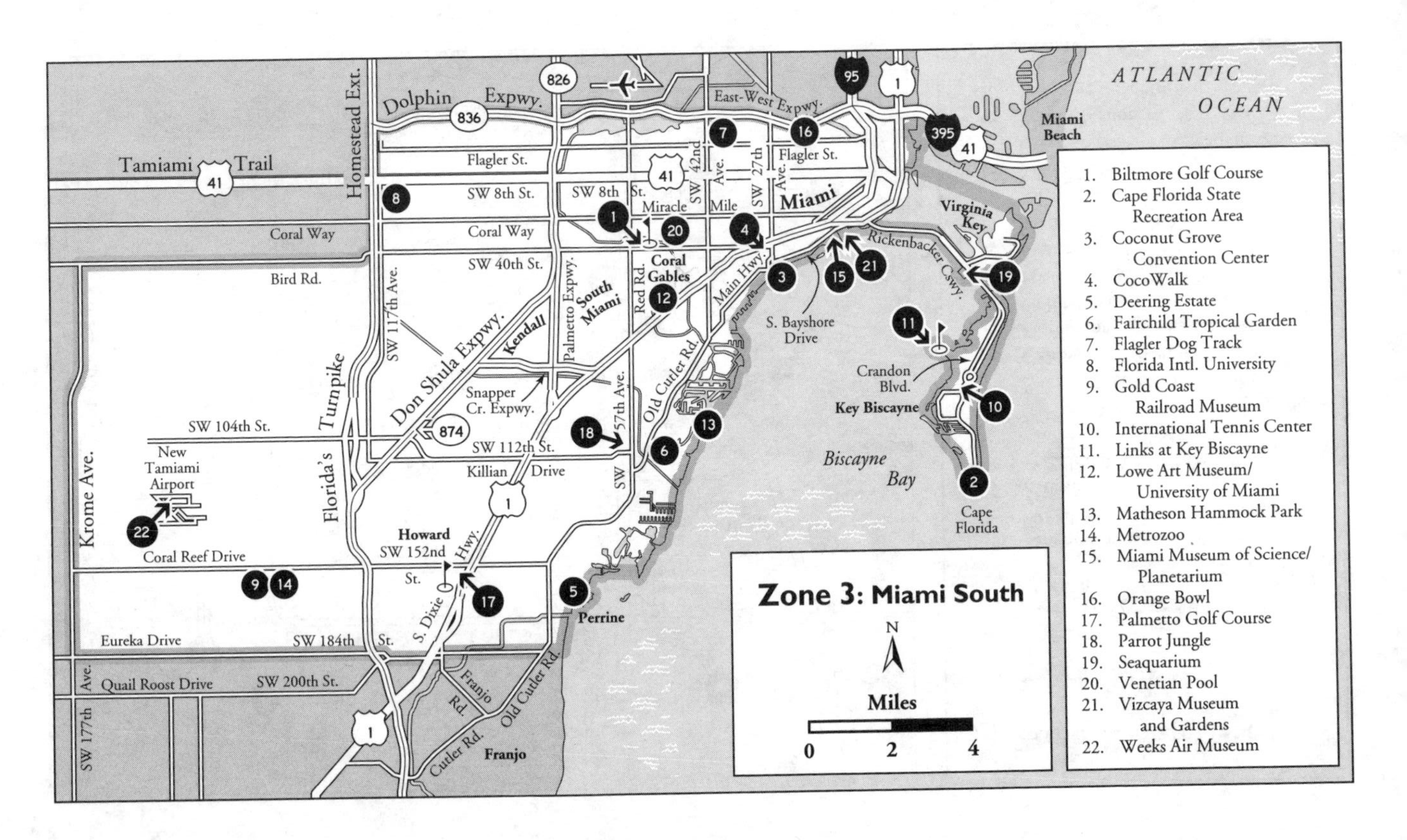
Zone 3: Miami South
ATLANTIC OCEAN
Miami Beach
Virginia Key
Key Biscayne
Biscayne Bay
Cape Florida
Crandon Blvd.
Rickenbacker Cswy.
S. Bayshore Drive
Miami
Coral Gables
South Miami
Kendall
Howard
Perrine
Franjo
Tamiami Trail
Dolphin Expwy.
East-West Expwy.
Homestead Ext.
Flagler St.
SW 8th St.
Coral Way
SW 40th St.
Bird Rd.
Miracle Mile
SW 42nd Ave.
SW 27th Ave.
Main Hwy.
Red Rd.
Palmetto Expwy.
Don Shula Expwy.
Snapper Cr. Expwy.
SW 117th Ave.
Florida's Turnpike
SW 104th St.
SW 112th St.
Killian Drive
SW 57th Ave.
Old Cutler Rd.
S. Dixie Hwy.
SW 152nd St.
Coral Reef Drive
Eureka Drive
SW 184th St.
Quail Roost Drive
SW 200th St.
SW 177th Ave.
Krome Ave.
Franjo Rd.
Cutler Rd.
New Tamiami Airport
N
Miles
0 2 4
1. Biltmore Golf Course
2. Cape Florida State Recreation Area
3. Coconut Grove Convention Center
4. CocoWalk
5. Deering Estate
6. Fairchild Tropical Garden
7. Flagler Dog Track
8. Florida Intl. University
9. Gold Coast Railroad Museum
10. International Tennis Center
11. Links at Key Biscayne
12. Lowe Art Museum/ University of Miami
13. Matheson Hammock Park
14. Metrozoo
15. Miami Museum of Science/ Planetarium
16. Orange Bowl
17. Palmetto Golf Course
18. Parrot Jungle
19. Seaquarium
20. Venetian Pool
21. Vizcaya Museum and Gardens
22. Weeks Air Museum

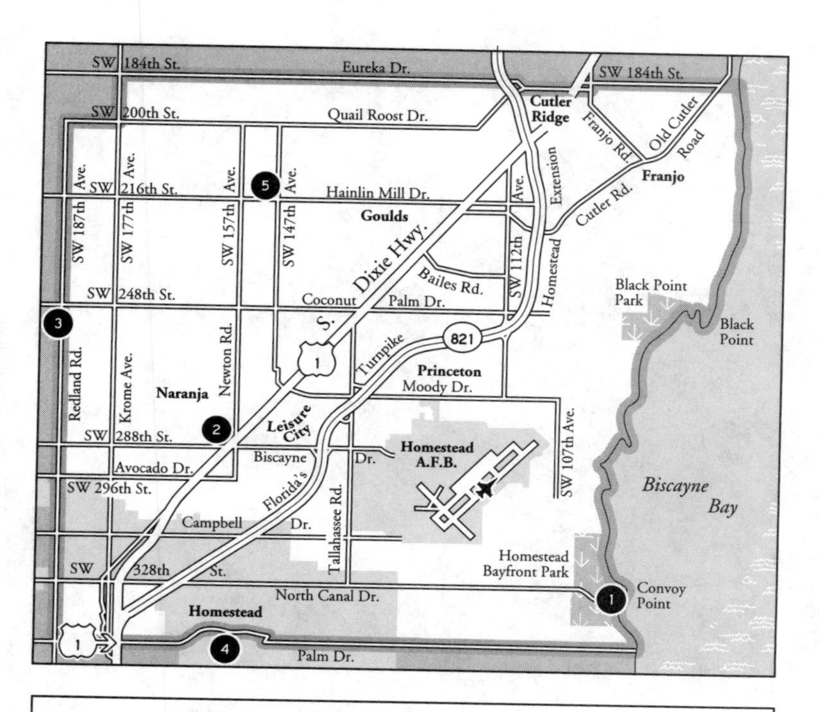

Zone 4: Southern Dade County

1. Biscayne National Park
2. Coral Castle
3. Fruit and Spice Park
4. Keys Gate Golf Club
5. Monkey Jungle

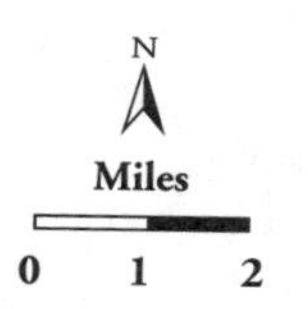

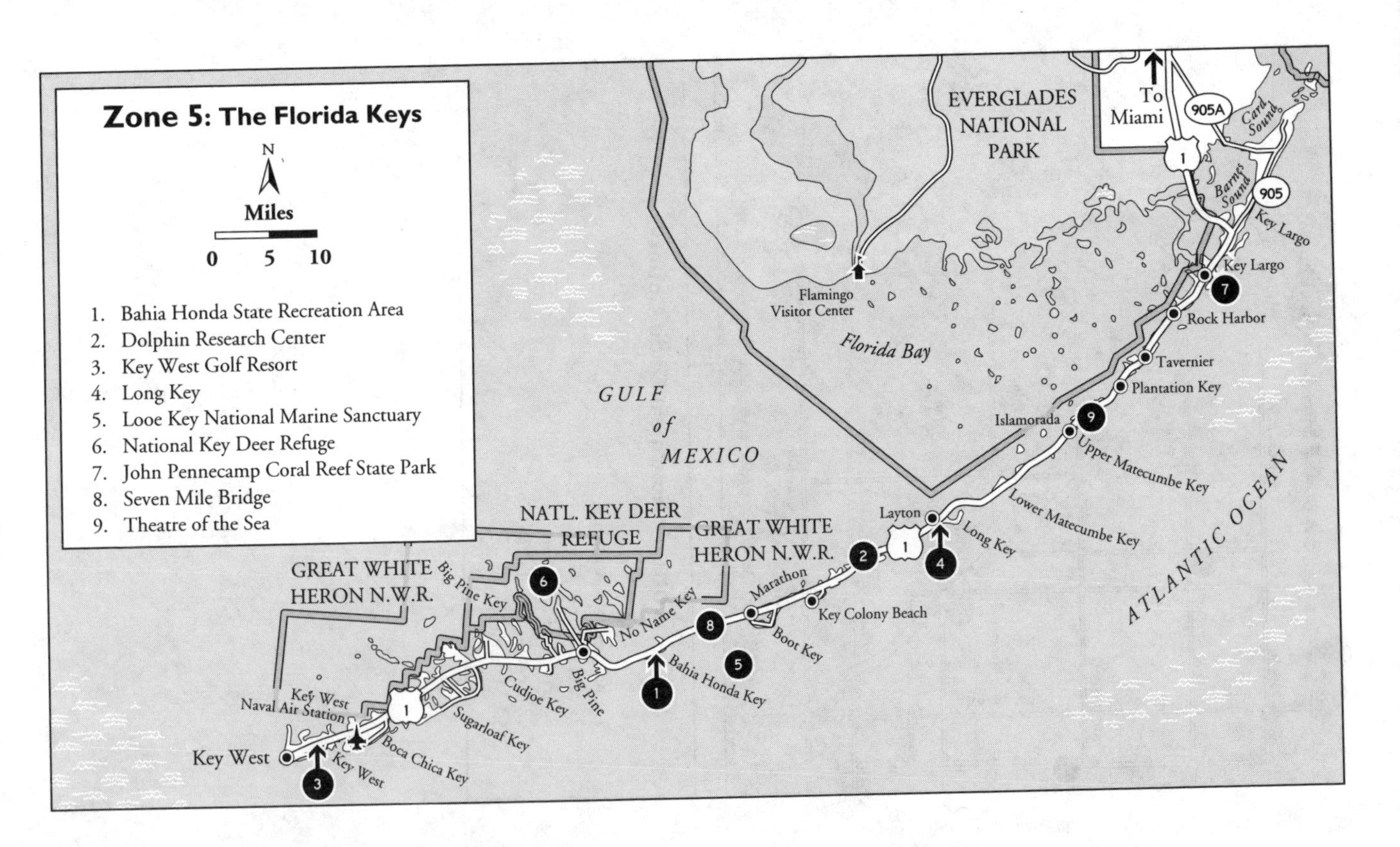
Zone 5: The Florida Keys
N
Miles
0 5 10
1. Bahia Honda State Recreation Area
2. Dolphin Research Center
3. Key West Golf Resort
4. Long Key
5. Looe Key National Marine Sanctuary
6. National Key Deer Refuge
7. John Pennecamp Coral Reef State Park
8. Seven Mile Bridge
9. Theatre of the Sea
EVERGLADES NATIONAL PARK
To Miami
905A
905
1
Card Sound
Barnes Sound
Key Largo
Key Largo
Rock Harbor
Tavernier
Plantation Key
Islamorada
Upper Matecumbe Key
Lower Matecumbe Key
Flamingo Visitor Center
Florida Bay
GULF of MEXICO
ATLANTIC OCEAN
Layton
Long Key
NATL. KEY DEER REFUGE
GREAT WHITE HERON N.W.R.
GREAT WHITE HERON N.W.R.
Marathon
Key Colony Beach
Boot Key
No Name Key
Bahia Honda Key
Big Pine Key
Big Pine
Cudjoe Key
Sugarloaf Key
Key West Naval Air Station
Key West
Key West
Boca Chica Key

Part One

Planning Your Visit to Miami

Understanding the City: A Brief History of Miami

For an American city, Miami is unique: the majority of the population is Hispanic and the city vibrates with an entrepreneurial spirit that drives Miami's breathtakingly—and, in traffic, nerve-wrackingly—frenetic pace. Dominated by Cuban entrepreneurs—from the more than 600,000 residents of Cuban birth or descent who live in South Florida—Hispanic-owned businesses set the high-pitched corporate rhythm of Miami.

The Cubans' fast-paced commercial spirit is embodied in everything from family-owned grocery stores to huge corporations and banks. The roots of this hard-charging business community go back to the first Cuban refugees fleeing the Castro regime in the late 1950s—people from the entrepreneurial and professional classes who often arrived penniless but brought with them the skills and drive to become successfully self-employed in the United States.

They came to the right place. Historically, the success of the hard-working new immigrants fits a Miami pattern of boom and bust that began not very long ago. After all, the city was founded only a century ago on a long-shot business gamble that paid off. Through the decades that followed, Miami's history was a roller-coaster ride of dizzying successes and precipitous declines.

A Woman with a Dream

While South Florida's mild winters had been attracting visitors from the north for years in the mid- and late 1800s, it took an idea from a woman from Cleveland named Julia Tuttle to create the city of Miami. After settling on the north bank of the Miami River in 1891, Tuttle began to plan her city—and worked to find a railroad magnate who would extend a line south to the tip of the Florida peninsula.

Henry M. Flagler was one of the railroad men Tuttle tried to entice. His line reached Palm Beach in 1893, but he said he wasn't interested in extending it another 66 miles to tiny Miami. That is, until the winter of 1894–95.

A killer freeze struck Florida that winter and destroyed most of the valuable citrus fruit crops—but the cold didn't extend as far south as Miami, where the orange blossoms continued to bloom. The legend is that Tuttle sent a simple, eloquent message to Flagler as a final plea to extend his railroad line—a single orange blossom. Whether the legend is true or not, Flagler changed his mind and the line to Miami was completed on April 15, 1896. All 300 residents of Miami turned out to greet the locomotive—and a new era.

The Early Twentieth Century

The pace of development started to pick up. Within a few months a newspaper rolled off the press, local citizens voted to incorporate the town, streets were laid out, and churches and schools were established. The city was already promoting itself as "America's sun porch."

A modest boom resulted in the early years of the twentieth century. Swamps were drained (marking the beginning of the demise of the Everglades), Government Cut (the future Port of Miami) was dug across the lower end of Miami Beach to improve access to Miami's harbor, and Flagler extended his railroad farther south to Key West in 1912.

Thousands of people made the move south to take advantage of the year-round warmth and sunshine of Miami. In 1915, the citizens of Miami Beach voted to incorporate and elected a mayor, J. N. Lummus. The south end of the island already boasted several casinos, and holiday hotels began sprouting up. In Miami, national advertising attracted more residents, including the rich and famous, who built fabulous waterfront estates. The most lavish was Vizcaya, finished in 1916 by James Deering, a founder of International Harvester.

The Roaring Twenties

Then the Roaring Twenties arrived, along with developers who carved up nearby farmland into subdivisions. The city's population doubled between 1920 and 1923. Soon, Miami's growth turned into a feeding frenzy as dozens of new communities sprang up. It was also the era of Prohibition—and rum runners had a field day along South Florida's impossible-to-patrol coast. Mobsters moved in and operated with virtual immunity from the law. The city's reputation as a place teetering on both the moral and geographical edge of America had begun.

The most famous community to spring up during the '20s was Coral Gables, a planned community of Mediterranean homes, wide boulevards, and meticulous landscaping. George Merrick, Coral Gables' developer, poured millions of dollars into the development—including a lot of money for advertising, further fueling the nation's fascination with Miami. Merrick paid silver-tongued orator William Jennings Bryan $100,000 to tout Coral Gables at the exclusive community's Venetian Pool, a former rock pit transformed into a tropical paradise of waterfalls, caves, and lush landscaping.

Miami in the early '20s was real-estate crazy. Prices spiraled as property changed hands once, twice, three times. But most of the profits were on paper. Toward the end of 1925 the bottom began to fall out of the boom, sales at Coral Gables began to decline, and railroads announced an embargo of all but essential freight so they could repair their tracks, cutting off the supply of building materials.

The Pendulum Swings

But it took an act of nature to deliver a near-knockout blow. A hurricane struck on September 17, 1926, killing more than 100 people and leaving Miami in chaos. Houses were smashed, businesses were destroyed, boats were thrown onto dry land. National headlines screamed, "Miami Is Wiped Out!"—which was nearly the case.

Over the next few years, Miami's population fled northward. Local leaders such as Merrick went bankrupt. But it wasn't all bad news: Some money came to Miami from outsiders who purchased Hialeah racetrack, the city's aviation industry was born, and airports were built. During the Great Depression, Greynolds and Matheson Hammock Parks were constructed by the Civilian Conservation Corps.

Slowly, tourism began to pick up in the '30s, especially in Miami Beach, where new, "modern" hotels and apartments proliferated on Collins Avenue. Northerners swarmed south again to escape cold winters—and the Depression. More than 500 Art Deco structures were built and tourists flocked to "futuristic" Miami Beach.

War . . . and Another Boom

The recovery didn't last long, however. The Japanese bombing of Pearl Harbor in 1941 and the U.S. declaration of war killed tourism. Nor did it help when a German U-boat torpedoed a tanker in full view of the Florida coast in February 1942. The city's hotels were empty.

That is, until the soldiers came to be trained in the warm climate of South Florida. By the end of 1942 the military had turned 147 hotels into barracks and many hotels into temporary hospitals for wounded soldiers. GIs trained on Miami Beach and German prisoners of war were interned at camps in suburban Kendall and Homestead.

After the war, thousands of former soldiers returned to South Florida with their families, became students on the GI Bill, and crowded the University of Miami. There was a new housing boom in Miami. Farms were transformed into suburbs, and by the end of the '50s the population of Greater Miami was nearing one million. Arthur Godfrey broadcast his national TV show from Bal Harbour; glamorous, oversized hotels were built on Miami Beach; and air conditioning, once a luxury, became a necessity that tamed the scorching Miami summers. The future of Miami looked good in the mid-'50s.

A Revolution Revolutionizes Miami

But it was to change radically after Fidel Castro deposed Cuban dictator Fulgencio Batista in 1959. After Castro declared himself a socialist, confiscated property, and nationalized many island businesses, thousands of Cubans left Havana every day—many with nothing more than the clothes they wore. Most of them came to Miami. Almost overnight, entire neighborhoods filled with people speaking only Spanish.

After the failed, CIA-led Bay of Pigs invasion of Cuba in 1961 (many exiled leaders still believe they were betrayed by the United States) and the Cuban missile crisis of 1962 (in which Russia agreed to remove its missiles in return for a U.S. promise not to invade Cuba), it looked like the Cubans were in Miami to stay. Over the years, thousands of political refugees fled Cuba on "freedom flights" to Miami, expanding the city's Hispanic population base. By 1973, the Cuban population of Miami had swelled to 300,000.

In the '60s and '70s, another wave of immigrants moved to Miami: Jewish retirees from the north. By 1975, 300,000 Jews lived in Greater Miami, making the city's Jewish community second only to New York's in size. Most are concentrated in Miami Beach, and today the city serves as the de facto capital for retired American Jews during the winter months.

Ethnic Tension and the White Powder Trade

Miami, alas, is no melting pot. Urban renewal and hard-charging Cubans were squeezing out—and putting the economic squeeze on—Miami's African American community as many jobs were taken by recent immigrants. In 1968, Miami had its first race riot when Liberty City exploded as Richard Nixon was giving his acceptance speech at the Republican National Convention in Miami Beach.

In the 1970s, drugs began playing a big role in Miami as big money poured into the city to satisfy America's demand for illegal drugs. Yet, at the same time, the legitimate business community prospered; the Cuban community, no longer made up of penniless refugees, thrived and ran successful businesses throughout Miami.

Although a recession in the early '70s was a setback, Miami was booming again at the end of the decade. The city had turned into an international banking center as money flowed in from Latin America, rapid transit construction was under way, and the downtown area was being revitalized.

Then, more setbacks. In 1980, more blacks and disadvantaged Miamians rioted after a Tampa jury acquitted a white policeman of murdering a black man, Arthur McDuffie. Haitian "boat people" were landing almost daily on South Florida beaches. Then Fidel Castro announced that anyone who wanted to leave Cuba could do so—and Miami Cubans sailed to Mariel Harbor in Cuba to help them. They were forced to bring back some unwanted passengers as well: criminals and inmates of Cuba's prisons and mental institutions. The city struggled under 125,000 new "Marielito" refugees, many of them undesirables who tarnished the city's reputation.

A lot of the new refugees settled in South Beach, further driving the neighborhood of 1930s hotels and apartments even closer to the brink of slumdom; Miamians avoided the neighborhood at night. Some Anglo residents of Miami were fed up and many cars sported bumper stickers that read: "Will the last American leaving Miami please bring the flag?" A variation of "white flight" had set in, and Anglo residents began to leave Miami, often heading north to Broward County and beyond.

The early '80s were turbulent years in Miami. Drug dealers pumped more than $10 billion into the economy and the sale of handguns soared—as did the city's murder rate. In 1981, 621 people died violent deaths in Dade County and Miami earned a national reputation as Murder Capital USA.

"Miami Vice" and a Jet-Set Destination

But just as with every other crisis that preceded this one, Miami bounced back. A new building boom started downtown. Next, the city's image improved dramatically in 1984 when "Miami Vice" premiered on national television and revealed a city steeped in glamorous danger and lush, tropical beauty. In 1985, the city elected its first Cuban-born mayor, Xavier Suarez. The new Bayside Marketplace attracted tourists and shoppers to downtown, and the Pope paid a visit in September 1987.

Professional and college sports prospered in the late '80s with the introduction of the Miami Heat professional basketball squad, and downtown reverberated with the sound of race cars during the Miami Grand Prix. The University of Miami football team claimed number-one ranking three times and the new Joe Robbie Stadium (now Pro Player Stadium), home of the Miami Dolphins, hosted Super Bowls in 1989 and 1995.

In the late '80s South Beach, once nearly deserted at night and blighted, made a spectacular comeback. Hundreds of millions of dollars were spent renovating the Art Deco hotels and apartment buildings built in the '30s. Inhabited in the '70s and early '80s by Jewish retirees from colder climates, today these whimsical buildings are home to hotels, artists' lofts, chi-chi restaurants, oceanfront cafés, art galleries, and theaters. Jet-set celebrities such as Madonna, Robert De Niro, Cher, Mickey Rourke, and Sylvester Stallone are South Beach regulars. Today, instead of a place to avoid, South Beach is a place to be seen.

An International Destination

More changes: Miami is increasingly popular with tourists from outside the United States. The city is the gateway for U.S.–Latin American trade and swarms with visitors from Brazil, Colombia, and other countries surrounding the Caribbean basin. Miami's hot international reputation also draws tourists from Europe, especially Germans, Brits, and Scandinavians. (The only major tourist group that's yet to descend on Miami in large numbers is the Japanese—and that could change at any time.)

Even 1992's Hurricane Andrew—which devastated southern Dade County, left more than 150,000 homeless, and uprooted much of the region's lush foliage—couldn't put a dent in the city's economic revival. Except for Key Biscayne, the storm spared Miami.

More Crime . . . and Tourists Are the Targets

But the violent deaths of foreign tourists in Florida, a recession in Europe and Canada, and competition from other sunny destinations have put a crimp in the state's $32-billion-a-year tourist business. In 1993, nine foreign tourists were murdered in Florida, including a German visitor who was shot in his car after leaving Miami International Airport—as he was reading directions on how to avoid crime in Miami. In December 1993, tourism was down 7.6% compared to the previous December.

Miami has cleaned up its act somewhat—as we go to press, crime is down, even against tourists who continue to besiege the city in the winter. But there are other problems that won't go away any time soon: Miami is a complicated city beset with serious social problems. Ethnic divisions between Anglos, Cubans, Haitians, Central Americans, and African Americans are often appallingly clear. Riots and violent expressions of rage have been a staple of Miami's civic life since the '60s.

Compounding the problems are nonstop waves of immigration that began with Cubans in the late 1950s, continued with Nicaraguans in the 1970s and 1980s, and in the 1990s brought Haitians escaping economic deprivation and repression.

Miami on the Rebound

Travel industry experts say that in spite of the problems, Miami's and Florida's futures as tourist destinations look rosy: South Americans are a rapidly expanding market for Florida tourism, and safety and security in the state far surpasses that of most Latin American countries. Meanwhile, police and tourism agencies are beefing up police patrols around Miami International Airport (MIA), installing better highway signs (including 427 new directional signs featuring an orange sunburst logo to direct visitors toward major tourist destinations), stripping rental cars of identifying markings, and implementing awareness campaigns to help visitors avoid becoming crime statistics. These and other visitor safety programs have reduced crimes against tourists by about 60% . . . and in 1997, Miami tourism authorities reported that 10 million tourists visited Miami, a 4% increase over the previous year.

More Than Just Beaches

Obviously, Miami is more than a tourist destination boasting white, sandy beaches and a warm, sunny climate. It's also a commercial and convention center that draws a lot of business travelers. More than 1.4 million delegates attended conventions in Greater Miami in 1996, and that's just a fraction of the millions of business visitors who come to South Florida each year. The city's status as an international banking center draws visitors from throughout the world; Miami is a major United States gateway for Latin American and European travelers. Miami is also a jumping-off point for visits to vast expanses of Florida wilderness and wildlife preserves—a paradise for fishermen and boaters, as well as sun and beach worshipers.

As a transportation hub, Miami boasts two notable facilities. Miami International Airport serves approximately 100 airlines with more than 1,500 flights daily. The Port of Miami is the world's largest cruise port and is home to 15 cruise ships. A drive across MacArthur Causeway on a Friday night treats visitors to an unforgettable sight: long rows of brightly lit passenger liners framed by the impressive downtown Miami skyline.

In the '90s, it's a younger, more cosmopolitan breed of visitor that's energizing Miami and adding to the city's surge of optimism and affluence. As many pundits point out, Miami—a city that has undergone drastic changes as a result of Hispanic immigration over the last 30 years—could be a blueprint for the rest of the United States in the twenty-first century. Today, it's one of the hottest travel destinations in the world.

Miami Neighborhoods

Miami is a big city with a wide array of cultures, including Cuban, Haitian, and Nicaraguan—a reflection of the city's close proximity to the Caribbean. About half of Miami's two million residents speak Spanish as their native language; the warm, gregarious Latin culture prevails throughout Greater Miami. Listen carefully, however, and in a single block you can also overhear people speaking Yiddish, Russian, Creole, and German.

Many of Miami's neighborhoods are officially cities on their own, and each has a distinctive background and character. Most can be explored on foot, but a car is still indispensable to get from one neighborhood to another. Keep in mind that the character of a neighborhood can change rapidly in sprawling Miami, making it all too easy to stray into hostile territory.

The following list of Miami's most popular neighborhoods (all of which are safe for exploration by visitors on foot, except where noted) starts in South Miami Beach, continues north along the ocean to Sunny Isles, crosses Biscayne Bay to North Miami, and turns south to Little Haiti, downtown, Coral Gables, and other towns and neighborhoods in south Dade County.

South Beach (Zone 1)

Created 50 years ago as a place for Northerners to escape cold winters and the Great Depression, South Miami Beach (usually called South Beach or SoBe) is a 23-block area on the southern tip of Miami Beach. The architecture is intentionally whimsical—a collage of Art Deco, streamlined moderne, and Spanish Mediterranean–revival styles adapted to the South Florida climate. Over the decades, the old neighborhood has had its ups and downs, but today, South Beach is very much on a roll.

A preservation movement that began in the 1970s has resulted in a kaleidoscope of restored old buildings—mostly hotels, also some apartment buildings, restaurants, and condos—in lollipop colors, as well as streets filled with fashion models and slim-hipped Euro boys and girls, international photographers, Lycra-clad Rollerbladers and mountain bikers, and a few retirees hanging on as prices keep going up. See it all from a table at a sidewalk café, where you can relax with a drink and enjoy the best people-watching in the western hemisphere. In South Beach, the balance between voyeurs and exhibitionists is nearly perfect.

South Beach is also a popular stop with the jet set. Singer Gloria Estefan and her hubby own a restaurant on Ocean Avenue (Lario's), Academy Award–winner Robert De Niro's apartment takes up the entire floor of an Art Deco apartment building, and the late fashion designer Gianni Versace spent $8 million to renovate the oceanfront, circa-1930 Mediterranean Revival villa on Ocean Drive (where he was murdered in July 1997). No wonder a group of major magazine editors dubbed South Beach the "American Riviera."

It's also a neighborhood with some problems, many of which soon become apparent to visitors. On weekends, traffic slows to a crawl and finding a place to park induces heartburn. If you luck into a parking space, it's one of those good news/bad news scenarios.

The good news: If you're short on quarters to feed the meter, don't worry. The fine is only $18 if paid in 30 days, and as the number of cars you'll see parked at expired meters attests, enforcement isn't a high priority with Miami Beach cops.

The bad news: While South Beach has a reputation for being safe, car break-ins are a problem. Don't leave anything of value in your car. Finally, keep this in mind: Many Miami residents who own a car routinely take a taxi to South Beach for an evening on the town. Parking, they say, is too much of a hassle.

Thinking of renting a room? Accommodations tend toward the funky, with rooms and amenities right out of the '50s. (Don't assume that a South Beach hotel's nifty, recently renovated Art Deco exterior is an indication that the rooms got a face-lift, too.) The nightclub and street scene goes on all night, seven nights a week: light sleepers, beware.

Everyone who visits Miami, however, should come to South Beach at least once. If the constant procession of hardbodies, neo-hippies, permatanned geriatrics, punk rockers, and portfolio-carrying fashion models isn't enough to keep you entertained, then SoBe's eclectic spread of boutiques, outdoor cafés, nightclubs, art galleries, restaurants, and bookstores will.

And don't miss an evening stroll down Ocean Drive, where the best Art Deco architecture faces the sea and the beautiful people strut their stuff; walk down the street side for up-close, elbow-to-elbow people-watching, then cruise back on the Lummus Park (ocean) side for the best views of the architecture.

Central Miami Beach (Zone 1)

While the architecture of South Beach is rooted in the 1930s, the mile-long stretch of Miami Beach above 21st Street has its feet firmly planted in the '50s. Outrageous, ostentatious hotels loom over the beach and Collins Avenue—and the most outré is the Fontainebleau Hilton, at 4441 Collins Avenue, a curving mass of '50s kitsch.

You can't miss it as you drive north on Collins Avenue—the trompe l'oeil mural on the wall "exposes" the hotel behind it: the huge painting depicts a direct view of the ocean as you head north on Collins Avenue. The sweeping lobby of the 1,206-room hotel and spa, with its oversized chandeliers, is worth a peek. Legend has it that Frank Sinatra started a scrambled-egg fight in the coffee shop.

Across Collins Avenue and Indian Creek is where Miami Beach's wealthiest residents live. Drive, stroll, or rent a bike to view exclusive homes along pine tree–lined roads such as Alton Road, Pine Tree Drive, Bay Drive, and La Gorce Drive. Famous names residing in the neighborhood include Julio Iglesias, Cher, and Sylvester Stallone. Boat cruises of Biscayne Bay are available at the marina across from the Eden Roc Hotel.

Some folks are confused by Miami Beach's strange mix of commercial properties—hotels, restaurants, bars, grocery stores, travel agencies, etc.—and residential properties—mostly large condominium and apartment buildings sprinkled throughout the town. And it does create a problem for some short-time visitors who are stymied in their search for, say, a restaurant or bar within walking distance of their hotel, which is surrounded by anonymous-looking apartment buildings. The reason for the odd mixture—odd for a resort town, anyway—is that Miami Beach is a year-round working city, not just a vacation mecca.

North of Miami Beach (Zone 1)

North of the procession of glitzy '50s hotels in central Miami Beach a lot of the scenery gets uninspiring. Yet, for many people, that's okay: This stretch of Miami Beach is almost a purer Florida that lets up on the unrelenting trendiness to the south.

The communities of Surfside, Bal Harbour, and Sunny Isles are respectively dominated by Jewish and Canadian tourists and retirees, rich people living in an exclusive enclave, and middle-of-the-road tourists who don't know any better—or only care about easy access to the beach. With their seemingly endless succession of high-rise buildings, these neighborhoods comprise what's often called the "condo corner" of Miami.

Yet these communities offer a comfortable, low-key ambience that contrasts to the high-octane pulse of South Beach. Along Harding Avenue, Surfside's main commercial drag, people of all ages—retirees, young professionals, families—stroll streets full of small shops, delicatessens, jewelers, dress shops, luggage stores, and beauty parlors.

Surfside, surprisingly enough, also has its literary side. The town was home to Isaac Bashevis Singer, the Yiddish writer who learned that he had won the Nobel Prize for literature at Sheldon's Drugstore, Harding Avenue and 95th Street, where he regularly stopped for meals. Singer lived on Collins Avenue in Surfside from 1973 until his death in 1991.

Some of the other bright spots along this stretch of US A1A are the North Shore State Recreation Area (between 91st and 95th streets; reputed to be one of the few places in Miami Beach to officially allow topless bathing—although our sharp reporters note that European women tend to ignore local conventions and doff their tops all along Miami Beach's shoreline); Haulover Beach Park (featuring uncrowded beaches—including a nude beach—a marina, kayak rentals, and a great place to fly kites); and Bal Harbour Shops, full of expensive designer stores as tony as any on Rodeo Drive.

Located at the northern end of Miami Beach, Sunny Isles offers folks out for a drive a throwback to American culture in the '50s: a busy commercial strip along Collins Avenue filled with hotels and motels with "theme" motifs. The Safari features life-size terra cotta camels and Arabs guarding the lobby; the Suez has miniature pyramids; the Hawaiian Isle sports Easter Island statues to impart a sense of the exotic. For visitors age 40 and older, the kitschy hotels are a nostalgia trip to an earlier era; enjoy the whimsy before the chain hotels take over and homogenize the view.

Wolfie Cohen's Rascal House, a restaurant and sandwich shop in Sunny Isles, is considered by many to be one of Miami Beach's quintessential monuments to eating (along with Joe's Stone Crab in South Beach). As one longtime Miami resident put it, "The way people line up to get in, you'd think they're giving something away." They're not: The restaurant is successful because of its good food, great service, and staff of blue-haired waitresses who are brusque and funny. Wolfie's is reputed to serve the best corned beef sandwich south of New York City.

North Miami (Zone 2)

Communities east of Biscayne Bay (across from Miami Beach) range from the bland to the truly dangerous. Yet scattered around are a few worthwhile destinations, some of them world-famous: Hialeah Park (and 400 pink flamingos), Opa-Locka (an economically depressed neighborhood filled with restored, Moorish-influenced architecture that was founded by real estate genius and aviation pioneer Glenn Curtiss in the 1920s), and Miami Jai-Alai. Not so famous, but still worth seeing, are places such as the Ancient Spanish Monastery and the new, 23,000-square-foot Museum of Contemporary Art.

This is where you find major sporting venues such as Calder Race Track (horse racing), Pro Player (formerly Joe Robbie) Stadium (home of the Miami Dolphins), and the Golf Club of Miami.

Little Haiti (Zone 2)

Immigrants from Haiti are a major ethnic group in Miami, and a visit to Little Haiti gives visitors a chance to encounter this rich Caribbean culture. Yet the neighborhood's name promises more than it can deliver: this is no well-defined Chinatown or Little Italy, but an amorphous community with few architectural features to make it stand out from the rest of sprawling Miami.

The best bet for first-time visitors is the Caribbean Marketplace (5927 NE 2nd Avenue). The open-air marketplace was designed to resemble the Iron Market in Port-au-Prince and houses food booths, record stores, tropical clothing, and Haitian arts and crafts. During the day, visits to the neighborhood are safe, but unfortunately we can't recommend visiting the area at night.

Downtown Miami (Zone 2)

Downtown Miami, easily identifiable by its distinctive skyline of modern high-rises, is the small nerve center of this vibrant city. On weekdays in the morning through the early afternoon, the streets are jammed with sidewalk vendors, dazed-looking tourists, businesspeople in suits, and street people pushing shopping carts. They're all a part of a surging throng of humanity that contributes to Miami's sophisticated character and international ambience.

Relaxing, it's not. The streets are lined with countless cut-rate shops hawking electronics, luggage, jewelry, and clothes. Mini shopping malls, exotic eateries offering Brazilian fare, small Cuban cafés (stop in for a quick *cafe Cubano* when the street scene gets overpowering and your energy level needs a boost), and a few honest-to-God tourist attractions (the Metro-Dade Cultural Center is the best) make downtown a must-see place for visitors.

Just make sure your visit is in the morning or during lunch; by midafternoon, the crowds are gone. And don't even think about coming downtown at night: it's dead.

South of Downtown Miami/Brickell Avenue (Zone 3)

Running from the Miami River (the southern border of downtown) to Coconut Grove along Brickell Avenue is the largest group of international banks in the United States—a parade of high-rises perched among sculpture-filled piazzas, fountains, and lush South Florida foliage. The collection of banks is partially the result of political instability throughout Latin America in the late 1970s. Miami became a safe haven for corporate money and a new corporate banking center.

A little farther along Brickell Avenue is a collection of impressive high-rise condominiums. The buildings, home to many seasonal Latin American visitors with bucks and mostly done in bold primary colors, are immediately identifiable to fans of "Miami Vice." The most famous is the Atlantis, a truly outrageous piece of architecture: A gaping square hole in the center of the building includes a palm tree, Jacuzzi, and a red spiral staircase. It was designed by the firm Arquitectonica, renowned for creating Miami's new breed of distinctive, post–Art Deco buildings; see page 89 for a listing of more striking buildings designed by this avant-garde company.

Little Havana (Zone 3)

The impact of Cubans on Miami over the last three decades is incalculable; they are unquestionably the largest and most visible ethnic group in the city. Some background: Following Fidel Castro's takeover of Cuba in 1959, a flood of middle-class refugees settled in Little Havana. They rose quickly through Miami's social strata and now wield considerable clout in the city's affairs, both civic and social.

Today, however, the streets of Little Havana (located a few miles west of downtown) don't offer visitors a whole lot to see. In fact, the name "Little Havana" is misleading; while the words suggest a self-contained, ethnic enclave such as the Chinatown or Little Italy found in many large American cities, the reality is different in Miami. Just like Little Haiti, Little Havana is an amorphous neighborhood without strict boundaries that doesn't look a whole lot different from other parts of Miami.

Yet this neighborhood *does* offer visitors a taste of another culture, such as old men in *guayaberas* (billowing cotton shirts) playing dominoes in the park, exotic restaurants, and sights and sounds that are distinctly Cuban. You'll also see plenty of examples of what locals call "Spanglish": signs and billboards that charmingly mix English and Spanish, like one motel's boast, "Open 24 Horas."

The best place for a stroll in Little Havana is Calle Ocho (pronounced KAH-yeh OH-cho, Spanish for 8th Street), where streetside counters sell *cafe Cubano* (thimble-sized cups of sweet, highly charged Cuban coffee that Anglos call "jet fuel"), and the odor of cigars being rolled and baking bread fills the air. Our advice: Visit Little Havana for lunch or dinner at Versailles Restaurant (3555 SW 8th Street; open daily 8 a.m. to 2 a.m.). It offers great Cuban fare, it's cheap, easy to find, and parking is easy. Versailles is a Little Havana institution that shouldn't be missed. (See page 180, "Dinner in Little Havana," for specific instructions on visiting this Miami landmark.)

Coral Gables (Zone 3)

One of America's first planned communities, Coral Gables is a fascinating town filled with gorgeous, Mediterranean-style homes, manicured lawns, and lush foliage. The layout of the place, however, resembles a maze, with street names in Spanish written on small white stones at ground level that are hard to read. As a result, it's easy to get lost. Yet this classy old neighborhood, where many of Miami's most successful citizens live, is perfect for exploration by foot or bicycle.

Intriguing sights to be discovered on an informal tour of Coral Gables include the Venetian Pool, a freshwater coral rock lagoon called the best swimming hole in the world (bring a swimsuit, a towel, and five bucks); the Biltmore Hotel, fabulously restored after decades of neglect; and the Miracle Mile, a four-block stretch of expensive shops and boutiques where you can give your credit cards a real workout. Take a peek inside the recently restored Omni Colonnade Hotel; the rotunda is beautiful and the lobby features lots of cool marble. The building was the former office of George Merrick, the man who built Coral Gables.

Note: While it's easy to get lost in Coral Gables, at least you'll be able to tell you're in the right place. Look for those white street stones on the ground with the Spanish names.

Coconut Grove (Zone 3)

To natives, it's "The Grove." Miami's former Bohemian quarter today is a mix of expensive shops, trendy bars and restaurants, and decidedly upscale galleries and boutiques: think of it as a bit of California trendiness gone astray. Although not as outrageous as South Beach, Coconut Grove offers people-watchers another outstanding opportunity to sit at an outdoor café and watch fashion magazine victims strut their stuff, in-line skaters weave through bumper-to-bumper traffic, and hip-looking cops ride by on mountain bikes.

Shoppers can browse in New Age bookstores, lingerie shops (including the ubiquitous Victoria's Secret), a surfboard boutique, a Harley-Davidson dealership, and flower shops. CocoWalk, a multilevel mall done in pink and beige, features a courtyard with live music on evenings and weekends. Who are the neighbors? Residents include Madonna, who paid $4.9 million for her Coconut Grove mansion. Sylvester Stallone plopped down $7 million for eight acres on nearby South Miami Avenue that were part of the Vizcaya estate.

Key Biscayne (Zone 3)

Unless you've got a yacht, the only way to reach this beautiful island is via the Rickenbacker Causeway ($1 toll). Once there, you'll see how well-off

Miamians live their plush lifestyles off the beaten track. The late President Richard Nixon had his "winter White House" here.

Yet there's more to Key Biscayne than ogling the rich: The island features some of the best beaches in the Miami area—and most of them are open to the public. Seaquarium, Miami's sea mammal emporium, is located on Virginia Key, the island the causeway crosses before reaching Key Biscayne. On the five-mile-long causeway, visitors can pull over, park their cars, and rent sailboards and jet skis for zooming around the placid waters of Biscayne Bay. A note for those who travel with their pets: These are the only beaches in the Miami area that allow dogs.

Two state parks are located on the island. On the tip is Bill Baggs Cape Florida State Park, devastated by Hurricane Andrew in 1992. We're glad to report the foliage in the 406-acre park is recovering from its beating. Yet we recommend Crandon Park, with its wide, open beaches, as a better bet for visitors. Pack a lunch and swimming gear for a day at a Key Biscayne beach.

South Miami (Zone 3)

Stretching south along US 1 below downtown, Miami turns into a sprawl of tract suburban houses with two-car garages, strip shopping centers featuring discount waterbed stores, some golf courses—and a few tourist attractions located off the highway.

If you've got the time, however, it's an area worth exploring—just get off US 1. Old Cutler Road, which meanders between the highway and Biscayne Bay, offers visitors a scenic drive through lush tropical foliage—at least as far south as Coral Reef Drive (SW 152nd Street), where the damage from Hurricane Andrew is still evident. Worthwhile stops while exploring the neighborhood include Fairchild Tropical Garden, Parrot Jungle, and (after it reopens) the Charles Deering Estate.

Kendall and Perrine (Zone 3)

Continuing south, Dade County gets less and less interesting, yet a few attractions are worth the drive. The premier tourist destination is Metrozoo, still a world-class zoo even after the devastation wrought by Hurricane Andrew in 1992. Other nearby attractions will appeal to train and airplane buffs, respectively: the Gold Coast Railroad Museum and the Weeks Air Museum.

Homestead and Florida City (Zone 4)

Neither of these southern Dade County towns are neighborhoods worth exploring by short-term visitors, but both serve as jumping-off points for three areas that shouldn't be missed if you've got the time: Everglades and

Biscayne National Parks, and the Florida Keys. Nearby attractions include Monkey Jungle, the Coral Castle, and the Fruit and Spice Park.

The Beaches

"Life is a beach": you heard it here first. For many visitors, South Florida is strictly a beach destination—and no wonder. With more than 10 miles of wide, sandy, palm tree–studded beaches, Miami Beach is a sun-worshiper's paradise. All the beach is open to the public and staffed by lifeguards during daylight hours from 1st to 14th streets; at 21st, 35th, 46th, 52nd, 64th streets; and at North Shore State Recreation Area and Haulover Beach Park.

Question: What's the best way to the beach?

Answer: If you're staying at a Miami Beach hotel located on the ocean, you're an elevator ride away from the sand and surf. If you're staying at a motel or condo across Collins Avenue, it's a few minutes' stroll to the beach.

Other folks—people staying in hotels, motels, or condos that aren't within walking distance of the beach—have a decision to make before jumping in the car and heading to the ocean.

Where to Put the Car

Parking is one consideration when choosing a beach location to spend a few hours or the day. The farther south along Miami Beach you go, the harder it is to find a place to leave the car; on weekends, it can be nearly impossible unless you arrive early. Along Miami Beach, metered public parking lots, beach access, and rest rooms are provided along Collins Avenue at these locations:

Miami Beach Public Parking Lot, Beach Access, and Rest Room Locations
1st Street (at Washington Avenue, South Pointe Park)
6th to 14th streets, Lummus Park
21st Street
35th Street
46th Street (next to the Eden Roc Hotel)
53rd Street
64th Street
73rd Street (across from the North Shore Community Center)
79th to 87th streets (North Shore State Recreation Area)
93rd Street (Surfside)
96th Street (Bal Harbour)
108th Street (Haulover Park)
167th Street (next to the Holiday Inn)

Who Goes Where?

The beaches of Miami Beach can also be broken down by the kinds of folks who congregate at them.

South Beach, especially 10th through 12th streets, is topless, while gays tend to favor the beach around 18th Street. South Beach also attracts Germans, Italians, the young and the restless, Eurotrash, and glitterati from the world over.

The War Zone is the old name for the tip of land below 5th Street down to Government Cut (the shipping channel leading to the Port of Miami). Just a few years ago this was mostly surfer turf, but the neighborhood is undergoing rapid change as the Art Deco District trendiness pushes south. Today the Zone is being developed as heavily as the rest of South Beach, rents are just as high, and the area is losing its identity as SoBe grooviness takes over. A massive, cathedral-sized club called Amnesia started the trend a few years ago—and as we go to press, high-rises are springing up throughout the old neighborhood. But for now, anyway, the Zone boasts a higher percentage of ungentrified residents than the rest of South Beach. There's a park on the oceanside between 2nd and 3rd streets where folks gather at sunup for tai chi.

Families, on the other hand, tend to flock to the 20s, 30s, and 40s—and north. A wooden boardwalk extends from the 20s to the 50s behind many of the huge hotels that line the beach; you'll see a wide array of people strolling and jogging.

Miami Beach is a city of many different communities featuring a wide range of ethnic groups. For example, **mid-Miami Beach,** centered around 41st Street, is the city's commercial strip and has one of the largest concentrations of Lubovitch Jews in the state. Most are very conservative (even more conservative than Hassids). They can be seen walking to one of the temples in the area in family groups during weekends.

Farther north, **Surfside** attracts an older population and is also a popular destination for Canadian and Scandinavian tourists. The epicenter of Canadian tourism is Hollywood, Florida, just over the line in Broward County. There's even a newspaper in Hollywood published in French for Canadian visitors. Canadians stream down into Florida and inhabit northern Dade County from Surfside northward. For folks looking to sunbathe in the raw, **Haulover Beach Park** (just past Bal Harbour) has a "clothing optional" (nude) section along its more than one-mile length. It's a beautiful park that features a marina and plenty of parking.

Sunny Isles, located above Haulover Beach, has a lovely park beach with sea grape trees and sand dunes (which are about as high above sea level as you'll get in Miami). It's a popular spot for families.

Beyond Miami Beach

Miami Beach, however, isn't your only beach option. Key Biscayne's **Crandon Park** offers miles of wide, white Atlantic Ocean beach and no parking problems; it's a popular destination for families and picnickers.

For swimming, windsurfing, or jet skiing in the shallow, placid waters of Biscayne Bay, pull over on the **Rickenbacker Causeway** that connects Key Biscayne to the mainland. It's a popular beach destination for local residents that features shade trees and picnic tables close to the water. And it's okay to bring the dog.

In North Miami Beach (which, confusingly enough, is a suburb of Miami located on the mainland), the **Oleta River State Recreation Area** has a small, sandy, man-made beach on the shores of Biscayne Bay and the Intracoastal Waterway. It's an oasis of quiet surrounded by condos. South of Coral Gables and east of the Miami suburb of Kendall, **Matheson Hammock Park** offers a small beach on Biscayne Bay with a terrific view of the Miami skyline.

When to Go: Two Main Tourist Seasons . . . and Two Shoulders

They don't call Florida the Sunshine State for nothing: During the winter months, Miami is a mecca for sun-seeking vacationers escaping icy blasts in less temperate climes. From November through April, South Florida's subtropical climate offers—but doesn't guarantee—blue skies, warm sunshine, and low humidity.

So it's no surprise that the winter months are Miami's peak tourist season. The "winter season" generally starts just before Christmas and ends just after Easter. Christmas week, the busiest week of the year, pushes tourist facilities, restaurants, and hotels throughout South Florida to their limit. Lines get long at major tourist destinations, small attractions get inundated, and finding a hotel room that's both convenient and affordable is difficult.

Our advice: Avoid touring the Miami area during Christmas week and major holidays such as Easter and Thanksgiving. Late November (after Thanksgiving) through the week before the holidays, however, offers manageable crowds at attractions, beaches, and restaurants—and finding a convenient, reasonably priced hotel room is easier then.

While the crowds recede after New Year's Day, things really pick up in mid-January as affluent Northerners who own property in South Florida stream for the remainder of the winter. The winter season remains in full swing through Easter, and Easter week is almost as crowded as the weeks before and after Christmas. The winter months are the best time to visit the Everglades (it's the dry season, so mosquitoes are usually scarce and animal life congregates around the remaining water). The period between Easter and the beginning of the summer season (Miami's other major tourist season) is slow in South Florida.

The Summer Season

The action picks up toward the middle of June with the arrival of families on vacation with school-aged children. The "summer season" continues through mid-August when the kids head back to school. While Miami doesn't get as crowded during the summer as it does in the winter months, summer is South Florida's other major tourist season.

If you plan to visit this subtropical region during the summer, keep two things in mind: This is Miami's rainy season too, characterized by ferocious, though usually brief, afternoon thunderstorms, near-tropical heat, and stifling humidity. Comfort, as well as crowd avoidance, dictates early day touring and sight-seeing.

Here's another caveat to summer visits to Miami. Natives (usually defined as residents who have lived here at least five years) think of South Florida summers the way folks in Maine think of their winters: You really haven't arrived until you've survived at least one. Keep that in mind if you've never ventured farther south than Orlando between June and September, and you're contemplating a summer trip to Miami. The intensity of the sun, high temperatures, and wall-like humidity are often oppressive. Keep in mind that high temperatures don't tell the whole story: most natives pay more attention to a weather forecast's humidity levels than the day's high temperature (80% is comfortable; the high 90s are hellish).

The Shoulder Seasons

More advice on when to visit Miami: Mid-April through early June and September through mid-December, the two "shoulder" periods between the major tourist seasons, offer visitors the best chance of avoiding large crowds, packed attractions, and expensive lodging. The weather is usually pleasant and dry (though rainier than the winter months).

Note, however, that South Florida's hurricane season lasts from June to November. Statistically, there's not much chance that one of the huge tropical storms will hit during your visit—and if it does, there will be plenty of warning. Evacuation routes are well marked throughout Miami.

Miami's Average Monthly Temperatures

	High	Low
January	74	63
February	76	63
March	77	65
April	79	68
May	83	72
June	85	76
July	88	76
August	88	77
September	86	76
October	83	72
November	79	67
December	76	67

Avoiding Crowds

In general, popular tourist sights are busier on weekends than weekdays, and Saturdays are busier than Sundays. The winter season is by far the busiest time of year at most attractions, with some exceptions: the relatively low number of school-aged children in town during the winter means that kid-friendly places such as the Seaquarium may not be as crowded, compared to summer.

Driving in Miami's rush-hour traffic, especially on I-95 and on US 1, should be avoided. Much of the freeway is elevated and when an accident ties up traffic downtown, often there's no place to escape the backup.

If you're driving to Miami on a weekday, avoid hitting town between 7:30 a.m. and 9 a.m., and 4 p.m. to 6 p.m. Expect equally heavy traffic on the two east-west expressways that connect with I-95 near downtown: the Dolphin Expressway (Route 836) and the Airport Expressway (Route 112). US 1 below downtown is the only route to Coconut Grove, Coral Gables, and points south; rush-hour gridlock is the norm.

How to Get More Information on Miami Before Your Visit

For additional information on entertainment, sight-seeing, maps, shopping, dining, and lodging in Greater Miami, call or write the **Visitor Ser-**

vice Center at the Greater Miami Convention and Visitors Bureau (701 Brickell Avenue, Suite 2700, Miami, Florida 33131; (800) 283-2707 or (305) 539-3000).

Ask for a free copy of **Greater Miami & The Beaches Visitor Guide,** a biannual publication with nearly 200 pages of information, including basic stuff such as post office locations, annual rainfall, language services, colleges and universities, hospitals, and real estate agents.

If you need specific information, ask for it when you call or write. For example, if you're planning on staying in a hotel or motel away from traditional tourist haunts and need to know if it's in a safe neighborhood, the folks at the Visitor Service Center can help.

Part Two

Visiting Miami on Business

Not All Miami Visitors Are Headed to the Beach

While most of the more than 13 million visitors a year who flock to Miami come to bask in the tropical sun, to enjoy the Latin culture, and to see and be seen in South Beach, not everybody has an itinerary centered around leisure-time activities. In fact, in 1996 more than three million visitors came to Miami for conventions and business.

In many ways, the problems facing business visitors on their first trip to Miami don't differ much from the problems of folks in town on a vacation. People visiting on business need to locate a hotel that's convenient, want to avoid the city's worst traffic hassles, face the same problems when the drawbridge on the MacArthur Causeway is up, and want to know the locations of Miami's best restaurants. This book can help.

For the most part, though, business visitors aren't nearly as flexible about the timing of their visit as folks who pick Miami as a vacation destination. While we advise the best times for coming to South Florida are the shoulder seasons between winter and summer, the necessities of business may dictate that January is when you pull into town—or even worse, the weeks before and after Christmas, when services in the Miami area are strained to the max.

Yet much of the advice and information presented in the *Unofficial Guide* is as valuable to business visitors and convention-goers as it is for tourists. As for our recommendations on seeing South Florida's many attractions—who knows? Maybe you'll find the time to squeeze a morning or an afternoon out of your busy schedule, grab this book, and spend a few hours exploring some of the places that draw the other nine million or so visitors to Miami each year.

The Miami area is home to two major convention centers. The massive, million-square-foot *Miami Beach Convention Center* is South Florida's major exhibition venue. The smaller *Coconut Grove Convention Center,* located in the hip neighborhood south of downtown Miami, specializes in consumer-oriented exhibitions such as home shows, health and fitness expos, and gun and knife shows.

Other Convention Venues

Other convention sites that draw national conventions include:

- *Miami Convention Center* in downtown Miami: 37 meeting rooms and the 28,000-square-foot Riverfront Hall
- adjacent *Hyatt Regency Miami:* 80,000 square feet of meeting and banquet rooms and the 12,000-square-foot Regency Ballroom
- *Radisson Centre* near Miami International Airport: 120,000 square feet of meeting, exhibition, and banquet space
- *Doral Ocean Beach Resort* in Miami Beach: 45,000 square feet of meeting space
- *Doral Resort and Country Club* in Miami: 75,000 square feet of meeting and banquet facilities
- *Fontainebleau Hilton* in Miami Beach: 190,000 square feet of meeting and exhibit space
- *Sheraton Bal Harbour* in north Miami Beach: 70,000 square feet of meeting and conference rooms

The Miami Beach Convention Center

Expanded and renovated in 1990 at a cost of more than $92 million, the Miami Beach Convention Center is South Florida's premier convention locale. The 1.1-million-square-foot center is one of the best designed and modern facilities for conventions in the United States and can handle up to four conventions at a time.

Spanning four city blocks near Miami Beach's Art Deco District, the center is only minutes from the beach and great restaurants, and is less than a half-hour from Miami International Airport (allow more time during rush hour). The center is located on Washington Avenue between 17th Street and Dade Boulevard; unfortunately, although it's a massive building, it's not visible from Miami Beach's main drag, Collins Avenue.

With all of its meeting rooms on one level, the center's main floor, with 500,000 square feet, either can be configured as a vast, centralized facility with four points of access or can be subdivided into four separate halls of approximately 125,000 square feet each. A skywalk with lounges, bars, and meeting rooms spans the halls, giving convention-goers a bird's-eye view of the hall.

Surrounding the exhibit area are 70 separate meeting rooms for a total of 145,000 square feet of flexible space. All are fully carpeted and divided by soundproof walls. The meeting rooms can accommodate as few as 100 or as many as 2,000 convention-goers.

Thirty-nine ground-level truck bays divided between the north and south ends of the center allow large and small exhibitors to unload and set up their exhibits with minimal effort. Direct truck access to the exhibit floor is via a dedicated ramp and a 30-by-24-foot roll-up door in each hall.

Equipment can be carried or wheeled directly to the exhibit area. The exhibit areas and meeting rooms are well marked and easy to find. Parking around the center, however, is difficult; the 800-space lot adjacent to the center fills up quickly. We suggest you take advantage of hotel shuttle buses or take a cab during large conventions.

If you must drive and the lot is full, head for the 2,000-space parking garage on 17th Street (a block south toward the Lincoln Road Mall); trying to find street parking within walking distance is frustrating at best. For more information on the Miami Beach Convention Center, call (305) 535-0238.

On a happier note, places to dine around the Miami Beach Convention Center are plentiful; head down Washington Avenue into the heart of South Beach, where a wide range of high-quality eateries, bistros, and fast-food venues are close by. In addition, Lincoln Road Mall, a block south of the convention center between 16th and 17th streets, is another nearby destination with a wide range of trendy restaurants, bars, and shops.

ElectroWave, a new mini-bus service, makes a stop near the convention center on Washington Street and provides easy, free transportation south into the Art Deco District; the electric buses run about every 10 minutes. Now more than ever, making an escape from the exhibit floor for a quick bite or for a quiet meal with clients is easy.

The Coconut Grove Convention Center

Located south of downtown Miami at 2700 Bayshore Drive in the trendy enclave of Coconut Grove, this 150,000-square-foot hall was completely renovated and expanded in 1989 and accommodates shows of up to 18,000 attendees. It's in a striking location on the shores of Biscayne Bay, features a backdrop of sailboats in the nearby marina, and is located only 10 minutes from downtown Miami and less than half an hour from Miami International Airport.

The main hall is divisible into five halls measuring from 7,000 to 50,000 square feet and features an eight-window ticket booth. Two 30-foot-wide doors roll up to ceiling height at the north and south ends of the hall to enable easy access for service vehicles and exhibitors. All the exhibition space is on the ground level, making it easy to roll or carry equipment through the doors from the parking lot. In addition, two concession stands are located in the main hall and a full-service restaurant is located on the premises. A 700-car parking lot surrounds the hall. For more information on the Coconut Grove Convention Center, call (305) 579-3310.

Hotels near the convention center include the Doubletree Hotel at Coconut Grove (190 rooms), the Grand Bay Hotel (177 rooms), and the Mayfair House Hotel (178 rooms). In nearby Coral Gables, major hotels include the Biltmore Hotel (279 rooms), the Omni Colonnade Hotel (157 rooms), the Holiday Inn Coral Gables (168 rooms), and the Hyatt Regency Coral Gables (242 rooms).

Coconut Grove offers some of Miami's best dining and night life, so getting away from the exhibit floor for a meal is easy.

Part Three

Hotels

Deciding Where to Stay

Miami's Confusing Hotel Scene

Over the years, Miami and Miami Beach have been through so many boom and bust cycles that the hotel scene tends to remain in constant flux. On the ocean, hotel development began in South Beach, the southernmost part of the barrier island known collectively as Miami Beach. Over the years, as Miami Beach's popularity spiraled, new hotel development worked its way north along the Atlantic coast in a seemingly unstoppable wave. At first times were good, and each new hotel was larger and grander than its older neighbors to the south.

Miami Beach reached its zenith in the late '50s during the halcyon days of the Fontainebleau, Eden Roc, Diplomat, and Kennilworth. These were among the largest and most resplendent hotels in America. Their opulent, cathedral-sized lobbies, enormous swimming pools, and formal gardens signaled Miami's arrival as the preferred playground of the wealthy and influential.

As it turned out, the supply of luxury hotel rooms eventually outran demand, and the developers shifted their attention to the vacation needs of people of more modest means. A new crop of hotels sprang up along the coast north of Bal Harbour. These properties were smaller (glorified motels really) and employed fanciful themes to compete with their more established competitors to the south. Desert-themed hotels such as the Sands and the Dunes stationed a small caravan of fiberglass camels at their entrances. Other properties drew inspiration from the Sputnik satellite and space exploration craze of the time. Though faddish and outlandish, these smaller hotels prospered, along with the more established large hotels, throughout the '60s.

During this period, South Beach, the cradle of Miami tourism, fell into decline. Unable to compete with the Fontainebleaus, Eden Rocs, and mod-

theme hotels, the smaller inns at the southern end of Miami Beach became the permanent residences first of Jewish retirees from the northeast, and later of Cuban emigrés and refugees.

In the 1970s Walt Disney World opened near Orlando. At first, Disney's impact on Miami tourism was minimal, with motoring vacationers stopping at Disney World for a one-day visit before continuing south to Miami. With the opening of Epcot Center in 1982, however, South Florida tourism was changed forever. Walt Disney World had become a destination instead of merely a stopover. For South Florida and particularly Miami, it was as if a wall had been constructed in the center of the state, a Disney wall that blocked the flow of American tourists to destinations south of Orlando.

Overbuilt and underfed, Miami tourism fell on hard times. Luxury hotels failed by the score or plugged along in a state of increasing disrepair. Tourists were supplanted by legions of retirees, and many of Miami's and Miami Beach's most notable hostelries were razed to make way for high-rise condominiums.

By the end of the '80s, Miami had recovered some of its tourist base by targeting Latin Americans and Europeans. British and the German travelers especially were ready to initiate a love affair with Miami. In the early '90s, the Miami Beach Convention Center expanded to become one of the largest and most well-designed meeting venues in the United States. This resurgence in tourism and convention traffic coincided with an upswing in commerce to trigger the most explosive growth seen in greater Miami since the 1950s.

In downtown Miami, Coral Gables, Coconut Grove, and around the airport, growth largely addressed the needs of business. Here, the presence of national chain hotels created a recognizable standard. Catering primarily to business travelers, hotels on the mainland kept pace with Miami's growing stature as the financial, trade, and transportation capital of the Caribbean. Across the bay in Miami Beach, however, it was (and is) a different story entirely.

In the boom of the late '40s and the '50s, Miami Beach's growth and development were at least geographically organized: there was a predictable march of new construction heading due north, right up the beach. Since those days, some hotels have survived, some have failed, others have been renovated or replaced entirely by high-rise condos. For the most part, there has been precious little discernible logic to all of this change.

To an outsider, particularly, it seems as if Miami and Miami Beach have evolved almost randomly since the mid-'60s. You'll find new luxury resorts sharing the same block with 1980s condominiums and ramshackle hotels from the 1940s. Properties of every conceivable size, and with vastly different clientele, populate the same stretch of oceanfront. In a half-mile stroll along Collins Avenue in Miami Beach, you will see small residential hotels with inhabitants clustered in lawn chairs on canvas-covered porches. Next door might be a recently restored Art Deco hotel with a sidewalk café, and across the street, a modern condominium tower.

The practical lesson to be derived from this bit of history is that Miami Beach is a pretty mixed-up place. If you want to find nice accommodations, you have to dig a little deeper than a hotel's ad promising "an established hotel right on the ocean in the heart of Miami Beach." Though dozens of hotels can truthfully make that claim, there are many among them you would not wish on your worst enemy.

Some Considerations

1. When choosing your Miami or Miami Beach lodging, cross-reference your candidate hotel's address with our profiles of the various Greater Miami neighborhoods and communities. Make sure your hotel is situated in a location convenient to your recreational or business needs, and that it is in an area where you will feel safe and comfortable. Please note that the areas we profile below are those most frequented by visitors to Miami. If a hotel you are considering is located elsewhere, check out its environs with the Greater Miami Convention & Visitors Bureau, (800) 283-2707, Monday through Friday, 9 a.m. to 5 p.m.
2. Find out how old the hotel is and when the guest rooms were last renovated. Request that the hotel send you its promotional brochure. Ask if brochure photos of guest rooms are accurate and current.
3. If you plan to have a car, inquire about the parking situation. Some hotels offer no parking at all, some charge extra for parking, and others offer free parking.
4. Be aware that many hotels, particularly hotels in Miami Beach, serve a narrowly defined clientele. Some hotels cater almost exclusively to Latin Americans, others to Germans, and still others to Jewish or British guests. If you are worried about not fitting in, ask about the hotel's clientele before you book a room.

Location

Your main reason for visiting Miami will help frame your choice of hotel. Your primary consideration should be location. Traffic is so bad in Miami that you do not want to commute to your business or touring destination, or to the beach. If you have come to Miami to shop along the Miracle Mile in Coral Gables, choose a Coral Gables hotel. If you plan to spend your time on the beach, book a Miami Beach or Key Biscayne hotel. If you are in town on business, lodge as close to your business destination as possible.

While there are hotels all over the Greater Miami area—with some stuck in quite improbable places—we deal primarily with those hotels that are located in areas of concentrated tourist activity, business activity, or both.

The Mainland

Downtown Miami Hotels in downtown Miami are close to the Port of Miami, the Orange Bowl, city government, the airport, and Miami's business and financial center. The Miami Beach Convention Center is a 15-minute commute under optimal traffic conditions. Downtown Miami is not particularly active after business hours, and the choice of restaurants and nightspots is decidedly limited compared to Miami Beach, Coral Gables, or Coconut Grove. Though downtown Miami is generally safe for visitors on foot, we recommend walking in groups or taking a cab after dark.

Miami International Airport Area The airport is located inland just west of downtown Miami. Hotels situated near the airport are convenient to Coral Gables, downtown Miami, major expressways leading south to the Keys and north toward the Hialeah Race Track, Pro Player Stadium (home of the Miami Dolphins), and Fort Lauderdale. Commuting time from airport area hotels to Miami Beach or to the Miami Beach Convention Center is about 20 to 30 minutes if the traffic isn't bad. Accommodations near the airport are scattered around a 16-square-mile area crisscrossed by expressways. If you need to travel beyond your hotel you will need a car or a cab.

Coral Gables Coral Gables is about two miles south of the airport, four miles southwest of downtown, and extends south to Biscayne Bay. A banking and trade center as well as one of Miami's nicest residential areas, Coral Gables is also home to the University of Miami and the Miracle Mile, one of Florida's best shopping venues. Likewise, many of Miami's finest restaurants are located in Coral Gables. Hotels in Coral Gables are convenient to the University of Miami, the airport, Coconut Grove and Biscayne Bay, and several attractions. Miami Beach and the Miami Beach Convention Center are a complicated 30- to 50-minute commute from Coral Gables. Downtown Coral Gables and the Miracle Mile are safe for pedestrians both day and evening, though normal safety precautions should be observed.

Coconut Grove Coconut Grove is an upscale bayside community framed on the west and south by Coral Gables. Coconut Grove is convenient to a number of southern Dade County attractions, including Parrot Jungle, Miami Seaquarium, Fairchild Tropical Garden, and Vizcaya. Key Biscayne and various Biscayne Bay marinas are also easily accessible from Coconut Grove. Miami Beach and the Miami Beach Convention Center are 30 to 50 minutes away via I-95 and I-195 or the MacArthur Causeway. Coconut Grove is considered safe for visitors on foot throughout the day and evening.

Miami Beach

Miami Beach is situated on a barrier island roughly across upper Biscayne Bay from downtown Miami. Collins Avenue (also US A1A) is the main north-south thoroughfare. East-west thoroughfares are numbered streets, running from 1st Street in the south to 96th Street in the north. Contiguous with Miami Beach as you head north on Collins Avenue past the city limits (at 87th Street) is Surfside, followed by Bal Harbour, then Sunny Isles. Four causeways connect Miami Beach to the mainland. Hotels between 5th and 61st streets are about a half-hour drive from the Miami International Airport.

The Historic Art Deco District The Art Deco District, extending from 5th Street northward along the beach to 15th, represents Miami Beach at its finest. Hotels here are small, independently owned, and architecturally distinctive in the Deco/Caribbean style of Miami Beach's original tourist boom. Many of these hotels have been lovingly restored and provide a glimpse of a bygone era. The feel here is hot, sultry, and very active. Diners in open-air cafés watch an endless parade of in-line skaters, joggers, models, and young, hip nightclubbers. While parking is virtually nonexistent, dozens of restaurants and clubs are within easy walking distance—and so is the beach. The Miami Beach Convention Center is a 20- to 30-minute walk or 5- to 10-minute cab ride away. Hotel rooms in the Art Deco District may be smaller than you would find in a chain hotel. Though the baths are generally small and modest by modern standards, the guest rooms themselves are often beautifully appointed. If you opt to stay in this area, you will enjoy the quintessential Miami Beach experience. Be forewarned, however, that the Art Deco District is a party zone: clubs rock long into the night and quiet is sometimes hard to come by. The Art Deco District is well patrolled by the Miami Beach Police and is pretty safe both day and night, though you may have to contend with some panhandlers or hustlers.

Miami Beach North of the Historic Art Deco District to Arthur Godfrey Road (I-195) While the officially designated, historic Art Deco District runs from 5th to 15th Street, there are many hotels in the Art

Deco style all the way up to 43rd Street. North of 15th, however, they tend to be larger hotels, and may or may not have been recently renovated. Development from 15th north to 43rd Street has been somewhat erratic, with little emphasis on artistic or historic preservation. Art Deco–era hotels in this area are sprinkled among more modern hotels, condominiums, and whole blocks of small retailers.

To muddy the water for travelers and travel agents, many hotels north of the designated historic district claim in their promotional literature, AAA guides, and the *Hotel & Travel Index* to be in the Art Deco District. If you want to stay in one of the small Art Deco hotels in the historic district, confirm that your hotel is located across from Lummus Park (beach front) or on Collins Avenue (one block west of the beach) between 5th and 15th streets.

Above 15th Street are many good hotels and quite a few rundown ones. This area is improving each year, however, by virtue of its close proximity to the Miami Beach Convention Center. Businesspeople staying at beach hotels between 15th and 23rd Streets are within a 5- to 12-minute walk of the Convention Center.

So far, most of the renovation north of the Art Deco District has taken place between 15th and 31st Street. Above 31st, up to 43rd Street, there are about five grubby hotels for every nice one. For specific recommendations of hotels, check out our hotel ratings and rankings to find the nicest rooms and the best deals.

Miami Beach above the Art Deco District is safe days and evenings during business hours for visitors on foot. Those enjoying the local after-hours night life scene should walk in groups, drive, or take a cab between clubs.

Miami Beach North of Arthur Godfrey Road (I-195) to the John F. Kennedy Causeway Driving north on Collins Avenue from South Miami Beach, you cross Arthur Godfrey Road, also known as 41st Street. Running east-west, this road directly links Miami Beach to Miami via I-195, and dead-ends into Collins Avenue. Collins Avenue, north of Arthur Godfrey to the Kennedy Causeway (71st Street), is the home of Miami Beach's fabled hotel giants. Though many of the great hotels are gone and others have been renamed or replaced by skyward-stretching condominiums, the Fontainebleau and the Eden Roc, among others, still invite visitors to relive the zenith of Miami Beach's golden age.

Huge, commanding, and magnificent after 40 years, these hotels almost single-handedly saved this area of Miami Beach from decline. Sandwiched between the Intracoastal Waterway on the west and the Atlantic Ocean on the east, hotels here offer stunning views in all directions. Each of the great

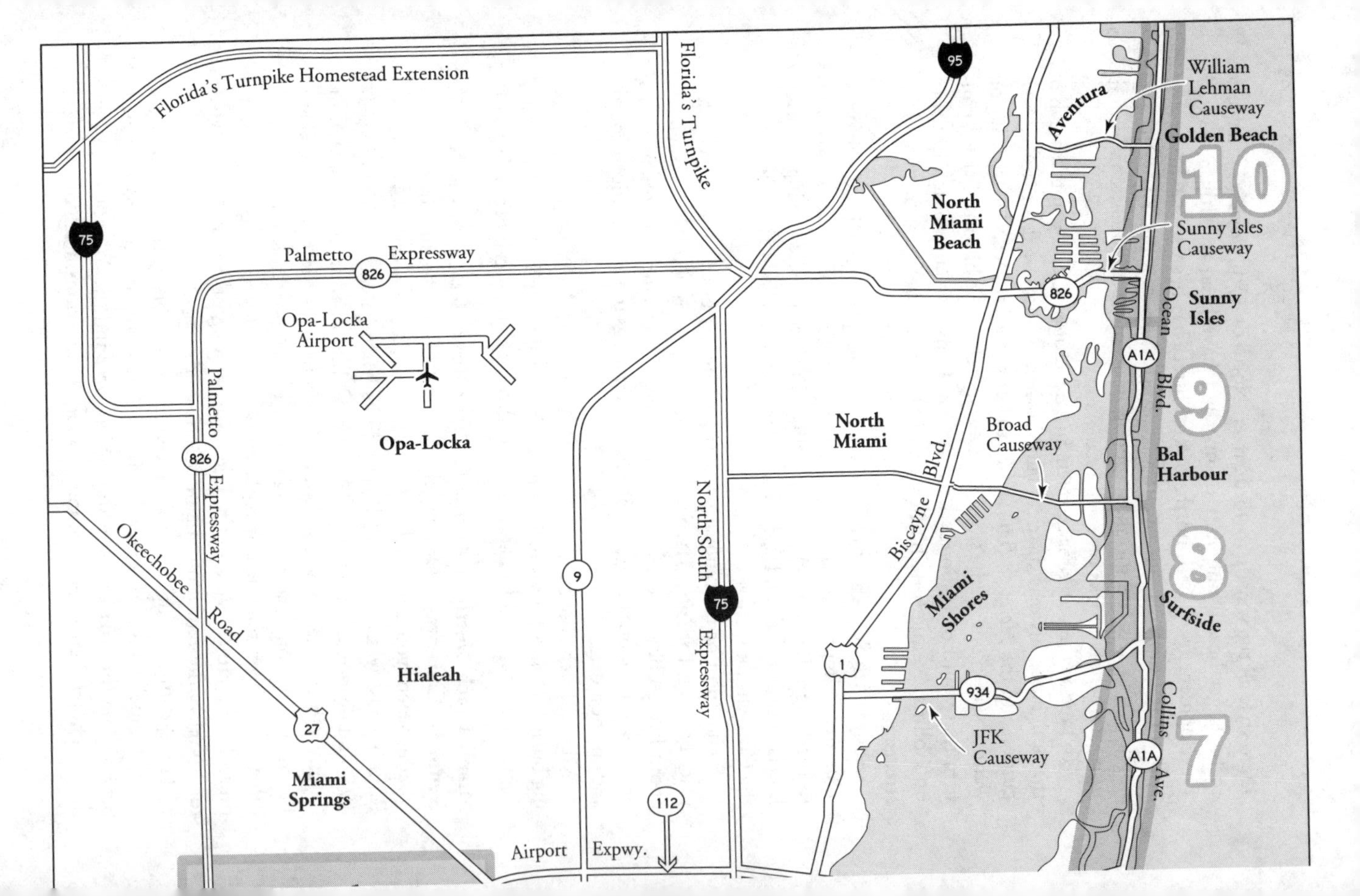

Florida's Turnpike Homestead Extension
Florida's Turnpike
95
William Lehman Causeway
Aventura
Golden Beach
10
North Miami Beach
Sunny Isles Causeway
75
Palmetto
826
Expressway
826
Sunny Isles
Ocean
A1A
Blvd.
Opa-Locka Airport
9
Opa-Locka
North Miami
Broad Causeway
Bal Harbour
Palmetto
826
Expressway
Blvd.
Biscayne
8
Okeechobee
Road
9
North-South
75
Expressway
Miami Shores
Surfside
1
Hialeah
934
27
JFK Causeway
Collins
A1A
Ave.
7
Miami Springs
112
Airport
Expwy.

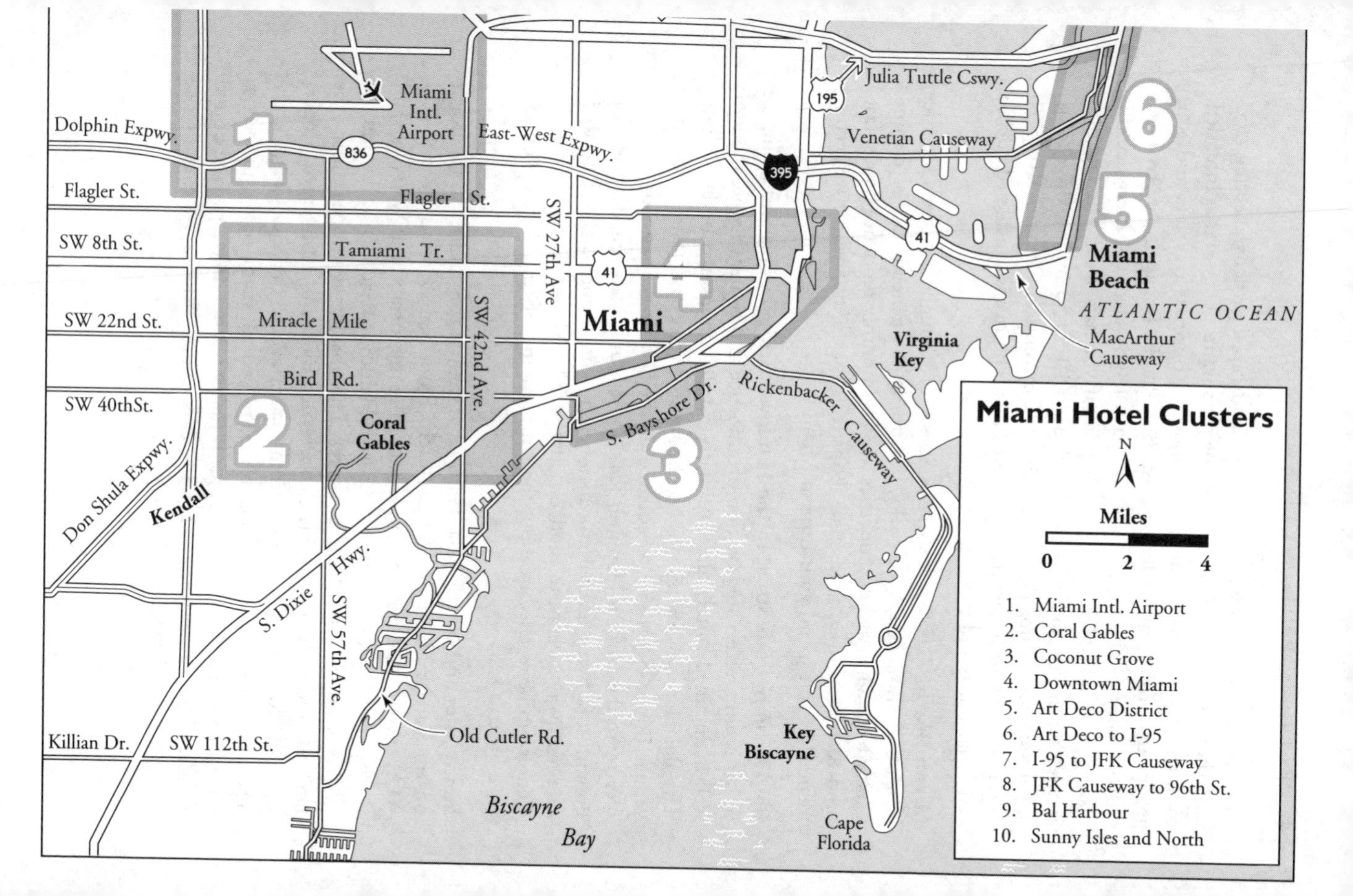

Miami Hotel Clusters
N
Miles
0
2
4
1. Miami Intl. Airport
2. Coral Gables
3. Coconut Grove
4. Downtown Miami
5. Art Deco District
6. Art Deco to I-95
7. I-95 to JFK Causeway
8. JFK Causeway to 96th St.
9. Bal Harbour
10. Sunny Isles and North
Miami Intl. Airport
Dolphin Expwy.
836
East-West Expwy.
Julia Tuttle Cswy.
195
Venetian Causeway
395
41
Miami Beach
ATLANTIC OCEAN
MacArthur Causeway
Virginia Key
Flagler St.
Flagler St.
SW 8th St.
Tamiami Tr.
SW 27th Ave
41
Miami
SW 22nd St.
Miracle Mile
SW 42nd Ave.
Bird Rd.
SW 40thSt.
Coral Gables
S. Bayshore Dr.
Rickenbacker Causeway
Don Shula Expwy.
Kendall
S. Dixie Hwy.
SW 57th Ave.
Old Cutler Rd.
Killian Dr.
SW 112th St.
Key Biscayne
Biscayne Bay
Cape Florida

hotels offers elaborate swimming pools, landscaped gardens, meeting facilities, shopping arcades, and a variety of restaurants. They are, as intended, complete resorts. Today they cater more to business travelers and tour groups than to the individual tourist. But like the hotels of the Art Deco District, they offer a taste of a world past. If you elect to experience this slice of Florida history, you will be happier if you have a car. The night life and restaurants of South Miami Beach are a 10- to 30-minute drive away, depending on traffic. The Miami Beach Convention Center is 10 to 20 minutes by cab or convention-sponsored bus. The area is considered safe for pedestrians days and evenings.

Miami Beach, 71st Street to 96th Street Although there are a few nice hotels and also a couple of parks, the area is in a general state of decline. Characterized by smaller properties, weekly/monthly residence hotels, fast-food eateries, and eclectic retail shops, this area is not where we recommend that you spend your time in Miami.

Bal Harbour, 96th Street to the Haulover Bridge This area along the ocean is another isolated bastion of affluence and beauty. Large, modern, well-maintained hotels alternate with equally imposing condominiums. The Bal Harbour Shops, one of the most diverse and tasteful shopping venues in the Southeast, is situated at the 96th Street end of the area. Nearby to the north is Haulover Park and Marina, featuring deep-sea fishing and kite flying as well as a nice beach. The airport is about 40 to 55 minutes away in light to moderate traffic. The Miami Beach Convention Center can be reached in about the same amount of time. Visitors on foot have little to fear.

Sunny Isles and North Bal Harbour is the last community to the north on the barrier island of Miami Beach. From here, Collins Avenue (US A1A) crosses the Haulover Cut (connecting the Intracoastal Waterway and the Atlantic Ocean) and passes through Haulover Beach Park. Beyond the park is Sunny Isles and Golden Shores. This area was developed during the late '50s and early '60s and is characterized by small, motel-sized properties with exotic themes ranging from space travel to the Suez Canal. Once again, while there are some nice rooms to be had, many of the properties have seen better days. Plus, the area is pretty remote unless you are bound for the Calder Race Track or Pro Player Stadium. Walking is generally safe during day and evening business hours.

Getting a Good Deal on a Room

High Season vs. Low Season

High season in Miami is from Christmas through Easter. Additionally, some hotels observe a second high season from mid-June through mid-August, known as the Family Season. Room rates for many hotels are 25 to 50% higher during these times of year. September, October, November (excluding the Thanksgiving holiday), and the first two weeks of December are the best times for obtaining low rates. Be aware, though, that a large convention at the Miami Beach Convention Center can drive rates up regardless of the season. Check with the Miami Convention and Visitors Bureau to make sure your visit does not fall during a big meeting or trade show.

Special Weekend Rates

While well-located Miami hotels are tough for the budget-conscious, it's not impossible to get a good deal, at least relatively speaking. For starters, most downtown hotels that cater to business, government, and convention travelers offer special weekend discount rates that range from 15 to 40% below normal weekday rates. You can find out about weekend specials by calling the hotel or consulting your travel agent.

Getting Corporate Rates

Many hotels offer discounted corporate rates (5 to 20% off rack rates). Usually you do not need to work for a large company or have a special relationship with the hotel to obtain these rates. Simply call the hotel of your choice and ask for their corporate rates. Many hotels will guarantee you the discounted rate on the phone when you make your reservation. Others may make the rate conditional on your providing some sort of *bona fides,* for instance a fax on your company's letterhead requesting the rate or a company credit card or business card on check-in. Generally, the screening is not rigorous.

Half-Price Programs

The larger discounts on rooms (35 to 60%), in Miami or anywhere else, are available through half-price hotel programs, often called travel clubs. Program operators contract with an individual hotel to provide rooms at deep discount, usually 50% off rack rate, on a "space available" basis. Space available, in practice, generally means that you can reserve a room at the discounted rate whenever the hotel expects to be at less than 80% occupancy. A little calendar-sleuthing to help you avoid city-wide conventions and special events will increase your chances of choosing a time for your visit when the discounts are available.

Most half-price programs charge an annual membership fee or directory subscription charge of $25 to $125. Once enrolled, you are mailed a membership card and a directory listing all the hotels participating in the program. Examining the directory, you will notice immediately that there are a lot of restrictions and exceptions. Some hotels, for instance, "black out" certain dates or times of year. Others may only offer the discount on certain days of the week, or require you to stay a certain number of nights. Still others may offer a much smaller discount than 50% off rack rate.

Some programs specialize in domestic travel, some specialize in international travel, and some do both. The more established operators offer members between 1,000 and 4,000 hotels to choose from in the United States. All of the programs have a heavy concentration of hotels in California and Florida, and most have a very limited selection of participating properties in New York City or Boston. Offerings in other cities and regions of the United States vary considerably. The programs with the largest selection of hotels in Miami are *Encore, Travel America at Half Price (Entertainment Publications), International Travel Card,* and *Quest.* Each of these programs lists 14 to 45 hotels in the Greater Miami area.

Encore	(800) 638-0930
Entertainment Publications	(800) 285-5525
International Travel Card	(800) 342-0558
Quest	(800) 638-9819

One problem with half-price programs is that not all hotels offer a full 50% discount. Another slippery problem is the base rate against which the discount is applied. Some hotels figure the discount on an exaggerated rack rate that nobody would ever have to pay. A few participating hotels may deduct the discount from a supposed "superior" or "upgraded" room rate, even though the room you get is the hotel's standard accommodation. Though hard to pin down, the majority of participating properties base discounts on the published rate in the *Hotel & Travel Index* (a quarterly reference work used by travel agents) and work within the spirit of their agreement with the program operator. As a rule, if you travel several times a year, you will more than pay for your program membership in room rate savings.

A noteworthy addendum to this discussion is that deeply discounted rooms through half-price programs are not commissionable to travel agents. In practical terms this means that you must ordinarily make your own inquiry calls and reservations. If you travel frequently, however, and run a lot of business through your travel agent, he or she will probably do your legwork, lack of commission notwithstanding.

Preferred Rates

If you cannot book the hotel of your choice through a half-price program, you and your travel agent may have to search for a lesser discount, often called a "preferred rate." A preferred rate could be a discount made available to travel agents to stimulate their booking activity or a discount initiated to attract a certain class of traveler. Most preferred rates are promoted through travel industry publications and are often accessible only through an agent.

We recommend sounding out your travel agent about possible deals. Be aware, however, that the rates shown on travel agents' computerized reservations systems are not always the lowest rates available. Zero in on a couple of hotels that fill your needs in terms of location and quality of accommodations, then have your travel agent call for the latest rates and specials. Hotel reps are almost always more responsive to travel agents because travel agents represent a source of additional business. There are certain specials that hotel reps will disclose *only* to travel agents. Travel agents also come in handy when the hotel you want is supposedly booked. A personal appeal from your agent to the hotel's director of sales and marketing will get you a room more than half the time.

Wholesalers, Consolidators, and Reservation Services

If you do not want to join a program or buy a discount directory, you can take advantage of the services of a wholesaler or consolidator. Wholesalers and consolidators buy rooms, or options on rooms (room blocks), from hotels at a low, negotiated rate. They then resell the rooms at a profit through travel agents, tour packagers, or directly to the public. Most wholesalers and consolidators have a provision for returning unsold rooms to participating hotels, but are disinclined to do so. The wholesaler's or consolidator's relationship with any hotel is predicated on volume. If they return rooms unsold, the hotel might not make as many rooms available to them the next time around. Thus, wholesalers and consolidators often offer rooms at bargain rates, anywhere from 15 to 50% off rack, occasionally sacrificing profit margin in the process, to avoid returning the rooms to the hotel unsold.

When wholesalers and consolidators deal directly with the public, they frequently represent themselves as "reservation services." When you call, you can ask for a rate quote for a particular hotel, or alternatively ask for their best available deal in the area where you prefer to stay. If there is a maximum amount you are willing to pay, say so. Chances are the service will find something that will work for you, even if they have to shave a dollar or two off their own profit. Sometimes you will have to pay for your room when you make your reservation using your credit card. Other times you will pay as usual, when you check out. Listed below are several services that frequently offer substantial discounts:

Budget Reservations	(800) 681-1993
Central Reservation Service	(800) 950-0232
Hotel Reservations Network	(800) 964-6835
Florida Hotel Network	(800) 538-3616

Exit Information Guide

A company called EIG (Exit Information Guide) publishes a book of discount coupons for bargain rates at hotels throughout the state of Florida. These books are available free of charge in many restaurants and motels along the main interstate highways leading to the Sunshine State. Since most folks make reservations prior to leaving home, picking up the coupon book en route does not help much. For $2 ($5 Canadian), however, EIG will mail you a copy (third class) before you make your reservations. If you call and use a credit card, EIG will send the guide first class for $3. Write or call:

Exit Information Guide
4205 NW 6th Street
Gainesville, FL 32609
(352) 371-3948

Condominium Deals

There are a large number of condo resorts and timeshares in the Greater Miami area and the Keys that rent to vacationers for a week or even less. Bargains can be found, especially during off-peak periods. Reservations and information can be obtained from Condolink, (800) 733-4445.

The majority of area condos that rent to visitors also work with travel agents. In many cases the condo owners pay an enhanced commission to agents who rent the units for reduced consumer rates. It's worth a call to your travel agent.

How to Evaluate a Travel Package

Hundreds of Miami package vacations are offered to the public each year. Packages should be a win-win proposition for both the buyer and the seller. The buyer only has to make one phone call and deal with a single salesperson to set up the whole vacation: transportation, rental car, lodging, meals, attraction admissions, and even golf and tennis. The seller, likewise, only has to deal with the buyer once, eliminating the need for separate sales, confirmations, and billing. In addition to streamlining selling, processing, and administration, some packagers also buy airfares in bulk on contract like a broker playing the commodities market. Buying a large number of airfares in advance allows the packager to buy them at a significant savings from posted fares. The same practice is applied also to hotel rooms. Because selling vacation packages is an efficient way of doing business, and because the packager can often buy individual package components (airfare, lodging, etc.) in bulk at discount, savings in operating expenses realized by the seller are sometimes passed on to the buyer so that, in addition to convenience, the package is also an exceptional value. In any event, that is the way it is supposed to work.

All too often, in practice, the seller realizes all of the economies and passes nothing in the way of savings on to the buyer. In some instances, packages are loaded additionally with extras that cost the packager next to nothing, but that run the retail price of the package sky-high. As you might expect, the savings to be passed along to customers are basically nil.

When considering a package, first choose one that includes features you are sure to use. Whether you use all the features or not, you will most certainly pay for them. Second, if cost is a greater concern than convenience, make a few phone calls and see what the package would cost if you booked its individual components (airfare, rental car, lodging, etc.) on your own. If the package price is less than the à la carte cost, the package is a good deal. If the costs are about the same, the package is probably worth it for the convenience.

Helping Your Travel Agent Help You

When you call your travel agent, ask if he or she has been to Miami. Firsthand experience means everything. If the answer is no, either find another agent or be prepared to give your travel agent a lot of direction. Do not accept any recommendations at face value. Check out the location and rates of any suggested hotel and make certain that the hotel is suited to your itinerary.

Because some travel agents are unfamiliar with Miami, your agent may try to plug you into a tour operator's or wholesaler's preset package. This essentially allows the travel agent to set up your whole trip with a single phone call and still collect an 8 to 10% commission. The problem with this scenario is that most agents will place 90% of their Miami business with only one or two wholesalers or tour operators. In other words, it's the line of least resistance for them, and not much choice for you.

Often, travel agents will use wholesalers who run packages in conjunction with airlines, like Delta's Dream Vacations or American's Fly-Away Vacations. Because of the wholesaler's exclusive relationship with the carrier, these trips are very easy for travel agents to book. However, they will probably be more expensive than a package offered by a high-volume wholesaler who works with a number of airlines in a primary Miami market.

To help your travel agent get you the best possible deal, do the following:

1. Determine where you want to stay in Miami (Miami Beach, downtown, Coral Gables, Key Biscayne, etc.) and, if possible, choose a specific hotel. This can be accomplished by reviewing the hotel information provided in this guide and by writing or calling hotels that interest you.
2. Check out the Miami travel ads in the Sunday travel section of your local newspaper and compare them to ads running in the newspapers of one of Miami's key markets, i.e., New York, Philadelphia, or Boston. Often you will be able to find deals advertised in these newspapers that beat the socks off anything offered in your local paper. The best source of all is the "Sunday Travel" section of the *New York Times.* See if you can find some packages that fit your plans and that include a hotel you like.
3. Call the wholesalers or tour operators whose ads you have collected. Ask any questions you might have concerning their packages, but do not book your trip with them directly.
4. Tell your travel agent about the packages you find and ask if he or she can get you something better. The packages in the paper will serve as a benchmark against which to compare alternatives proposed by your travel agent.
5. Choose from among the options uncovered by you and your travel agent. No matter which option you elect, have your travel agent book it. Even if you go with one of the packages in the newspaper, it will probably be commissionable (at no additional cost to you) and will provide the agent some return on the time invested on your behalf. Also, as a travel professional, your agent should be able to verify the quality and integrity of the package.

If You Make Your Own Reservation

As you poke around trying to find a good deal, there are several things you should know. First, always call the hotel in question as opposed to the hotel chain's national 800 number. Quite often, the reservationists at the national number are unaware of local specials. Always ask about specials before you inquire about corporate rates. Do not be reluctant to bargain. If you are buying a hotel's weekend package, for example, and want to extend your stay into the following week, you can often obtain at least the corporate rate for the extra days. Do your bargaining, however, before you check in, preferably when you make your reservations.

Miami Lodging for Business Travelers

The primary considerations for business travelers are affordability and proximity to the site or area where you will transact your business. Identify the zone(s) where your business will take you, then find the hotels in the Hotel Chart that are situated there. Once you have developed a short list of possible hotels that are conveniently located, fit your budget, and offer the standard of accommodation you require, you (or your travel agent) can make use of the cost-saving suggestions discussed earlier to obtain the lowest rate.

Where to Stay for Meetings at the Miami Beach Convention Center

If you are attending a meeting or trade show at the Miami Beach Convention Center, the most convenient lodging is in South Miami Beach. Hotels located between 15th and 24th streets are within walking distance. Hotels south of 15th and north of 24th up to 53rd Street are about 5 to 15 minutes from the convention center by cab or shuttle. While some downtown hotels are a fast 10- to 15-minute drive from the Miami Beach Convention Center via the MacArthur or Tuttle Causeways, most are more remote.

Commuting to Miami Beach from the mainland during rush hour is something to be avoided if possible. At the moment, there are not nearly enough hotel rooms on South Miami Beach to accommodate attendees of a large convention or trade show. If you want a room near the Miami Beach Convention Center, book early—very early. If you need a room at the last minute, try a wholesaler or reservation service, or one of the strategies listed below.

Convention Rates: How They Work and How to Do Better

If you are attending a major convention or trade show, it is probable that the meeting's sponsoring organization has negotiated "convention rates" with some hotels. Under this arrangement, hotels agree to "block" a certain number of rooms at an agreed-upon price for the use of convention attendees. Sometimes, as in the case of a small meeting, only one hotel is involved. In the event of a large, city-wide convention at the Miami Beach Convention Center, however, almost every downtown and airport hotel, and many Miami Beach hotels, will participate in the room block.

Because the convention sponsor is bringing a lot of business to the city and reserving a large number of rooms, it usually can negotiate a volume discount on the room rates, a rate that should be substantially below rack rate. The bottom line, however, is that some conventions and trade shows have more bargaining clout and negotiating skills than others. Hence, your convention sponsor may or may not be able to obtain the lowest possible rate.

Once a convention or trade show sponsor has completed negotiations with participating hotels, it will send its attendees a housing list that includes all the hotels serving the convention, along with the special convention rate for each. When you receive the housing list, you can compare the convention rate for hotels where you might like to stay with the rates obtainable using the strategies covered in the previous section. If the negotiated convention rate doesn't sound like a good deal, you can try to reserve a room using a half-price club, a consolidator, or a tour operator. Remember, however, that many of the deep discounts are available only when the hotel expects to be at less than 80% occupancy, a condition which rarely prevails when a big convention is in town.

Strategies for Beating Convention Rates

There are several strategies for getting around convention rates:

1. Reserve early. Most big conventions and trade shows announce meeting sites one to three years in advance. Get your reservation booked as far in advance as possible using a half-price club. If you book well ahead of the time the convention sponsor sends out the housing list, chances are good that the hotel will accept your reservation.
2. Compare your convention's housing list with the list of hotels presented in this guide. You might be able to find a hotel that suits your needs that is not on the housing list.
3. Use a local reservations agency or consolidator. This is also a good strategy to employ if, for some reason, you need to make reservations at the last minute. Local reservations agencies and consolidators almost always control some rooms, even in the midst of a huge convention or trade show. One Miami-based wholesaler is Florida Hotel Network, (800) 538-3616.
4. Stay in a condominium. Reservations and information can be obtained from Condolink, (800) 733-4445.

Hotels and Motels: Rated and Ranked

Room Ratings

To separate properties according to the relative quality, tastefulness, state of repair, cleanliness, and size of their standard rooms, we have grouped hotels

Hotel and Motel Toll-Free 800 Numbers	
Best Western	(800) 528-1234 U.S. & Canada (800) 528-2222 TDD (Telecommunication Device for the Deaf)
Clarion	(800) 424-4777 U.S.
Comfort Inn	(800) 228-5150 U.S.
Courtyard by Marriott	(800) 321-2211 U.S.
Days Inn	(800) 325-2525 U.S.
Doubletree	(800) 528-0444 U.S.
Econo Lodge	(800) 424-4777 U.S.
Embassy Suites	(800) 362-2779 U.S. & Canada
Fairfield Inn by Marriott	(800) 228-2800 U.S.
Doubletree Guest Suites	(800) 424-2900 U.S. & Canada
Hampton Inn	(800) 426-7866 U.S. & Canada
Hilton	(800) 445-8667 U.S. (800) 368-1133 TDD
Holiday Inn	(800) 465-4329 U.S. & Canada
Howard Johnson	(800) 654-2000 U.S. & Canada (800) 654-8442 TDD
Hyatt	(800) 233-1234 U.S. & Canada
Loew's	(800) 223-0888 U.S. & Canada
Marriott	(800) 228-9290 U.S. & Canada (800) 228-7014 TDD
Quality Inn	(800) 228-5151 U.S. & Canada
Radisson	(800) 333-3333 U.S. & Canada
Ramada Inn	(800) 228-3838 U.S. (800) 228-3232 TDD
Residence Inn by Marriott	(800) 331-3131 U.S.
Rodeway	(800) 424-4777 U.S
Sheraton	(800) 325-3535 U.S. & Canada
Wyndham	(800) 822-4200 U.S.

and motels into classifications denoted by stars. Star ratings in this guide apply to Miami-area properties only, and do not necessarily correspond to ratings awarded by Mobil, AAA, or other travel critics. Because stars have little relevance when awarded in the absence of commonly recognized standards of comparison, we have tied our ratings to expected levels of quality established by specific American hotel corporations.

Room Star Ratings		
★★★★★	*Superior Rooms*	Tasteful and luxurious by any standard
★★★★	*Extremely Nice Rooms*	What you would expect at a Hyatt Regency or Marriott
★★★	*Nice Rooms*	Holiday Inn or comparable quality
★★	*Adequate Rooms*	Clean, comfortable, and functional without frills (like a Motel 6)
★	*Super Budget*	

Star ratings apply to room quality only, and describe the property's standard accommodations. For most hotels and motels a "standard accommodation" is a hotel room with either one king bed or two queen beds. In an all-suite property, the standard accommodation is either a one- or two-room suite. In addition to standard accommodations, many hotels offer luxury rooms and special suites, which are not rated in this guide. Star ratings for rooms are assigned without regard to whether a property has restaurant(s), recreational facilities, entertainment, or other extras.

In addition to stars (which delineate broad categories), we also employ a numerical rating system. Our rating scale is 0 to 100, with 100 as the best possible rating, and zero (0) as the worst. Numerical ratings are presented to show the difference we perceive between one property and another. Rooms at the Sonesta Beach Resort, the Miami Beach Ocean Resort, and the Riande Continental are all rated as three and a half stars (★★★½). In the numerical ratings, the Sonesta Beach Resort is rated an 80, the Miami Beach Ocean Resort a 79, and the Riande Continental a 75. This means that within the three-and-a-half-star category, the Sonesta Beach Resort and the Miami Beach Ocean Resort are comparable, and both have slightly nicer rooms than the Riande Continental.

Cost estimates are based on the hotel's published rack rates for standard rooms. Each "$" represents $40. Thus a cost symbol of "$$$" means a room (or suite) at that hotel will be about $120 a night.

How the Hotels Compare

Here is a hit parade of the nicest rooms in town. We've focused strictly on room quality, and excluded any consideration of location, services, recreation, or amenities. In some instances, a one- or two-room suite can be had for the same price or less than that of a hotel room.

If you use subsequent editions of this guide, you will notice that many of the ratings and rankings change. We'll include new properties, as well as reflecting in our ratings such positive developments as guest room renovation or improved maintenance and housekeeping in hotels already listed. A failure to properly maintain guest rooms or a lapse in housekeeping standards can negatively affect the ratings.

Finally, before you begin to shop for a hotel, take a hard look at this letter we received from a couple in Hot Springs, Arkansas:

> *We canceled our room reservations to follow the advice in your book [and reserved a hotel highly ranked by the* Unofficial Guide*]. We wanted inexpensive, but clean and cheerful. We got inexpensive, but [also] dirty, grim, and depressing. I really felt disappointed in your advice and the room. It was the pits. That was the one real piece of information I needed from your book! The room spoiled the holiday for me . . .*

Needless to say, this letter was as unsettling to us as the bad room was to our reader. Our integrity as travel journalists, after all, is based on the quality of the information we provide our readers. Even with the best of intentions and the most conscientious research, however, we cannot inspect every room in every hotel. What we do, in statistical terms, is take a sample: we check out several rooms selected at random in each hotel and base our ratings and rankings on those rooms. The inspections are conducted anonymously and without the knowledge of the property's management. Although it's unusual, it is certainly possible that the rooms we randomly inspect are not representative of the majority of rooms at a particular hotel. Another possibility is that the rooms we inspect in a given hotel are representative, but that by bad luck a reader is assigned a room which is inferior. When we rechecked the hotel our reader disliked so intensely, we discovered our rating was correctly representative, but that he and his wife had unfortunately been assigned to one of a small number of threadbare rooms scheduled for renovation.

The key to avoiding disappointment is to do some advance snooping around. We recommend that you ask to be sent a photo of a hotel's standard guest room before you book, or at least get a copy of the hotel's promotional brochure. Be forewarned, however, that some hotel chains use the same guest room photo in their promotional literature for all hotels in the chain, and that the guest room in a specific property may not resemble the photo in the brochure. When you or your travel agent call, ask how old the property is and when the guest room you are being assigned was last renovated. If you arrive and are assigned a room inferior to that which you had been led to expect, demand to be moved to another room.

How the Hotels Compare in Miami

Hotel	Zone	Quality Rating	Star Rating	Cost ($=$40)
Mayfair House Hotel	3	98	★★★★★	$$$$$$+
Marlin	1	97	★★★★★	$$$$$$$$–
Casa Grande Suite Hotel	1	96	★★★★★	$$$$$$$–
Grove Isle Club and Resort	3	96	★★★★★	$$$$$$$$+
Ocean Front Hotel	1	95	★★★★½	$$$$$+
Alexander Hotel	1	94	★★★★½	$$$$$$$$
Hotel Intercontinental	3	94	★★★★½	$$$$$+
Biltmore Hotel	3	93	★★★★½	$$$$$$$$
Grand Bay Hotel	3	93	★★★★½	$$$$$$$+
Hotel Sofitel	2	93	★★★★½	$$$$$+
Omni Colonnade Hotel	3	93	★★★★½	$$$$$$+
Hotel Astor	1	92	★★★★½	$$$$$
Hyatt Regency Coral Gables	3	91	★★★★½	$$$$$$$$–
Hotel Delano	1	90	★★★★½	$$$$$$$$$+
Westin Resort Miami Beach	1	90	★★★★½	$$$$$$$–
Doral Golf Resort & Spa	2	89	★★★★	$$$$$$$+
Hotel Impala	1	89	★★★★	$$$$$–
Hotel Place St. Michel	3	89	★★★★	$$$$+
Cardozo on the Beach	1	88	★★★★	$$$$
Embassy Suites	2	87	★★★★	$$$$$$$+
Wyndham Miami	3	87	★★★★	$$$$$$$+
Doubletree Grand Hotel	3	86	★★★★	$$$$+
Hyatt Regency Miami	3	86	★★★★	$$$$$
Don Shula's Hotel & Golf Club	2	85	★★★★	$$$$$$–
Doubletree at Coconut Grove	3	85	★★★★	$$$$$$$+
Marriott Biscayne Bay	3	85	★★★★	$$$$$–
Miami Airport Hilton & Towers	2	85	★★★★	$$$$$$–
Sheraton Bal Harbour Resort	1	85	★★★★	$$$$$$$$–
Blue Moon Hotel	1	84	★★★★	$$$$$–
Fontainebleau Hilton Resort & Spa	1	84	★★★★	$$$$$$$$$–
Radisson Mart Plaza	2	84	★★★★	$$$$$$–
David William Hotel	3	83	★★★★	$$$$$–

How the Hotels Compare in Miami (continued)

Hotel	Zone	Quality Rating	Star Rating	Cost ($=$40)
Eden Roc Hotel	1	83	★★★★	$$$$$$$–
Sea View Hotel	1	83	★★★★	$$$$$$–
Club Hotel by Doubletree	2	82	★★★½	$$$$–
Club Hotel & Suites by Doubletree	3	81	★★★½	$$+
Miami Airport Marriott	2	81	★★★½	$$$$
Sheraton Gateway	2	81	★★★½	$$$$$–
Courtyard Airport	2	80	★★★½	$$$+
RIU Pan American Ocean Resort	1	80	★★★½	$$$$$–
Sonesta Beach Resort	3	80	★★★½	$$$$$$$$+
Miami Beach Ocean Resort	1	79	★★★½	$$$$$–
Indian Creek Hotel	1	78	★★★½	$$$$–
Miami Airport Courtyard South	2	78	★★★½	$$$+
Cavalier Hotel	1	77	★★★½	$$$$
Kent Hotel	1	77	★★★½	$$$$–
Newport Beachside Crowne Plaza Resort	1	77	★★★½	$$$$$–
Shelborne Beach Hotel	1	77	★★★½	$$$$$$–
Brigham Gardens	1	76	★★★½	$$$–
Lily Guesthouse	1	76	★★★½	$$$$–
Sheraton Biscayne Bay	3	76	★★★½	$$$$$
Riande Continental	1	75	★★★½	$$$$–
Best Western Beach Resort	1	74	★★★	$$$+
Comfort Inn and Suites Airport	2	74	★★★	$$$–
Park Central Imperial Hotels	1	74	★★★	$$$$
Best Western Marina Park	3	73	★★★	$$$+
Holiday Inn Select LeJeune Center	2	73	★★★	$$$$+
National Hotel	1	73	★★★	$$$$$$+
Holiday Inn Downtown	3	72	★★★	$$$+
Riande Continental Miami Bayside	3	72	★★★	$$$+
Airport Regency Hotel	2	71	★★★	$$$+
Days Inn Art Deco	1	71	★★★	$$+
Leslie Hotel	1	71	★★★	$$$$$
LTI Seville Beach Hotel	1	71	★★★	$$$$

How the Hotels Compare in Miami (continued)

Hotel	Zone	Quality Rating	Star Rating	Cost ($=$40)
Best Western Miami Airport Inn	2	70	★★★	$$+
Essex House Hotel	1	70	★★★	$$$$$$$$–
Tudor Hotel	1	70	★★★	$$$+
Governor Hotel	1	69	★★★	$$+
Mermaid Guest House	1	68	★★★	$$$–
Ritz Plaza Hotel	1	68	★★★	$$$$$$+
Wellesley Inns Airport West	2	68	★★★	$$$–
Marseilles Hotel	1	67	★★★	$$$+
Waldorf Towers Hotel	1	67	★★★	$$$+
Di Lido Beach Resort	1	66	★★★	$$+
Howard Johnson Port of Miami	3	66	★★★	$$+
Majestic Hotel	1	66	★★★	$$$+
Avalon Hotel	1	65	★★★	$$$$–
Days Inn Oceanside	1	65	★★★	$$$–
Sol Miami Beach Hotel	1	64	★★½	$$$$–
Hampton Inn Downtown	3	63	★★½	$$+
Boulevard Hotel Art Deco	1	62	★★½	$$$$–
Budgetel Inn Airport	2	62	★★½	$$
Colony Hotel	1	62	★★½	$$$$+
Dezerland Surfside Beach Hotel	1	62	★★½	$$$$$$–
Comfort Inn Airport	2	61	★★½	$$+
Holiday Inn Coral Gables	3	61	★★½	$$$$
Howard Johnson Airport West	2	61	★★½	$$+
Beacon Hotel	1	60	★★½	$$$$+
Holiday Inn Airport	2	60	★★½	$$$+
Howard Johnson Miami Airport	2	60	★★½	$$$–
Miami Airport Fairfield Inn South	2	60	★★½	$$+
Red Roof Inn Airport	2	60	★★½	$$$–
Beachcomber	1	59	★★½	$$$
Crown Hotel	1	59	★★½	$$+
Best Western Surf Vista	1	58	★★½	$$$–
Betsy Ross Hotel	1	58	★★½	$$$$–
Comfort Inn Hotel	1	58	★★½	$$+
Dorchester	1	58	★★½	$$$+
La Quinta Miami Airport	2	57	★★½	$$+
Penguin Hotel	1	56	★★½	$$$

How the Hotels Compare in Miami (continued)

Hotel	Zone	Quality Rating	Star Rating	Cost ($=$40)
South Beach Resort	1	56	★★½	$$$$
Beach Plaza Hotel	1	54	★★	$$+
Everglades Hotel	3	54	★★	$$$–
Winterhaven Hotel	1	54	★★	$$$+
Days Inn North Beach	1	53	★★	$$$$–
Princess Ann Hotel	1	53	★★	$$+
Carlton Hotel	1	52	★★	$$+
Paradise Inn	1	52	★★	$+
Raleigh Hotel	1	48	★★	$$$$$$+
Edison Hotel	1	42	★½	$$$$+

How the Hotels Compare in the Keys

Hotel	Quality Rating	Star Rating	Cost ($=$40)
The Gardens Hotel	90	★★★★½	$$$$$$+
Sheraton Suites Key West	89	★★★★	$$$$$$$$$$–
Hyatt Key West Resort & Marina	88	★★★★	$$$$$$$$–
Marriott's Reach Resort	88	★★★★	$$$$$$$–
Cheeca Lodge	87	★★★★	$$$$$$$$–
Marriott's Casa Marina Resort	86	★★★★	$$$$$$$–
The Artist House	85	★★★★	$$$$–
Marriott Key Largo Bay Beach Resort	85	★★★★	$$$$$+
Ocean Key House Suite Resort & Marina	85	★★★★	$$$$$$$$$–
Bayside Key West Resort (suites)	84	★★★★	$$$$–
Heron House	84	★★★★	$$$$–
Island City House Hotel	84	★★★★	$$$$$–
La Mer Hotel	83	★★★★	$$$$$–
Pier House	82	★★★½	$$$$$$$$$–
Best Western Suites at Key Largo	81	★★★½	$$$$$–
Duval House	79	★★★½	$$$$$–
Seascape	79	★★★½	$$$+
Banyon Resort	78	★★★½	$$$$$

How the Hotels Compare in the Keys (continued)

Hotel	Quality Rating	Star Rating	Cost ($=$40)
Eaton Lodge	78	★★★½	$$$$+
Holiday Inn La Concha	77	★★★½	$$$$$$$–
La Te Da	77	★★★½	$$–
Westin Beach Resort Key Largo	75	★★★½	$$$$$$$$$$–
Best Western Key Ambassador	70	★★★	$$$–
Best Western Hibiscus Motel	69	★★★	$$$$$+
Faro Blanco Marine Resort	69	★★★	$$+
Quality Inn Key West	69	★★★	$$$$–
Chesapeake Resort	68	★★★	$$$$
Eaton Manor Guesthouse	68	★★★	$$$+
Ramada Limited Resort & Marina	68	★★★	$$$$
Breezy Palms Resort	67	★★★	$$
Holiday Inn Beachside	67	★★★	$$$$–
Howard Johnson Resort Key Largo	66	★★★	$$$$$–
Holiday Inn Marathon	65	★★★	$$$+
South Beach Oceanfront Motel	64	★★½	$$$$+
Atlantic Shores Motel	63	★★½	$$$$$$+
Bayside Key West Resort (rooms)	63	★★½	$$$$–
Santa Maria Motel	63	★★½	$$$–
Southernmost Motel in the USA	63	★★½	$$$$$–
Comfort Inn Key West	62	★★½	$$$$$
Econo Lodge Resort Key West	62	★★½	$$$$$–
Hampton Inn Key West	62	★★½	$$$
Ramada Inn Key West	62	★★½	$$$$
Blue Marlin Motel	61	★★½	$$$$+
Days Inn Key West	61	★★½	$$$$$$–
Pelican Cove Resort	61	★★½	$$$$$–
Fairfield Inn Key West	60	★★½	$$$$+
Holiday Inn Key Largo	60	★★½	$$$$+
Howard Johnson Motor Lodge	59	★★½	$$$+
Marina Del Mar Resort	57	★★½	$$$+
Nancy's William Street Guest House	56	★★½	$$$$+
Popp's Motel	52	★★	$$+
Key Lodge Motel	51	★★	$$$$–
Islander Motel	50	★★	$$+

THE BEST DEALS

Having listed the nicest rooms in town, let's reorder the list to rank the best combinations of quality and value in a room. As before, the rankings are made without consideration of location or the availability of restaurant(s), recreational facilities, entertainment, or amenities. Once again, each lodging property is awarded a value rating on a 0 to 100 scale. The higher the number, the better the value.

We recently had a reader complain to us that he had booked one of our top-ranked rooms in terms of value and had been very disappointed in the room. We noticed that the room the reader occupied had a quality rating of ★★½. We would remind you that the value ratings are intended to give you some sense of value received for dollars spent. A ★★½ room at $50 may have the same value rating as a ★★★★ room at $100, but that does not mean the rooms will be of comparable quality. Regardless of whether it's a good deal or not, a ★★½ room is still a ★★½ room.

Listed below are the best room buys for the money, regardless of location or star classification, based on averaged rack rates. Note that sometimes a suite can cost less than a hotel room.

The Top 30 Best Deals in Miami

Hotel	Zone	Quality Rating	Star Rating	Cost ($=$40)
1. Club Hotel & Suites by Doubletree	3	81	★★★½	$$+
2. Brigham Gardens	1	76	★★★½	$$$–
3. Best Western Miami Airport Inn	2	70	★★★	$$+
4. Cardozo on the Beach	1	88	★★★★	$$$$
5. Governor Hotel	1	69	★★★	$$+
6. Courtyard Airport	2	80	★★★½	$$$+
7. Hotel Place St. Michel	3	89	★★★★	$$$$+
8. Days Inn Art Deco	1	71	★★★	$$+
9. Hotel Astor	1	92	★★★★½	$$$$$
10. Hotel Intercontinental	3	94	★★★★½	$$$$$+
11. Comfort Inn and Suites Airport	2	74	★★★	$$$–
12. Di Lido Beach Resort	1	66	★★★	$$+

The Top 30 Best Deals in Miami (continued)

Hotel	Zone	Quality Rating	Star Rating	Cost ($=$40)
13. Howard Johnson Port of Miami	3	66	★★★	$$+
14. Ocean Front Hotel	1	95	★★★★½	$$$$$+
15. Doubletree Grand Hotel	3	86	★★★★	$$$$+
16. Miami Airport Courtyard South	2	78	★★★½	$$$+
17. Indian Creek Hotel	1	78	★★★½	$$$$–
18. Budgetel Inn Airport	2	62	★★½	$$
19. Club Hotel by Doubletree	2	82	★★★½	$$$$–
20. Hotel Sofitel	2	93	★★★★½	$$$$$+
21. Mayfair House Hotel	3	98	★★★★★	$$$$$$+
22. Paradise Inn	1	52	★★	$+
23. Marriott Biscayne Bay	3	85	★★★★	$$$$$–
24. Wellesley Inns Airport West	2	68	★★★	$$$–
25. David William Hotel	3	83	★★★★	$$$$$–
26. Mermaid Guest House	1	68	★★★	$$$–
27. Casa Grande Suite Hotel	1	96	★★★★★	$$$$$$$–
28. Blue Moon Hotel	1	84	★★★★	$$$$$–
29. Riande Continental	1	75	★★★½	$$$$–
30. Kent Hotel	1	77	★★★½	$$$$–

The Top 30 Best Deals in the Keys

Hotel	Quality Rating	Star Rating	Cost ($=$40)
1. La Te Da	77	★★★½	$$–
2. Breezy Palms Resort	67	★★★	$$
3. The Artist House	85	★★★★	$$$$–
4. Faro Blanco Marine Resort	69	★★★	$$+
5. Heron House	84	★★★★	$$$$–
6. Best Western Key Ambassador	70	★★★	$$$–
7. Seascape	79	★★★½	$$$+
8. La Mer Hotel	83	★★★★	$$$$$–
9. Island City House Hotel	84	★★★★	$$$$$–
10. Eaton Lodge	78	★★★½	$$$$+

The Top 30 Best Deals in the Keys (continued)

Hotel	Quality Rating	Star Rating	Cost ($=$40)
11. The Gardens Hotel	90	★★★★½	$$$$$$+
12. Eaton Manor Guesthouse	68	★★★	$$$+
13. Best Western Suites at Key Largo	81	★★★½	$$$$$–
14. Marriott Key Largo Bay Beach Resort	85	★★★★	$$$$$+
15. Duval House	79	★★★½	$$$$$–
16. Holiday Inn Marathon	65	★★★	$$$+
17. Santa Maria Motel	63	★★½	$$$–
18. Quality Inn Key West	69	★★★	$$$$–
19. Banyon Resort	78	★★★½	$$$$$
20. Marriott's Reach Resort	88	★★★★	$$$$$$$–
21. Holiday Inn Beachside	67	★★★	$$$$–
22. Marriott's Casa Marina Resort	86	★★★★	$$$$$$$–
23. Hampton Inn Key West	62	★★½	$$$
24. Chesapeake Resort	68	★★★	$$$$
25. Ramada Limited Resort & Marina	68	★★★	$$$$
26. Popp's Motel	52	★★	$$+
27. Howard Johnson Motor Lodge	59	★★½	$$$+
28. Islander Motel	50	★★	$$+
29. Cheeca Lodge	87	★★★★	$$$$$$$$–
30. Hyatt Key West Resort & Marina	88	★★★★	$$$$$$$$–

Part Four

Arriving and Getting Oriented

A Geographic Overview of Miami and South Florida

Situated only two degrees above the Tropic of Cancer, Miami is a subtropical city on the same latitude as the Sahara Desert. Located near the southeastern tip of Florida on the Atlantic Ocean and Biscayne Bay, Greater Miami (as the whole metropolis is often called) is a conglomeration of 26 municipalities with a total population of around two million.

But don't think of Miami as an isolated city perched on the end of the Florida peninsula. It's actually the southern terminus of a long, skinny mass of suburban sprawl that stretches north along I-95 and the Atlantic coast to West Palm Beach. The northern suburbs of Miami merge with Fort Lauderdale, the next major city up the coast.

Many first-time visitors don't realize that Miami and Miami Beach are two different cities. Miami Beach is located on a narrow barrier island, with the Atlantic Ocean on one side and Biscayne Bay on the other. The rejuvenated Art Deco District and hip South Beach are on the southern tip of the island; condo canyons stretch along its northern end. Miami Beach is often touted as America's Riviera.

Miami, featuring one of the most distinctive and beautiful skylines in the United States, is directly across the bay on the mainland. It's the most important commercial city in Florida and, because of its strong financial connections to Latin America, is called the Capital of the Caribbean. The two cities are connected by a number of causeways that cross wide, but shallow, Biscayne Bay.

Geographically, Greater Miami is longer than it is wide and hugs the coast; think of I-95 as the city's spine. The interstate runs north-south just to the west of downtown Miami, easily recognizable by its cluster of glitzy high-rise office and bank buildings.

The Major Highways

Immediately south of downtown, I-95 ends and merges with US 1, also called South Dixie Highway. US 1 swings southwest along Biscayne Bay through congested suburbs that include the cities of Coral Gables, Coconut Grove, Kendall, South Miami, Perrine, Cutler Ridge, and Homestead. South Dixie Highway is infamous for its seemingly endless number of traffic lights and horrendous traffic jams.

Forming Greater Miami's western border is Florida's Turnpike, Homestead Extension. Folks heading south from Miami and Miami Beach to visit southern Dade County's attractions—or to tour the Florida Keys and Biscayne, and Everglades National Parks—should skip US 1 and take Route 836 (the Dolphin Expressway) to Florida's Turnpike and head south toward Homestead on this toll road; for more on driving around Miami, read on.

Other major highways that visitors to Miami need to know about are:

- Route 112, the Airport Expressway (a toll road that links Miami International Airport with I-95 and Miami Beach)
- Route 836 (*the* major east-west link connecting Florida's Turnpike, MIA, I-95, downtown Miami, and South Miami Beach)
- Route 826, the Palmetto Expressway (a major commuter route that runs north to south between MIA and Florida's Turnpike before heading east to I-95 in North Miami)
- Route 874, the Don Shula Expressway (which links the Palmetto Expressway and Florida's Turnpike in South Miami)

South and west of Miami, drab housing tracts and strip malls (many of them rebuilt since 1992's Hurricane Andrew, which wreaked havoc on southern Dade County) give way to monotonous—and spectacularly productive—agricultural fields growing citrus, avocados, and decorative foliage. Continue south to reach the Florida Keys; head west on Route 41 (the Tamiami Trail) to reach the Everglades. Neither destination, by the way, is monotonous.

The Layout

Most of Dade County is organized on a grid, which makes finding your way around fairly easy. "Avenues," "Courts," and "Places" are oriented north to south and "Streets" go east to west. Downtown, Miami Avenue and Flagler Street divide the Miami area into four quadrants: SW, NW, SE, and NE. Watch out, though—some numbered streets and avenues also have names. For example, Bird Road is also SW 40th Street; the Tamiami Trail is also known as Calle Ocho, Route 41, and SW 8th Street.

Some of the major highways that crisscross Miami also sport several names. Route 836 is also known as the Dolphin Expressway and, appropriately enough, the East-West Expressway. East of I-95, the highway crosses Biscayne Bay on the MacArthur Causeway (which connects the mainland to Miami Beach) and changes names again to I-395; once the highway lands on Miami Beach, it becomes 5th Street. The polyglot of names is often confusing to first-time visitors.

Topographically, Dade County is flat and hardly rises above sea level. Most folks don't seem to mind, however. The terrain makes for panoramic sunsets and offers residents and visitors beguiling vistas and a decidedly nonclaustrophobic feeling. Spectacular beaches, terrific views of downtown Miami and gorgeous Biscayne Bay, abundant wildlife (especially colorful and exotic birds such as flamingos), and verdant subtropical plant life make most people forget that South Florida is as flat as a pancake.

Coming into the City

By Car

Most people who drive to Miami arrive on I-95, which begins south of downtown and continues north along the Atlantic seaboard all the way to Maine; it's the major north-south expressway on the East Coast. Another major route for visitors traveling by car is Florida's Turnpike, a toll highway that starts near Orlando and Walt Disney World, runs down the center of the Florida peninsula, then heads east to Fort Pierce on the Atlantic coast; from there the turnpike parallels I-95 south to Miami. The Homestead Extension of Florida's Turnpike skirts Greater Miami to the west. It's the route to take if you're headed to the Keys.

Another major highway, I-75, funnels motorists to Miami from Naples, Fort Myers, St. Petersburg, Tampa, and other points along Florida's west coast. It's better known by another name: the Everglade Parkway. US 41, also called the Tamiami Trail and Alligator Alley, connects Miami and the Everglades to the west.

US 1 is the stoplight-laden road that I-95 and Florida's Turnpike replaced, but the old highway is still intact, and is a diversion from boring highway driving if you're not in a hurry. Though it's not a practical route for visitors on a tight schedule (traffic lights, shopping centers, and congestion often slow traffic to a crawl and the road is rated as one of the most unpleasant driving experiences in South Florida), US 1 still affords glimpses of beaches, palm trees, occasional Florida kitsch, and plenty of strip shopping centers.

US A1A, the alternate Route 1, is an even better alternative for folks weary of interstates—and even slower. Much of this venerable old highway runs directly along the beach. Hint: for visitors who fly into Fort Lauderdale/Hollywood International Airport and are headed to Miami Beach, A1A is the way to go . . . if you're not in a rush.

If you're driving north to Miami from the Keys on US 1, take Florida's Turnpike, Homestead Extension in Florida City; US 1 between here and Miami is often unpredictably congested. Then take Route 874 north (the Don Shula Expressway) to Route 826 north (the Palmetto Expressway); next, go east on the Dolphin Expressway (Route 836), which goes past Miami International Airport and links up with I-95 near downtown Miami. It may sound complicated, but it's much faster.

The Penalty for Getting Lost: More on Driving Around Miami

Greater Miami is a sprawling metropolis crisscrossed by busy expressways passing through neighborhoods that can change character from gentrified to seedy within a block. Sooner or later—probably sooner—most visitors to the city fall victim to Miami's infuriating lack of street signs and inadequate highway signs and find themselves taking an unplanned detour. Since you'll be hard put to forget all the bad publicity you've heard about Miami as you frantically drive along unfamiliar streets in search of an interstate ramp, it can be a very scary experience.

How concerned about safety should you be on an unplanned detour?

"Some neighborhoods look grim but aren't necessarily unsafe," reports one Miami native who regularly drives through some of the city's worst areas without incident. "But the lack of visual clues, especially to Anglo visitors not used to different cultures, makes it hard to discern if a neighborhood is truly 'dangerous' or just different. To a lost tourist, a house with a yard full of junk might look threatening in Miami—but the same house could be considered 'charming' if it were in Jamaica."

In addition, many visitors aren't prepared for the sharp contrasts that exist between trendy places near the beach and economically disadvantaged neighborhoods west of Biscayne Boulevard in Miami. Don't be fooled; the difference in safety may not be as wide as you think (both areas are relatively safe).

Yet our advice is to stay in areas that you know are safe (granted, that's not very helpful advice if you're lost) and not to wander around the city. "Neighborhoods change radically, and areas with crack and prostitution exist next to areas being renovated," our friend adds. "Check with one of the police vans stationed around the city or someone you know before wandering into an area that you don't know."

If you *do* get lost, it helps to think positive. Remember that during daylight you are much safer than at night, and if you avoid looking like a lost tourist, you're less likely to become a crime statistic. (Read on for more information on how to avoid crime.) And remember that property values around interstates fall—and it shows. The streets that you're frantically driving on as you try to find that entrance ramp back to the highway may look bad, but they're not necessarily the most dangerous areas in the city.

By Plane

Virtually all foreign visitors flying into Miami must fly into Miami International Airport. Domestic flyers, however, have a choice: Fort Lauderdale/Hollywood International Airport, a smaller facility, is a viable option and worth considering. It's only 30 minutes north of downtown Miami, close to I-95, and convenient for folks headed to Miami Beach because you can skip the major highways by taking US A1A south.

Miami International Airport (MIA) MIA is the eighth-largest airport in the United States, and number two in the number of international passengers it handles. More airline companies fly into MIA (100) than to any other airport in the country, averaging more than 1,500 take offs/landings a day. MIA has service to every major city in Latin America and the Caribbean, as well as connections to Europe and the Middle East. All told, MIA makes connections to 200 cities on 5 continents; more than 33 million passengers fly in and out of MIA each year.

MIA boasts 118 aircraft gates and 8 concourses; anticipating more growth, the Dade County–owned facility embarked on a $4 billion expansion program scheduled to be completed in 2007. Improvements will include increasing the number of gates to nearly 140, adding 3 new passenger concourses, upgrading baggage handling systems, and doubling the amount of retail space. But the place is already huge: the second-floor departure level of the horseshoe-shaped terminal is jammed with boutiques, bookstores, a hotel (with 260 rooms), bars, gift shops, restaurants, and a culturally diverse flow of people from around the world.

In spite of its size, however, MIA is an easy airport to get around in. From your gate, follow the signs to the baggage area on the lower level; bus, taxicab, SuperShuttle service, passenger car pickup, and rental car limos are outside the door. (See page 98 for more information on van and cab service from MIA.) Directly across the street is a multilevel garage for short-term parking. If you're faced with a long walk between terminals, take the elevator to Level 3, where a "horizontal escalator" will save wear and tear on your feet.

Fort Lauderdale/Hollywood International Airport This is a small, modern, easy-to-get-around facility only minutes off I-95. While not as convenient for Miami-bound travelers as its big brother to the south, this airport offers peace of mind to visitors who are anxious about safety when they drive to and from Miami International Airport. Unlike MIA, it's not located near unsafe, economically distressed neighborhoods and it's virtually impossible to get lost trying to find I-95. A lot of domestic flyers headed for Miami have switched to Fort Lauderdale and the airport has launched a $1 billion expansion that will add a new terminal, entrance road, and 5,000 additional parking spaces as early as 2000.

From the gate, go to the lower level and claim your baggage at the baggage carousels. Then exit the terminal on the ground level to the curb, where you can meet someone picking you up or find ground transportation out of the airport. Rental car shuttle buses are located at both ends of the terminal; call your rental car company on your way to the baggage claim area to let them know that you've arrived and that you need a lift to their office to pick up your car. Most of the rental car offices are located on nearby US 1; getting to I-95 from them is very easy.

By Train

Amtrak operates a small, modern terminal located near Hialeah Park, northwest of downtown Miami. It's not very convenient if your destination is the beach or downtown Miami—and it's in a neighborhood that's not very safe.

If you're not being picked up by someone with a car, however, you're not out of luck: a Metrorail station is about eight blocks away. Outside the terminal, board Metrobus "L," which takes you to the elevated-train station; the fare is $1.25 plus $.25 for a transfer to the above-ground train. Check the bulletin board inside the train station for current bus, Metrorail, Metrobus, and driving information.

The terminal is located at 8303 NW 37th Avenue; for recorded arrival and departure information, call (305) 835-1200. For ticket prices and reservations, call Amtrak at (800) 272-7245. To reach the station by car from I-95, take NW 79th Street west to NW 37th Avenue and turn right; the station is a few blocks north where the street dead ends. Signs will help direct you.

The Port of Miami

Miami is the "Cruise Capital of the World," with more than three million passengers a year sailing from the Port of Miami, the home of 17 cruise ships—the world's largest year-round fleet. Cruise passengers can choose from the world's most popular ports of call on sea vacations ranging from one-day excursions to voyages up to three months in length. In addition, in 1998 one-day cruises are scheduled to return to the Port of Miami.

Destinations include exotic ports in the Caribbean, South America, the coastal resorts of Mexico, the Bahamas, and Key West. With the recent addition of Cunard's ships sailing out of Miami, the port now offers cruises around the globe, with stops in the Far East, Europe, and South America. Year-round, passengers enjoy tropical weather virtually from the start of their voyages—a big attraction for vacationers from northern climates and a key to Miami's leadership in the cruise industry.

For cruise passengers flying into Miami International Airport who booked a cruise with airfare included, getting to the ship is easy: representatives from cruise ship operators, holding signs, greet passengers as they enter the passenger terminal. Luggage is transferred automatically to the ship and passengers board motorcoaches for the quick (less than 30 minutes) trip to the dock. Your luggage is later delivered to staterooms aboard ship.

If you booked your own flight to Miami, don't expect to be greeted by an official from the cruise line. Instead, proceed to the lower level, pick up your luggage, step outside, and take a cab to the Port of Miami. Taxi rates range from $12 to $16 for up to five passengers.

If you're driving, the Port of Miami is easy to find: it's located on Dodge Island in Biscayne Bay between Miami and Miami Beach, and can be reached from Miami via Port Boulevard. From I-95, take Exit 3 to downtown and follow signs to Biscayne Boulevard; Port Boulevard is next to Bayside Marketplace. From I-395 (Exit 5 east on I-95, toward Miami Beach), take the Biscayne Boulevard south exit to downtown and follow signs to the Port of Miami. Parking is located in front of the terminals for $8 a day, payable prior to embarking. Have your cruise tickets handy and drop off your luggage at the terminal before parking your car; the luggage will be sent to your cabin.

The Port of Miami has 12 air-conditioned cruise passenger terminals that are wheelchair-accessible and feature duty-free shopping, ground-level customs clearance, and easy access to cars, buses, and taxis. In addition, the terminals are color-coded and marked with the name of the ship, which makes it easy for folks driving to the port to find the right one. Long-term parking is across from the terminals; luggage handed over to porters at the terminal entrances will be delivered to your stateroom. Unfortunately, due to an increase in terrorism in the past few years, security measures have been adopted that prevent noncruising visitors from boarding the cruise ships before they sail.

Note: Folks who drive to the Port of Miami or who booked their own airfare and aren't whisked to their ship in a bus can take advantage of a wider range of duty-free goods at Miami Duty Free (MDF), a clean, uncluttered shop located at 125 NE 8th Street in downtown Miami. Just present your cruise or flight ticket to the security guard, select and pay for your goods, and MDF will deliver them to your plane or ship on the day of departure. Items include liquor, perfumes, Wedgwood china, Waterford crystal, and Rolex watches, all at prices 20 to 40% below retail. Salespeople at MDF speak seven languages; the shop is open 10 a.m. to 6 p.m. daily. For more information, call (305) 358-9774.

Where to Find Tourist Information in Miami

If you're short on maps or need more information on sight-seeing, restaurants, hotels, shopping, or things to do in the Greater Miami area, there are several places to stop and pick up maps and brochures:

- in downtown Miami at the kiosk in front of Bayside Marketplace on Biscayne Boulevard.
- at the Miami Beach Chamber of Commerce located across from the Holocaust Memorial at 1920 Meridian Avenue, Miami Beach. Phone: (305) 672-1270. Hours: 8:30 a.m. to 6 p.m. weekdays and 10 a.m. to 4 p.m. Saturdays; closed Sundays.
- at the Miami Visitors Center at Aventura Mall, 19501 Biscayne Boulevard, Aventura. Phone: (305) 935-3836. Hours: 10 a.m. to 9:30 p.m. Monday through Saturday, 11 a.m. to 6 p.m. Sundays.
- at the Sunny Isles Visitor Information Center, 17100 Collins Avenue, Suite 208, at the Harrison Supermarket shopping center. Phone: (305) 947-5826. Hours: 9 a.m. to 2 p.m. weekdays.
- in Surfside at 9301 Collins Avenue in the community center. Phone: (305) 864-0722. Hours: 9 a.m. to 5 p.m. Monday, Wednesday, and Thursday.
- at the Greater Homestead/Florida City Chamber of Commerce, 160 Highway 1 in Florida City. Phone: (305) 254-9180 (Miami), (800) 388-9669 (Florida and U.S.). Hours: 8 a.m. to 6 p.m. daily.
- at Sears, Coral Gables, 3655 SW 22nd Street (Coral Way at Douglas Road), Coral Gables. Phone: (305) 460-3477. Hours: 9:30 a.m. to 9 p.m. Monday through Saturday, 10 a.m. to 6 p.m. Sundays.
- at Sears, Miami International Mall, 1625 NW 107th Street, Miami. Phone: (305) 470-7863. Hours: 10 a.m. to 9 p.m. Monday through Saturday, 10 a.m. to 6 p.m. Sundays.
- at Sears, Westland Mall, 1625 W. 49th Street, Hialeah. Phone: (305) 364-3827. Hours: 10 a.m. to 9 p.m. Monday through Saturday, noon to 6 p.m. Sundays.

- at Miami International Airport; there is a Tourist/Information Center on Level 2, Concourse E, across from the hotel; it's open 24 hours a day.

Finally, check the Greater Miami Convention and Visitors Bureau at 701 Brickell Avenue, Suite 2700. It's not particularly convenient for visitors who just want to pick up a map, but the view from these 27th-floor offices is spectacular. Park in the basement of the building—and don't forget to have your parking ticket stamped before you leave.

How to Avoid Crime and Keep Safe in Public Places

Crime in Miami

You don't have to be a fan of "Miami Vice" reruns to know that Miami is renowned for glamorous, over-the-top crime. Blame it on a lot of things: the city's geographical and (some say) moral position on the edge of the continent; a drug-smuggling industry that turns over as much as $12 billion a year; a proliferation of guns in the hands of its citizenry (the bloodiest shoot-out in FBI history took place in Miami, and Florida has *the* most liberal gun ownership laws in the country); a crush of immigrants fleeing dictatorial bad guys throughout Latin America (a situation which also spawned several racial disturbances in the last two decades); rising crime against tourists.

Inevitably you will ask yourself, Just how safe is Miami, anyway? Am I going to end up being another statistic?

The fact is, most deadly violence that occurs in Miami is either the result of domestic strife or a drug deal gone wrong. By steering clear of both situations, visitors can leave safely on the same airplane they came in on. Some experts even say that Miami is safer now than in the 1920s, when gangsters like Al Capone were muscling in on illegal nightclubs and casinos. A local historian notes that Miami's crime rate was three times higher per capita in 1925 than in the early '80s, when the town earned its title as "Murder Capital USA." If that's true, bystanders have never been safer in South Florida.

Surviving Miami International Airport

And what about all the bad press about the killing of tourists leaving the airport? The problem is simple: Miami International Airport is located in an economically distressed, high-crime neighborhood. And while the Airport Expressway whisks you the eight miles to Miami in about as many minutes (except during rush hour), getting to the expressway isn't so easy if your rental car agency is located on a side street outside the airport—and a lot of them are.

The solution? There are several, depending on your degree of concern about crime. You could choose a rental car company based on its easy access to the expressway instead of its rates (see page 94). Or make sure your rental car has a cellular phone. (A lot of Miami car rental agencies provide a car phone at no additional charge; you pay for the phone calls by the minute; they can also be rented.) Or take a taxi or shuttle van to your hotel and have your rental car delivered to you there.

Our opinion? We think most people overreacted to the spate of bad publicity Miami received in 1993 when nine foreign tourists were murdered in Florida. As tragic and frightening as these deaths might be, that's nine unfortunate people killed out of the 20 million visitors who came to Florida that year. While the neighborhoods around the airport can be dangerous and confusing, signs to the expressway have been improved recently and car rental agencies are providing detailed directions when they send you on your way.

In fact, car rental agencies take the crime threat *very* seriously. Today, all rental cars are virtually indistinguishable from private vehicles; they carry regular license plates and no stickers. Most car rental offices are equipped with TVs that continuously show videos instructing customers how to avoid becoming a crime victim; the offices also provide customers with detailed written information on avoiding crime.

More reassuring news: In 1995, more than 400 new directional highway signs were erected at a cost of nearly $3 million. The signs feature an orange sunburst logo and direct visitors toward major tourist areas. Finally, Dade County has inaugurated a new police force, the Tourist Oriented Police Squad (TOPS), to patrol the airport area; look for the marked squad cars patrolling the roadways and neighborhoods surrounding MIA. In addition, the Tourist Robbery Abatement Program (TRAP) assigns police officers to patrol areas frequented by tourists such as the airport, car rental parking lots, and nearby neighborhoods.

Public Service Aid Shane Maguffy, a police cadet with 900 hours of criminal justice education, is one of the pros patrolling the area. He regularly doles out advice, information, and reassurance to first-time visitors. What, we asked him, should a visitor do if he or she gets lost after leaving MIA?

"Don't read a road map at an intersection—it attracts people's attention," he says. "Instead, go to a restaurant or well-lighted parking lot and read the map there. You can also call 579-6111, the police department's nonemergency number, for help on finding your way; they'll even send an officer out to help."

What if you're in a minor accident—say, if you're bumped from behind by another car? "It could be a bad guy trying to trick you into pulling over by staging a fake accident," Maguffy says. "Keep going." Another scam: Criminals will wave and point at your tires, acting like good samaritans who only want to warn you that one of your tires is bad. Their goal is to get you to stop and get out of your car—so that they can rob you, or worse. Use your imagination and you'll think of other methods that bad guys will use to set up unsuspecting tourists for a mugging. The key is to avoid becoming a victim by *not* pulling over on the side of the road, where you're most vulnerable. Drive to a safe, lighted area before stopping and leaving your car.

More advice for visitors: keep your luggage in the trunk. "Bad guys look inside cars at traffic lights and if they see luggage, they know you're a tourist," Maguffy explains. "At stoplights, leave room between you and the vehicle ahead. If someone approaches your car, you have room to make a U-turn."

Some final advice for drivers in South Florida: do whatever it takes to avoid becoming a crime victim. "If you have to run a red light to avoid someone who approaches you, do it," Maguffy adds. "And don't 'sleep' drive. Always look in the rearview mirror and all around you. Crime can happen anywhere."

The increased presence of the City of Miami police on the roads has, in fact, reduced crime: in late 1995, crimes against tourists dropped approximately 60% compared to the previous year. Visitor robberies decreased 80% between 1992 and 1996; a whopping 26% drop occurred between 1995 and 1996. As a result, we think Miami is no more dangerous than any other big U.S. city. Here are some more suggestions on how to avoid crime that applies to Miami and any other large urban center.

Having a Plan

Random violence and street crime are facts of life in any large city. You've got to be cautious and alert, and plan ahead. Police are rarely able to actually foil a crime in progress. When you are out and about you must work under the assumption that you must use caution because you are on your own; if you run into trouble, it's unlikely that police or anyone else will be able to come to your rescue. You must give some advance thought to the ugly scenarios that might occur, and consider both preventive measures that will keep you out of harm's way and an escape plan just in case.

Not being a victim of street crime is sort of a "survival of the fittest" thing. Just as a lion stalks the weakest member of the antelope herd, muggers and thieves target the easiest victims. Simply put, no matter where you are or what you are doing, you want potential felons to think of you as a bad risk.

On the Street For starters, you always present less of an appealing target if you are with other people. Secondly, if you must be out alone, act alert and always have at least one of your arms and hands free. Felons gravitate toward preoccupied folks, the kind found plodding along staring at the sidewalk, with both arms encumbered by briefcases or packages. Visible jewelry (on either men or women) attracts the wrong kind of attention. Men, keep your billfolds in your *front* trouser or coat pocket, or in a fanny pack. Women, keep your purses tucked tightly under your arm; if you're wearing a jacket, put it on *over* your shoulder bag strap.

Here's another tip: carry two wallets, including one inexpensive one, carried in your hip pocket, containing about $20 in cash and some expired credit cards. This is the one you hand over if you're accosted. Your real credit cards and the bulk of whatever cash you have should be in either a money clip or a second wallet hidden elsewhere on your person. Women can carry a fake wallet in their purses and keep the real one in a pocket or money belt.

If You're Approached Police will tell you that a criminal has the least amount of control over his intended victim during the first few moments of his initial approach. A good strategy, therefore, is to short-circuit the crime as quickly as possible. If a mugger starts by demanding your money, for instance, quickly take out your billfold (preferably your fake one), and hurl it as far as you can in one direction while you run shouting for help in the opposite direction. The odds are greatly in your favor that the criminal will prefer to collect your billfold rather than pursue you. If you hand over your wallet and just stand there, he will likely ask for your watch and jewelry next. If you're a woman, the longer you hang around, the greater your vulnerability to personal injury or rape.

Secondary Crime Scenes Under no circumstances, police warn, should you *ever* allow yourself to be taken to another location—a "secondary crime scene," in police jargon. This move, they explain, provides the criminal more privacy and, consequently, more control. A mugger can rob you on the street very quickly and efficiently. If he tries to remove you to another location, whether by car or on foot, it is a certain indication that he has more in mind than robbery. Even if the thief has a gun or knife, your chances are infinitely better running away. If the criminal grabs your purse, let him have it. If he grabs your jacket, come out of it. Hanging onto your money or jacket is not worth getting mugged, sexually assaulted, or murdered.

Another maxim: never believe anything a criminal tells you, even if he's telling you something you desperately want to believe, for example, "I won't hurt you if you come with me." No matter how logical or benign he sounds, assume the worst. Always, *always,* break off contact as quickly as possible, even if that means running.

In Public Transport When riding a bus, always take a seat as close to the driver as you can; never ride in the back. Likewise, on the subway or elevated train, sit near the driver's or attendant's compartment. These people have a phone and can summon help in the event of trouble.

In Cabs While it is possible, though not likely, you'll hail a cab on the street in Miami, you are somewhat vulnerable in the process. Particularly after dusk, call a reliable cab company and stay inside while they dispatch a cab to your door. When your cab arrives, check the driver's certificate, which must, by law, be posted on the dashboard. Address the cabbie by his last name (Mr. Jones or whatever) or mention the number of his cab. This alerts the cab driver to the fact that you are going to remember him and/or his cab. Not only will this contribute to your safety, it will keep your cabbie from trying to run up the fare.

If you are comfortable reading maps, familiarize yourself with the most direct route to your destination ahead of time. If you can say, "South Beach via Washington Avenue, please," the driver is less likely to run up your fare by taking a circuitous route so he can charge you for extra mileage.

If you need to catch a cab at the train station or at one of the airports, always use the taxi queue. Taxis in the official queue are properly licensed and regulated. Never accept an offer for a cab or limo made by a stranger in the terminal or baggage claim area. At best, you will be significantly overcharged for the ride. At worst, you may be abducted.

Personal Attitude

While some areas of every city are more dangerous than others, never assume that any area is completely safe. Never let down your guard. You can be the victim of a crime and it can happen to you anywhere. If you go to a restaurant or night spot, use valet parking or park in a well-lighted lot. Women leaving a restaurant or club alone should never be reluctant to ask to be escorted to their cars.

Never let your pride or sense of righteousness and indignation imperil your survival. This is especially difficult for many men, particularly when in the presence of women. It makes no difference whether you are approached by an aggressive drunk, an unbalanced street person, or an actual criminal, the rule is the same: forget your pride and break off contact as quickly as possible. Who cares whether the drunk insulted you, if everyone ends up back at the hotel safe and sound? When you wake up in the hospital with a concussion and your jaw wired shut, it's too late to decide that the drunk's filthy remark wasn't really all that important.

Criminals, druggies, some street people, and even some drunks play for keeps. They can attack with a bloodthirsty hostility and hellish abandon that is beyond the imagination of most people. Believe me, you are not in their league . . . nor do you want to be.

Self-Defense

In a situation where it is impossible to run, you'll need to be prepared to defend yourself. Most policemen insist that a gun or knife is not much use to the average person. More often than not, they say, the weapon will be turned against the victim. Additionally, concealed firearms and knives are illegal in most jurisdictions. The best self-defense device for the average person is Mace. Not only is it legal in most states, it's nonlethal and easy to use.

When you shop for Mace, look for two things: it should be able to fire about eight feet, and it should have a protector cap so it won't go off by mistake in your purse or pocket. Carefully read the directions that come with your device, paying particular attention to how it should be carried and stored, and how long the active ingredients will remain potent. Wearing a rubber glove, test-fire your Mace, making sure that you fire downwind.

When you are out about town, make sure your Mace is someplace easily accessible, say, attached to your keychain. If you are a woman and you keep your Mace on a keychain, avoid the habit of dropping your keys (and your Mace) into the bowels of your purse when you leave your hotel room or your car. *The Mace will not do you any good if you have to dig around in your purse for it.* Keep your keys and your Mace in your hand until you have safely reached your destination.

More Things to Avoid

When you do go out, walk with a minimum of two people whenever possible. If you have to walk alone, stay in well-lighted areas that have plenty of people around. And don't walk down alleys. It also helps not to look too much like a tourist when venturing away from places such as beaches and the Art Deco District. Don't wear a camera around your neck and don't gawk at buildings and unfold maps on the sidewalk—or thumb through guidebooks, including this one. Be careful about who you ask for directions. (When in doubt, shopkeepers are a good bet.) Don't count your money in public, and carry as little cash as possible. At public phones, if you must say your calling card number to make a long-distance call, don't say it loud enough for strangers around you to hear. And avoid public parks and beaches after dark.

Carjackings

With the recent surge in carjackings, drivers also need to take special precautions. Stay alert when driving in traffic and keep your doors locked, with the windows rolled up and the air-conditioning on. Leave enough space to the car in front of you so that you're not blocked in and can make a U-turn if someone approaches your car and starts beating on your windshield. Store your purse or briefcase under your knees when you are driving, rather than on the seat beside you.

The Homeless

If you're not from a big city or haven't been to one in a while, you're in for a shock when you come to Miami. It seems like every city block is filled with shabbily dressed people asking for money. Along beaches, near waterfront areas on Biscayne Bay, and near large public buildings in downtown Miami, you will see people sleeping in blankets and sleeping bags, their possessions piled up next to them.

Who Are These People? "Most are lifelong residents who are poor," responds Joan Alker, assistant director of the National Coalition for the Homeless, an advocacy group headquartered in Washington, D.C. "The people you see on the streets are primarily single men and women. A disproportionate number of them are minorities and people with disabilities—they're either mentally ill or substance abusers or have physical disabilities."

Are They a Threat to Visitors? "No," Alker says. "Studies show that homeless men have lower rates of conviction for violent crimes than the population at large. We know that murders aren't being committed by the homeless. I can't make a blanket statement, but most homeless people you see are no more likely to commit a violent crime than other people."

Should You Give the Homeless Money? "That's a personal decision," Alker says. "But if you can't, at least try to acknowledge their existence by looking them in the eye and saying, 'Sorry, no.'" While there's no way to tell if the guy with the Styrofoam cup asking for a handout is really destitute or just a con artist, no one can dispute that most of these people are what they claim to be: homeless.

Ways to Help It's really a matter for your own conscience. We confess to being both moved and annoyed by these unfortunate people; moved by their need and annoyed that we cannot enjoy Miami without running a gauntlet of begging men and women. In the final analysis, we found that it is easier on the conscience and spirit to get a couple of rolls of quarters at the bank and carry a pocket full of change at all times. The cost of giving those homeless who approach you a quarter really does not add up to all that much, and it is much better for the psyche to respond to their plight than to deny or ignore their presence.

There is a notion, perhaps valid in some cases, that money given to a homeless person generally goes toward the purchase of alcohol or other drugs. If this bothers you excessively, carry granola bars for distribution, or, alternatively, buy some inexpensive gift coupons that can be redeemed at a McDonald's or other fast-food restaurant for coffee or a sandwich.

We have found that a little kindness regarding the homeless goes a long way, and a few kind words delivered along with your quarter or granola bar brightens the day for both you and someone in need. We are not suggesting a lengthy conversation or prolonged involvement, but something simple like, "Sure, I can help a little bit. Take care of yourself, fella."

Those moved to get more involved in the nationwide problem of homelessness can send inquiries—or a check—to the National Coalition for the Homeless, 1612 K Street, NW, Suite 1004, Washington, D.C. 20006.

Keep It Brief Finally, don't play psychologist. All the people you encounter on the street are strangers. They may be harmless, or they may be dangerous. Either way, maintain distance and keep any contacts or encounters brief. Be prepared to handle street people in accordance with your principles, but mostly, just be prepared. If you have a druggie in your face wanting a handout, the last thing you want to do is pull out your wallet and thumb through the twenties looking for a one-dollar bill. As the sergeant used to say on "Hill Street Blues": Be careful out there.

Things the Natives Already Know

Miami Customs and Protocol

With its tropical climate and reputation as a vacation capital, Miami takes casualness to extremes that can startle folks from colder, stuffier climes—and we're not referring to the profusion of topless bathers on South Beach.

It's hard not to think of a situation where shorts, a loud print shirt, and a straw hat wouldn't be appropriate—with the exception of a small number of exclusive restaurants and clubs that require jackets and ties for men and equally formal attire for women. Casual, cool, lightweight, and colorful clothing is the norm in Miami.

Eating in Restaurants Miami and its environs, as an emerging capital of Latin America and an international mixing bowl of cultures, boasts an astounding variety of restaurants. In fact, the emergence of a new cuisine in town could be an indicator of political unrest somewhere in the world. The first thing new immigrants do when they hit Miami, it seems, is open a restaurant.

Again, casual is the byword when it comes to eating in Miami restaurants. Don't feel intimidated about unfamiliar menus or a wait staff that doesn't speak English—many Latin restaurants offer menus in both Spanish and English and you only need to point to place your order.

Tipping Is the tip you normally leave at home appropriate in Miami? The answer is yes. Just bear in mind that a tip is a reward for good service. Here are some guidelines:

Porters and skycaps A dollar a bag.

Cab drivers A lot depends on the service and the courtesy. If the fare is less than $8, give the driver the change and a dollar. Example: If the fare is $4.50, give the cabbie fifty cents and a buck. If the fare is more than $8, give the driver the change and $2. If you are asking the cabbie to take you only a block or two, the fare will be small, but your tip should be large ($3 to $5) to make up for his wait in line and to partially compensate him for missing a better-paying fare. Add an extra dollar to your tip if the driver does a lot of luggage handling.

Parking valets $2 is correct if the valet is courteous and demonstrates some hustle. A dollar will do if the service is just OK. Only pay when you check your car out, not when you leave it.

Bellmen When a bellman greets you at your car with one of those rolling luggage carts and handles all of your bags, $5 is about right. The more luggage you carry yourself, of course, the less you should tip.

Waiters Whether in a coffee shop, an upscale eatery, or ordering room service from the hotel kitchen, the standard gratuity ranges from 15 to 20% of the tab, before sales tax. At a buffet or brunch where you serve yourself, leave a dollar or two for the folks who bring your drinks. Some restaurants, however, are adopting the European custom of automatically adding a 15% gratuity to the bill, so check before leaving a cash tip.

Cocktail Waiters/Bartenders In this case you tip by the round. For two people, a dollar a round; for more than two people, $2 a round. For a large group, use your judgment: Is everyone drinking beer, or is the order long and complicated? Tip accordingly.

Hotel Maids On checking out, leave a dollar or two per day for each day of your stay, providing the service was good.

How to Look and Sound Like a Native First, a definition: a Miami native is anyone who has lived in town for five years or longer. In other words, this is a city of transients. As a result, visitors to the city needn't feel concerned about not fitting in. Keep in mind that the city hosts more than 13 million visitors a year from all over the world.

Yet, if it's important to you not to look like A Visitor on Holiday in the Sun and Fun Capital of North America, we offer the following advice:

1. Pronounce the city's name "My-AM-uh," the way folks did when Miami was more Anglo than Latin. Problem is, a lot of natives may not understand what you're saying.
2. Never ever admit visiting the Everglades.
3. Be obsessive, if not maniacal, about the Dolphins or the Heat.
4. Be drop-dead beautiful and strut your stuff on Ocean Drive in South Beach. An eye-catching option for ladies: Strap on a thong bikini and cruise through Lummus Park on in-line skates.
5. Sit alone at a sidewalk café on Ocean Drive and engage in an intense conversation—on your cellular phone.
6. Men: For a night of clubbing on South Beach or the Grove, sport an earring, ponytail, and gold Rolex while attired in a tux jacket, gaudy Bermuda shorts, and no socks.
7. For women on the town, it's ego-dressing: An orchid behind the ear, a low-cut blouse, a skirt slit up the thigh or a silk nightgown; other options include anything in a bright floral pattern or leopard skin, or a tight leather miniskirt.
8. Leave the dog at home. A parrot perched on your shoulder or a boa constrictor draped over an arm is a sure indication you're not from Duluth.
9. Hire a hot-pink Rolls Royce and a driver and go clubbing on South Beach. Needless to say, as the hot wheels idle outside blocking traffic, you'll be making a statement. Icing on the cake: a retinue of white Harley-Davidson motorcycles.
10. Never eat green key lime pie.

Publications for Visitors

The reputable *Miami Herald* is the city's only daily newspaper; visitors should make a point of picking up the Friday edition—the Weekend section carries comprehensive information on entertainment, restaurants, nightclubs, happenings for kids, art reviews, and things going on around town. Try to grab a Friday edition before coming to Miami.

An even better source for listings is the weekly *New Times,* an "alternative" newspaper available free from street machines as well as from a wide variety of clubs, bars, and shops around town.

Other publications available at newsstands and hotel lobbies include *South Florida,* the area's main monthly magazine, *Ocean Drive,* a glossy South Miami Beach magazine that chronicles the comings and goings of celebrities and beautiful people, *South Beach,* a bimonthly with a more artistic slant on SoBe life, and *Travel Host,* a visitors guide with information on shopping, dining, clubs, pay-per-view television, and maps.

Miami on the Air

Aside from the usual babble of format rock, talk, easy listening, and country music stations, Miami is home to a few radio stations that really stand out for high-quality broadcasting. Tune in to what hip Miamians listen to.

Miami's High-Quality Radio Stations

Format	Frequency	Station
Jazz, Latin	88.9 FM	WDMA
Progressive rock, jazz, punk	90.5 FM	WVUM
Public radio	91.3 FM	WLRN
Classical, jazz	93.1 FM	WTMI

Tips for the Disabled

Most public places in South Florida offer generally impressive facilities for disabled visitors, because a lot of buildings are recent structures built with wheelchair access in mind. Plus, many buses have lowering platforms that allow wheelchair-bound passengers to board.

Metrozoo and the Seaquarium are accessible to people in wheelchairs and all parks in Dade County offer free parking for disabled people. Vizcaya, a 34-room Italian-style palace on Biscayne Bay, isn't wheelchair accessible, but the 10-acre formal gardens on the estate are. Beach access for wheelchairs is available at Crandon Park on Key Biscayne, and at Haulover Beach Park and North Shore State Recreation Area on Miami Beach.

In Everglades National Park, all the walking trails are wheelchair accessible. Due to the passage of the Americans with Disabilities Act in 1990, the issue of access for folks with disabilities has gotten a higher profile in Miami. Even small Art Deco hotels in South Beach now offer elevators, ramps, and bathrooms with railings to make their rooms wheelchair-accessible.

In addition, there are a number of services in Greater Miami to serve the needs of disabled folks. The *Deaf Services Bureau* (Gables One Tower, 1320 South Dixie Highway, Suite 760, Coral Gables, FL 33146; (305) 668-4407 voice/TDD, 668-4669 FAX) provides interpreter services, advocacy, information, personal counseling, special needs assistance, and a 24-hour crisis hotline: (305) 668-4694 (TDD). Open Monday, Tuesday, Thursday, and Friday, 9 a.m.–5 p.m.; Wednesday, 9 a.m.–noon.

The *Florida Relay Service* (200 S. Biscayne Boulevard, Suite 600; (305) 579-8644; (800) 955-8770; TDD is (800) 955-8771) serves as a liaison for deaf and hard-of-hearing visitors with TDDs who need to contact persons without TDD-equipped phones. Open 24 hours a day, seven days a week.

The *State of Florida Division of Blind Services* (401 NW 2nd Avenue, Suite S714, Miami; (305) 377-5339) provides services to visually impaired people.

Paraplegics and other physically disabled people needing referrals to services in the Miami area can contact the *Metro-Dade Disability Services and Independent Living* (D-SAIL) office located at 1335 NW 14th Street in Miami; phone (305) 547-5444.

Bugs

Miami's subtropical climate regularly soaks the city in extended stretches of heat, rain, and humidity. Because South Florida rarely experiences freezing temperatures, the result is a plethora of insect activity year-round. For people from more temperate climes, often the biggest shock they receive on a visit to the Miami area is the sight of *cockroaches.*

But visitors shouldn't be shocked or overly concerned about the bugs—because most sightings are brief glimpses at night as they scurry out of sight when a light is turned on. Unless you're staying at the Fontainebleau Hilton or some other ritzy resort that goes to the expense of protecting its guests from the sight of insects, you're bound to see an occasional roach during your stay in South Florida.

Relax.

"Just because you see roaches doesn't mean a place isn't clean," reports one longtime Miami resident who says she's as freaked out by bugs as anyone from more temperate climes. "They're only active at night, they don't crawl on you, and they don't bite or make noise. The really good news is that roaches don't like people. But roaches are a part of Florida."

Another local insect with a notorious reputation—this one more well-deserved—is the *mosquito.* But if your stay in South Florida revolves around the beach, mosquitoes aren't much of a problem: ocean breezes keep the pesky critters at a minimal level year-round.

On the other hand, if your visit to Miami isn't centered on the beach, or if you plan to make some inland sojourns, get ready to be attacked by mosquitoes. The worst place of all for mosquitoes is the Everglades, which we recommend only visiting in the winter—and even then, it's a good idea to use insect repellent. It is readily available at retail outlets and visitor centers.

During the summer, many Miami residents listen closely to local news broadcasts for reports of mosquito activity. Long, wet periods of rain often result in a predictable explosion in the mosquito population. If one is on the way, it's a good idea to reschedule any extended outdoor activities that you're planning away from the beach.

Miami residents who enjoy outdoor entertaining also have a secret weapon in the war against mosquitoes: Avon's *Skin-So-Soft* skin cream, which has a repellent effect on the bugs, doesn't make you smell like a science lab, and doesn't contain any harsh chemicals (so it's okay for babies and kids). Knowledgeable Miamians report that large bottles of the stuff are standard issue in South Florida and keep it handy throughout the summer months.

St. Louis Encephalitis

Although contraction of this disease occurs very rarely, St. Louis encephalitis is an ongoing concern for Florida's health officials. The disease is transmitted to humans by mosquito bites, and is often more severe in children and the elderly. In spite of regular warnings by state and county agencies, many people (including locals) are still unsure how much of a threat the mosquito-borne infection poses. A reader from New York City wrote:

> *Something very important to keep in mind: our resort's pools were closed by 6 p.m. every night. Why? Mosquitoes. We heard . . . that there was an encephalitis scare, so pools were closed early to protect guests from possible exposure. Alternately, we heard it was encephalitis season—implying that this wasn't an isolated scare, but an annual event. We couldn't substantiate either way, but you should inform your readers, even if it's not annual. People should know to bring bug spray, and they should plan on possibly not having any late night swims.*

Because mosquitoes flourish during periods of summer rain, it can be said that Florida undergoes an annual "encephalitis season." But 1997's El Niño rains particularly concerned public health officials because increased ground moisture causes even greater mosquito proliferation.

However, encephalitis is not a common disease in Florida, and most summers see no cases reported. Rather, health officials advise taking precautions during periods of warmth and moisture. Precautions include:

- Avoid outdoor activities between dusk and dawn when mosquitoes are most active.
- If you must be outside at night, wear long pants and long-sleeved shirts, as well as insect repellent on exposed skin.
- Avoid water—especially standing water—at night.

There is no vaccine for St. Louis encephalitis since it occurs in humans so rarely. The good news is that, due to conscientious preventive measures on the part of Florida locals and tourists, only a handful of cases were reported in 1997, in spite of El Niño.

An Informal Tour of Arquitectonica-Designed Buildings

Arquitectonica is the local avant-garde design firm that solidified the other Miami (read: non–Art Deco) style of architecture in the minds of millions of "Miami Vice" viewers.

The opening footage of the show panned Brickell Avenue, a downtown, tree-lined boulevard flanked by high-rise bank buildings and condominiums. Among the skyscrapers in the shot is the whimsical Atlantis, a tall building punctuated with a large opening in the center that contains a palm tree and a red spiral staircase. Atop the building and off-center rests a large red triangle.

Some of Arquitectonica's other buildings that put their stamp on Miami's landscape include the Imperial and the Palace, both on Brickell Avenue, and the Miracle Center, a mall near the corner of Coral Way and Douglas Road in Coral Gables.

Bring Lots of Quarters

After spending a day or two exploring Miami Beach and Miami by car, you'll discover this fact: Because of ubiquitous parking meters, you can't survive in Miami without quarters—lots of them. The demand for two-bit pieces is so intense, in fact, that retail businesses throughout Miami routinely charge each other $1 for a $20 roll of quarters. One shop owner on Miami Beach pointed out that the only places that drop the surcharges are banks and Publix food stores. Our advice: Buy a few rolls before hitting town, tuck them in a corner of your luggage, and generously resupply your pocket or purse with quarters each day.

A Cuban Coffee Primer

You'll see crowds huddling around an open window in front of the restaurants that line Calle Ocho in Little Havana and dot the rest of the city. It's the café window, presenting the same aroma of Cuban coffee that hits you when you enter the MIA terminal and stays curled in your nostrils as you tour the city. It's as ubiquitous as the palm trees.

In the mornings workers stop by the windows for a Styrofoam cup of *cafe con leche,* espresso with steamed milk. In late afternoon, the men in their *guayaberas* (loose-fitting shirts) gather to talk politics and drink thimblefuls of black, sweetened espresso. Some of the local Anglos call it "jet fuel."

Here's a java glossary of *cafe Cubano* in ascending order of potency.

Cafe con leche—usually a morning drink. About one part coffee to four parts steamed whole milk. Usually served *con azucar* (with sugar) and very sweet. Ask for it *sin azucar* (without sugar) and add your own to taste. For more of a kick, ask for it *oscuro* (dark).

Cortadito—smaller than a *cafe con leche.* About one part espresso to two parts milk.

Colada—a cup of straight, hypersugared espresso served with about five plastic thimble-sized cups for sharing. Only the truly intestinally fortified would venture to drink one solo.

For gifts or to replicate *cafe Cubano* in your espresso machine at home, Cafe Bustelo and Cafe Pilon are two of the most popular brands of espresso and are available in almost all local supermarkets and stores; stock up before you leave Miami.

¿Habla espanol? A Crash Course in Spanish for Anglos

Though many would say otherwise, the official language of Miami *is* English. Most locals speak rudimentary English, although their native tongue often is Spanish. But it's possible, on rare occasions (say, your car breaks down or you're in a small shop or restaurant), to find yourself in a situation where there's no one around who speaks English. Of course, you'll have this book at hand.

If you find yourself trying out your rudimentary Spanish with a non-English speaker, keep these hints in mind: Speak slowly and clearly. Charades and hand gestures have been known to bridge language gaps. And the critical ingredient to cross-cultural communication is a sense of humor.

Hola. Como estas? (Oh-lah. Como es-tahs?)
Hello. How are you?

Donde esta la playa? El aeropuerto? (Don-day es-tah lah ply-yah? El arrow-pwerto?)
Where is the beach? The airport?

Es muy lejos? (Es moo-ey lay-hohs?)
Is it very far?

Esta bien. (Es-tah bee-en.)
Okay.

Quiero el cafe sin azucar, por favor. Quiero arroz con pollo y una cerveza. (Key-err-o el cah-fey seen azoo-car, pour fah-vor. Key-err-oh-rose cone poy-yo ee oon-a ser-vay-sah.)
I would like a coffee without sugar, please. I'd like chicken with rice and a beer.

No puedo hablar espanol. (No pway-doh ab-lar es-pan-nyol.)
I can't speak Spanish.

No se. (No say.)
I don't know.

Dime. (Dee-may.)
Tell me.

Dame. (Dah-may.)
Give me.

Gracias. (Grah-see-ahs.)
Thank you.

Cuanto cuesta? (Kwan-toe kwes-tah?)
How much is it?

Part Five

Getting around Miami

Driving Your Car

Getting Out of Miami International Airport

Due to a flurry of bad publicity in late 1993, most visitors on their first visit to Miami International Airport are more concerned about personal safety after they leave the airport than they are in the air. While we think Miami's bad reputation for visitor safety is largely undeserved, there is cause for concern at MIA: the airport is located about eight miles west of downtown Miami in a confusing, economically depressed, and crime-ridden area.

If it were simply a matter of leaving the airport by car and jumping on the freeway, there would be no problem . . . and there isn't one if you're being picked up by a friend or business colleague, if you take public transportation or the SuperShuttle, or if you're being picked up by a cruise ship company and being whisked to the dock in a motor coach.

The problem is when you rent a car. Most of the rental car agencies are located outside the airport proper . . . and that's where the confusion begins. Poor highway signs and a landscape with few landmarks (at least to out-of-town visitors) compound the problem of finding your way out of a car rental agency. Our advice: When you rent your car, get a map and explicit directions from the car rental agency clerk to the closest highway that leads to your final destination (the rental agencies, you'll discover, take the threat of violence against visitors very seriously). And read "How to Avoid Crime and Keep Safe in Public Places" on page 76 for advice on how to avoid being an easy mark for crooks as you drive around Miami. And hang on to the rental car agency map: When returning your car it will come in handy on the confusing and poorly signed roadways around MIA.

I-95

It's not just another superhighway. Interstate 95, which starts below downtown and goes north all the way to Maine, is the Big Enchilada of expressways in car-crazy Miami. The north-south route connects all the major highways in South Florida . . . and when traffic isn't backed up ten miles by construction delays or an accident, travelers can breeze from Coconut Grove in the south to North Miami, the airport, and Miami Beach in minutes. When I-95 is working right, getting around Miami is a breeze.

The problem, as you've probably gathered, is that I-95 frequently *doesn't* work right. The aforementioned construction delays can leave trapped motorists seething for hours (because a lot of the highway is elevated, there's often no escape to a side street). Almost as bad is the temptation to take an exit you're not familiar with to avoid a backup . . . and get hopelessly lost in an unsafe neighborhood. Unfortunately, I-95 passes through some pretty rough territory.

More problems: Dealing with poorly marked highways is a way of life for drivers in Miami, and I-95, being the Numero Uno transportation artery, has more than its fair share of sign problems. Often, signs are misleading, ambiguous, or just don't exist. Detours around construction projects are particularly irksome: with the high volume of traffic, it's easy to miss the one sign that gives you the information you need to make a quick decision. The result is an unplanned side trip. See Part Four: Arriving and Getting Oriented, page 68, for more information on unscheduled detours around Miami.

Further complicating a cruise on I-95 is the peculiar mix of drivers indigenous to South Florida. Frustrated jet-fighter-pilot wannabes weaving in and out of rush-hour traffic in expensive sports cars, "Third-World" drivers (easily recognizable by their refusal to use turn signals and a tendency to make multiple lane changes on a whim), retirees driving big cars (easily identified as they slowly drift into your lane), high-strung yuppies in Volvos and BMWs tailgating while they yack on car phones and pound the steering wheel. . . .

Maybe it's those little cups of *cafe Cubano* jet fuel regularly consumed by Miamians that make this such a high-strung city to drive around in.

To sum up: I-95 in Miami often induces soaring blood pressure and moments of pure terror—even in experienced drivers who routinely handle the frustrations of driving in other big American cities. The solution for first-time visitors is to study a road map carefully before venturing out, check the *Miami Herald* for a listing of construction delays and lane closures (often scheduled at night, causing backups that rival rush-hour traffic snarls), avoid driving in rush-hour traffic, and drive very defensively.

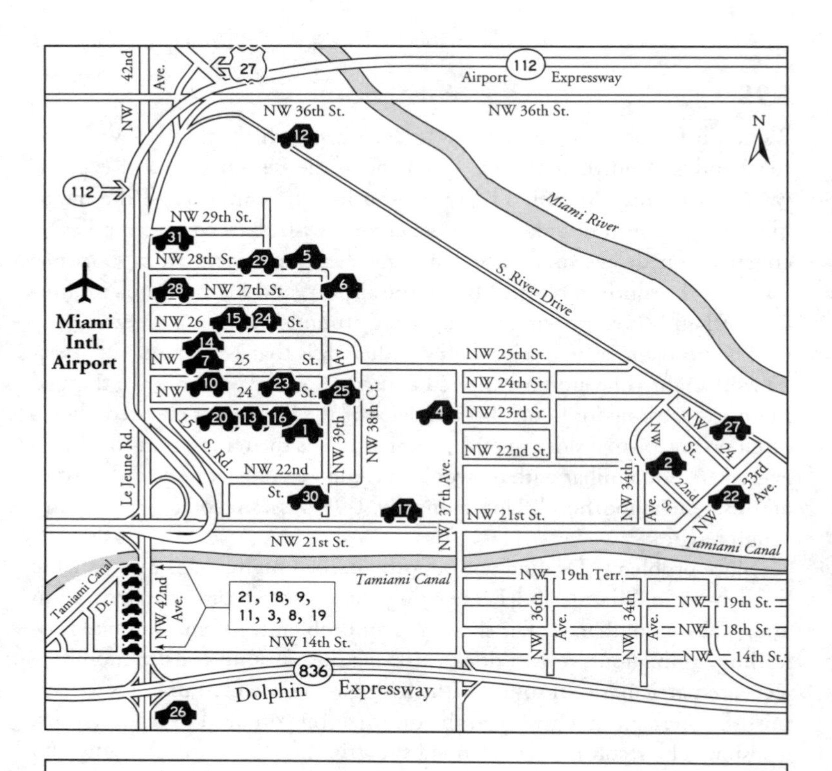

Car Rental Agencies near Miami International Airport

1. ABC Rent-A-Car
2. Alamo Rent-A-Car
3. Andres Rent-A-Car
4. Avis Rent-A-Car
5. Budget Rent-A-Car
6. Capital Rent-A-Car
7. Delta Auto Rental
8. Demo Rent-A-Car
9. Dollar Rent-A-Car
10. Doral Rent-A-Car
11. Elegant Rent-A-Car
12. Enterprise Rent-A-Car
13. Excel Rent-A-Car
14. First Class Rent-A-Car
15. Florida Auto Rental
16. Freedom Spirit
17. Hertz Rent-A-Car
18. InterAmerican Car Rental
19. Intercontinental Rent-A-Car
20. Laser Rent-A-Car
21. Moonan Rent-A-Car
22. National Rent-A-Car
23. Pass Rent-A-Car
24. Payless Car Rental
25. Quality Car Rental
26. Royal Rent-A-Car
27. South Florida VIP Rent-A-Car
28. Thrifty Car Rental
29. Total Rent-A-Car
30. Unidas Rent-A-Car
31. Value Rent-A-Car

Causeways to Miami Beach

The city of Miami Beach is on a barrier island across Biscayne Bay from Miami. Getting on and off the island means crossing long bridges, called causeways, that link the island to the mainland. You've got a number of choices to make.

Getting to South Beach

The best-known link between Miami and its sister city across the bay is the *MacArthur Causeway.* This toll-free (but not drawbridge-free) road provides a high-speed link between downtown Miami and South Beach (the southern end of Miami Beach). From downtown, the MacArthur Causeway is easy to find. Take Biscayne Boulevard (US 1) north a few blocks past Bayside Marketplace and bear right onto the multilane highway that crosses the bridge. (A landmark: the ugly, orange *Miami Herald* building anchors the causeway to the mainland on the left.) From I-95, take I-395 (Exit 5 east), which puts you directly on the MacArthur Causeway to Miami Beach.

Along the way you cross Watson Island (the future home of Parrot Jungle), pass the Port of Miami on the right, and pass Palm and Star islands on the left. When you reach Miami Beach, 5th Street and the Art Deco District is straight ahead; bear left onto Alton Road if your destination is farther north and you want to miss the congestion of Collins Avenue (Miami Beach's main drag); bear right to reach the Miami Beach Marina, South Pointe Park, and Joe's Stone Crab.

One final note: the return trip from Miami Beach to Miami at night offers one of the most impressive and beautiful cityscapes in the world—especially on weekends when cruise ships lit up like Christmas trees are framed by multicolored high-rises in the background.

Getting to Mid-Miami Beach

The *Julia Tuttle Causeway* (I-195) is the main link between I-95, Biscayne Boulevard, and mid-Miami Beach; it's definitely the route to take if you want to avoid the congestion of downtown Miami and the almost 'round-the-clock insanity of South Beach. It's also a straight shot from MIA; Route 112, the Airport Expressway, changes route numbers when it crosses I-95 and becomes I-195 as it heads east over the Julia Tuttle Causeway toward Miami Beach.

The causeway drops you off at 41st Street (Arthur Godfrey Road) on Miami Beach; continue straight to Indian Creek Road and turn right if you're going south. If you're headed north, turn left on Collins Avenue (US A1A). The Julia Tuttle Causeway is a very convenient and usually uncongested way to get on and off Miami Beach, and the one the *Unofficial Guide* research team used the most (we roomed on Miami Beach). Although the view of Miami's skyline is good from the Julia Tuttle Causeway, it isn't as impressive as the MacArthur Causeway's up-close, heart-stopping panorama of cruise ships and high-rises.

Farther north, the *John F. Kennedy Causeway* (Route 934) connects NE 79th Street in Miami with 71st Street in Miami Beach (surprise: the street-numbering systems in the two cities are close, but don't quite match). While this is a good route to take if you're traveling to or from Biscayne Boulevard and Miami Beach, it's not a good choice for hooking up with (or leaving) I-95. Getting on and off the interstate from 79th Street in Miami is confusing at best—and it's a grim-looking neighborhood that most out-of-town visitors would rather avoid. Take the Julia Tuttle Causeway instead.

Getting to Miami Beach North

The *Broad Causeway* (NE 123rd Street) links North Miami to Surfside and Bal Harbour at 96th Street on Miami Beach. It passes through a congested downtown shopping district on the mainland, then crosses northern Biscayne Bay before reaching Bay Harbor Islands and Miami Beach. Due to the traffic lights and congestion along NE 125th Avenue on the mainland side, it's not a fast way to reach I-95 from Miami Beach.

Farther north, the *Sunny Isle Causeway* (Route 826) connects NE 163rd Street in North Miami Beach (which, confusingly enough, is on the mainland) to Sunny Isles on Miami Beach around 170th Street. It's a major route to and from Haulover Beach Park, the Oleta River State Recreation Area, and Florida International University's Bay Vista campus. The *William Lehman Causeway* (Route 856), just below the Broward County line, connects Biscayne Boulevard in North Miami Beach to 192nd Street on Miami Beach. Neither of these two causeways are major routes for out-of-town visitors.

An Alternative Route to South Beach

There's one other route to Miami Beach we need to mention: the *Venetian Causeway,* the original bridge that linked the two cities. It's located just north of the MacArthur Causeway, and is a narrow, two-lane bridge that crosses several artificial islands in Biscayne Bay. While not a particularly convenient route (the MacArthur Causeway is usually faster), it's a pretty drive, a great bicycling or jogging route, and worth exploring if you have the time. The Venetian Causeway is also the route to take during rush hour when traffic is backed up for miles on the MacArthur Causeway. Unfortunately, bridge repairs will keep this link between Miami and Miami Beach closed until late 1999; you can still reach the Venetian Islands from Miami Beach, but not the mainland.

The Miami side of the Venetian Causeway is tucked in behind condos and shopping malls just north of the *Miami Herald* building; it can be tough to find the first time. The Miami Beach side connects drivers with Dade Boulevard, just above the Lincoln Road Mall. Turn right on Washington Avenue to reach South Beach; go straight along Dade Boulevard to Collins Avenue.

Parking

Miami is a city that forces people to use their cars: public transportation is limited and the city is too spread out to make walking convenient. With all those cars in circulation, a question becomes obvious very quickly, especially on a trip to South Beach or Coconut Grove on a Saturday night: where do you park the car?

The answer is also obvious: you don't—or, at least, a lot of people don't. Instead, they endlessly cruise around the block in a nearly hopeless search for a parking space. The parking problems in and around Miami's most popular districts are a big political issue—and no immediate solutions are in sight.

Yet there is one solution to the problem—and it's one that many Miami residents use when they go out for a night on the town: call a cab.

"If you don't take a cab, you just cruise and cruise and cruise looking for a parking space," reports one Miami Beach native who enjoys an occasional night out on the town. "If you give up and decide to park illegally in South Beach, avoid parking in alleys. There's a much higher probability of getting a ticket. But taking a cab is the best way to beat the problem."

Downtown Miami, we're glad to report, offers plenty of parking—unfortunately, most of the spaces are in expensive high-rise parking garages. But you're not obliged to park in them, at least if you're not in a rush. If you're visiting downtown Miami and don't mind walking, park at the garage at Bayside Marketplace, which is easy to find, cheaper than the high-rise garages, and easier to get in and out of. Then cross Biscayne Boulevard by foot to explore downtown. When your feet give out, take the "People Mover" to the College/Bayside station and walk down NE 4th Street to your car.

Back to the Beach The farther north you go away from South Beach, the easier the parking. Above 27th Street (which is where the worst of the South Beach traffic congestion lets up), metered street parking is usually easy to find on Collins Avenue and the numbered streets that intersect it. Around 71st Street, the parking gets even easier, although be careful: The commercial strip around 71st Street and Collins Avenue has a reputation for car break-ins and theft.

Taxis, Shuttles, and Public Transportation

Taxis

With a population highly dependent on private cars for getting around, Miami isn't a great town for hailing cabs. If you need one, a phone call is your best bet.

Taxis are usually plentiful outside the terminals at Miami International Airport; the rate is $3 for the first mile, $2 a mile thereafter, with a $1.50 surcharge added to airport fares. Expect to pay about $18 for a trip from the airport to downtown and $23 to Coconut Grove. Flat-rate fares are available to Miami Beach south of 63rd Street ($22 to $24), Miami Beach between 67th Street and 87th Terrace ($27 to $29), Miami Beach between 87th Terrace and Haulover Park ($32 to $34), Miami Beach between Haulover Park and the Broward County line ($38 to $41), and Key Biscayne ($29 to $31). Trips to other destinations in and around Miami can range from $25 on up.

Popular Cab Companies	
Metro	(305) 888-8888
Super Yellow	(305) 885-1111
Tropical	(305) 945-1025
Yellow	(305) 444-4444

SuperShuttle

Another alternative for getting out of MIA without your own car or ride from a friend is *SuperShuttle,* a van service that can accommodate up to 11 passengers at a clip. It operates 7 days a week, 24 hours a day, and fares are lower than taxis. Rates begin around $9 per person (free for children age three and under) for downtown hotels, $12 for Coral Gables, $11 for South Beach, and $12 for mid–Miami Beach destinations. Call (305) 871-2000 the day before your return flight to arrange a ride back to the airport; keep in mind the shuttle typically makes two additional stops before heading to MIA, so schedule your pickup time accordingly.

Water Taxis

The *Biscayne Bay Water Taxi* shuttles visitors and downtown workers on lunch breaks to attractions, hotels, restaurants, shops, and beaches along Miami's waterfront and Biscayne Bay. Stops include the Biscayne Marriott, Watson Island, Bayside Marketplace, the Hard Rock Cafe, the Intercontinental Hotel, the Dupont Plaza Hotel, the Sheraton Biscayne, Barnett Plaza, Brickell Key, and the Hyatt Regency. Daytime-only stops include

Vizcaya and Seaquarium. Continuous service runs every 25 to 30 minutes from 11 a.m. to 9 p.m. Monday–Thursday; 9:30 a.m. to 9 p.m. Friday–Sunday. Children ride free on Sundays. In addition, the Water Taxi offers on-call service from the Miami Beach Marina. An all-day pass is $15 from any location. Children under age 12 with an adult pay half price. Call (305) 467-6677 for more information or for a pickup from the Miami Beach Marina.

Buses and Public Transportation

Miami, like a lot of large cities, jumped on the mass-transit bandwagon and built an elevated train system (in lieu of a subway, an engineering no-no in South Florida due to the region's high water table, which also rules out basements) and a downtown "People Mover." Yet the fledgling systems have a long way to go before native Miamians—and visitors to the area—can abandon their cars and rely on public transportation to get around. Our advice to visitors is to come in your own car or rent one after you reach Miami.

Metrorail, Miami's futuristic, above-ground train system, is a 21-mile-long, one-line system that runs from Hialeah in northwest Miami south through downtown to Kendall, a suburb southwest of the city. It's clean and modern, but really doesn't go where most visitors want to be—Miami Beach and the airport being two prime examples.

Moreover, the limited system hasn't really caught on with the local clientele (many of whom refer to the system as "MetroSnail"—the trains run about every 20 minutes). While Metrorail was once burdened with an unsafe reputation, security guards have since cleaned up most of the crime. Still, the line passes through some neighborhoods that visitors should avoid.

On the other hand, a ride on downtown's *Metromover*—called the "People Mover" by almost everyone—should be on every visitor's list of things to do on a Miami visit. It's really neat: a Disneyesque, automated monorail scoots people around downtown, treating them to spectacular views of the city, Biscayne Bay, and, off in the distance, the Atlantic Ocean. The system has recently been expanded with two out-and-back connections (in spite of their names, they're not "loops") to the Brickell Avenue business district to the south (Brickell Loop) and to the Omni Hotel to the north (Omni Loop). It's a very practical, clean, and safe system for getting around downtown Miami. Plus, it's air-conditioned.

Priced at a quarter a trip, the "People Mover" is the best tourist bargain in South Florida—and it hooks up with the Metrorail system. But unless you're staying downtown and don't plan to venture to other parts of Miami, this small transportation system won't replace your need for a car.

Miami's *Metrobus* system operates throughout Dade County, serving about 200,000 riders a day on 65 routes. Most of the lines radiate out of downtown Miami and run at least twice per hour between 6 a.m. and 7 p.m. weekdays, less often on weekends. The bus system is also the only public transportation in Miami Beach. Our advice: Short-term visitors should stick to their cars and leave the complicated, relatively slow bus system to commuters.

Visitors can cruise South Beach on the *ElectroWave*, Florida's first electric shuttle system. Shuttles stop every 6 to 11 minutes at 30 designated stops on Washington Street and at Lincoln Road Mall between 5th and 17th Streets. The mini-buses seat up to 22 passengers with wraparound seating and air-conditioning, and will allow visitors more convenient access between municipal parking lots and local hot spots. Hours of operation are 8 a.m. to 2 a.m. Monday through Wednesday, 8 a.m. to 4 a.m. Thursday through Saturday, and 10 a.m. to 2 a.m. Sunday. And you can't beat the price—it's free.

Part Six

Entertainment and Night Life

Miami Night Life: An Overview*

Miami is a city that never sleeps, even when the sun comes up. Whether it's because the residents and visitors of this dynamic city are easily bored or easily amused is a toss-up. The fact is, Miami's social side is like a multifaceted theme park, full of wondrous amusements for all ages that bring out the child in everyone.

There are enough worthwhile diversions in Miami to literally keep people busy around the clock, which could explain the city's extreme fondness for *colada,* the Cuban espresso coffee so eye-opening it is doled out in thimble-size cups. There are parties, and then after-parties, and then after-hour parties, which start at the hour most good suburbanites are already in the carpool lane.

Miami is one of those spicy, late-night towns where the diversity of expression is reflected in the ethnic eclecticism of its community. The melting pot image is not quite right for Miami. It is more like a human paella.

There are supper clubs, coffeehouses, dance companies, symphonies, dragshows, discos, strip joints, comedy clubs, concert halls, jazz boites, gay clubs, gallery walks, and rock pubs to suit every taste, and then some. It's only a matter of finding the time. Miami night life can be divided into three basic categories: theater and other cultural pursuits; live jazz, Latin, R & B, or rock music; and the restaurant-cum-disco scene. Noteworthy establishments are described in the following pages. After that, we list individual club profiles of the best places Miami has to offer. For those venues with live music, we advise calling ahead for scheduling information and reservations.

Nightly, weekly, and monthly schedules of live music clubs, theatrical productions, and special events are printed in the *Miami Herald* Weekend

* The night-life chapter was researched and written by *Miami Herald* night-life columnist Tara Solomon, known locally as "The Queen of the Night." Her column appears every Friday in the *Herald's* Weekend section.

sections as well as community newspapers, including *Entertainment News & Views*, and free local hip sheets such as *Wire*.

Theater and Other Cultural Pursuits

The performing arts world in Miami boasts a broad array of offerings, from legitimate local theater to national touring companies. Tickets tend to be reasonably priced for evenings and events, and the venues run the gamut from offbeat playhouses to grander locales, such as the renovated **Jackie Gleason Theater** (1700 Washington Avenue, Miami Beach; (305) 673-7300), the site of touring Broadway productions and national ballet companies. Miamians take full advantage of the cultural possibilities, so make every effort to investigate ticket availability early.

Quality theater abounds. The **Coconut Grove Playhouse** (3500 Main Highway, Coconut Grove; (305) 442-4000) is a popular venue for national tours, such as "Death of a Salesman," starring Hal Holbrook. You'll find more intimate theater in the Playhouse's Encore Room, (305) 442-4000. For local talent and productions with an edge, **New Theater** (65 Almeria Avenue, Coral Gables; (305) 443-5909) offers first-class production values with a sense of the avant garde, under the direction of Rafael de Acha. Very worthy is the award-winning **Area Stage** (645 Lincoln Road, Miami Beach; (305) 673-8002), which combines stellar local talent with the works of poignant playwrights such as Harold Pinter.

Classical music spills out from a number of renowned concert halls and associations. The highly acclaimed **New World Symphony** (541 Lincoln Road, Miami Beach; ticket office: (305) 673-3331) is the country's largest training orchestra and offers a wide range of concerts, including a Sunday afternoon series. The **Concert Association of Florida (CAF)** (offices at 555 17th Street, Miami Beach; (305) 532-3491) has been Miami's foremost presenter of symphonies, ballets, and opera divas for the past 28 years. CAF concerts are held at various venues throughout Miami.

The dance divine can be caught at the **Miami City Ballet** (performances at the Jackie Gleason Theater, 1700 Washington Avenue, Miami Beach; call (305) 532-4880 for tickets) under the inspired artistic direction of Edward Villella. For fluid moves, try the **Momentum Dance Company** at La Salle High School (3601 S. Miami Avenue, Coconut Grove; (305) 858-7002).

For a more modern approach to the performing arts, **Miami Light Project** (at various venues; call (305) 531-3747) imports the freshest talents in the worlds of dance, music, and theater.

Once a year, for ten days in February, the Miami Film Society presents the **Miami International Film Festival**. An internationally acclaimed event that showcases brilliant filmmaking from around the world, the festival has featured many avant-garde directors, including new-wave Spanish filmmaker Pedro

Almodovar, who was introduced to American audiences at the festival in 1984 with his film *Dark Habits.* **The Miami Beach Film Society** (presentations at various venues on Miami Beach; call the hotline at (305) 673-4567) feeds South Beach's hunger for the unusual with special cinema-themed events such as its "Movies to Dine For" gourmet dinner-cum-movie nights at South Beach's hottest restaurants. The propaganda arts-themed **Wolfsonian Museum** (1001 Washington Avenue, Miami Beach; call (305) 531-1001) features exhibitions and screenings of movie classics such as Fritz Lang's *Metropolis.*

Live Entertainment: Café Clubs and Concert Clubs

Miami offers not only the unusual small concert clubs, but also the café-cum-club, and these are some of the best night life bets in the area. Restaurants that feature live performances of salsa, jazz, and just about everything else run rampant. Impromptu dancing on tabletops is not uncommon. Local, regional, and less mainstream national talent can be found every night, all over Dade county. Miami being Miami, the Latin music is unbeatable, and the Latin jazz is among the best in the world. **Yuca** (501 Lincoln Road, Miami Beach; (305) 532-9822), a restaurant whose name is not only a popular root vegetable used in Cuban cuisine but also an acronym for its clientele (Young Urban Cuban Americans), serves up Latin vocalists in its upstairs concert space; on weekends, renowned Cuban folk singer Albita performs with her band—a true Miami experience not to be missed.

In the café club category, **Monty's Raw Bar** (2550 South Bayshore Drive, Coconut Grove; (305) 856-3992) is an oasis of fun with calypso and reggae throughout the week and weekends, right on the waterfront. **John Martin's** (253 Miracle Mile, Coral Gables; (305) 445-3777) features fantastic and hard-to-find Irish music on Saturdays and Sundays. **Cafe Iguana** (8505 Mills Drive, Miami; (305) 274-4948) sheds its modern disco duds on Sundays with a wild Western Night featuring food, music, and costume contests with a country flair; line dance lessons start at 6 p.m. **Taurus** (3540 Main Highway, Coconut Grove; (305) 448-0633), in the heart of Coconut Grove, showcases blues talent and more in its terraced locale, Tuesday through Saturday. Also in the Grove is the **Improv Comedy Club and Cafe** (3390 Mary Street, Coconut Grove; (305) 441-8200) where you can catch stand-up acts every night of the week while enjoying a drink or dinner (Tuesday and Wednesday are two-for-one entree nights). On weekends, the tropically appointed **Cardozo Cafe**—within the Cardozo Hotel, which is owned by Gloria and Emilio Estefan—turns into a disco until 2 or 3 in the morning (1300 Ocean Drive, Miami Beach; (305) 538-0553).

In South Beach, check out **Mangoes Tropical Cafe** (900 Ocean Drive; (305) 673-4422), **Clevelander Hotel** (1020 Ocean Drive; (305) 531-3485), and **I Paparazzi** (940 Ocean Drive; (305) 531-3500). At the exotic restaurant-lounge **Tantra** (1445 Pennsylvania Avenue, Miami Beach; (305) 672-4765), diners can have a taste of fabulosity with their meal (the place is swarming with models, trendies, and movie stars on any given night); of special note is the Sod Lounge with the tented banquettes and fresh grass floor.

Concert clubs in Miami feature an eclectic and diverse selection of performers. **The Cameo Theater** (1445 Washington Avenue, Miami Beach; (305) 532-0922), a popular DJ-driven club, also headlines national talent like Sister Hazel and underground heavy metal bands. **Tobacco Road** (626 South Miami Avenue, Miami; (305) 374-1198) is undeniably lively, and even holds the title of being Miami's oldest club. The nightly live music ranges from Latin jazz to rock and R & B.

The Nightclub Connection

Now that Miami (and particularly South Beach) has gained a national reputation as the nightclub capital of the world, celebrities mingle with models and the uncommonly beautiful dance with boys-and-girls-next-door. Club life is always volatile, so keep your ears open for news on the hot clubs du jour. The scene shifts and regroups constantly. Our advice is ask your servers at dinner what they recommend that evening. Miami's wait staff—many of whom are models and actors, at least on South Beach—is extremely well informed on life in the demimonde. Whenever possible, call ahead for information on theme nights andspecials.

Most of the action, of course, is on South Beach. Fortunately, most clubs are concentrated along Washington Avenue, South Beach's main commercial artery. While there are very few clubs per se on famed Ocean Drive, there are numerous restaurants with sidewalk seating that feature a jazz or blues vocalist. A sprightly walk along the oceanfront strip reading the menus and sidewalk marquees will give you all the info you need. The nightclub circuit is unpredictable at best, with new developers taking over spaces at a moment's notice, so there's a good chance that your favorite dance club last year is now a parking lot, or will be soon.

Since most of the area nightclubs don't get going until at least 11 p.m., an afternoon nap (or, as locals call it, a disco coma) is advised. Once refreshed, venture out to one of the many options. **Lua** (409 Espanola Way, Miami Beach; (305) 534-0061) is intimate, elegant—a little bit of Paris in the '20s, by the sea; they also offer a separate dance room. **Bash** (655 Washington Avenue, Miami Beach; (305) 538-2274) is a dance club that attracts celebs and trendies; reggae is played in the outdoor garden bar. **Liquid** (1439 Washington Avenue, Miami Beach; (305) 532-9154) caters to the trendier-than-thou crowd, offering a dimly lit, urban dance club that may seem spartan to those seeking plusher quarters. **The Living Room at the Strand** (671 Washington Avenue, Miami Beach; (305) 532 2340) is the definitive upscale lounge for the '90s—plenty of models and celebs, with the *de rigueur* attitude from the doormen who guard the velvet ropes. **Shadow Lounge** (1532 Washington Avenue, Miami Beach; (305) 531-9411) is one of the few dance clubs on South Beach where a suit and tie on gentlemen is actually appreciated; two levels provide plenty of niches for roaming. At **Chaos** (743 Washington Avenue, Miami Beach; (305) 674-7350), celebs mix with in-the-know locals in a bustling dance scene whose aptly chosen name comes from its well-known sister club in New York.

When it's so late you don't think you can stay awake another second, the crowd is just sauntering in at **Groove Jet** (323 23rd Street, Miami Beach; (305) 532-2002), which bills itself as "the only club that matters." The truth of the matter is that it's one of the trendiest hot spots you're likely to encounter; even the most jaded of souls will marvel at the outdoor Crystal Lounge (named for the thousands of mirror shards decorating every last surface) and the celebrity clientele.

In Coconut Grove, you'll find **Bar 609** (3338 Virginia Street, Coconut Grove; (305) 444-6096), booming with Top 40 music and a mix of locals, University of Miami students, and visitors. **Marco's in the Grove** (3339 Virginia Street, Coconut Grove; (305) 444-5333) is perfect for a dressier night out on the town; dine in the club's nouvelle restaurant before descending to the glitzy basement disco.

On a less wholesome note, there are the clubs where the charm is measured by how much skin is showing. Most of these clubs are concentrated on Biscayne Boulevard, just north of 163rd Street. **Madonna** (1527 Washington Avenue, Miami Beach; (305) 534-2000) is slick and stocked with lovely ladies, including centerfold celebs. **Deja Vu** (2004 Collins Avenue, Miami Beach; (305) 538-5526) offers a most interesting menu—hundreds of beautiful girls and three ugly ones.

Doing the Keys

In Key West, where laid-back bars rule over the flashy disco scene favored in Miami, some of the more popular haunts include the open-air **Schooner Wharf Bar** (202 Williams Street; (305) 292-9520), open 8 a.m. to 4 a.m. with live music Thursday through Saturday. **The Green Parrot Bar** (profiled in the following section) is another good choice for a little piece of Key West, with prime people-watching. The Sunday evening tea dance at the **Atlantic Shores Motel** (510 South Street; (305) 296-2491), a sixteen-year institution, features a disco overlooking the pier and a largely gay clientele.

The Gay Scene

Miami, especially South Beach, has been described as a gay mecca. Its active and involved gay community is evident on many levels. From lawyers to drag divas, the crowds congregate in a variety of bars and clubs. Endless theme offerings at these clubs include boys' nights, women's nights, drag shows, strip shows, and many things you might not have ever heard of.

South Beach serves as a central spot for much of Miami's gay society. A cute corner bar, **West End** (942 Lincoln Road, Miami Beach; (305) 538-9378) has a casual, chatty crowd. An always-happening boite is **Twist** (1057 Washington Avenue, Miami Beach; (305) 538-9478), whose two floors of bar space make it perfect for late-night gossip and cocktails. **Salvation** (1771 West Avenue, Miami Beach; (305) 673-6508), a large club known for its high-energy Saturday night party, caters to a crowd that considers dancing integral to survival. Disco mall **Amnesia** (136 Collins Avenue, (305) 531-5535), which looks not unlike a very decadent Club Med, is the site of a disco-fueled tea dance on Sundays from 6 p.m. The internationally known **Warsaw** (1450 Collins Avenue; (305) 531-4555) is a dance club renowned for its music and beefy patrons; quite a hoot is its Wednesday night amateur strip contest, which starts at the fragile hour of 1 a.m.

And off the Beach, the action continues at a number of clubs. **Ozone** (6620 SW 57th Avenue; (305) 667-2888) draws devotees from all over Miami with excellent dance music, nightly specials, and a powerful pace.

For the Entire Family

Planet Hollywood, a 17,900-square-foot restaurant/bar-cum-movie-memorabilia franchise, gives cinema buffs a new reason to go to Coconut Grove (Mayfair Shops, off Grand Avenue, between Virginia and Mary Streets; (305) 445-7277). Of course, the star association doesn't hurt (shareholders include Sly Stallone, Bruce Willis, Arnold Schwarzenegger, and Demi Moore). Perfect for large gatherings or birthday celebrations, dinner at Planet Hollywood can become an event in itself. Also in Coconut Grove is **Virtua Cafe** (3390 Mary Street in the Streets of Mayfair complex; (305) 567-3070), an 11,000-square-foot, high-tech-themed entertainment restaurant and bar where there's something for everyone in the family. Let Junior knock himself out in the numerous virtual reality rooms while Mom, Dad, and the grandparents grab a pizza and order of "Martian beef medallions" in the futuristic dining room that boasts a view of the solar system. After 10:30 p.m., though, it's 21 and older.

AMNESIA INTERNATIONAL

Euro megaclub/disco mall

Who Goes There: 21–45; models, sometimes in the company of heavily tanned older men, heavyweights who know the owner, Causeway kids in search of love, visiting celebs

136 Collins Avenue
(305) 531-5535 Miami Beach Zone 1

Cover: Varies, $7–10
Minimum: None
Mixed drinks: $3–6
Wine: $4–5
Beer: $3–5
Dress: Trendy, but not too extreme; sexy slip dresses or updated sausage casings for females, and leather jackets and jeans for the male contingency are always acceptable. For Sunday afternoon tea dance, a good body is the best accessory.
Specials: Sunday afternoon tea dance ($5 cover)
Food available: Casual food on the ground floor.

Hours: Thursday–Sunday, 10 p.m.–5 a.m.; Sunday, 6 p.m. tea dance

What goes on: Patterned after its namesake in Cap D'Agde, France, Amnesia has taken Miami Euro madness to the next level. By all standards a megaclub for the '90s, Amnesia has achieved instant success.

Setting & atmosphere: The space is so huge (32,000 feet) that getting separated from the person you came with will surely translate into acquiring new friends. Since nine-tenths of the club is open-air with lots of polished blonde wood and Caribbean-print cushions, club rats usually shy away, claiming it reminds them of Club Med or a shopping mall. A giant phosphorescent waterfall and four-color skywriting laser add that megaclub touch.

If you go: With a club this big, it becomes, at one point, about the numbers. Meaning, dress decently and you shouldn't have a problem getting in, at least eventually (weekends draw lines down the block, even with the 2,500-person capacity). Expect a predominantly straight crowd, except at tea dance, which is favored by muscle boys, drag queens, and assorted freaks. Great fun, huh?

BASH

Euro dance club with bohemian streak

Who Goes There: 23–40; well-heeled straight couples, NFL players on vacation, reggae fans, celeb friends of owners Sean Penn and Mick Hucknall

655 Washington Avenue
(305) 538-BASH Miami Beach Zone 1

Cover: $10–15; Tuesday, none
Minimum: None
Mixed drinks: $5–6
Wine: $5
Beer: $5
Dress: Better wear a designer outfit, unless you care to show the doorman six forms of ID; no running shoes, even if they're by Gaultier; jackets for men on weekends strongly recommended.
Specials: None
Food available: None

Hours: Tuesday–Saturday, 10 p.m.–5 a.m.; Sunday, 11 p.m.–5 a.m.

What goes on: Smoky, dark, and sexy, Bash has all the energy of a really good private party. It's not about the decor, because one barely remembers the black velvet banquettes or undulating steel bar (too dark inside) or the sexy cocktail servers (everyone on South Beach looks like a model, anyhow). It might have something to do with the celeb owners who, when in town, have been known to travel in an entourage that includes filmmaker Oliver Stone and actors Dennis Hopper and Johnny Depp—the ultimate PR weapon for a hot club.

Setting & atmosphere: Partner Mick Hucknall of the English rock group Simply Red has described Bash as being "three clubs in one," and rightly so. The main room has a smallish, eternally packed dance floor pumping Euro/house music at unearthly decibels and three VIP lounges. The long, narrow bar is separated by structural columns and is demimonde unto itself. In the back, the outdoor patio serves as an island-themed escape valve, where couples with happy feet bounce to reggae, salsa, and the Gipsy Kings.

If you go: Unattached males would be wise to bring an attractive female or two; guys in testosterone-rich packs don't stand a chance. Dressing within an inch of one's life is rewarded here, especially on weekends when the door scene becomes a major pick-and-choose nightmare, partially due to the club's close proximity to numerous other nighttime establishments. Valet parking available.

BERMUDA BAR

Singles bar and dance club for those who just can't forget the 1980s

Who Goes There: 21–50; big-haired girlfriends looking for Mr. Rightstein, local beer buddies hoping to score, restless locals, curious businessmen looking for a scene

3509 NE 163rd Street
(305) 945-0196 Miami North Zone 2

Cover: $5
Minimum: None
Mixed drinks: $5–6
Wine: $5 and up
Beer: $4 and up
Dress: Women: Bimbo Barbie: high hair, big earrings. Men: open-neck shirts and designer sportswear.
Specials: Happy hour, every day at 5 p.m.; ladies' night on Wednesday.
Food available: Casual American fare.

Hours: Wednesday–Sunday, 5 p.m.–5 a.m.

What goes on: Lots of loud, venting energy pumping throughout this North Miami dance club, which caters to a post-college day job (and, at times, much older) crowd. On weekends, it's packed by midnight, with gaggles of revelers equally dispersed on the dance floor, around the bars, and in the various lounges. Mercifully, there is no VIP room, allowing normal folk to mill about unrestricted. The DJ spins Top 40 and disco tunes, with Latin music on Thursday.

Setting & atmosphere: From the outside with its two-story coral and white stucco facade, you'd swear Bermuda Bar was a giant theme restaurant. (The unglamorous strip mall location doesn't help matters any.) Inside, oversized palms and beachy props give you that Frankie and Annette in Discoland feel. A plus: lots of free parking and bright, crime-deterring lighting in the never-ending lot out front.

If you go: Call for a schedule of special theme nights, such as the pajama and lingerie parties, so that you can dress accordingly.

CAFÉ NOSTALGIA

Miami version of a Cuban nightclub of yore

Who Goes There: 21–50; lots of Latin locals or visiting Latin Americans out to conquer the town Cuban-style

2212 SW 8th Street
(305) 541-2631 Miami South Zone 3

Cover: Varies by event; call to inquire
Minimum: None
Mixed drinks: $6–8
Wine: $6 and up; bottle service available
Beer: $5 and up

Dress: Casual glitz: "Miami Vice" meets the '90s for the men with dark jackets, jeans, and cellular phones; tight things with a touch of glitter for the girls
Specials: None
Food available: None

Hours: Thursday–Saturday, 9 p.m.–3 a.m.; call for events schedule

What goes on: Many will reminisce about the heyday of Havana, even those born after the fall of Cuba. In Miami, it's all luscious legend and remembrance of things past, and Café Nostalgia is appropriately named. People come for comfort, entertainment, or to dance madly to live Afro-Cuban bands that take the stage at 10:30 p.m. If you can't manage to fudge some odd version of salsa or merengue, just wiggle in your seat and smile a lot. The music is infectious, though.

Setting & atmosphere: All nightclubs once looked like this—tiny tables, dark corners, intimate lighting, and an inviting bar that patrons sit at because they choose to, not because they're waiting for a table to open. Cuban songsters from the '50s are featured in original campy videos on an overhead screen. Spanish is by far the language of choice among patrons and staff, but feel free to order your drinks in English. There is an extensive list of wines and liquors by the bottle.

If you go: Latins in Miami have a strong sense of propriety and ethnic pride—no sweatshirts naming Anglo-sounding universities will be appreciated. Also, while you may argue that you are technically still in the continental United States, you are in a foreign land. Don't be an ugly American. This is not a club in a suburban mall, so space is limited. Thus, try to make a reservation. Valet parking is available.

CAMEO THEATRE

Nightclub and concert hall for the young and reckless

Who Goes There: 18–28; punksters and heavy metal fans, Beavis and Butthead types, clean-cut college kids on disco night

1445 Washington Avenue
(305) 532-0922 Miami Beach Zone 1

Cover: Varies, usually $5–10; free for ladies before midnight
Minimum: None
Mixed drinks: $5–6
Wine: $4
Beer: $3

Dress: Denim, all forms of street wear, anything you'd see in *Paper* or *Vibe* magazines.
Specials: None
Food available: None

Hours: Friday–Sunday, 11 p.m.–5 a.m.

What goes on: One of Miami's more popular small concert spaces catering to the youthquake set. Prepubescent punksters sporting pierced body parts and shellacked mohawks line Washington Avenue when a heavy metal act is in town, alerting shocked motorists to what's inside. On Friday nights the venue joins forces with local Top 40 station Power 96 for the hugely popular "Hot Bodies Contest." Most nights feature reggae, hip-hop, and alternative acts. Silver jewelry and fake tattoo vendors serve as lobby entertainment.

Setting & atmosphere: Outside, the glass-block and neon-lit facade spotlights one of South Beach's most historic Art Deco buildings. Inside, it has all the allure of a black hole, but for what it is, it works. This former movie theater features a cavernous dance floor and stage at the bottom level, with a three-level tier of bars and seating climbing to nosebleed heights. The atmosphere is provided by smoke machines, lasers, and bizarre images projected onto the walls.

If you go: Leave mom at home.

CAPTAIN TONY'S

Local watering hole with eclectic live music

Who Goes There: 25–40; locals and tourists, spring breakers

428 Greene Street, Key West
(305) 294-1838 The Florida Keys Zone 5

Minimum: None
Mixed drinks: $3–5
Wine: $3.50
Beer: $2–3.25
Dress: So casual you can wear cut-offs and flip flops; shoes and shirts are requested at night.

Specials: Live music daily and the house pirate's punch, a gin/rum/fruit-juice concoction served in a 22-ounce souvenir jug.
Food available: None

Hours: Monday–Saturday, 10 a.m.–2 a.m.; Sunday, noon–2 a.m.

What goes on: This is one of the Keys' legendary bars, owned since the 1960s by local character Captain Tony, who is 77, has been married seven times, has 13 children, and was even elected mayor (1988–91). Captain Tony, who originally came to the Keys as a fisherman in the 1940s, occasionally drops by the bar, amusing patrons with incredible stories, such as how he used to give Jimmy Buffett $10 a day, plus all he could drink. In case Captain Tony doesn't show, there are live musical acts daily, starting in the afternoons. Music is truly eclectic, ranging from Nirvana to the Top 40 hits of the '50s. In case you experience déjà vu, the bar site is the former location of the original Sloppy Joe's, before it moved to Duval Street.

Setting & atmosphere: An amusing hodge-podge of bar patrons past, with mementos stuffed everywhere. Wall-to-wall business cards, musical instruments, license plates, celebrity bar stools, a plane propeller, and even a bra dangling from the ceiling. Folklore has it that the bar's tip bell was stolen from an old Key West fire truck by none other than Hemingway himself, according to Captain Tony.

If you go: Bring some mad money for Captain Tony T-shirts, hats, and glasses, which are sold in a separate retail area.

CHURCHILL'S HIDEAWAY

Rock and roll bar showcasing local bands

Who Goes There: 21+; rockers, locals, blue-collar boys, office workers, big college crowd on weekends

---

5501 NE 2nd Avenue
(305) 757-1807 Miami North Zone 2

Cover: Varies, usually $3
Minimum: None
Mixed drinks: None
Wine: $3
Beer: $1.25 for draft; $3–5 for bottled
Dress: Very casual.

Specials: 70 types of bottled beer, 7 drafts, good wine selection; live bands on weekends.
Food available: Traditional pub grub; fish 'n' chips, shepherd's pie, burgers.

Hours: Every day, 11 a.m.–3 a.m.

What goes on: An English-themed rock and roll pub where good-at-heart bad boys get together to down a brew and play a game of snooker. British-owned and operated, the pub, established in 1946, provides the ideal backdrop to catch a local band, shoot a few darts, or snag some barbecue on the patio—a Friday afternoon tradition.

Setting & atmosphere: Fitting of any decent English pub, there's a game room equipped with dart boards and pool and snooker tables. Much of the 350-person capacity, though, flows into the Key West–esque bar area where local rock groups perform on Friday and Saturday nights. For an escape, there's the patio bar with barbecue grill and laundry room, where on Sundays you can catch a local newscaster doing his wash. Two satellite dishes ensure clear coverage of major sports events, shown on TVs inside.

If you go: If you're visiting in the summer months, you'll coincide with the English soccer season, during which time the bar opens at 9 a.m. to televise the games. Parking is available on the street or, safer, in the bar's adjacent lot.

THE CLEVELANDER BAR

Oceanfront hotel bar, gym, and outdoor nightspot

Who Goes There: 21–45; restless youth, locals, European tourists, Causeway crawlers, bikini babes

1020 Ocean Drive
(305) 531-3485 Miami Beach Zone 1

Cover: None
Minimum: None
Mixed drinks: $4–5
Wine: $4–5.75
Beer: $3–4
Dress: All forms of beachwear, from bikinis with sarongs to shorts and sandals; on a breezy night, Levis; this is one place where less is more.

Specials: Weekday happy hour, 5–7 p.m., with 2-for-1 drinks; nightly drink specials; live music every night.
Food available: Full menu until 3 a.m., from burgers to surf 'n' turf; live lobster tank.

Hours: Bars, every day, 11 a.m.–5 a.m.

What goes on: The '90s version of *Beach Blanket Bingo,* with scantily clad babes and bronzed hunks parading around the pool/bar of this popular oceanfront hotel. Live bands nightly and omnipresent DJs keep the rambunctious spirit going. Needless to say, this is prime cruising territory.

Setting & atmosphere: Smack on trendy Ocean Drive, this outdoor bar is studded with palm trees and cartoonish, Jetsonian obelisks. Ten TVs inside and out ensure you'll never miss a music video or major sporting event, not that you won't get distracted by the onslaught of physical beauty on display. The glass-enclosed gym, appropriately suspended above the stage and dance floor, stays open till 11 p.m. Less active types can always shoot a game of pool on one of the four tables located inside and out.

If you go: This is a great spot for people-watching, as the covered outdoor bar is located just microsteps from Ocean Drive, just across the street from the ocean. Metered parking is limited; valet is always available, for a price (we recently paid $10 on a Saturday afternoon).

CLUB TROPIGALA

1950s Havana-inspired supper club and salsa parlor

Who Goes There: 21–60; Latins who know how to dance, stylemongers, tourists, condo groups, locals with a sense of adventure

4441 Collins Avenue (Fontainebleau Hilton Resort and Spa)
(305) 538-2000 Miami Beach Zone 1

Cover: Show only, $15; dinner and show, prices vary
Minimum: None
Mixed drinks: $5.25–7.50
Wine: $4.75
Beer: $3
Dress: Jackets for men; ladies, semiformal.
Specials: Special entertainment.
Food available: Full menu; continental standards.

Hours: Showtimes: Wednesday, Thursday, and Sunday, 8:30 p.m.; Friday and Saturday, 8 and 10 p.m.; dancing until the wee hours

What goes on: This world-renowned supper club draws an eclectic crowd of all ages and looks, from discerning trendies who think it's the ultimate in camp, to older Latin couples who've made it their Saturday night tradition for years. Thirty performers and special acts, plus a 10-piece orchestra for dancing.

Setting & atmosphere: Right out of the *Jungle Book*, with extravagant tropical murals, palm fronds, bamboo, waterfalls, and color-enhanced dancing fountains. The truly huge room is successfully tiered for greater intimacy. What's really amazing is that every seat is filled.

If you go: One of the few times where two generations can spend the evening together without complaints. Wear your dancing shoes and get ready to salsa—or watch in envy.

821

Your friendly corner club for gay-friendly neighbors

Who Goes There: Lots of locals looking for fun, but not necessarily *that* kind of fun

821 Lincoln Road
(305) 534-0887 Miami Beach Zone 1

Cover: None
Minimum: None
Mixed drinks: $5 and up
Wine: $5

(821)

Beer: $4 and up
Dress: Whatever makes you happy.
Specials: Happy hour, 3–9 p.m.
Food available: None

Hours: Every day, 3 p.m.–3 a.m.

What goes on: This is a chatty place—locals talk to tourists, tourists talk to the staff, and everyone talks about the same person they all know in New York. Undeniably friendly, 821 with its laughter and silliness is conducive to expressive dancing and such. Thursday nights are popular with everyone, although they're billed as Mary D's cabaret night for women. Music ranges from '70s trash disco to current dance hits (it doesn't really matter, as the patrons will dance to anything). Coolest night is Sunday's Jetset Lounge, which celebrates the cocktail revolution in high lounge style with the best music around.

Setting & atmosphere: It's a narrow little space for broad-minded people right on Lincoln Road. The decor is not memorable, but this club is all about the crowd. People pop in throughout the night on the way to dinner, coming from dinner, and while arguing over where to have dinner. There are occasional art exhibits and special performances.

If you go: There are no caveats to 821. Stop in for a drink while shopping or gallery-hopping or slate it for the evening. While you could easily go in evening dress or jeans, there's no need to plan attire. The more comfortable you are, the more comfortable you'll be.

GREEN PARROT BAR

Key West's oldest bar

Who Goes There: 21–75; locals, tourists, New Yorkers escaping the rat race

601 Whitehead Street, Key West
(305) 294-6133 The Florida Keys Zone 5

Cover: None
Minimum: None
Mixed drinks: $3–3.50
Wine: $2.75
Beer: $1.50–2.75
Dress: Key West casual.
Specials: Happy hour, 4–7 p.m., 7 days a week, with $2.25 mixed drinks, $1 draft, and $1.50 domestic beer.
Food available: Standard Tex-Mex fare from the Gato Gordo restaurant next door.

Hours: Monday–Saturday, 10 a.m.–4 a.m.; Sunday, noon–4 a.m.

(Green Parrot Bar)

What goes on: Open since 1890, this popular bar features live entertainment every Saturday with reggae, rock, and blues from 10 p.m. to 2 a.m. Once a month poetry slams liven up Sundays with open readings. Occasionally, single acts perform on Saturday afternoons. Several years back the bar's propensity for attracting the most eligible bachelors in town was noted in *Playboy* magazine.

Setting & atmosphere: This is an open-air bar, known to display bold, if not quality, art, with the outside walls covered in various themes (i.e., sports, slice-of-life, Jamaica). Two pool tables, two deluxe pinball machines, three dart boards, and an eclectically stocked juke box add to the bar's breezy, laid-back charm.

If you go: If you're a people-watcher, try to get a seat by the street for a unique view of humanity.

GROOVE JET

Ultratrendy dance club for genetically gifted youth

Who Goes There: 21–35; models, sports figures, local personalities without a curfew

323 23rd Street
(305) 532-2002 Miami Beach Zone 1

Cover: $10, Tuesday and Thursday, $15 on weekends
Minimum: None
Mixed drinks: $5–7
Wine: $6–7
Beer: $4–5
Dress: Upscale casual chic (no shorts, tank-tops, or tennies) with a touch of something overtly hip, whether it be a Gucci belt, Todd Oldham mules, or worn leather jeans; Goth attire (all black—clothes, lips and nails, attitude) for Sunday's "The Church" theme night.
Specials: None
Food available: None

Hours: Tuesday, Thursday–Sunday, 11 p.m.–5 a.m.

What goes on: This is where the coolest of the cool go to party on South Beach, which would include Hollywood brat packers (Matt Dillon, Leonardo Di Caprio) and rock stars (Sean "Puffy" Combs, Marilyn Manson). There's dancing and cocktailing inside and out, but most of the VIP activity takes place under the wise old Groove Tree in the funky Crystal Lounge.

Setting & atmosphere: However fresh-faced the crowd, the interior dance floor still reminds us of a big black box. Better is the sleek '50s-themed inside bar area. Best is the bohemian Crystal Lounge area—a roomy, wood-decked patio with a massive round bar and various seating areas, all covered with broken mirror shards. The effect is not unlike that of several hundred disco balls, all spinning at once (or is that just us after one martini too many?).

If you go: Don't overdress. Go late (take an afternoon disco nap if you need to); it doesn't even get good until 2 a.m. Really.

HARD ROCK CAFE

International restaurant chain of rock and roll memorabilia

Who Goes There: The easily amused of all ages, rock and roll fanatics, tourists, party animals

401 Biscayne Boulevard, Bayside Marketplace
(305) 377-3110 Miami North Zone 2

Cover: None
Minimum: None
Mixed drinks: $6–9.50
Wine: $4–5.50
Beer: $3–6
Dress: No fashion police here; you'll feel at home in jeans, Bermuda shorts, or a business suit worn after hours.
Specials: Food specials are available; call ahead.
Food available: Basic, moderately priced American-themed food—burgers, wings, salads, and the like.

Hours: Sunday–Wednesday, 11 a.m.–midnight; Thursday–Saturday, 11 a.m.–2 a.m.

What goes on: Rock and roll memorabilia with a view of the Miami Bay. Smack in the middle of a tropical shopping mall (can't miss the café—it's the one with the vintage convertible plunged through the roof); this hot spot gets lots of curious tourists and locals with out-of-towners in tow.

Setting & atmosphere: A toybox for adults. All walls and corners are saturated with trappings of rock stars throughout the ages, such as Axl Rose's tour jacket and personal letters from the Beatles. A largely chaotic decor scheme includes wooden floors, brass railings, loud print tablecloths, and separate rooms for private parties. Thirsty mall rats of drinking age favor the long, winding bar that hugs one entire wall.

If you go: Don't tell anyone it's your birthday, unless you want the DJ to announce it over the PA system. Wear sensible shoes; bring money for souvenirs. Plenty of parking, both valet and garage.

THE HUNGRY SAILOR

Neighborhood institution doubling as reggae bar

Who Goes There: 21–45; college kids, locals, tourists passing through Coconut Grove; mostly men, some with dates

3426 Main Highway, Coconut Grove
(305) 444-9359 Miami South Zone 3

Cover: $3–5, when live entertainment is featured
Minimum: None
Mixed drinks: None
Wine: $3.50–4.50
Beer: $2–3

Dress: Very casual; shirt and shoes are recommended.
Specials: Thursday, $5 cover and penny drafts.
Food available: None

Hours: Every day, 6 p.m.–4 a.m.

What goes on: While not the place for the girls to sip chardonnay after a hard day at the mall, this rustic, nautical-themed bar is deserving nonetheless. Distinguished a decade ago as one of Coconut Grove's gay bars, the Hungry Sailor has successfully made the transition to being a straight bar where reggae is the chosen melody and darts are taken seriously.

Setting & atmosphere: Small and dark, with old wooden tables and a makeshift stage for the reggae bands that play twice a week. Anchors and other nautical objects serve as theme decor.

If you go: This is one of those Coconut Grove institutions to tell your friends back home about.

JIMMY'Z AT CUBA CLUB

Euro disco/trance, disco, Top 40

Who Goes There: 21–50; Fellini-esque mix of models, Euroboys in crested blazers, celebs, upscale barflies, young women with bionic décolleté

432 41st Street
(305) 604-9798 Miami Beach Zone 1

Cover: $10 on weekdays, $15 on weekends (waived for members)
Minimum: None

Mixed drinks: $8–10
Wine: $7.50
Beer: $6

(Jimmy'z at Cuba Club)

Dress: Anything currently shown in *French Vogue/Vogue Homme.* The wilder the better for this crowd.

Specials: None

Food available: Memorable gourmet cuisine in a private dining room.

Hours: Tuesday–Saturday, 8 p.m.–5 a.m.

What goes on: Regine Choukroun, the legendary Queen of the Night, is the impresario of the club, which caters to the junior jetset. There are theme nights galore, from Tuesday jazz nights with combos and full Latin bands to whimsical soirees named for exotic destinations the average Joe will never get to but the privileged know first-hand. Wednesday is alarmingly popular, with a loyal contingent for the weekly disco night, as well as spill-over from the adjoining luxury restaurant, the Forge.

Setting & atmosphere: Sophisticated yet full of character—like Regine herself—Jimmy'z doesn't lack for color. There are red walls, gilt-edged mirrors, a chandelier as large as a Subaru in the Champagne Jazz Room, a bed done up in rich jewel tones by one of the bars, and an extravagant walk-in humidor that houses the VIP stogies of celebs including Madonna, Sly Stallone, and Michael Jordan.

If you go: This is the only place in Miami where a Wednesday night is that much wilder (and more fun) than your typical Saturday night. Call the week ahead for dinner reservations. Valet available.

LIQUID

Late-night club that prides itself on its razor-sharp attitude and crowd; owned by New York club impresario Chris Paciello and Madonna pal Ingrid Casares

Who Goes There: 21–29 (last admitted age); those whose fabulousness is secure such as Madonna, Jack Nicholson, and models Kate, Naomi, Helena, and Claudia

1439 Washington Avenue
(305) 532-9154 Miami Beach Zone 1

Cover: $10, weeknights; $15, Friday and Saturday

Minimum: None

Mixed drinks: $5–6

Wine: $5

Beer: $5

Dress: Club couture. Most aim for very chic or very freak. Comfort is not a consideration.

Specials: None

Food available: None

(Liquid)

Hours: Wednesday–Monday, 11 p.m.– 4 a.m.

What goes on: This is just a tiny step away from a restrictive country club on acid, so be prepared for real entertainment and fashion industry faces if you get in. While you may not recognize the owners by name, you'd kill for a chance to photocopy their address books. Monday nights are legendary, as Liquid is host to Miami's longest running one-nighter, Fat Black Pussycat. The music is high funk, and you have to enter through the alley. Sunday is the big gay night, but in this crowd, as the saying goes, "What night isn't it?"

Setting & atmosphere: It's sleek, stark, and mean inside Liquid. Basically everything you'd hate in a pet—but love in a club à la Manhattan. Everyone checks everyone out, but pretends they don't care. The music is as intense as the space and clientele, with DJs flown in from New York for deep house sounds. Celebs congregate in VIP and VVIP rooms with convenient economy-size bottles of champagne.

If you go: Dress. If you don't get on the good side of the door guardian, you won't get off the curb. Thus be calm, confident, comfortable with people who don't have last names, and once again, dress! If you haven't seen it in a magazine, it won't be seeing the inside of Liquid.

THE LIVING ROOM AT THE STRAND

Euro-flavored lounge with dancing, dining and (much) posing

Who Goes There: Sprite models with deeply tanned playboys; urban sophisticates from 20 to 40; visiting celebs and rock stars after their Miami concert gigs

651 Washington Avenue
(305) 532-2340 Miami Beach Zone 1

Cover: None
Minimum: None
Mixed drinks: $6 and up
Wine: $6 and up; bottle service available
Beer: $4 and up
Dress: Gucci, Prada or Chanel will cut down the risk of your having to wait in line, an unfortunate (and unfortunately very common) occurrence here. And don't even think of wearing denim unless you happen to be very good looking or very famous.
Specials: None
Food available: None

Hours: Thursday–Sunday, 11 p.m.– 4 a.m.

(The Living Room at The Strand)

What goes on: Dancing, necking and champagne-consumption among beautiful, attitudinal, and somewhat reckless types who care not what tomorrow brings. The young are gorgeous and know it, the aged are beautiful and paid for it, so everyone's basically happy, if rather clannish, preferring that you keep to your side of the double banquette, thank you very much. If being in the middle of such vulgarity makes you nauseous, make a reservation in the dining area along the back wall—the steak au poivre is terrific.

Setting & atmosphere: As its name implies, the spacious club is plush and overstuffed, with cozy velvet couches. The catch, though, is that you have to buy a bottle (vodka or champagne are typical) in order to qualify to sit in one, and it doesn't come cheap, starting at $80. The lighting is mercifully dim, which, with the rampant hedonism in this crowd, could be a very good thing.

If you go: Look and act sharp. A quick "Hey, how are you" to the doorman and a hint of smile will do better than asking who's there on a given night. Packs of single men don't stand a chance unless the normal guy–to–stunning female ratio is no less than 1:2. Do not valet park in a rental vehicle.

LUA

Clandestine piano bar/cabaret/Euro mini-disco

Who Goes There: 21–55; trust-fund kids, models, film and TV people, local celebutantes, cabaret fans, celebs

409 Espanola Way
(305) 534-0061 Miami Beach Zone 1

Cover: Thursday, $7; Friday and Saturday, $10
Minimum: None
Mixed drinks: $6–7
Wine: $6
Beer: $4
Dress: Elegant or of-the-moment trendy; vintage cocktail dresses with gloves, anything by Vivienne Westwood, Polo blazers with the family crest.
Specials: None
Food available: None

Hours: Thursday–Monday, 10 p.m.–5 a.m.

What goes on: Passionate conversations are a constant at this trendy, tiny hideaway. Dancing is relegated to the adjacent disco room, where the throbbing beat rocks the entire place. Popular bar scene for those who don't like the formality of the living room–like VIP area.

(Lua)

Setting & atmosphere: Very camp fin de siècle, with plump love seats paired with teeny cocktail tables, lamps with fringe that extends inches too long from their shades, and a trompe l'oeil fireplace mural. The type of club where Miss Havisham would surely be a charter member.

If you go: Weekends get saturated, so go early (or late) to take in all the nuances of this charming spot.

MAC'S CLUB DEUCE

Oldest, least pretentious locals bar on South Beach

Who Goes There: Hip and not-so-hip locals, pool junkies, barflies, tattooed bikers, drag queens, film crews, unfazed normal folk, New Yorkers

222 14th Street
(305) 673-9537 Miami Beach Zone 1

Cover: None
Minimum: None
Mixed drinks: $2.50–4.50
Wine: $3
Beer: $2.50–3.25
Dress: Inexplicably casual, although we once saw a woman wearing a pink taffeta pea coat.
Specials: None
Food available: Miniature pizzas, pickled eggs.

Hours: 8 a.m.–5 a.m., 7 days a week, 365 days a year

What goes on: A neo–Fellini-esque documentary waiting to happen. Since 1926, the constant stream of nightcrawlers taking their place at the wrap-around bar has served as the main attraction. The best training a novice barfly could get.

Setting & atmosphere: Wouldn't win any design awards, but then, it's not that kind of place. Assorted neon beer signs dot the walls; a worn pool table sits off to a corner. A decently stocked juke box and cigarette machine get lots of use. The big-screen TV is the only trace of modernism. Smoky and dim, but not so dark that you can't see the elements around you, which is a good thing.

If you go: You'd best use the rest room at a prior stop; the last time we checked out the facilities we noticed a gaping hole in the wall leading to the main room. No valet, of course, but street parking is not as bad as it could be. Conveniently located across from a late-night tattoo parlor and 24-hour French sandwich stand.

MARCO'S IN THE GROVE AND CLUB TAJ

A place for professional partiers to dine, dance, and talk about tomorrow

Who Goes There: 21–40; people who proudly lease BMWs and dress a bit (much) to go out

3339 Virginia Street, Coconut Grove
(305) 444-5333 Miami South Zone 3

Cover: Varies
Minimum: None
Mixed drinks: $5 and up
Wine: $4 and up
Beer: $4 and up
Dress: Urban yuppie meets Latin chic. Men wear jackets because they look better; women don't because they know better. Lots of hair and shoulder-baring dresses are frequently spotted.
Specials: Nightly dinner specials; happy hour.
Food available: Classic Italian menu.

Hours: Tuesday–Saturday, 8 p.m.–1 a.m.; dancing, Thursday–Saturday, 10 p.m.–3 a.m.

What goes on: Table hopping, table dancing, what's the difference? In this bustling restaurant and its adjacent nightclub, everyone's either young or pretending to be so, and they're out for fun. Folks will dance at the drop of a hat (or plate), and the art of flirting is mastered by many who frequent Marco's and Club Taj. Dinner hour is definitely not sedate—it's more of a feed-yourself-well-before-the-frenzy approach, and everyone dances as if the fiddler of doom is up next.

Setting & atmosphere: It's club American-style, with tropical colors and a techno-hip light show that illuminates the dance floor. While theme nights are popular, they're not restrictive. The DJ does what it takes to keep people dancing—thus the mix of Latin music, house, and Top 40 throughout the night.

If you go: Be prepared for theme parties—particularly anything Latin where your feet may be rendered useless by stomping experts. This is a great spot for groups looking to entertain themselves as a crowd within a crowd. Free valet parking is worth noting in the congested Coconut Grove area, and reservations couldn't hurt.

SLOPPY JOE'S BAR

Famous and infamous Key West watering hole that Ernest (Poppa) Hemingway used to call home

Who Goes There: A mix of humanity, from local barflies to midwestern tourists

201 Duval Street, Key West
(305) 294-5717 The Florida Keys Zone 5

Cover: None, unless it's a special event.
Minimum: None
Mixed drinks: $3.75–5.50
Wine: $3.25
Beer: $2.75–3.50
Dress: Very casual.

Specials: Constant drink specials, including the bar's Pop Double, Hemingway Hammer, and Key Lime shooter, priced from $2.25–6.
Food available: Light menu.

Hours: Monday–Saturday, 9 a.m.–4 a.m.; Sunday, noon–4 a.m.

What goes on: Famed for being the local watering hole of Ernest Hemingway, this bar has gained a following with both locals and the international tourist crowd. The Hemingway Days Festival, which originated at the bar in 1981, has now become a world-renowned week-long event. The bar continues to host the outrageous Hemingway Look-A-Like Contest in mid-July. Entertainment goes on all day and night, with a varied selection of country duets, rock, and blues vocalists.

Setting & atmosphere: Everything about the bar reads "sit back, relax, and have fun." There is an enormous amount of memorabilia on Hemingway and George Russell (Hemingway's friend and owner of the bar). The original long, curving bar, ceiling fans, and jalousie doors open on busy Duval Street. Note the Depression-era mural of Russell, Hemingway, and Skinner.

If you go: T-shirts are a must-purchase to take back home. There are mugs, magnets, clothes, and much more. Vacationing businessmen and women should note that franchises are available for future Sloppy Joe's.

TOBACCO ROAD

Noted Miami institution, neighborhood bar featuring live music/concert venue/home of annual blues festival

Who Goes There: 21–45; hep cats, rockers, bikers, modern bohemians

626 South Miami Avenue
(305) 374-1198 Miami South Zone 3

Cover: Usually $3, weekends only
Minimum: None
Mixed drinks: $3.25–3.75
Wine: $3.25
Beer: $2.75–3.25
Dress: Tuxedoes to Harley gear; anything goes.

Specials: Weekday happy hour, 5–8 p.m. with $1–2 appetizer plates. Live music nightly.
Food available: Lunch and dinner in the American vein: steaks, burgers, chicken wings, and nachos, plus daily specials.

Hours: Every day, 11:30 a.m.–5 a.m.; kitchen is open until 2 a.m.

What goes on: A Miami hot spot since 1912, this New Orleans–type bar is the city's oldest, and holds Miami's first liquor license. Perennially popular with locals, Tobacco Road was among the first to showcase local and national blues acts. The theme nights are among the best: Monday night is blues jam; Wednesday, live jazz. Once a year, in October, the bar sponsors a Blues Fest, showcasing 20 bands in the rear parking area.

Setting & atmosphere: Charmingly quaint, the wooden frame structure has the feel of a roadhouse. There are two stories, each with a stage. Often, both stages are in use simultaneously. Outside, the wooden deck patio is shaded by a huge oak tree; thatched tiki-style huts and colored patio lights complete the bohemian picture.

If you go: This is the kind of place best enjoyed in a group. Not recommended for lovelorn singles or first dates. Parking is available in the lot behind the bar.

TWIST

Party palace just for the boys

Who Goes There: 21–45; the young, tan, and built—your basic gay Greek gods

1057 Washington Avenue
(305) 538-9478 Miami Beach Zone 1

Cover: Varies; call to inquire
Minimum: None
Mixed drinks: $4 and up
Wine: $5 and up
Beer: $4 and up
Dress: South Beach casual—jeans, T-shirts (frequently removed), or more exotic apparel announcing availability such as a scrap of leather.
Specials: Generally something every day—call, ask, or just order it.
Food available: None

Hours: Every day, 1 p.m.–5 a.m.

What goes on: Twist yourself into a quiet corner or contort yourself on the dance floor. Twist offers a number of very different atmospheres to suit your mood. Very popular with locals, this relatively long-standing gay bar/club satisfies a wide variety of tastes. Depending on the area you select, it can be a place for a romantic drink on a first date or a spot to let loose to throbbing music on the packed dance floor. And, of course, this being Florida, there's an outdoor deck bar that makes you realize Key West is only several hours away. Essentially, all kinds of people go for all kinds of reasons.

Setting & atmosphere: There's chrome and leather and some strong wall colorations—but, frankly you won't remember much about the decor because it will be packed to the gills. You'll probably have too much fun, too. Nonetheless, don't end your experience at the first-level bar, which is where the chatty locals hang out with flippant (but cute) bartenders and overhead videos. Venture up the staircase, and you can scam drinks, play pool, or dance before heading outside to the terrace.

If you go: Like they say, "No rules, just right." Twist hardly ever gets a bad comment, probably because it's a likable locale with likable locals. Definitely a smart choice on the tour, since you're unlikely to become a victim of attitude or unfriendliness. Don't overdress and you'll blend with the melange of types that patronize Twist.

Part Seven

Exercise and Recreation

Handling Florida Weather

Most of the folks on our *Unofficial Guide* research team work out routinely. Some bike, some run, some lift weights, while others play tennis or do aerobics. While visiting Miami's subtropical climate, it didn't take us long to figure out that exercising during the hot, humid, and rainy summer months—and under the powerful rays of the South Florida sun—presented some problems.

The best months for outdoor recreation are November through March, the "dry" season of warm days, low humidity, and infrequent rain. During late spring, summer, and early fall, you must get up very early to beat the heat—and you'll still have to deal with the climate's formidable humidity. The winter months can bring temperatures that reach up into the 80s, but the weather is usually delightful for outdoor recreation. During the summer months, unless you get up very early, we recommend working out indoors.

First, A Reality Check: Sunburn

There's a downside to frolicking in Miami's sun-drenched beauty—getting fried by the tropical sun. Folks from milder climes routinely underestimate the power of the subtropical sun . . . and pay the price in misery that can ruin a vacation. Before setting out for a long afternoon in the sun, keep in mind that Miami shares the same latitude as the Sahara Desert.

To avoid a blistering sunburn, take it *very* easy on the first few days in South Florida. Spend no more than five or ten minutes sunbathing or exercising outside on your first day; you can increase the amount of time under the sun by about 15 minutes each subsequent day. After a week, most visitors can spend an hour sunbathing or working out in the sun without getting a burn. It's especially important in the beginning not to expose yourself to the sun between 11 a.m. and 2 p.m., when its rays are at their most powerful. Finally, don't forget to apply a liberal amount of sunblock with a *Sun Protection Factor* (SPF) of 25 or higher—and reapply often, especially if you're engaging in water sports.

Our Secret Weapon Against Sunburn

What should you do if you forget our advice and get a bad burn? While there are plenty of nonprescription pain relievers on the market that will take the edge off the pain, consider trying our secret weapon: *aloe.*

Stop by any *Woolworth's* in Miami or Miami Beach and pick up a live aloe plant—prices typically start around $3. Crushing a leaf and gently rubbing the gel that oozes from the leaf on your burn works better than anything else we've tried for relieving the pain of sunburn. (It also works well on scratches and scrapes and makes an excellent tea.) In North Miami Beach, the *Log Cabin Nursery* at 8128 Collins Avenue usually stocks aloe plants; prices start at $1.50. This nonprofit plant store is open daily from 9 a.m. to 4:30 p.m. Sunday through Friday; 10 a.m. to 4:30 p.m. on Saturdays.

Indoor Sports

Free Weights and Nautilus

Many of the major hotels in the Miami area have a spa or fitness room with weight-lifting equipment. For an aerobic workout, most of the fitness rooms offer a Lifecycle, Stairmaster, or rowing machine.

Fitness Centers and Aerobics

Many Miami fitness centers are co-ed and accept daily or short-term memberships. The *Olympia Gym & Fitness Center,* located at 20335 Biscayne Boulevard in North Miami Beach, features two free-weight areas, fixed weights, Stairmasters, and aerobics classes. Daily membership is $10; the weekly rate is $30. Call (305) 932-3500 for more information.

The *Downtown Athletic Club* at 200 South Biscayne Boulevard (on the 15th floor of the Southeast Financial Building) boasts a 32,000-square-foot facility that includes free weights, exercise bikes, treadmills, an indoor track, a basketball court, a whirlpool, and racquetball. The daily rate is $13. Members qualify for two and a half hours of free parking a day while working out; for more information, call (305) 358-9988.

World Gym of Coral Gables at 3737 SW 8th Street offers free and fixed weights, Stairmasters, Lifecycles, and a treadmill. Membership is $10 a day and $30 a week; call (305) 445-5161 for more information.

On South Beach, *The Gridiron Club* at 1676 Alton Road offers daily memberships for $9 a day and $43 a week. Facilities include a complete gym (with both free and fixed weights) and aerobic studios, but no sauna or whirlpool. For more information call (305) 531-4743.

Land Sports

Walking

By and large, Miami is as car crazy as any other large American city—maybe a bit more. When an errand requires a trip of two or three blocks or longer, most residents reach for their car keys. In fact, most Miamians think it strange that anyone would want to walk anywhere. As a result, Miami isn't a very friendly city for strolling or walking. Folks looking for a place to stretch their legs may have to drive to get there.

Nor is the city's decentralized layout conducive to long walks. While many neighborhoods are great for strolling—Coral Gables, Coconut Grove, South Beach, and downtown on a busy weekday morning immediately come to mind—they're too far apart to walk between them.

There is, however, one great walking destination in South Florida: *Miami Beach.* From sunup to sundown, the sparkling white beach is a great place for a long walk or a leisurely stroll. (After the sun sets, stay off the beach—it's not safe after dark.) From 21st Street to 51st Street, the wooden *boardwalk* behind the hotels is a favorite destination for all kinds of people, ranging from religious Jews to vacationing Europeans and South Americans and even an occasional homeless person.

For a more structured walking tour that's also informative and fun, take the *Art Deco walking tour* of South Miami Beach, which starts every Saturday morning at 10:30 a.m. and every Thursday at 6:30 p.m. The cost is $10 (tax deductible), and the tour lasts 90 minutes. It begins at the Art Deco Welcome Center at the Ocean Front Auditorium located at 1001 Ocean Drive; reservations aren't required. Hint: For the Saturday morning tour, get to South Beach at least an hour before the tour starts, find a parking place, and eat breakfast before showing up for the walk.

On the mainland, *Coconut Grove* and *Coral Gables* are good places to stretch your legs. The Grove offers unlimited opportunities for people-watching and window shopping; for a longer walk, take the paved *bicycle path* that follows Biscayne Bay south along Bayshore Drive, Main Highway, Ingraham Highway, and Old Cutler Road. Just watch out for bikes.

In Coral Gables, start walking from the Miracle Mile west toward City Hall. The neighborhood gets really lush; energetic strollers can view famous landmarks such as the Merrick House (the former home of Coral Gables' founder), the ritzy Colonnade Hotel, the Venetian Pool, and the Biltmore Hotel.

For spectacular views of Biscayne Bay and downtown Miami, take a long walk along the *Rickenbacker Causeway*, which connects the mainland with Key Biscayne. If your legs can handle it, a long walk along the causeway's combination walkway/bike path leads past Windsurfer Beach, Seaquarium, the Miami Marine Stadium, and Crandon Beach, located near the end of Key Biscayne. There's plenty of public parking near the beaches that line the causeway or at the marina on Virginia Key.

Although it costs $8 to get in, *Fairchild Tropical Garden* is filled with paths that make for excellent walking. The park is tranquil, filled with beautiful plants and trees, man-made lakes, manicured greens—and no cars are allowed inside. Go in the morning or late afternoon when it's cool and the light is at its best.

Farther from Miami, *Everglades National Park* offers unlimited opportunities for walks—at least, during the winter months when the mosquitoes won't eat you alive. *Shark Valley*, about 35 miles west of Miami on Route 41, has a long, wide, paved path that makes a 15-mile loop into the glades, as well as a short nature path near the visitor center. You'll see plenty of wildlife along the way. On weekends, arrive early before the parking lot fills up.

Near the park's southern entrance outside Florida City, strollers can choose from a wide number of paved and wooden pathways that show off the best of the glades' unique topography, flora, and wildlife. *The Anhinga Trail* is the closest and offers a half-mile boardwalk famous for its scenery and wildlife; expect to see gators, birds (including the eponymous anhinga drying its wings after a dive), and fish.

Running

Both casual and serious joggers face the same problems as folks in search of a good destination to take a stroll: in Miami, the car reigns supreme. As a result, it's tough to find a place for a long run that doesn't require dodging automobile traffic.

On Miami Beach, the *boardwalk* between 21st Street and 51st Street, as well as anywhere along the beach itself, offers the best—and safest—running surfaces. Above 30th Street, the beach gets narrow and it's often hard to find a packed track through the sand (unless you don't mind getting your feet wet near the surf where the sand is packed down by the waves). North of North Shore State Recreation Area (between 79th and 87th streets), a path runs parallel to the beach behind the narrow boardwalk toward Bal Harbour; its wide, packed surface is excellent for running.

On the mainland, the best destination for runners and joggers is the *bike path* that starts in Coconut Grove and continues south along Biscayne Bay; watch out for cyclists and cars as you cross the many intersections along the route. *Coral Gables* offers plenty of shaded, low-traffic back streets for serious joggers. The *Rickenbacker Causeway* to Key Biscayne has a path—and great views—that's excellent for a run that can reach marathon lengths if you continue around the island.

TENNIS

If you're not staying in a posh hotel or resort that offers free tennis, you're not entirely out of luck: the area abounds with plenty of public tennis courts.

The premier public tennis facility in the Miami area may be *The Tennis Center at Crandon Park* on Key Biscayne (phone (305) 365-2300), which offers 17 hard courts, 8 clay courts, and 2 grass courts. Hourly rates during the day for hard courts are $3 per person/per hour and $6 per person/per hour for clay. At night, only the hard courts are lighted; the rate is $5 per person/per hour. Advance reservations are accepted.

The Key Biscayne Tennis Association at 6702 Crandon Boulevard has seven clay and two hard courts that can be rented up to two days in advance. The courts are open 8 a.m. to 9 p.m. Monday through Thursday; until 6 p.m. Friday through Sunday; rates are $5 per person/per hour; only two clay courts and the two hard courts have lights. Call (305) 361-5263 for more information.

On Miami Beach, *Flamingo Park Center* at 1000 12th Street has 19 clay courts, all lighted for night play. The daytime rate is $5.50 per couple/per hour; at night, it's $6.50 per couple/per hour. Reservations for that day only may be made in person, not by phone. Call (305) 673-7761 for more information.

Farther up the beach in Surfside, the *A&M Tennis/Surfside Tennis Center and Pro Shop* at 88th Street and Collins Avenue features three hard courts and a fully staffed pro shop. Hours are 10:30 a.m. to 9 p.m. Monday through Friday, 9 a.m. to 5 p.m. on Saturday, and 9 a.m. to 5 p.m. on Sunday. The fee is $3 per person/per hour ($3.75 at night); reservations are accepted and the staff will find you a playing partner if you need one. Lessons and programs are available. Call (305) 866-5176 for more information.

In addition, the City of Miami and the Metro-Dade County Park and Recreation Department operate more than 250 tennis courts between them. Court locations include popular visitor destinations such as Haulover Park and North Shore Park (Miami Beach), Peacock Park (Coconut Grove), Tamiami Park (next to Florida International University), and Tropical Park (at the Palmetto Expressway).

GOLF

The peak season for golf in South Florida is Thanksgiving through mid-April. Midmornings are the most popular tee time and usually require reservations made well in advance. During the week, singles can frequently catch up with a game because of no-shows. Weekends, when local residents hit the links, are always busy (regardless of season), and getting a morning reservation is difficult. Plan on teeing off before 1 p.m. so you're not racing the sun, which sets around 5 p.m. in midwinter.

The summer months are ferociously hot and humid, so reserve a tee time either before 9 a.m. or after 4 p.m. to play nine holes; avoid the links between 1 and 3 p.m. In addition, afternoon thunderstorms frequently roll across Dade County. Greens fees, however, are reduced at many courses during the off-season.

Vacationers should reserve tee times when booking their hotels; some hotels block off tee times at nearby courses for their guests. During the summer, many golf courses offer discounts to local residents. Reservations at two municipal courses (Biltmore and Grenada) can be secured up to 24 hours in advance at no charge by calling the service at (305) 669-9500 on a touch-tone phone. Golfers on extended stays in Dade County might consider subscribing to the service to secure preferred times further in advance; the fee is $35 a year.

Biltmore Golf Course

Established: 1926

Address: 1210 Anastasia Avenue, Coral Gables FL 33134

Phone: (305) 460-5364

Status: Municipal course

Tees:

Championship: 6,624 yards, par 72, USGA 71.5, slope 119.

Men's: 6,213 yards, par 72, USGA 69.7, slope 116.

Ladies': 5,600 yards, par 72, USGA 73.3, slope 122.

Fees: Daily, $44; Twilight (after 2 p.m.), $15; Early bird (before 8 a.m.), $15. Cart fee is $15 (18 hole); $8.25 (9 hole).

Facilities: Clubhouse, full-service pro shop with custom club building and club repair capabilities, restaurant, locker rooms, driving range, putting greens, sand trap area, lessons from pros, tennis courts, Biltmore Hotel.

Comments: Redesigned in 1992, the Biltmore Golf Course is in excellent shape. Today, the course hosts the Coral Gables Open and the Orange Bowl International Junior Golf Championship.

California Club

Address: 20898 San Simeon Way, North Miami FL 33179

Phone: (305) 651-3590

Status: Semiprivate course

Tees:

Championship: 6,670 yards, par 72, USGA 70.9, slope 125.

Men's: 6,264 yards, par 72, USGA 68.6, slope 120.

Ladies': 5,675 yards, par 72, USGA 69.7, slope 117.

Fees: Weekdays, $37 after 12 p.m.; Twilight (after 2 p.m.), $25; $16.50 (9 holes) after 3 p.m. Call for weekend rates. Carts are mandatory.

Facilities: 18-hole championship course, driving range, restaurant, locker rooms.

Comments: A tight course with sharp doglegs. There are three great finishing holes with water on the left.

City of Miami Country Club (Miami Springs)

Established: 1923

Address: 650 Curtiss Parkway, Miami Springs FL 33166

Phone: (305) 888-1918

Status: Public course

Tees:

Championship: 6,741 yards, par 71, USGA 71, slope 122.

Men's: 6,476 yards, par 71, USGA 72, slope 122.

Ladies': 5,836 yards, par 73, USGA 72.5, slope 122.

Fees: Daily, $15; Twilight (after 3 p.m.), $11. Cart fee is $20.

Facilities: Pro shop, restaurant, banquet facility for up to 700, lounge, lighted driving range, lessons from pros.

Comments: The Country Club in Miami Springs was opened by the City of Miami in 1923. The 18-hole championship par 71 course features challenging sand traps and a tropical ambience throughout its 6,741 yards. Home of the original Miami Open from 1925 until 1955, Miami Springs is now the annual host of the prestigious North-South Tournament. Less than five minutes from Miami International Airport and area hotels, Miami Springs has become a favorite among business travelers in Miami. With its low seasonal rates and extensive facilities, the manicured championship course welcomes visitors to Miami's tropical world of golf.

Costa del Sol Golf Course

Address: 100 Costa del Sol Boulevard, Miami FL 33178 (Entrance NW 41st Street E 102nd Avenue)

Phone: (305) 592-9210

Status: Semiprivate course

Tees:

Championship: 6,400 yards, par 72, USGA 70, slope 118.

Men's: 5,978 yards, par 72, USGA 68, slope 114.

Ladies': 5,487 yards, par 72, USGA 70, slope 115.

Fees: Please call for rates and tee times. Club rentals, $10.

Facilities: Pro shop, driving range, putting green, restaurant/lounge, locker rooms, lessons.

Comments: Play this Palm Springs–style course and experience the relaxed, private atmosphere that prevails here. No two holes play the same. Doglegs, some tight fairways, and interesting water holes make club selection the key at Costa.

Doral Resort & Country Club

Established: 1961

Address: 4000 NW 87th Avenue, Miami FL 33178

Silver Course Clubhouse: 5001 NW 104th Avenue

Phone: (305) 592-2000

Status: Resort course

Tees:

Course One (The Blue Monster)

Championship: 7,125 yards, par 72, USGA 74.5, slope 130.
Men's: 6,701 yards, par 72, USGA 72.2, slope 125.
Ladies': 5,392 yards, par 72, USGA 73, slope 124.

Course Two (The Gold Course)

Championship: 6,602 yards, par 70, USGA 73.3, slope 129.
Men's: 6,209 yards, par 70, USGA 70.7, slope 124.
Ladies': 5,179 yards, par 70, USGA 71.4, slope 123.

Course Three (The Red Course)

Championship: 6,146 yards, par 70, USGA 70.2, slope 121.
Men's: 6,058 yards, par 70, USGA 69.9, slope 118.
Ladies': 5,096 yards, par 70, USGA 70.6, slope 118.

Course Four (The White Course)

Championship: 6,208 yards, par 72, USGA 69.7, slope 117.
Men's: 5,913 yards, par 72, USGA 68.4, slope 113.
Ladies': 5,286 yards, par 72, USGA 70.1, slope 116.

Course Five (The Silver Course)

Championship: 6,614 yards, par 71, USGA 72, slope 131.
Men's: 6,315 yards, par 71, USGA 70.5, slope 128.
Ladies': 5,567 yards, par 71, USGA 72, slope 130.

Course Six (The Green Course)

Nine holes: 1,085 yards, par 3.

Fees: In season (December 22–May 3): Hotel guests—Blue course, $190; White course, $95; Red course, $160; Gold course, $170; Silver course, $170. Nonguests—Blue course, $225; White course, $110; Red course, $180; Gold course, $200; Silver course, $180. Green course, $25 all the time for all guests.Greens fees are significantly lower off-season.

Facilities: One of the world's largest pro shops, driving range, four putting greens, world-class Doral Spa, on-course snack bar, three full service restaurants, 15-court tennis facility, Doral golf learning center with Jim McLean, caddies available, fishing in the course lakes. The clubhouse for the Silver Course was under renovation at press time. The new facilities will be extensive.

Comments: The home of the famous Doral "Blue Monster" and the Doral-Ryder Open. This is one of the premier golf courses in the country. The Gold Course has recently been redesigned by Raymond Floyd (original designer of the "Blue Monster"). With the tropical Miami climate and four championship courses, this Florida destination is one that should not be missed by the avid golfer. Serene lakes and Cypress trees line the fairways of this wonderful setting, as you challenge the "Blue Monster."

Fontainebleau Golf Club

Established: 1970

Address: 9603 Fontainebleau Boulevard, Miami FL 33172

Phone: (305) 221-5181

Status: Public course

Tees:

Course One (West)

Championship: 7,035 yards, par 72, USGA 73.3, slope 122.
Men's: 6,647 yards, par 72, USGA 71.57, slope 117.
Ladies': 5,586 yards, par 72, USGA 71.45, slope 119.

Course Two (East)

Championship: 6,944 yards, par 72, USGA 72.54, slope 120.
Men's: 6,650 yards, par 72, USGA 71.2, slope 118.
Ladies': 5,565 yards, par 72, USGA 71, slope 118.

Fees: For two people. Winter: $50 weekdays ($40 after noon); $60 weekends ($46 after noon). Call for summer rates. Includes cart fee.

Facilities: 36-hole championship course, driving range, snack bar, pro shop, lessons from PGA professional.

Comments: Mark Mahanna design.

Golf Club of Miami

Established: 1990

Address: 6801 Miami Gardens Drive, Miami FL 33015

Phone: (305) 829-8449

Status: Public course

Tees:

Course One (West)

Championship: 7,017 yards, par 72, USGA 73.5, slope 130.
Men's: 6,139 yards, par 72, USGA 69.4, slope 124.
Ladies': 5,300 yards, par 72, USGA 70.1, slope 123.

Course Two (East)

Championship: 6,353 yards, par 70, USGA 70.3, slope 124.
Men's: 5,810 yards, par 70, USGA 67.9, slope 118.
Ladies': 5,025 yards, par 70, USGA 68.8, slope 117.

Course Three (South)

Men's: 4,240 yards, par 62, USGA 60.6, slope 95.
Ladies': 3,281 yards, par 62, USGA 58.9, slope 89.

Fees: In season (December–April 15): $55 weekdays, $75 weekends.

Off-season (April 16–December): $24–40. Rates include cart and green fees. Twilight fees are available. All fees subject to 6.5% Florida tax.

Facilities: Two grass driving ranges (one lighted), two pro shops, on-course beverage service, lessons from PGA professionals, Turn Key tournament operation, full-service restaurant, banquet room, men's and women's locker rooms.

Comments: South Florida's premier public golf facility. Site of former National Airlines Open, the 1991 Senior PGA Tour National Qualifying School, and Regional USGA events such as the Mid-AM qualifier.

Hollywood Golf Hotel

Established: 1930

Address: 1600 Johnson Street, Hollywood FL 33020

Phone: (954) 927-1751

Status: Public course

Tees:

Championship: 6,336 yards, par 70, USGA 70, slope 117.
Men's: 6,024 yards, par 70, USGA 70, slope 117.
Ladies': 5,484 yards, par 70, USGA 70, slope 117.

Fees: Winter: $34; Summer: $25. Cart included.

Facilities: Pro shop, clubhouse restaurant, 35-room full-service hotel, locker rooms, pool.

Comments: Famous Florida club designed by Donald Ross in 1930. It was completely renovated in 1995.

International Links of Miami (Formerly the Melreese Golf Course)

Established: 1960

Address: 1802 NW 37th Avenue, Miami FL 33125

Phone: (305) 633-4583

Status: Public course

Tees:

Championship: 7,173 yards, par 71, slope 132.
Men's: 6,613 yards, par 71, slope 125.
Ladies': 5,534 yards, par 71, slope 118.

Fees: $75 before 3 p.m.; $30 after 3 p.m.; includes cart.

Facilities: Pro shop, restaurant/lounge, banquet facility for up to 200, lighted driving range, lessons from pros, rental equipment.

Comments: International Links of Miami is an outstanding 18-hole championship par 71 course with 14 holes bordering the water. It is rated as one of the finest municipal golf courses in the country. International Links has hosted the Ladies' PGA, Public Links Qualifying, the National Clergymen's Tournament, the National Baseball Players' Tournament, and the Regional Handicapped Tournament.

Miami National Golf Club
(Formerly the Kendale Lakes Golf Course)

Established: 1970

Address: 6401 Kendale Lakes Drive, Miami FL 33183

Phone: (305) 382-3930

Status: Semiprivate course

Tees:

Marlin Course
Blue Tees: 3,359/3,334 yards, par 36.
White Tees: 3,120 yards, par 36.
Red Tees: 2,743 yards, par 37.
Dolphin Course
Blue Tees: 3,319 yards, par 36.
White Tees: 3,060 yards, par 36.
Red Tees: 2,579 yards, par 36.
Barracuda Course
Blue Tees: 3,360 yards, par 36.
White Tees: 3,092 yards, par 36.
Red Tees: 2,702 yards, par 37.

Fees: Winter: $39–45; $35–45 after 10 a.m.; $20–25 after 2 p.m. Cart fee: $20 weekdays; $30 weekends. Call for summer rates.

Facilities: Three championship 9-hole courses, 40-stall driving range (lighted), 12-court tennis facility (6 lighted), 2 Olympic-size pools, infant wading pool, swimming lessons from professionals, men's and women's locker rooms, banquet facility, and grill bar.

Comments: Miami National Golf Club was built in 1970 and is considered one of the best courses in Greater Miami. It was remodeled after Hurricane Andrew, with $2 million going to repair the clubhouse and golf course. It has been host to several LPGA tour events and PGA qualifiers for the Doral-Ryder Open and the Honda Classic.

Miami Shores Country Club

Established: 1937

Address: 10000 Biscayne Boulevard, Miami Shores FL 33138

Phone: (305) 795-2366

Status: Public course

Tees:

Championship: 6,373 yards, par 71, USGA 70.6, slope 120.
Men's: 6,094 yards, par 71, USGA 69.1, slope 116.
Ladies': 5,442 yards, par 72, USGA 71.3, slope 121.

Fees: Winter: $60; Twilight (after 3 p.m.): $25. Carts mandatory.

Facilities: Clubhouse with three banquet rooms seating up to 450, pool, tennis courts, pro shop, lighted driving range, golf school, men's and women's locker rooms, spacious lounge area available for lunch and dinner.

Comments: Miami Shores is one of the oldest clubs in Miami. It is characterized by elevated tees and greens that are small and well bunkered.

Normandy Shores Golf Course

Established: Early 1940s

Address: 2401 Biarritz Drive, Miami Beach FL 33141

Phone: (305) 868-6502

Status: Public course

Tees:

Championship: 6,402 yards, par 71, USGA 70.5, slope 120.
Men's: 6,055 yards, par 71, USGA 68.9, slope 116.
Ladies': 5,527 yards, par 73, USGA 71, slope 119.

Fees: Winter: Residents: $30 before 11 a.m.; $21 after 11 a.m. Nonresidents: $40 before 11 a.m.; $25 after 11 a.m. Call for summer rates. Walking is allowed on weekdays at any time and on weekends after 1 p.m.

Facilities: Snack bar, locker rooms, driving range, chipping and putting greens.

Comments: Normandy Shores is located just off Biscayne Bay, five minutes from Miami Beach. This well-bunkered course presents a challenge to golfers of all skill levels.

Palmetto Golf Course

Established: 1959

Address: 9300 SW 152nd Street, Miami FL 33157

Phone: (305) 238-2922

Status: Public course

Tees:

Championship: 6,698 yards, par 70 USGA 72.7, slope 128.

Men's: 6,214 yards, par 70 USGA 70.2, slope 123.
Ladies': 5,710 yards, par 73 USGA 73.4, slope 125.

Fees: Winter: $30 weekdays, $34 weekends. Call for summer rates. Twilight rates available during both seasons.

Facilities: Pro shop, driving range, putting green, snack bar.

Comments: This course was designed by Dick Wilson and purchased by Dade County in 1967 for public use. It is an extremely challenging course with many water holes. The recently built canopy over the hitting area of the driving range allows protection from the sun.

Bicycling

First, the good news: Dade County is flat.

And the bad? With its congestion and a decentralized layout that makes devising a long ride problematic, Miami is not a very bike-friendly town. Road riders out for a long-distance spin must often negotiate bumper-to-bumper traffic, share the road with rude drivers, and deal with the city's infuriating lack of street signs.

Nor are fat-tired cyclists immune to the problem of finding problem-free riding in South Florida: Unless you're into beach riding (which is *very* hard on equipment), mountain bikers will find little off-road cycling—and certainly no mountains.

In the summer, cyclists should keep a wary eye peeled for approaching afternoon thunderstorms, which can be fearsome. During the summer months' extreme heat and humidity, try to confine long rides to the early morning hours or risk heat exhaustion; carry plenty of water and take sunblock along for the ride. Away from breezes on the beach, mosquitoes can be a problem when you're not pedaling. On the other hand, the winter months offer excellent cycling conditions.

Where to Rent a Bike

Mountain bikes and beach cruisers are available for rental at *Miami Beach Bicycle Center,* 601 5th Street (at Washington Street, phone (305) 674-0150). Rental rates start at $14 for 24 hours. *Grove Cycles* at 3226 Grand Avenue in Coconut Grove (phone (305) 444-5415) rents beach cruisers, tandems, and in-line skates. Beach cruisers rent for $5.50 an hour, $15 a day, and $25 for 24 hours; tandems rent for $10 an hour and $30 a day; in-line skates rent for $6 an hour and $30 a day; the price includes protective padding. Helmets rent for $3 a day; children 15 years old and younger receive free helmet rental. *Mangrove Cycles* at 260 Crandon Boulevard on

Key Biscayne (phone (305) 361-5555) rents one-speed bikes for $7 for 2 hours, $10 a day, and $35 a week; mountain bikes rent for $12 for 2 hours, $18 a day, and $55 a week. The shop is open every day 10 a.m. to 6 p.m. but is closed on Mondays.

Road Riding

Before Hurricane Andrew, Miami-area cyclists in the know would throw their bikes on the car and drive south to Homestead, where they would unload and put in many long, flat miles riding around *The Redlands*. It's a locale adjacent to the Everglades renowned for sparse traffic, farms, lush foliage, and coral-rock walls.

No more; the storm wiped out the trees and years will go by before the area recovers enough greenery to attract road riders in search of triple-digit rides and some shade. While riders in search of long rides can still churn out relatively traffic-free miles around Homestead, it's not very scenic—or particularly safe. An influx of unsavory characters attracted by construction jobs as the area rebuilds has made the crime rate soar. But you're okay on a moving bike.

Nowadays, for eye-pleasing scenery and enough tree cover to ward off the effects of the subtropical sun, most riders head for *Coconut Grove*. The streets are pretty, dense foliage such as bougainvillea and hibiscus keep the worst of the sun's effects at bay, and the area's eclectic architecture entertains the eye.

For a longer spin on skinny tires, follow the *bike path* south along Bayshore Drive, Main Highway, Ingraham Highway, and Old Cutler Road—although most serious riders will want to stay off the path and ride in traffic: the paved path is often broken up by tree roots and is better suited for fat tires and one-speed rental bikes. Figure on turning back around 152nd Street (Coral Reef Drive). From this point south, the foliage is sparse as the greenery continues to recover from Hurricane Andrew.

For a more energetic ride—and the biggest climb in Dade County—take the *Rickenbacker Causeway* to Key Biscayne. The climb to the top of the bridge offers stunning views, and a ride around the island is long enough to provide a real workout. You can still spot damage from Hurricane Andrew at the southern end of the island, but the foliage is starting to come back. Yet a ride to and around Key Biscayne remains a Sunday morning favorite with area roadies.

Mountain Biking

Local hammerheads report that all is not lost in mountainless Dade County—although the good riding that's available emphasizes handling over aerobics.

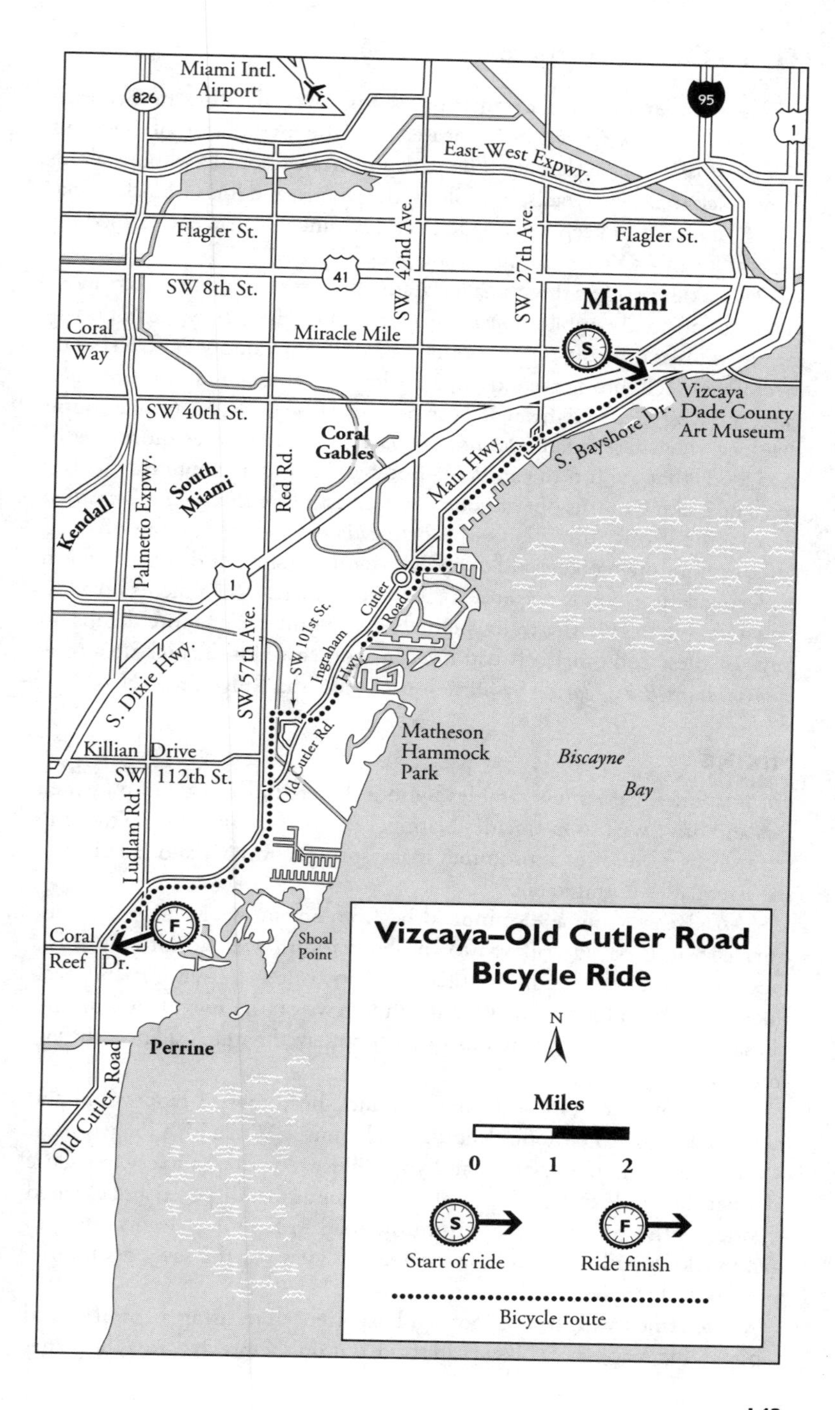
Miami Intl. Airport
826
95
1
East-West Expwy.
Flagler St.
Flagler St.
41
SW 8th St.
SW 42nd Ave.
SW 27th Ave.
Miami
Coral Way
Miracle Mile
S
SW 40th St.
Vizcaya Dade County Art Museum
S. Bayshore Dr.
Coral Gables
Main Hwy.
Red Rd.
South Miami
Kendall
Palmetto Expwy.
1
Cutler Road
SW 101st St.
Ingraham Hwy.
S. Dixie Hwy.
SW 57th Ave.
Old Cutler Rd.
Matheson Hammock Park
Biscayne Bay
Killian Drive
SW 112th St.
Ludlam Rd.
F
Coral Reef Dr.
Shoal Point
Perrine
Old Cutler Road
Vizcaya–Old Cutler Road Bicycle Ride
N
Miles
0
1
2
Start of ride
Ride finish
Bicycle route

The premier off-road destination is just over the line in Broward County: *Markham County Park,* located near the intersection of I-75 and I-59, west of Fort Lauderdale. The park features whoop-de-whoops along single-track trails, jeep roads, real hills in the woods, and lots of black, sticky mud guaranteed to keep intermediate and advanced riders entertained for hours. There's a $1 entrance fee to the park.

Dade County offers three smaller destinations for mountain bikers looking for an off-road ramble. *Amelia Earhart Park* in Hialeah, while not offering any trails as difficult as those found in Markham County Park, has some nice single-track through woods, open fields, soft sand, and mud. *Greynolds Park,* off West Dixie Highway in North Miami Beach, has a 1.6-mile course that local riders like to jam around. *Haulover Park* offers three short rides in the woods that are fun to explore—but avoid riding through the field or you'll be picking thorns out of your inner tubes. *Oleta River State Recreation Area* (across from Sunny Isles in North Miami) is constructing off-road paths for mountain bikers and offers an extensive system of dirt roads worth exploring. Admission to the area is $3.25 per vehicle. While there's no additional charge to ride the trails, helmets are required. For more details on some of these and other off-road rides in southeast Florida, pick up a copy of *Mountain Bike! Florida* by Steve Jones (Menasha Ridge Press).

HIKING

For unspoiled wilderness rambles by foot, hikers must first jump in their cars and drive west to Everglades National Park—but only during the winter months. Clouds of mosquitoes make spring, summer, and fall visits to the Everglades unthinkable.

Shark Valley, about a 90-minute drive from downtown Miami, offers visitors a 15-mile paved walkway to an observation tower; admittedly, this a long trek for all but the most ardent walkers. But a shorter, out-and-back hike still offers glimpses of wildlife and views of the Everglades' unique fauna and topography. There's also a short, unpaved nature trail near the visitor center.

For a more varied look at the Everglades, head toward Homestead and the park's southern entrance leading to Flamingo. While it's a longer drive, it's still a manageable day trip, and you will leave with a much better sense of what the subtle Everglades are all about. A number of paved and elevated wooden pathways that radiate from the road to Flamingo lead visitors to hammocks (small islands of elevated land), views of the sawgrass prairie, and tropical jungles.

Once armed with heavy boots and experienced in using a compass and topographic map, savvy hikers can strike out on their own across the glades during the winter months (which is also the dry season; don't try this during the summer). The rewards include sightings of wildlife and a unique view of the sawgrass prairie that most visitors miss. Pull over anywhere along the road, and head off toward a hammock. Park rangers at the main visitor center near the entrance can offer advice and suggestions for exploring on your own.

KITES

Go fly a kite at *Skyward Kites,* located at Haulover Beach Marina (between Bal Harbour and Sunny Isles on Miami Beach). You can't miss it: just look up as you approach the bridge over the channel on Route A1A near Bal Harbour and you'll see an astounding array of kites, windsocks, and air bags floating in the breeze overhead. A wide array of windborne items are for sale. The retail outlet is open from 9 a.m. to sunset daily. Call (305) 945-1681 for more information.

Water Sports

SWIMMING

The Miami area features two well-known swimming destinations: the *Atlantic Ocean* and *Biscayne Bay.* Miami Beach offers 10 miles of sandy white beaches along the ocean from South Pointe Park in South Beach north to Sunny Isles Beach at 192nd Street.

If you're not staying at a hotel close to the beaches, public beaches with metered parking, bathrooms, and outside showers are available along Route A1A (Collins Avenue) in Miami Beach at: 1st Street and Washington Avenue (South Pointe Park); 3rd Street; 6th to 14th streets (Lummus Park); 21st Street; 35th Street; 46th Street (next to the Eden Roc Hotel); 53rd Street; 64th Street; 73rd Street (across from the North Shore Community Center); 79th to 87th streets (North Shore State Recreation Area); 93rd Street (Surfside; a very small lot across Collins Avenue from the beach); 96th Street (another small lot); and a small lot next to the Holiday Inn on 167th Street (Sunny Isles) that charges $3.50 to park your car.

Other options for ocean swimming include *Haulover Beach* (just north of Bal Harbour between 163rd and 192nd streets; $3 per car), *Crandon Park* on Key Biscayne ($3.50 per car; $1 toll on the Rickenbacker Causeway), and *Bill Baggs Cape Florida State Park* (also on Key Biscayne; $3.50 per car). Haulover is renowned for its "clothing optional" (nude) area on the north end of the beach; Crandon Park is popular with families.

The clear waters of Biscayne Bay are shallow and usually calm; the most popular beaches are along the Rickenbacker Causeway. Picnic tables, shade trees, and no restrictions on pets make these beaches extremely popular with local residents; the waters are also popular with windsurfers (the beach after the first bridge on the causeway is informally called *Windsurfer Beach*).

If you're looking for a nonsaltwater experience, but your hotel doesn't have a pool, the *Venetian Pool* at 2701 DeSoto Boulevard in Coral Gables (phone (305) 460-5356) should be on your itinerary.

Originally excavated to supply limestone for early Coral Gables homes, this large, coral-rock, outdoor pool offers a tropical lagoon–like setting, with caves, waterfalls, and stone bridges. The pool is open Tuesday through Sunday from 10 a.m. to 4:30 p.m.; closed Mondays. Admission for adults is $5; teens age 13 to 17 get in for $4, children age 12 and under are admitted for $2, and no children under age 3 are permitted. A new café offers a full luncheon menu.

Swimming Hazards: It's a Wild Ocean Out There

Folks on a visit to the shores of the Atlantic Ocean at Miami Beach or other South Florida beaches need to keep a few things in mind to guarantee a safe and pleasant trip. To get the low-down on beach hazards and commonsense safety guidelines, we called Larry Pizzi, operations supervisor of the Miami Beach lifeguards.

On the Beach "The biggest hazard on the beach is the sun," Pizzi reports. "Even on cloudy days, the sun's ultraviolet rays filter through and you can get a really bad sunburn. Unfortunately, I hear people all the time say they can't go home without a sunburn—or no one will believe they came to Miami Beach!"

Next hazard: theft. "Be careful of your belongings on the beach," Pizzi warns. "Don't take jewelry, billfolds, and large sums of cash to the beach. Cameras are generally okay if you don't take a long walk and leave them. Just take normal precautions with your valuables."

In the Water Jellyfish, Pizzi says, top the list of hazards here. "Jellyfish can appear anytime, but are more common in the winter," he says. "Portuguese men-of-war, which are really beautiful creatures, are more common in the summer. We put out yellow warning flags to warn folks if they're in the water."

If you get stung, use a pocketknife or credit card to carefully scrape the tentacle away from the skin. "Don't rub it," Pizzi warns. "Pull it off carefully, then treat it with vinegar. Better yet, if you get stung, go to a lifeguard for help."

Sea lice—actually, the spores of Portuguese men-of-war—are invisible creatures that cause an itchy rash that's best treated with cortisone lotions.

The rash can last about a week. "It's also called 'swimmers' eruption,'" Pizzi adds. "It's pretty rare. But it's a good idea to avoid seaweed or anything else floating in the water, since the spores usually come into the beach on something else."

Rip tides, also called undertow, usually occur when easterly winds are blowing from 15 to 20 miles an hour, creating a break in an off-shore sandbar that sends water draining away from the beach.

"If you get caught in a rip tide, even if you're a strong swimmer, don't fight it," Pizzi advises. "Swim parallel to the beach in the direction the water is pushing. Eventually, you'll break free. Remember that panic is the killer, and don't swim against a rip tide."

When there's a rip tide, a red warning flag is posted at lifeguard stations located continuously on Miami Beach from 1st to 14th streets; at 21st, 35th, 46th, 53rd, and 64th streets; and at North Shore State Recreation Area. A red flag is a warning not to swim, although beaches are rarely closed and swimmers may choose to ignore the warning. Yellow flags mean caution; ask the lifeguard to tell you the specific hazard (jellyfish, rip tide, etc.).

Another hazard is stingrays, which bury themselves in the sand—and occasionally get stepped on by swimmers. "They have a barb on the end of their tails which isn't poisonous, but is usually dirty, so infection is a problem," Pizzi says. "There's nothing you can do to avoid stepping on a stingray, but it's very rare."

Finally, what about everybody's favorite beach hazard—sharks?

"Shark attacks are incredibly rare, not just in Miami Beach but all over the world," Pizzi reports. "But when we get a reported sighting, we send out a boat to investigate, get the Coast Guard to send up a helicopter, and clear the beach, if necessary. We check out all the reports."

Other hazards: sport concession areas (marked with buoys), getting lost (most of the beach looks the same and lots of children and adults manage to lose the location of their cars or possessions), snorkeling and diving (mark your location with a diving flag so you're not run over by a boat), and exceeding your physical limits when swimming. "A lot of people come here when it's winter at home and they think they're in good physical shape—but they're not," Pizzi notes.

If You Need Help . . .

What should you do if you or another swimmer gets in trouble and needs help? "Try to float or tread water, remain calm, and don't exhaust yourself by screaming," he advises. "Wave for help and someone will be there soon."

Tides cause the most problems for inexperienced ocean swimmers—and the lifeguards who rescue them. "People go out at low tide to play on the sandbars, then the tide comes in. Water that was four feet deep becomes six or seven feet deep," Pizzi explains. "Weak swimmers step into a hole and panic."

Pizzi emphasizes that the safest place to enjoy the beach is near one of the lifeguard stations (see list of locations above). "It's always better to swim near a guard—even if it means leaving your oceanfront hotel and walking, driving, or taking public transportation," he says. "Lifeguards have first-aid kits, radios, and access to police and fire departments for any emergency."

Folks on the beach between the guarded areas aren't completely unprotected. Four-wheel vehicles operated by the Miami Beach lifeguards regularly patrol all of Miami Beach and keep an eye out for swimmers.

Canoeing and Kayaking

Visitors to Miami can rent canoes and kayaks to explore the backwaters of Biscayne Bay. The visual rewards range from close-up views of gorgeous waterfront estates to glimpses of Everglades-worthy wilderness located in Miami's backyard.

While 854-acre *Oleta River State Recreation Area* is virtually surrounded by high-rises, visitors can rent canoes and explore the quiet waters that surround the park—and possibly sight a manatee. Admission to the park is $3.25 per car (up to 8 people); canoe and paddleboat rentals are $10 per hour. One-person kayaks rent for $8 per hour. A $20 deposit and a driver's license are also required. Boat rentals are available weekdays noon to 5 p.m. and weekends 9 a.m. to 5 p.m. The park is located off Sunny Isles Boulevard between Miami Beach and the mainland (North Miami Beach). For more information, call (305) 947-6707.

At Haulover Beach Park, the *Urban Trails Kayak Company* offers guided and unguided tours of the Oleta River area and its mangrove-shrouded waterways and uninhabited islands. That's not all: to the south, kayakers can explore the man-made backwaters and sumptuous estates bordering Biscayne Bay. Guided group tours ($35 per person) are by appointment; self-guided trips can start anytime. One-person kayak rental rates are $8 an hour, $20 for a half-day, and $25 a full day. Tandem (two-person) kayaks are $12 an hour, $30 a half-day, and $35 all day; no paddling experience required. Call (305) 947-1302 for more information.

Some of the world's most extensive mangrove forests can be explored by canoe at *Biscayne National Park,* near Florida City in southern Dade County. Canoe rentals are available from 9 a.m. to 4:30 p.m. for $8 an hour and $22 a half-day; the price includes paddles and life jackets. Folks with their own canoes can launch for free. Call (305) 230-1100 for more information.

Scuba Diving: Learning How

Every year, more than a million people travel to the Florida Keys to scuba dive at the only coral reef in the United States. Should you be one of them?

"Scuba diving is the most fun thing you can do outside of a bed," quips Captain Ed Sides, a master diver trainer who has instructed thousands of people how to dive safely over the last 20 years. "It's a wonderful, wonderful thing to do."

Intrigued? The requirements to become a certified scuba diver are minimal. You must be at least 12 years old, able to pass a swimming test, and fit enough to take on the rigors of handling and donning scuba gear in a rocking boat.

"Diving is fun and relatively easy," Captain Sides says. "The hardest part is getting dressed out on the dive boat. Once you're in the water, you're nearly weightless. It's a lot easier than snorkeling."

In addition to the reef, the Keys offer divers a chance to explore shipwrecks, see a wide variety of brilliantly colored fish, and swim in clear, warm, protected waters. "Also, there's no money or passport problems, because you're still in the U.S.," points out the dive instructor. "Theoretically, an hour and a half after touching down at Miami International Airport, you can be on a dive boat in Key Largo." If you checked your baggage or traffic is heavy, it will probably take a little longer.

How to Get Certified

To become a scuba diver, you need to be certified by an organization such as the Professional Association of Diving Instructors (PADI), the YMCA, or the National Association of Underwater Instructors (NAUI). Certification requires classroom work, passing a written final exam, "pool work," and two check-out dives with your instructor. Then you get a diving card that lets you rent equipment and dive anywhere in the world.

If your trip to South Florida is leisurely, you can become certified in three to four days. "I tell potential divers to buy the PADI dive manual and a dive table at a local dive shop and read it before they come down," Captain Sides says. "After they get to Key Largo, in two long morning sessions we can go through the text, watch some videotapes, take a few quizzes to make sure they're getting the information they need, and take the final exam."

Next comes the pool work, where new divers learn how to assemble their gear, practice underwater rescue, learn how to clear their masks, and learn other skills necessary to master the sport. If there are no more than four students in the class, it usually takes a long afternoon to complete the session.

Next, and finally, come two two-tank practice dives with the instructor. "We do all the little drills in the ocean that we learned in the pool," Captain

Sides explains. "There are no surprises. After you've sucked four tanks of air, you're certified." Total cost? Around $300, which includes all equipment except a mask, fins, and snorkel—and anyone interested in diving should make this $60 to $120 investment for personal gear.

What if you're on a tighter schedule—and don't want to spend valuable time in South Florida sitting in a classroom and swimming in a pool?

"Do everything but the check-out dive at home and get a transferral document from your instructor that states you've completed all your course work and pool work," Captain Sides says. "Then come here to do your check-out dives." The total cost to become certified, however, is usually higher that way, he adds.

Another option is a "resort" diving course. Captain Sides explains: "I take you to a swimming pool and teach you the minimum things you need to know. Then I take you out on a dive boat, we jump in, and I stay with you for the whole dive. It gets you down there and shows you the experience." It's not cheap—prices range from $120 to about $175. But if you've got the money and want to find out whether or not scuba diving is for you, it's the way to go.

After You're Certified

After certification, how much does it cost to go diving? A typical price is $35 to $50 for a two-tank trip—a half-day outing with two 60-minute dives, usually at two locations. A novice will also have to rent diving gear—a weight belt, two tanks, a regulator (the critical device that fits in your mouth and controls airflow from the air tank), and a buoyancy-control device (an inflatable vest usually called a "BCD"). Figure on another $32 a day.

Needless to say, if you've been bit by the diving bug and took the time and expense to get certified, it pays to start buying your own gear. The key component is the regulator, and list prices for quality units start around $600. "It's something you put in your mouth and something that your life depends on," Captain Sides notes. "It's a very personal piece of gear and the first thing you should buy. You can get good units on sale for around $450."

A good vest will cost around $300—and with the exception of mask, fins, and snorkel, that's all that most divers need to purchase. "Most people don't buy weight belts and tanks, because flying with them isn't a good idea," Captain Sides explains. "Unless, of course, you live next to the water or you have your own boat."

Is diving dangerous? "It's a very safe sport," the dive master responds. "But it also provides you with the opportunity to do horrible things to yourself. It's not unlike driving a car. So I take it seriously and make sure my students get good at what they do—and that they act responsibly. I drill it into people: you always dive with a buddy and always watch that person." His advice: find a dive instructor who's certified by one of the major diving organizations and make sure they have the same attitude toward safety.

For folks happy just to paddle around on the surface of the water with a snorkel in their mouths and dismiss the idea of scuba diving—and the possibility of getting nose to nose with a grouper—Captain Sides has this to say: "Scuba diving is different from snorkeling because you won't get a sunburn when you're under the surface. And with a snorkel in your mouth, you'll take in a lot of saltwater—which isn't a problem with scuba diving."

Where to Dive: The Keys

After earning their certification, novice divers can dive anywhere on their own. The Keys, however, offer beginning divers plenty of great scenery in protected waters that are relatively shallow (60 feet deep and less). It's the site of the only living coral reef in the North American continent: giant brain coral grows up to six feet in height; elkhorn corals are six to ten feet high; and mountainous star coral grows to five feet or more across and up to ten feet high. There's lots to see and explore.

Popular dive sites include *John Pennecamp Coral Reef State Park* in Key Largo (see page 240 for more information), *Looe Key National Marine Sanctuary* (near Big Pine Key in the Lower Keys), and the *Marquesas* (22 miles west of Key West). Dive shops are located all along US 1 and throughout Key West.

Where to Dive: Miami

For certified divers with more experience, Miami is a destination that offers a chance to explore an extensive line of natural reefs that parallels the entire length of Dade County. Miami is also home to one of the largest artificial reef programs in the world.

It started in 1972 with the sinking of the *Biscayne,* a 120-foot-long freighter that formerly hauled bananas from South America. The ship was the first of many wrecks (including barges, tugboats, naval vessels, and private yachts) that have been sunk for the enjoyment of sport divers. While the shallowest reefs near Miami are 30 feet down, wreck diving starts at 35 feet and goes down to about 130 feet. Private dive boats can lead visiting divers on tours of the wrecks and reefs, including night dives.

Up the coast in Sunny Isles, the *Diving Locker* offers a three-and-a-half-hour, two-dive trip every morning and afternoon, weather permitting. The cost, including tanks and weights, is $45. Most trips visit a wreck and a shallow reef. In addition, the shop offers a certification course (four-day private course is $250) and a one-hour introduction to scuba diving ($45, pool only). For more information and to schedule a dive trip, call (305) 947-6025.

Also in Sunny Isles is *H2O Scuba,* which offers four-hour, two-tank dive trips at 8:30 a.m. and 1 p.m. on weekends and at noon on weekdays; the cost is $80 per person plus equipment rental. A four-day certification course is $300, a one-day resort course is $175, and referral courses are $175 (class) and $300 (private). For more information, call H2O at (305) 956-3483.

SNORKELING

The closest place to Miami with reefs close enough to the surface for snorkelers to enjoy is *Biscayne National Park,* an underwater park located a few miles east of Florida City in southern Dade County; it's about an hour's drive from downtown Miami. Unlike scuba diving, which requires participants to be certified before they can dive, the requirements for snorkeling are minimal. You only need the ability to swim and a desire to see aquatic life up close.

At Biscayne National Park, three-hour snorkeling trips (two hours of travel, one hour exploring the reef) leave daily at 1:30 p.m., weather permitting; the cost is $27.95 per person and includes all the equipment you need. Call (305) 230-1100 to make a reservation. See our write-up on Biscayne National Park (page 208) for more information.

If you can't make it to Biscayne National Park, you're not completely out of luck. There's a small reef located off Miami Beach between 3rd and 6th streets in South Beach. The reef is 70 yards offshore and 16 feet down. Check with a lifeguard for the exact location and be sure to take out a diving flag to warn boaters that you're swimming in the area.

SAILBOARDS AND JET SKIS

The sparkling blue-green waters that surround Miami Beach are a constant temptation to frolic on the waves . . . and when the urge is overpowering, there are many ways to surrender. To windsurf or bounce around on jet skis—even if you're a novice—head toward Key Biscayne. After the first bridge on the Rickenbacker Causeway, turn right: you're on Windsurfer Beach.

Sailboards Miami on Windsurfer Beach is open daily from 10 a.m. to 5:30 p.m. and offers a guaranteed two-hour course in windsurfing for $49. If you're not happily beating to windward at the end of the course, your money is refunded. A one-hour sailboard rental is $20; two hours is $37. Advanced windsurfers can polish their technique with a private, half-hour lesson for $25. Single kayaks rent for $13 an hour; $18 an hour for two-seaters. For more information, call (305) 361-SAIL (7245).

For jet ski rentals, continue down the causeway a mile or so and turn left at the Miami Marine Stadium and follow the signs to *Tony's Jet Ski Rentals.*

Rides on the protected waters of Biscayne Bay start at $45 for a half-hour rental of a Waverunner; an hour will set you back $70. A Superjet (a jet ski for one person who stands instead of sits) costs $37.28 for a half-hour rental; the hourly rate is $63.90. Jet skis are rented daily from 10:30 a.m. to sunset; for more information, call (305) 361-8280.

Sailboats and Sailing Schools

To set sail on the calm, shallow waters of Biscayne Bay, head for *Sailboats of Key Biscayne,* located in the Crandon Park Marina on Key Biscayne. Catalina 22-footers rent for $27 an hour and $81 a half-day; Catalina 25-foot, J-24, and Hunter 23-foot sailboats rent for $35 an hour, $110 for a half day, and $170 for a full day. Bareboat (no crew) charters on sailboats from 30 to 54 feet are also available. For more information, call (305) 361-0328; if there's no answer, call (305) 279-7424.

Never sailed? Then sign up for a 10-hour sailing course offered at Sailboats of Key Biscayne that will turn you into a certified skipper. There's no classroom time—all instruction is on the water—and graduates of the course qualify for a 15% discount on boat rentals. The cost of the private, one-on-one course is $250; add $100 for a spouse or friend for one-on-two instruction. After completing the course, graduates are qualified to rent a cruising sailboat and embark on an overnight sailing trip.

More options: *Dinner Key* in Coconut Grove is another nearby destination well known for sailboat rentals and sailing lessons, and is a good jumping off point for sailing Biscayne Bay.

Deep-Sea Fishing

If the allure of battling the elements in a small boat and hooking the elusive Big One escapes you, it's time to bone up on your Hemingway. For a lot of visitors to Miami, however, going to sea to do battle with glamour fish such as marlin, tuna, sailfish, or shark is a major attraction to visiting the Sunshine State. In fact, Florida is called the Sportfishing Capital of the United States.

Trolling

The premier way of satisfying the primal urge to see a sailfish do an aerial rhumba eight feet above the water while hooked to the end of your line is by *charter boat,* sometimes called *trolling.* Fifty-foot power boats leave once and twice daily with groups of six to eight anglers on full- or half-day trips from marinas up and down the South Florida coast and the Keys. A half-day charter averages around $350, and no experience is necessary.

On the way out to the fishing grounds—only a few minutes away from most marinas around Miami and the Keys—the mate baits the hooks, arranges the lines on outriggers on the side of the boat (to prevent individual lines from tangling), and talks to the customers about the vagaries of hooking the Big One. He also gives explicit instructions on what to do when a fish strikes.

Once all the lines are out and the boat is over the fishing grounds, the boat "trolls" at a slow speed until a fish is hooked. Depending on the bait, tackle, and depth of the hook, rods react differently when a fish strikes; it's up to the mate to spot the action, set the hook, and get the rod into the hands of a customer. The captain will slow the boat until the fish is landed—or cuts the line and escapes. In fact, with the declining population of most billfish such as marlin and sailfish, catch-and-release is the norm on most charter boats these days.

"It's a very passive type of fishing—you sit in the fighting chair and if a fish strikes, the mate sets the hook and passes the rod to the angler, who just has to work the reel," explains Captain Jeff Cardenas, who has guided deep-sea fishing trips in the Florida Keys for more than 10 years. "For some people, it's very relaxing."

The goal of a fishing charter is to catch fish, and the captain will use his local knowledge of reefs, wrecks, currents, and weather to put the boat where he suspects the fish are. (He's also on the radio talking to other skippers doing the same thing.) The kind of fish you can expect to catch include mako shark, barracuda, bonita tuna, king mackerel, bluefin tuna, and wahoo. Caveat: while the captain will move the boat from location to location in search of fish, there are no guarantees you'll come back from your trip with a trophy to grace your rec room wall.

Finding a Charter Boat

Question: How do you select a charter boat?

A referral, Captain Cardenas says, is your best bet. But first-time visitors without local contacts still have a chance of finding a charter boat with a crew that works hard and shows a good attitude.

Here's how: At least a day before you plan to go on a deep-sea charter, head for a marina around 5 p.m. and hang out. That's when the charter boats are returning from their afternoon and all-day runs. Killing time, watching the pelicans, and hanging out around the docks watching the post-trip action is a South Florida tradition—and your key to locating a good charter boat.

As the boats pull in, happy or disgruntled customers (sometimes both) disembark. Depending on the success of the trip, the mate will unload a variety of fish for admiration by folks like you. (Note: If you're staying at a place with a kitchen, this is the time to buy some *very* fresh fish fillets.) "Walk the docks and talk to the captains and mates," advises Captain Cardenas, who recently retired as a fishing guide and now owns *The Saltwater Angler*, a tackle and custom rod shop in Key West.

Note which boats are bringing in big sport fish, ask about rates, and try to find a crew you're comfortable with. But before you select a charter boat and leave a deposit for the trip, Captain Cardenas suggests you do one more thing that can elevate your fishing charter from a passive experience to a really memorable event.

"Make an arrangement with your captain that you'd like to set the hooks and release the fish," he says. "In other words, negotiate terms of the trip to enhance the experience. Otherwise, the mate hooks the fish and all you do is crank it in."

Drift Boats

Charter boats aren't your only deep-sea fishing alternative: *Drift boats* (also called *party boats*) are larger than charter boats and transport 30 to 40 anglers at a time out to an off-shore reef. Once there, the captain turns off the engine, the boat begins to drift in the current, and the fishing lines go over the side—often with amusing results, as the lines begin to cross.

"It's the least expensive way to deep-sea fish," Captain Cardenas points out. "You use a conventional rod and reel baited with squid or mullet for bottom fishing, throw the line over the side and wait for a bite. Most people who go out on drift boats are fishing for their dinner." Not, he could have added, for trophy fish to hang on the wall. Species typically caught from a drift boat include redtail and yellowtail snapper, flounder, barracuda, grouper, and pompano.

You'll also get to know your neighbor as you stand elbow to elbow on the side of the large drift boat and pass your rods back and forth in an effort to untangle your lines. When things get really complicated, a crew member shows up to straighten it all out.

Just like a charter boat, drift boats have a crew that baits the customers' hooks and "gaffs" (spears) the catch after it's reeled in close to the boat. Beginners get plenty of help and advice—from both the crew and fellow party boaters—and tackle is available for rent on the boat. Bring your own rod and a typical three-and-a-half-hour drift boat excursion is $20; if you rent tackle, it's around $25.

A bad sign: a poker game starts up in the cabin of the drift boat, a sure indication that the fish aren't biting. "The fishing has declined a thousand percent over the last few years," moaned one glum fisherman between hands on a recent excursion out of Miami Beach. "It used to be that after an hour you caught your limit and were sick of reeling fish in."

Light-Tackle Fishing

More fishing options: In *light-tackle fishing,* a style popular in the Keys, a guide takes up to four anglers out in an open, 25-foot boat. Using LORAN coordinates (a long-range navigation system that allows a boat to reach a precise location), the guide will go anywhere from 10 to 70 miles off-shore looking for reefs and wrecks. Many guides take customers to their own "secret spots."

After reaching a promising location, the guide throws out chum (cut or ground bait) to attract fish: blackfin tuna, permit, cobia, and other hard-fighting species. "Light-tackle fishing offers good, fast action," says Captain Cardenas. "The fish come up right behind the boat and it doesn't take a high level of skill to land them. The captain baits the hook, the angler tosses the hook into the melee and hooks up." The total cost for an all-day trip is typically $400 to $450 for up to four anglers.

Sight Fishing

Sight fishing is another option for anglers, although technically it's not deep-sea fishing. Also called *saltwater flats fishing,* this type of angling calls for skill and patience.

It works like this: One or two customers and a guide in a 17-foot open boat are "poled"—pushed by the guide, who sits in an elevated chair with a long pole—through water that's only 18 inches deep (or shallower).

"This is what I get excited about," Captain Cardenas says. "Flats fishing takes place in a wonderful period of calm, wading birds, and clear water—so you can see an incredible amount of sea life. The lack of a motor lets you approach all kinds of creatures."

When a large predator such as a barracuda, bonefish, or permit is spotted—remember, this is called "sight" fishing—it's up to the angler to present the bait or fly to the fish.

"You see them way in advance, so you stalk the fish," he explains. "It's primarily done with a fly rod and the guides are teachers, so it's fully participatory by the customer. It's immensely rewarding."

Sight fishing, however, isn't for anglers who judge a trip by the number of fish they catch. "There isn't a strong emphasis on catching a fish—it's more of a backcountry experience," Captain Cardenas explains. "And there's no killing for glory. The fish are so hard to catch, it seems to diminish the quality of the experience to whack them over the head. Most people practice catch and release."

But there can be plenty of action: "It's really exciting to see a barracuda on the flats," Captain Cardenas says. "It's a very aggressive fish and shallow water is its territory. When you cast a fly in front of a barracuda, it charges. It's a very predatory moment happening right in front of your eyes as the fish jumps and does figure eights out of the water! It's an experience." Typical costs for sight fishing trips are $350 for a full day and $250 for a half-day; no more than two anglers can split the cost because the boats are so small.

Seasons

A word about seasons: In South Florida, charter and drift boats go out every day and customers have a good chance of catching something at any time of year. But spring and fall offer better chances of landing a big fish—or at least seeing more action. May and June, in particular, are excellent for tarpon, fish that are all muscle. As Captain Cardenas says, "Catch a 100-pound tarpon on a fly line and they go nuts." Needless to say, guides are booked a year in advance during the tarpon season.

In general, better fishing occurs when the water temperature is above 72°. In the winter, when the sea temperature drops below 70°, the only thing that will usually bite is barracuda, Captain Cardenas adds. A lot of people we spoke to said that most deep-sea fishing was better in the Keys than in the ocean off Miami.

How to Judge a Fishing Trip

With four major styles of deep-sea fishing to choose from, anyone with the time, interest, and money can experience high-quality saltwater angling in South Florida, especially if you heed these final words of advice:

"A lot of people get wrapped up in judging a fishing trip by the number of fish they caught," Captain Cardenas says. "That's not the way to do it, though. It's better to meet your own challenges and have a good time. The guy who caught 20 fish didn't necessarily have a better day. It's all in how you approach it: Like any sport, more involvement increases the enjoyment."

Spectator Sports

More well-known as a tropical paradise, Miami is also a great sports destination. South Florida probably got its big start in sports when the opening of the railroad made it possible for major league baseball teams to come south for spring training. Next, the construction of the Orange Bowl brought in top-level college and professional football teams. To take full advantage of this cornucopia of team sports, check the *Miami Herald*'s sports section for a daily listing of local games.

Pro Teams

Leading the list of attractions is the AFC East *Miami Dolphins* football team, which packs 'em in every season at Pro Player Stadium (formerly Joe Robbie Stadium). Successful? You bet—the Dolphins have played in the Super Bowl five times and in 1972 achieved everlasting glory with the only all-win, no-tie season in NFL history. The season is from August through December; ticket prices range from $24 to $130 and are available from the stadium box office or Ticketmaster at (954) 523-3309. The stadium is located at 2269 NW 199th Street in North Miami; phone (305) 620-2578 for more information.

Pro Player Stadium, which hosted its second Super Bowl in 1995, also hosts the annual *Blockbuster Bowl* football championship. It's also home to the newest addition to baseball's National League, the *Florida Marlins*, the 1997 World Series champs. General admission tickets for Marlins games range from $2 to $110; children's tickets are $1.50 on game day only. Call the stadium at (305) 626-7400 for home game dates and additional information on obtaining tickets.

The Miami Arena, located at 721 NW 1st Avenue in downtown Miami, hosts the *Miami Heat*, an NBA team offering fast-paced basketball action. The squad debuted in 1988 and recently completed a trip to the NBA's Eastern Conference Finals. Ticket prices are $15 to $135. Call (305) 577-HEAT for ticket information. The 15,000-seat Miami Arena is also home to the National Hockey League's *Florida Panthers*, who made an incredible run to the Stanley Cup finals in just their third season. For information, ticket prices, and dates for home hockey games, call (954) 768-1900.

Amateur Sports

Top-flight collegiate sports teams in South Florida include the *University of Miami Hurricanes* football, baseball, and basketball teams. Hurricanes football is played at the famous Orange Bowl from September through November; get a seat high up in the stands and you'll get a great view of Miami while watching exciting gridiron action: The team has won three national championships in the last decade. The stadium is located at 1400 NW 4th Street, west of downtown. Tickets are $18 and $22. For tickets to any Hurricane events, call (305) 284-CANE or (800) GO-CANES. For game information, call (305) 284-2263.

The University of Miami Hurricanes baseball team plays about 50 home games a year at Mark Light Stadium on the school's Coral Gables campus. The season lasts from February to May, with both day and evening games on the schedule. Tickets are $5 for adults and $3 for children and seniors.

The University of Miami basketball squad plays at the Miami Arena, 701 Arena Boulevard in downtown Miami. Tickets are $9 to $18. For more information on Hurricanes baseball and basketball, call (305) 284-2263.

Florida International University's *Golden Panthers* field a wide range of teams. Basketball is played November through March at the Golden Panther Arena, SW 8th Street and 112th Avenue in Miami. The baseball season is January through May; home games are played at the University Park Complex, SW 8th Street and 112th Avenue. Golden Panthers soccer is played September through November at the University Park Complex. For schedules, call (305) 348-4263.

Car Racing and Pro Tennis

The *Grand Prix of Miami* is South Florida's premier auto racing event. Each spring, international drivers compete at speeds of more than 100 mph at Metro-Dade Homestead Motorsports Complex in Homestead. Tickets for three days of racing action range from $40 to $200. For ticket information call the Homestead-Miami Speedway ticket office at (305)-230-RACE.

To see the best in top-notch international tennis competition, don't miss the *Lipton International Players Championship,* held for two weeks each March at the International Tennis Center, 7300 Crandon Boulevard, Key Biscayne, in a new, 7,500-seat stadium. The event draws more than 200,000 spectators and is broadcast live each year to more than 30 countries as top players compete for more than $4.5 million in prize money. Call (305) 446-2200 or (800) 725-5472 for dates and ticket information.

The Betting Sports: Horse Races, Greyhounds, and Jai Alai

Puppies and ponies and jai alai: South Florida is home to several sports that permit pari-mutuel wagering, the type of gambling where you bet against other bettors, not the house. For folks who can restrain themselves from wagering, the activities can be an inexpensive way to spend a fun afternoon or evening. *Note*: While no one under age 18 may bet in Florida, children may accompany adults to horse races, greyhound races, and jai alai.

Thoroughbred Horse Racing

For more than 50 years Florida has been a center of thoroughbred horse racing. Classy *Hialeah Park* (2200 E 4th Avenue, Hialeah; phone (305) 885-8000) trades racing dates with *Gulfstream Park* for winter racing. Gulfstream is located just over the Broward County line in Hallandale on US 1; phone (305) 931-RACE. *Calder Race Course's* weatherproof track permits racing during the rainy summer; it's located at 21001 NW 27th Avenue, near I-95 near the Dade-Broward border. The phone number is (305) 625-1311. To see where the ponies are running during your visit, check the sports section of the *Miami Herald*.

Dog Racing

Greyhounds reach speeds of more than 40 miles an hour; you can see the action at two tracks in the Miami area. Like horse racing, the venue rotates throughout the year, so check the *Miami Herald* before heading out. Racing starts around 7:30 p.m. six nights a week; several days during the week feature matinees starting at 12:30 p.m.

The *Flagler Greyhound Track* is located at 401 NW 38th Court near Seventh Street and 37th Avenue, southeast of Miami International Airport; the phone number is (305) 649-3000. In Broward County, the *Hollywood Greyhound Track* is located on US 1 a mile east of I-95, just over the county line in Hallandale; phone (305) 758-3647 from Dade County.

Jai Alai

For an unusual experience that recalls the Damon Runyun–esque days of early Miami, make a trip to the *Miami Jai Alai Fronton,* located at 3500 NW 37th Avenue, near Miami International Airport (phone (305) 633-6400). The crowd looks like it stepped out of the pages of a John Steinbeck novel and the atmosphere is redolent with the pungent smell of cigars and beer. A fronton, by the way, is the 176-foot-long court where jai alai (pronounced "high lie") is played; Miami's, built in 1926, is the oldest in the United States.

Don't forget to watch the action behind the big screen as teams compete in the world's fastest sport, a Basque game dating from the 15th century that's a cross between lacrosse, tennis, and racquetball. The hard ball (called a *pelota*) flung and caught in a long, curved wicker basket (a *cesta*) has been clocked at 180 mph. Teams of two or four compete and the first team to score seven points wins.

You can bet on a team to win or on the order in which teams finish. It's all utterly confusing to first-time visitors—yet fascinating to watch. Admission is $1; the first game is at 7 p.m. five nights a week. Matinees are on Monday, Wednesday, Friday, and Saturday, noon to 5 p.m.

Part Eight

Shopping in Miami

Strolling and Window Shopping

Downtown

Downtown Miami, a curious blend of Art Deco architecture and modern monoliths, contains a wondrous mix of shops, many owned and operated by second- and third-generation Latin families. As with most downtown metropolitan areas, the streets meander, but it's entirely possible to find everything you'll need by staying on the main drag, West Flagler, with a few side-street excursions. A word of caution: Most of what you've read about Miami is probably true, so wear sensible shoes, keep your jewelry in the hotel safe, and be home before the sun sets. You'll be fine.

Jewelry is really downtown Miami's main lure. For the real thing, visit the venerable **Seybold Building** (37 East Flagler Street), chock-full of jewelers and some wholesalers who sell rough stones and gold and silver by the ounce. If you're on a budget but don't want to sacrifice glamour, we suggest **Bijoux Terner** (22 NW 1st Street, (305) 371-4652), a jewelry chest of a store where you'll find everything from a modest pair of faux pearl earrings to a tiara for the Embassy Ball.

Small electronics stores are scattered about everywhere, with a deal or two to be found, but as far as returning your purchase should you change your mind, you'd be better off at Radio Shack.

Forgot your espadrilles? Not to worry. Head to the **Wild Pair** (78 East Flagler Street, (305) 358-0635), where much of Miami shops, for the best prices in fashionable footwear. Check out the $5 sale bin out front.

South Beach

The current hotspot of South Florida, as well as much of the world, South Beach is a fine destination for shopping on foot. While the entire district spans a mere 17 blocks, with trendy boutiques and quaint galleries in unlikely places such as hotel lobbies, there are certain streets the *au courant* shopper will not want to miss:

Lincoln Road (runs from the Ocean to the Bay, with nine blocks of shopping) In the 1940s, Lincoln Road was a chi-chi strip of elite retail stores, including Bonwit Teller, Saks Fifth Avenue, and Lillie Rubin. Today, like everything else on South Beach, it's hip. With a nod to New York's SoHo, Lincoln Road is a revamped, open-air, pedestrian mall that is home to artists, funky boutiques, and sidewalk cafés. Don't overlook the side streets, which are scattered with worthwhile stores, salons, and cafés one block north and south of Lincoln Road. Check out the funky studio of ceramic assemblagist **Carlos Alves** (1043 Lincoln Road, (305) 673-3824), whose colorful mosaics are collected by Gloria and Emilio Estefan, among others. **Flowers & Flowers** (925 Lincoln Road, (305) 534-1633) has the best blooms in Miami, plus intriguing gift items such as rose-scented beeswax candles and bitter orange potpourri. **Brownes Apothecary** (841 Lincoln Road, (305) 532-8703) offers a comprehensive selection of toiletries and up-to-the-minute beauty items, from old-fashioned hair pommade to lavender-scented soapstones. Attracted to things exotic? Stop by **World Resources** (719 Lincoln Road, (305) 673-5032) for everything from incense to Indonesian furniture. Just want a T-shirt to take back home? Try **Ete** (714 Lincoln Road, (305) 672-3265) for a witty, quality "T." Stop by **Pink Palm Co.** (737 Lincoln Road, (305) 538-8373) for an unusual greeting card or colorful gift item. Much fun is **Dish** (939 Lincoln Road, (305) 532-7737) where you can find original backstock of signature dishware from famous hotels and restaurants of yore. For designer clothing, try **En Avance** (734 Lincoln Road, (305) 534-0337), **Base** (716 Lincoln Road, (305) 672-0101) and **24 Collection** (744 Lincoln Road, (305) 673-2544). We like **Senzatempo** (1655 Meridian Avenue, (305) 534-5588) for its fascinating selection of vintage watches, furniture, and home accessories, as well as **Details at Home** (1031 Lincoln Road, (305) 531-1325), which has an excellent assortment of modern picture frames and other items for the well-decorated home, from upholstered furniture to dishware. **Yardware** (1021 Lincoln Road, (305) 531-2002) has everything the chic home garden requires, from fashionable tools to decorative hardware. Want to rent a video? Go where in-the-know locals and visiting celebs do—**New Concept Video** (749 Lincoln Road, (305) 674-1111) where you can find new releases as well as cult classics. Need a quick bite? Try **David's Cafe II** (1654 Meridian Avenue, one block north of Lincoln Road, (305) 672-8707) for inexpensive Cuban food; **Rosinella** (525 Lincoln Road, (305) 672-8777) for down-home Italian lunches and dinners without the glitz; and the **Van Dyke Cafe** (846 Lincoln Road, (305) 534-3600)—Lincoln Road's answer to the renowned News Cafe—a perennial favorite for casual dining and people-watching in a sidewalk café setting. In town the second Saturday of the month? Then you're in luck, for that's when Lincoln Road's Gallery Walk takes place. On a similar note, many visitors try scheduling their trips around the semi-weekly Lincoln Road Antiques and Collectibles Market, held along the intersection of Lincoln Road and Lenox Avenue the second and last Sunday of each month from October to late May.

Espanola Way (intersects Washington Avenue; situated between 14th and 15th streets) This quaint block of shops includes adorable gift and vintage boutiques, as well as avant-garde art galleries. Of special note are **Babalu** (500 Espanola Way, (305) 538-0679), which specializes in all things Cuban, from cigars to memorabilia; **South Beach Makeup** (439 Espanola Way, (305) 538-0805), which carries a plethora of makeup as well as the Kiehl's line of products; and the **Espanola Way Art Center** (409 Espanola Way, (305) 672-5305), where the resident artists always have several intriguing projects on display. On Sundays during tourist season, Espanola Way turns into a street fair–cum–block party, with vendors selling everything from handmade candles to vintage bric-a-brac.

Washington Avenue South Beach's main commercial artery, Washington Avenue is brimming with upscale boutiques, trendy restaurants, and the occasional hardware store. Some can't-miss stops are **My Uncle Deco Shop** (1570 Washington Avenue, (305) 534-4834) for $8 preworn Levis and other gear favored by models and locals and **Betsy Johnson** (805 Washington Avenue, (305) 673-0023) for up-to-the-microminute fashion for young women.

Ocean Drive At once scenic and chaotic, Ocean Drive is fine for people-watching while sipping overpriced cappuccino, but unless you're into T-shirts with slogans or another neon bikini, skip it. Music buffs will want to check out **Revolution Records** (1620-A Alton Road, (305) 673-6464) for new and used CDs, cassettes, and hard-to-find LPs. Also on Alton Road, which could be considered Washington Avenue–by-the-bay (the street is just east of Biscayne Bay): **Cy's Cigars** (1504 Alton Road, (305) 532-5301), which has a good selection of cigars, wines, and magazines; **Spiaggia** (1624 Alton Road, (305) 538-7949) for an eclectic and ever-changing offering of new and vintage home decor; and **Alton Road Nursery** (1239 Alton Road, (305) 532-7939) for a fantastic collection of not only plants but also glorious antiques that the owner accumulates on her travels.

Coral Gables

A picturesque business-cum-residential area, Coral Gables contains one of Miami's most historic shopping areas, Miracle Mile. This four-block stretch of outdoor shopping (don't neglect the side streets) contains more than 150 boutiques, with something to satisfy everyone's taste level and budget. The area is probably the safest in Miami, as well as the best manicured. Favorite destinations include **Leather World** (339 Miracle Mile, (305) 446-7888), for all types of small leather goods imaginable; **Luminaire** (2331 Ponce de Leon Boulevard, (305) 448-7367), for contemporary furnishings and accessories; and **Books & Books** (296 Aragon Avenue, (305) 442-4408), Miami's favorite independently owned bookstore.

COCONUT GROVE

Miami's hotspot hippie village of the 1970s, Coconut Grove has retained its anti-establishment charm while continuing to attract young sophisticates. Follow narrow sidewalks down the shady streets and browse the afternoon away. Our favorites include **La Capricieuse** and **La Capricieuse pour Homme** offering designer wear for both genders (3403 Main Highway, (305) 448-8806). Need a last-minute manicure, blow-out, or makeup application before dinner? Head to **Allure Express Salon** (3405 Main Highway, (305) 461-0020) for exceptional work at reasonable prices.

Mall Shopping

If it's a big, generic mall you want, Miami's got plenty. **Dadeland** and **Aventura** malls will do just fine, located respectively at 7535 North Kendall Drive, (305) 665-6226 and 19501 Biscayne Boulevard, North Miami Beach, (305) 935-1110. But it's that Miami flavor you crave, right? Okay, we know just where to send you.

Bal Harbour Shops, 9700 Collins Avenue, Bal Harbour, (305) 866-0311. If the thought of a $3,000 knit day dress doesn't send you into convulsions, you'll feel right at home at Bal Harbour Shops. A charming, two-floor mall with valet parking (self-parking by the hour is also available), a fleet of security guards, and French cafés serving $35 pasta entrees, Bal Harbour Shops is Miami's toniest mall. Offerings include Tiffany, Gucci, Chanel, Prada, Hugo Boss, Saks Fifth Avenue, Neiman Marcus, Ferragamo, and Versace. For the label-conscious, this is paradise found.

Bayside Marketplace, 401 Biscayne Boulevard (NE 4th–NE 9th streets), Miami, (305) 577-3344. Fun for the whole family, the tropical, indoor/outdoor Bayside is like an international carnival with stores. The lower level is teeming with stalls offering ethnic wares and cute, if largely useless, merchandise such as Flintstones coffee mugs and beach rafts in the image of the Venus de Milo. National chain stores include Brookstone, Victoria's Secret, The Limited, and The Gap. Great for gifts: the Disney Store, which stocks everything from Mickey Mouse silk boxer shorts to *101 Dalmatians* charm bracelets. Naturalists will appreciate Art by God, which carries oversized crystals to put on display at home, as well as zebra-skin rugs made from farm-raised herds. Just minutes from downtown Miami, Bayside is easy to find, safe, and clean, with plenty of sheltered, if slightly costly, parking.

CocoWalk, 3015 Grand Avenue, Coconut Grove, (305) 444-0777. Resembling a big Mediterranean birthday cake, CocoWalk is Miami's newest and most comprehensive shopping-cum-entertainment complex. Smack in the middle of Coconut Grove, the two-layer mall contains everything the Generation X mall rat craves: music, tapas, loud bands, a multiscreen cinema, and a Gap. Plus, grown-up choices including Victoria's Secret, JW Cooper for western wear, and a good bookstore.

The Falls, US 1 and SW 136th Street, Miami, (305) 255-4570. Probably Miami's most beautiful mall, The Falls is tropical and serene, with lots of wood, waterfalls, and leafy foliage. Bloomingdales is the big draw, but there are also 60 specialty and national boutiques, including Polo/Ralph Lauren, Banana Republic, Crate and Barrel, Pottery Barn, and Ann Taylor.

Specialty Shops

Antiques

You'll find the greatest concentration of antique stores on NW 27th Street, directly west of South Dixie Highway (an extension of US 1). Whether it's a delicate fauteuil chair or a replacement chandelier crystal you need, chances are you'll find it. We like **Southern Fine Arts** (3070 SW 38th Avenue, (305) 446-1641) for rarefied artifacts, fossils, and unique, antiquated furnishings, such as a tapestry-covered seventeenth-century footstool. **Corinthian Antiques** (2741 SW 27th Avenue, (305) 854-6068), which carries a mix of American English and continental collectibles, is your best bet for shopping the Queen Anne circuit.

North of town you'll find an inconspicuous strip mall littered with back-to-back antiques and collectibles stores on the 1600 block of 123th Street (just west of the traffic light at Biscayne Boulevard; it is on the south side of the street). One of our recent sprees yielded a minivan-full of cool stuff, from a golf-leafed writing desk from the mid-1960s to a shell-encrusted wall mirror. Be sure to check out **Mr. Bill's Antiques & Floral Emporium** (1648 NE 123rd Street, (305) 899-9924), where the eclectic contents of estate sales come in weekly.

Art

Besides Miami's Design District, which sells primarily to the design industry, Coral Gables, South Beach, and Bay Harbor Islands are your key areas for art. On the first Friday of every month, an air-conditioned minibus takes art lovers for a free tour of the Coral Gables galleries. There's no RSVP; just show up in the early evening hours at one of the galleries, such as **Artspace/Virginia Miller Galleries** (169 Madeira Avenue, (305) 444-4493). This area has a fine concentration of American and Latin American paintings.

On the trendy side, Lincoln Road on South Beach has become an art row of sorts. Local artists, some of whom attract international recognition, are located next to well-established Miami art specialists, including **Barbara Gillman** (939 Lincoln Road, (305) 534-7872) and artist Romero Britto, whose gallery, **Britto Central** (818 Lincoln Road, (305) 531-8821), attracts high-profile collectors including Arnold Schwarzenegger and Marisa Tomei. Lincoln Road's Gallery Walk is held the second Saturday of the month, 6–10 p.m.

Bargains

If it's labels like Armani and Moschino that entice you, we recommend **Loehmann's Plaza** (2855 NE 187th Street, (305) 932-0520) in North Miami. This location consistently carries the best selection of designer wear at the lowest prices.

In the gourmet food division, one of our secrets is **Alterman's Country Store** (12805 NW LeJeune Road, Opa-locka, (305) 688-3571), which sells undamaged high-end foodstuffs at a fraction of the retail cost. A friend of ours recently found a five-pound box of Godiva chocolates (retail: approximately $100) for $40. Revered goodies like imported cheeses and Maine lobsters turn up now and then. Expect a hit-or-miss inventory.

Bookstores

Any bookworm will tell you that everyone's favorite bookstore in Miami is **Books & Books** (two locations: 933 Lincoln Road, South Beach, (305) 532-3222; and 296 Aragon, Coral Gables, (305) 442-4408). A close second is **Borders Books & Music** (three locations: 9205 South Dixie Highway, Miami, (305) 665-8800; 3390 Mary Street, Coconut Grove, (305) 447-1655; and 19925 Biscayne Boulevard, Aventura, (305) 935-0027), which, like Books & Books, features meet-the-author readings and signings. For out-of-town news periodicals, try **Worldwide News** (1629 NE 163rd Street, (305) 940-4090) or **Plaza News** newsstand (7900 Biscayne Boulevard, (305) 751-6397) for the most comprehensive selections. Also good is **Joe's News** (1559 Sunset Drive, Coral Gables, (305) 661-2020). **Lambda Passages,** a gay bookstore, has a good selection of biographies, history, and art books (7545 Biscayne Boulevard, Miami, (305) 754-6900).

Cigars

Stogie aficionados will appreciate **Mike's Cigars** (1030 Cane Concourse, Miami Beach, (305) 866-2277), which carries more than 300 brands from all over the globe. Also worthy: **Cy's Cigars** (1504 Alton Road, (305) 532-5301) and the **News Cafe Store** on trendy Ocean Drive (800 Ocean Drive, (305) 538-6397), which is open 7 days, 24 hours—a real plus for the all-night set.

Classic Cars

South Florida is undoubtedly a car culture. More than just a mandatory transportation tool, in Miami cars are the ultimate accessory to reveal something about the driver's status and personality. For classics and exotics, South Florida is a healthy market. If you're scouting, here are a few places to begin.

Vantage Motor Works (1898 NE 151st Street, Miami, (305) 940-1161) specializes in Rolls Royce restorations.

Stephen Yanoshik Enterprises (Ft. Lauderdale, (954) 583-3400) specializes in British and Italian classics.

Designer Clothing

If you can't find it in Bal Harbour Shops (see "Malls"), chances are it doesn't exist. Do check out, however, the **Versace Jeans Couture Boutique** in South Beach (755 Washington Avenue, (305) 532-5993), for casual wear and home items such as china and lavish $700 silk throw pillows; **Magazine** (180 8th Street, South Beach, (305) 538-2704), specializing in cutting-edge European fashion for women and men; and **La Capricieuse** and **La Capricieuse pour Homme** (3403 Main Highway, (305) 448-8806) for some of the hippest labels around, including Katherine Hamnett, Dolce & Gabbana, Mark Eisen, and Prada.

Ethnic Goods

You might as well go to Bayside Marketplace, where you can find clothing and items from places as diverse as Jamaica, Africa, and India. The Caribbean Marketplace in Miami's Little Haiti district is interesting, but not so safe. Okay, so there's always **Pier 1 Imports** (various locations around Miami). **Island Trading Co.,** in the lobby of the Netherland Hotel (1332 Ocean Drive, South Beach, (305) 673-6300), is your answer for one-of-a-kind items collected from various locales around the world; everything from hand-woven tablecloths to crystal earrings and leather knapsacks. In the same vein is **World Resources** (two locations: 719 Lincoln Road, (305) 673-5032 and in the Miami Design District at 56 NE 40 Street, (305) 576-8799), where the selection includes exotic woods fashioned into furniture and other decorative arts.

Fresh Fish

Seafood is one of Miami's most reliable meals, and the waters around the city teem with more than 60 varieties of commercial fish that you can eventually find parked on a restaurant plate next to a lemon wedge. Some of the most popular saltwater catches are grouper, snapper, mahimahi, mullet, trout, pompano, and redfish.

To buy fresh fish, avoid supermarket fish counters; most of their goods have been frozen. Instead, opt for fish fresh off the boat at some of the docks around the city when fishermen come in with their day's haul. The best time to buy is late afternoon when all the fishing boats have returned.

On Key Biscayne, the boat docks next to Sunday's restaurant are usually lined with fishermen from about 3 p.m. The docks are easy to spot on this narrow island. They're on the left at about the midway point.

If you can't make it to the docks and still want to buy fresh fish, head to **Joe's Stone Crab Takeaway** (227 Biscayne Street, Miami Beach, (305) 673-4611) for stone crabs during the season, which is mid-October to mid-May.

Fruit Shipping

What's a trip to Florida without a box of rosy oranges and grapefruit to ship back home? **Norman Brothers Produce** (7621 SW 87th Avenue, South Miami, (305) 274-9363) will ship anything you wish from their amazing array of culinary exotica, which includes obscurities such as the dwarfed doughnut apple. Then there's always our favorite standby, **Publix** (numerous locations throughout Miami), which will do the shipping honors for you in season, November through February.

Jewelry

Besides downtown Miami, the **International Jeweler's Exchange** in North Miami (18861 Biscayne Boulevard, behind Loehmann's Plaza, (305) 935-1471) will fill the bill. Fifty stalls are stocked with gold, pearls, and diamonds. Open Monday through Saturday, 10 a.m. to 6 p.m., with extended holiday hours.

Swimwear

Finding a good swimsuit in Miami should be the least of your worries. **Alice's Day Off** (5900 Sunset Drive, South Miami, (305) 284-0301), **Swim n' Sport** (many locations, including The Falls and Bal Harbour Shops), and **Ritchie Swimwear** (800 Ocean Drive, Miami Beach, (305) 538-0201) are among the many fine options.

Spas

If shopping in Miami is just too much, take a break at one of the many day spas in the area. In about the same time it takes to pick up a pair of shoes in the city, you can enjoy the indulgence of an ultra-pampering massage and steam bath.

For ladies only, the Delano Hotel's rooftop **Agua Spa** (Collins Avenue at 17th Street, Miami Beach, (305) 674-6100) offers massages and full-body masks as well as stunning views of the ocean. Due to popular demand, the spa offers men's hours every night from 7:30 to 11 p.m., except Tuesdays.

For upscale personal care, from massage and facial to hair care and what is possibly the best manicure in Miami, try **White,** located within South Beach's famous coral-rock house (900 Collins Avenue, Miami Beach, (305) 538-0604).

The Cosmyl Spa and Beauty Center (4401 Ponce de Leon Boulevard, Coral Gables, (305) 442-9305) has full-day indulgence programs for tip-to-toe grooming and relaxing.

The Imagen Medical Day Spa (300 41st Street, Miami Beach, (305) 673-0666) offers beauty treatments, massage, and a full menu of medically supervised beauty procedures including laser surgery, collagen injections, and glycolic peels. Inclement weather? Try Imagen's tanning booth.

For the co-ed spa experience: **The Russian and Turkish Bath House** (5445 Collins Avenue, Miami Beach, (305) 867-8316) is co-ed every day except Thursday when it's for men only. You may romp topless through various steam rooms and saunas, take a synchronized massage (two therapists) or an aromatherapy jacuzzi, and then repair to the Relaxation Room.

Tropical Fish

The reefs that snake beneath the ocean and the nearby Caribbean Sea are home to a neon-colored patchwork of tropical fish. If you're looking to stock your aquarium back home, prices are more reasonable here in Miami, though transporting the fish may prove troublesome. Investigate thoroughly.

Biscayne Pet House (10789 Biscayne Boulevard, Miami, (305) 895-6164) offers a large inventory of freshwater fish, aquariums, and accessories.

Neighborhood Fish Farm (12150 SW 45th Street, Miami, (305) 221-8013) is a vast place with 137 freshwater ponds stocked with African chichlids, angelfish, and koi. It's worth a visit just to browse.

Tropical Furniture

To accommodate and adapt to the humidity and relentless sunshine of Miami, furniture is often made of rattan, wicker, or light woods. In many of the Art Deco hotels on South Miami Beach, '50s-style furniture—with its whimsy and clean lines—decorates rooms and lobbies. Miami is a furniture-producing mecca, though the most outstanding and truly local is tropical and vintage furniture. Shipping should present no problem, but be sure to verify with your furniture dealer and remember to insure your purchase.

Rattan Shack (9840 NW 77th Avenue, Hialeah Gardens, (305) 823-9800) is a vast place off the Palmetto Expressway with rattan and wicker furniture for indoors and outdoors.

J & J Rattan (4652 SW 72nd Avenue, Miami, (305) 666-7503) is another large warehouse exclusively selling rattan and wicker couches, dining sets, and chairs.

South Beach Furniture Showroom (180 NE 39th Street, Miami, (305) 858-4240) specializes in Heywood-Wakefield furniture.

Tropical Plants

South Florida's flora is part of its lure: the purple spray of bougainvillea, flowering hibiscus in primary colors, the royal poinciana trees that open a canopy of flaming orange blossoms. Before you purchase tropical plants with the hopes of recreating a patch of Miami in your backyard back home, make sure your climate and soil can support the vegetation.

CHC Garden Center (7901 SW 117th Avenue, Miami, (305) 595-1338) offers orchids, bromeliads, fruit trees, and expert advice on planting and maintenance.

Alton Road Nurseries (1239 Alton Road, Miami Beach, (305) 532-7939) is open seven days and is replete with plants and arty pots, decorative stones, and indigenous greenery.

Lester's Root Nursery (12000 West Dixie Highway, Miami, (305) 893-9948) sells indoor and outdoor plants at reasonable prices.

Correll Landscape Nursery (17091 Biscayne Boulevard, North Miami, (305) 947-4454) features a comprehensive selection of floral topiaries and hard-to-find herb plants, including lavender, chocolate-mint, and lemon verbena.

Used Yachts and Boats

South Florida is flush with used boats and yachts, and the rule of thumb is that boat buying is a soft market. The best place to get a feel for what's available and the range of prices is to pick up a copy of **Boat Trader,** a weekly black-and-white magazine that lists hundreds of photos and pertinent information. **Boat Trader** is available at most 7-11s and other convenience stores for $2.50. **Yacht Trader,** a sister publication, is also available for the same price in the same locations.

Also, you may want to visit one of the marinas or boatyards around Miami. Most have boaties who can fill you in on what's available and bulletin boards announcing sales.

Wine and Gourmet Foods

Whether you're browsing for a new imported mustard or in search of the definitive California cabernet sauvignon, chances are you'll find it at **Epicure Market** (1656 Alton Road, (305) 672-1861), where the local elite shop for foodstuffs, as well as the freshest of produce, tempting bakery items, and old-fashioned Jewish deli fare. **Lyon & Lyon** (1439 Alton Road, (305) 534-0600), a tiny but well-stocked French take-out market on South Beach, is perfect for that impromptu picnic on the beach. Select from a variety of delicious prepared foods seven days a week—and be sure to grab a frothy cappuccino on your way out. Also on South Beach is **Stephan's Gourmet Market & Cafe** (1430 Washington Avenue, (305) 674-1760), a gourmet Italian deli with a second-floor café. Stephan's carries a great selection of cheeses, wines, and champagnes, plus prettily packaged candies, nuts, and the like.

If you're a hard-core Italian food and wine fan, you'll spend hours at **Laurenzo's,** an Italian/American market and wine emporium (16385 West Dixie Highway, North Miami, (305) 945-6381). The award-winning wine department features wines from Bordeaux, Burgundy, Spain, California, and Italy, among other regions, as well as more than 40 weekly in-store wine specials. Another fine choice—where you can also sit down for dinner in the landscaped courtyard—is **Stephan's Gourmet Deli** (2 NE 40th Street in the Miami Design District, (305) 571-4070).

The stone crab is more than a seafood specialty in Miami—it's an obsession, almost. You can share this kingliest of crustaceans with friends back home—for a price. **Joe's Stone Crab Takeaway** will ship the iced crabs to the doorstep of your choice by the following morning (call (800) 780-2722).

Part Nine

Sight-Seeing Tips and Tours

Touring Miami

Residents of Miami are proud of their city and quick to point out that it has much more to offer than just great beaches, dazzling white light, and a famous downtown skyline. College and professional sports, art shows, street festivals, museums, film festivals, a book fair, a world-class zoo, and some fascinating attractions showcasing this subtropical paradise's flora and fauna make Miami a city well worth exploring, even if it means tearing yourself away from the beach for a day.

Specialized Tours

A number of local companies offer specialized tours of Miami and Miami Beach, usually in comfortable, air-conditioned motor coaches; trained tour guides provide the narration. In addition to bus tours—which take visitors to popular tourist areas such as South Beach, Coconut Grove, Brickell Avenue, Coral Gables, Little Havana, and downtown Miami—many of the guided tours are all-day or multi-day affairs that go to destinations well outside of Miami: the Florida Keys and Key West, the Bahamas, the Everglades, and Walt Disney World. Here's a run-down of some tours that are a little different. Most of the tours require advanced reservations and a deposit; most tour buses can pick you up and drop you off at your Miami or Miami Beach hotel.

Flamingo Tours offers daily narrated bus trips to Key West that pick you up at your Miami Beach hotel at 7 a.m. and bring you back around 11 p.m. The tour includes a breakfast stop at Key Largo, a brief stop at the Seven Mile Bridge, and an afternoon exploring Key West. Activities include visits to the Hemingway House, Mel Fisher's Treasure Exhibit, and a glass-bottom-boat ride. On the return trip, the bus stops in Islamorada. The price per person is $55; $25 for children ages 3–11.

Other tours offered by Flamingo include one-day cruises to the Bahamas from Fort Lauderdale that leave daily ($169 per person; price includes three all-you-can-eat meals); one-day motor-coach trips to Walt Disney World on Sunday, Monday, and Wednesday ($89 for adults and $65 for children ages 3–9); and a city bus tour of Miami that also stops at Parrot Jungle ($39 for adults and $25 for children ages 3–11, including admission). For more information, call Flamingo Tours at (305) 948-3822.

In addition to an all-day bus tour to Key West, *Miami Nice Excursions* offers bus tours to the Everglades on Tuesday and Saturday, narrated in English and German. The tours stop at the Everglades Alligator Farm near Florida City and include an airboat ride. The bus leaves at 8 a.m. and returns at 7 p.m.; $45 for adults and $29 for children ages 3–9. Call (305) 949-9180 for more information.

On Monday and Thursday, *Miami Nice* leads a popular combination bus tour to the Everglades and Parrot Jungle that picks you up at your Miami Beach hotel around 9 a.m. and drops you off at 5 p.m. Tickets are $45 for adults and $29 for children ages 3 to 9. On Tuesdays the tour company offers one-day excursions to Walt Disney World, Epcot, Universal Studios, or Disney MGM Studios in Orlando. The "Disney Blitz" leaves Miami Beach at 6 a.m. and returns around midnight. The motor-coach trip costs $89 for adults and $65 for children ages 3 to 9; the price includes the entrance fee to one of the parks.

Deco Tours of South Beach offers a wide range of tours, including citywide and shopping tours led by owner Dona Zemo. The most popular tour is the Art Deco Walking Tour, the official tour of the Miami Beach Chamber of Commerce (MBCC). The tour is available Monday through Friday. The cost of the two-hour tour is $10 per person; wear comfortable shoes. Call (305) 531-4465 for more information.

Touring on Your Own: Our Favorite Itineraries

If you've taken a guided tour of the city and you're looking for a less packaged experience, or if you've got only limited time to sight-see and want to experience the flavor of Miami, here are some suggested itineraries, along with some advice to get you into a South Florida state of mind.

Rent a convertible (c'mon, this *is* Miami), set the FM dial to some pulsating Latin rhythms, and crank up the volume. Wear your bathing suit beneath your clothes. Wear comfortable walking shoes. Carry only as much money as you'll need for the day. Pretend that you live like this every day of the year.

For a one-day hit of Miami-ness:

1. Breakfast at Parrot Jungle in South Miami.
2. Meander through Coral Gables in the early morning. Stop at the Biltmore Hotel and have a club soda. Drive by the Venetian Pool.
3. Visit Vizcaya.
4. On to The Grove for a stroll and some shopping.
5. Lunch at a Cuban restaurant on Calle Ocho. Order *arroz con pollo, cafe con leche,* and flan at La Carreta, Versailles, or Casablanca.
6. Head over to South Beach for a few hours of strolling, sunning, and beaching.
7. Enjoy a late-afternoon *cafecito.*
8. Back to the hotel for a shower and a nap.
9. Dinner at an oceanside restaurant on South Beach.
10. Dancing, nightclubbing on South Beach.

If you have two days, make this day two:

1. Breakfast at an oceanside café on South Beach.
2. Take a walking tour of the Art Deco District or rent a bike and explore the area.
3. Head downtown at lunchtime, the time when it is liveliest. Take the "People Mover" as it loops around Miami and offers great city views.
4. Eat lunch at one of the many crowded, but cheap, Cuban, Brazilian, or other ethnic eateries found throughout downtown. Wash it down with a caffeine-charged *cafe Cubano.*
5. On to Key Biscayne for an afternoon of windsurfing.
6. Head back downtown to take the Heritage of Miami sunset cruise from behind Bayside Marketplace and see the city at dusk from a sailboat.
7. A late-night dinner at one of the many restaurants that dot Coral Gables.

If your stay in Miami is longer than a couple of days, try to include the following not-to-be-missed attractions on your itinerary: Fairchild Tropical Garden, Metrozoo, Hialeah Park, the Historical Museum of South Florida, the Lowe Art Museum, snorkeling at Biscayne National Park or John Pennecamp Coral Reef State Park, a bike ride down Old Cutler Road, and a day trip to the Everglades and/or the Keys.

Miami for Children

Exotic Miami, world-renowned as an exotic vacation destination and a city that wears its reputation as a crime capital on its sleeve, isn't usually thought of as a great place to bring the kids.

We disagree. Although places like South Beach are definitely adult (some would suggest R-rated) in their appeal and the hustle and bustle of downtown will appeal only to adults and older children, Miami and its environs offer plenty to do for youngsters. Attractions include a world-class zoo, a marine-mammal emporium, a science museum designed for young folk, and some private "jungles" that will delight the kids.

Most families with children visit South Florida during the summer months, when school is out—and Miami bakes in heat and humidity. So, before starting off on a day of touring or a visit to the beach, parents should keep some things in mind.

Overheating, Sunburn, and Dehydration Due to South Florida's subtropical climate, parents with young children on a day's outing need to pay close attention to their kids. The most common problems of smaller children are overheating, sunburn, and dehydration. A small bottle of sunscreen carried in a pocket or fanny pack will help you take precautions against overexposure to the powerful subtropical sun. Be sure to put some on children in strollers, even if the stroller has a canopy. Some of the worst cases of sunburn we have seen were on the exposed foreheads and feet of toddlers and infants in strollers. To avoid overheating, rest at regular intervals in the shade or in an air-conditioned museum, hotel lobby, restaurant, or public building.

Don't count on keeping small children properly hydrated with soft drinks and water fountain stops. Long lines at popular attractions often make buying refreshments problematic and water fountains are not always handy. What's more, excited children may not inform you or even realize that they're thirsty or overheated. We recommend renting a stroller for children six years old and under, and carrying plastic water bottles.

The Beach To avoid a severe sunburn that can ruin a child's—and your—vacation, listen to this advice offered by Larry Pizzi, operations supervisor of the Miami Beach lifeguards: "Put your kids in light or pastel-colored T-shirts—they'll tan right through the shirts—gob the sunscreen on exposed skin, and give 'em little hats. Be particularly careful on windy days, because kids don't feel the sun burning."

More advice: "Don't let little kids swim alone—it's still the ocean out there," Pizzi says. "And don't leave your children alone on the beach—it's easy for them to get disoriented. Mark your street number so you don't get lost." For more advice on the hazards of the beach and ocean swimming, see our "Swimming" section in Part Seven: Exercise and Recreation, page 145.

Blisters Blisters and sore feet are common for visitors of all ages, so wear comfortable, well-broken-in shoes or sandals. If you or your children are unusually susceptible to blisters, carry some precut "Moleskin" bandages;

they offer the best possible protection, stick great, and won't sweat off. When you feel a hot spot, stop, air out your foot, and place a Moleskin over the area before a blister forms. Moleskin is available by name at all drugstores. Sometimes small children won't tell their parents about a developing blister until it's too late. We recommend inspecting the feet of preschoolers at least twice a day.

Sunglasses If you want your smaller children to wear sunglasses, it's a good idea to affix a strap or string to the frames so the glasses won't get lost and can hang from the child's neck while indoors.

Where to Go with Kids

The *Unofficial Guide* rating system for attractions includes an "appeal to different age groups" category indicating a range of appeal from one star (★): don't bother, up to five stars (★★★★★): not to be missed. To get you started, we've provided a list of attractions in Greater Miami most likely to appeal to children.

Top 10 Attractions for Kids
Biscayne National Park (Zone 4)
Everglades National Park/Shark Valley Tram Tour
Gold Coast Railroad Museum (Zone 3)
Historical Museum of South Florida (Zone 2)
Metrozoo (Zone 3)
Miami Museum of Science/Space Transit Planetarium (Zone 3)
Monkey Jungle (Zone 4)
Parrot Jungle and Gardens (Zone 3)
Seaquarium (Zone 3)
Weeks Air Museum (Zone 3)

Sight-Seeing Cruises

One of the best ways to see sun-dappled Miami is from a ship, and the cruise boats that depart from downtown Miami and the marina across from the Fontainebleau Hilton on Miami Beach give visitors a chance to see the town's most spectacular sights the way they ought to be seen: from the water. Most tours are narrated in English and Spanish, and snacks and beverages are sold on board.

From Bayside, the new, two-story shopping mall by the water in downtown Miami, several large, air-conditioned tour boats leave on the hour to whisk visitors on one-hour excursions around placid Biscayne Bay.

Tours generally leave every hour, starting at 11 a.m. until about 5:30

p.m. weekdays, and continuing until midnight on weekends. Ticket prices average $10 to $30 for adults and $5 to $20 for children ages 12 and under.

The sights include dazzling high-rise buildings downtown and the most conspicuous landmark on the water: the 65-foot Fender Stratocaster guitar rotating above the Hard Rock Cafe; its reported cost was a cool half-million dollars. Other sights on the cruise include the spiraling metal structure in Bayfront Park that's a monument to the crew of the space shuttle Challenger, and tugboats, freighters, and cruise ships tied up at the Port of Miami.

Next, the tour boats swing by Fisher Island, an exclusive community of high-rise condos that can only be reached by boat or helicopter, and Miami Beach. After passing under the MacArthur Causeway connecting Miami Beach and the mainland, a number of artificial islands is next, including the aptly named Star Island and Millionaires Row. Your guide will point out the former homes of Liz Taylor, Don Johnson and Melanie Griffith, Al Capone, and other Miami notables—it seems the elusiveness of fame and the high cost of real estate dictates who stays and who leaves Star Island—and the current home of mega-star Gloria Estefan.

After passing the Henry Flagler Monument and Palm Island, the tour boats swing back under the Venetian Causeway and complete their circuit of Biscayne Bay. It's a fun trip—and very scenic.

Sailing Aboard a Tall Ship on Biscayne Bay

For the nautically inclined, a sure bet is a two-hour cruise on Biscayne Bay aboard the Heritage of Miami II, an 85-foot topsail schooner. Once out on the placid waters of the bay, the engine goes off, the wind fills the sails . . . and the hustle and bustle of hectic Miami drops away. If the weather cooperates, the skipper lets passengers take the helm for a few minutes while under sail.

Two-hour sails depart at 1:30 p.m., 4 p.m., and 6:30 p.m. daily from Bayside Marketplace in downtown Miami. The cost is $12 for adults and $7 for children under age 12. One-hour sails depart on Friday, Saturday, and Sunday at various times. Call ahead for specific schedules on weekends. Prices are $7 per person. Our advice: In the winter, sign up for the 4 p.m. sail, which turns into a sunset cruise. For more information, call (305) 442-9697.

Helpful Hints: Travel Tips for Tourists

Great Views

If stunning panoramas turn you on, you've come to the right place: Miami offers visitors a wide array of great views to gladden the eye and quicken the pulse. Here are some of the *Unofficial Guide* research team's favorites.

Cruise Ships and High-Rises On a Friday, Saturday, or Sunday night, make the drive from Miami Beach to downtown Miami on the MacArthur Causeway and you're in for a treat: a magnificent panorama of glittering cruise ships tied up at the Port of Miami. The backdrop is another stunner: the knock-your-socks-off Miami skyline lit up like a Christmas tree. Many people consider it the most spectacular urban cityscape in the United States. Try to spot the CenTrust Building, a circular high-rise that changes color on command.

Downtown from a Slightly Different Angle Another great view of downtown is from the Rickenbacker Causeway to Key Biscayne. Park on the left side of the causeway. By the way, this is one of Miami's most popular make-out spots.

Art Deco Everyone loves the Art Deco District in South Beach. But for an unusual—and spectacular—view of the candy-colored architecture, try this: at sundown, put on a swimsuit, wade out into the surf until you're neck deep . . . and turn around. (Just don't inhale any salt water when you gasp at the view.) This is a popular diversion with hip Miami residents for beating the summer heat and cooling down for a torrid South Beach evening.

The "People Mover" It's a fun, automated transportation system that scoots people around a 26-block chunk of downtown and provides a spectacular, bird's-eye view of the city, Biscayne Bay, and the Atlantic Ocean. The new Omni Loop provides an excellent view of Government Cut and the Port of Miami. A ride on the People Mover only costs a quarter.

From a Boat Miami is married to the water, and much of the beauty of the city is best seen from a boat. Downtown high-rises, Bayfront Park, and the Port of Miami all take on a different, and beautiful, perspective when seen from the water. For more information on boat tours of the harbor and Biscayne Bay, see page 176. For information on Miami's water taxi service, another great way to see Miami from the water, turn to page 98.

The Everglades Although it's about an hour's drive west to Everglades National Park on Route 41, followed by a seven-mile tram or bicycle ride, your reward is one of the best views in South Florida, from the Shark Valley Observation Tower. The view from the top of the 50-foot tower (easily accessible from a ramp) stretches from horizon to horizon across stunning wilderness scenery. Directly below you lies a jungle scene featuring a wide array of bird life, huge fish, and giant turtles moving through the water.

Coral Way One of the most scenic drives in the city—aside from elevated superhighways where drivers really shouldn't let themselves be distracted by the view—is Coral Way (SW 24th Street), a broad avenue stretching from Coral Gables to Biscayne Bay below downtown. Start at the Miracle Mile and drive east; on the left at Douglas Road is the thoroughly spaced-out-looking Miracle Center, designed by Arquitectonica (see page 89 for more information on buildings designed by this avant-garde architectural design firm).

A Bird's-Eye View of Miami Stop by the Greater Miami Convention & Visitor Bureau's main office, located at 701 Brickell Avenue, Suite 2700, during regular business hours, pick up a free map, and check out the panoramic view of downtown Miami, the Miami River, Biscayne Bay, the Port of Miami, and the Atlantic Ocean from the office windows. Park in the basement of the high-rise, get your parking ticket validated, and parking is free.

Sunrise Make it a point to get up early one morning to view the sunrise over the ocean. Better yet, stay up all night and greet the rising sun.

Sunset From Key Biscayne, The Rusty Pelican Restaurant on the tip of the island has spectacular sunset views of downtown Miami. Also, from Miami Beach, sunsets over Biscayne Bay are a treat.

Cruise Ships and Freighters Navigating Government Cut See the action from South Pointe Park on the southern tip of Miami Beach. The 38-foot-deep channel means even the largest cruise and container ships can steam in and out of the Port of Miami. Fridays and Sundays are your best bets.

Scenic Drives

Driving is one of America's favorite pastimes, and because a car is a necessity for visitors in Miami, we've included a list of scenic and unusual routes for folks who like to jump in the car and go for a spin. Just don't leave during rush hour (7 a.m. to 9 a.m. and 3:30 p.m. to 6:30 p.m., weekdays).

One of the most memorable sights in Miami is the view of the city at night from the MacArthur Causeway—especially at night when cruise ships are tied up at the Port of Miami (see above, "Great Views").

Farther north on Miami Beach's Collins Avenue in the 40s is the stunning trompe l'oeil mural that greets drivers as they drive north toward the Fontainebleau Hilton. The huge painting "fools the eye" by "revealing" the curving, glitzy hotel that actually sits behind the brick wall. Continue north along US A1A as far as you want; cruising this venerable old highway is a South Florida tradition.

South of downtown, near the Rickenbacker Causeway, Vizcaya, and the Miami Museum of Science, take Bayshore Drive for a long, relaxing drive through Coconut Grove, Coral Gables, and points south. As you meander along Main Highway, Ingraham Highway, and Old Cutler Road, you'll pass some of the lushest tropical scenery in the Miami area, beautiful homes, and glimpses of sparkling Biscayne Bay. The best way to do this drive is to take a map and not worry about getting lost. A perfect destination—and a real treat for outdoor lovers—is Fairchild Tropical Garden; Parrot Jungle is another. A good turning-back point is Coral Reef Drive (SW 152nd Street). That's where the damage from Hurricane Andrew—a noticeable decrease in foliage—starts to appear.

For a look at what all of South Florida used to look like, go west on Route 41 toward the Everglades. (In Miami, just west of downtown, Route 41 is 8th Street, Calle Ocho, and cuts through the heart of Little Havana.) After you get past Florida's Turnpike, you'll start to see natural flora and an astounding amount of bird life in the canals along the side of the road. Past the Shark Valley entrance to Everglades National Park is Big Cypress National Preserve; the scenery is lush and you pass several Native American villages on the road.

Dinner in Little Havana

You really haven't experienced Miami's rich cultural mosaic until you've made the scene in Little Havana, a few miles west of downtown. Even for gringos whose entire Spanish vocabulary consists of "*hasta la vista,* baby" and "One *cafe Cubano,* please," a visit to this neighborhood is a no-brainer.

Need proof? Some members of the *Unofficial Guide* research team are wimps when it comes to exploring foreign cultures, not to mention self-conscious about their lack of foreign language skills. But their concern evaporated when, while cruising down Calle Ocho (SW 8th Street), they spotted . . . a Sam's Club warehouse store. Moral: You're still in the good old U.S.A.—and the neighborhood is safe.

One last reason to eat dinner in Little Havana: The food is not only great, it's cheap. Here are step-by-step directions to Versailles Restaurant, probably the most popular Cuban restaurant in Little Havana and a renowned Miami institution. (It also offers Anglo customers an English-language menu.) Other nearby Cuban restaurants you could try include La Carreta and Casablanca.

1. Using I-95 downtown as a reference point, go south on the interstate to Exit 2, Route 41 west. This will put you on SW 7th Street west. Note: You will eventually get to SW 8th Street—Calle Ocho—but because it's one-way eastbound as it nears I-95, you've got to take SW 7th Street for a few blocks. Read on.
2. See how easy it is to navigate Miami's grid system: At SW 22nd Avenue, turn left; it's one block to Calle Ocho (SW 8th Street),

where you turn right and continue west (it's a two-way street at this point). If you're aiming for a restaurant other than Versailles, check the address; if it's on Calle Ocho and the street number starts with a number lower than 22, turn left instead.

3. Versailles Restaurant is on your right at SW 36th Avenue; you can't miss it. Turn right and park in their lighted parking lot. Enter the restaurant and get a table.
4. The menu is huge, but if this is your first experience in a Cuban restaurant, here's what you order: the Cuban sampler, "The Classic" ($6 at lunch, $20 at dinner), with roast pork, beef, black beans, yucca, rice, and a tamale.
5. After dinner, dessert: order flan. Don't argue. Do it. It's great. Order a *cafe con leche* at the same time.
6. Pay the bill. You'll be amazed at how cheap it is.
7. After leaving the restaurant, turn left onto Calle Ocho and drive through the heart of Little Havana. I-95 is straight ahead. Another option: Turn right (south) at any major intersection to enter Coral Gables. At Coral Way, turn left (toward I-95) for a scenic drive through the town.

If you'd rather take a cab to Versailles, the address is 3555 SW 8th Street; phone (305) 445-7614. Trust us, however: driving to the restaurant is very easy, even for first-time visitors to Miami.

Part Ten

Attractions in Miami

Beyond the Beach

Miami is an exotic resort, a sports town, a shopping town, a jet-set destination, all located in a lush tropical climate. But that's not all—Miami and South Florida provide visitors with a potpourri of attractions that show off its history, flora and fauna, natural history, art collections, unique landscapes, and, last but not least, its penchant for the kitschy and commercial.

The following zone descriptions provide you with a comprehensive guide to South Florida's top attractions, along with listing a few dogs we think you should avoid. We give you enough information so that you can choose the places you want to see, based on your own interests. Each attraction includes a zone number so you can plan your visit logically, without spending a lot of valuable touring time crisscrossing the region.

A Time-Saving Chart

Because of the wide range of South Florida attractions, we've provided the following chart to help you prioritize your touring at a glance. In it, you'll find the zone, location, author's rating from one star (skip it) to five stars (not to be missed), and a brief description of the attraction. Some attractions, usually art galleries without permanent collections, weren't rated because exhibits change. Each attraction is individually profiled later in this section.

Attractions in Miami

Attraction	Description	Author's Rating
Zone 1: Miami Beach		
Bass Museum of Art	highbrow art	★★★
Holocaust Memorial	a moving memorial to Holocaust victims	★★★★

Attractions in Miami

Attraction	Description	Author's Rating
Jewish Museum of Florida	museum of Jewish culture, history	★★
The Wolfsonian	museum of early 20th-century design	★★★
Zone 2: Miami North		
Police Hall of Fame	cop museum	★½
Ancient Span. Monastery	oldest building in Am.	★★½
Miami Art Museum	traveling art exhibits	unrated
Hialeah Park	stately racetrack; flamingos	★★★
Hist. Museum/S. Fla.	10,000 years of history	★★★★
Museum of Contemporary Art	modern art gallery	★★★½
Zone 3: Miami South		
Art Museum at Florida International U.	changing art exhibits	unrated
The Barnacle State Historic Site	oldest home in Dade Co.	★★
Fairchild Tropical Garden	83-acre park	★★★★½
Gold Coast Railroad Museum	real trains and locomotives	★★½
Lowe Art Museum	diverse art collection	★★★★
Metrozoo	world-class zoo w/o cages	★★★★★
Miami Museum of Science	museum/planetarium	★–
Parrot Jungle	bird sanctuary and gardens	★★★★½
Seaquarium	sea mammal emporium	★★
Vizcaya Museum	lavish estate/ formal gardens	★★★–★★★★★
Weeks Air Museum	World War II aircraft on display	★★½
Zone 4: Southern Dade County		
Biscayne National Park	aquatic park	★★★★
Coral Castle	coral-block oddity	★
Fruit & Spice Park	fruit-bearing plants	★½
Monkey Jungle	primate zoo	★★★½

Zone 1: Miami Beach

Bass Museum of Art

Type of Attraction: A museum featuring artwork spanning the 14th to 20th centuries. A self-guided tour.

Location: 2121 Park Avenue (near Collins Avenue and 21st Street), Miami Beach. The museum is immediately behind the public library on Collins Avenue.

Admission: $5 for adults, $3 for seniors and students, free for children under age 6. Special exhibits may have additional charges.

Hours: 10 a.m. to 5 p.m., Tuesday through Saturday; 1 p.m. to 5 p.m., Sunday; 1 p.m. to 9 p.m. on the second and fourth Wednesday of the month; Monday, closed.

Phone: (305) 673-7533

When to Go: Any time.

Special Comments: A refreshing contrast to the drop-dead hipness and ultrabright colors of South Beach; a beautiful building constructed out of coral rock.

Overall Appeal by Age Group:

Pre-school	Grade School	Teens	Young Adults	Over 30	Senior Citizens
★	★★	★★½	★★★	★★★	★★★½

Author's Rating: A small, easy-to-digest collection of art that's worth seeing. ★★★

How Much Time to Allow: One to two hours.

Description and Comments Located in a beautiful Art Deco building that's only a block from the ocean, the Bass Museum displays European paintings, sculpture, and tapestries from the 14th century, as well as work by modern masters such as Toulouse-Lautrec. Don't expect to see a lot of drop-dead art in this compact museum, though. Much of the floor space is dedicated to special exhibits, and the surrounding grounds feature changing exhibits of contemporary sculpture.

Touring Tips Groups can call in advance to arrange a tour led by a docent (museum guide).

Other Things to Do Nearby Laze on the beach, ogle hard bodies on Ocean Drive, or try the corned beef at nearby Wolfies. If you can't find something interesting to do on South Beach, it's time to pack up and go home.

Holocaust Memorial of Miami Beach

Type of Attraction: A memorial to the 6 million Jews killed in the Holocaust. A self-guided tour.

Location: Dade Boulevard and Meridian Avenue (near the Miami Beach Convention Center) in Miami Beach.

Admission: Free.

Hours: 9 a.m. to 9 p.m., daily.

Phone: (305) 538-1663

When to Go: Any time.

Special Comments: While this is a hard area to find parking (especially if a convention is taking place), reserved street parking is available on Meridian Avenue for Holocaust Memorial visitors *only.*

Overall Appeal by Age Group:

Pre-school	Grade School	Teens	Young Adults	Over 30	Senior Citizens
★	★★	★★½	★★★	★★★★	★★★★½

Author's Rating: A moving experience. ★★★★

How Much Time to Allow: One hour.

Description and Comments Dedicated in 1990 in a ceremony that featured Nobel Prize laureate Elie Wiesel, the Holocaust Memorial utilizes contrasting elements to deliver an emotional punch: bright Jerusalem stone, somber black granite, the stillness of a reflecting pool, the backdrop of an azure sky, and a stunning, 42-foot sculpture of a giant outstretched arm (tattooed with a number from Auschwitz) rising up from the earth. Miami Beach is home to one of the world's largest populations of Holocaust survivors.

Touring Tips There's more to the memorial than just the dramatic sculpture that seems to rise from the reflecting pool—but you must get out of your car to experience it. Black granite panels contain a concise history of the Holocaust plus pictorial representations, text, and maps. After walking through an enclosed, shrinelike space and a narrow passage, the visitor is greeted with a stunning sight: a circular plaza surrounded by shining black granite that mirrors the 42-foot bronze sculpture.

Other Things to Do Nearby The Bass Museum of Art is located at 21st Street and Park Avenue, a few blocks north and east. The Miami Beach Chamber of Commerce Visitor Center is across the street from the Holocaust Memorial; dash in to pick up maps and tourist information.

The Jewish Museum of Florida

Type of Attraction: 230 years of Florida Jewish life on display in a 1936 Art Deco–style building. Guided and self-guided tours.

Location: In South Beach; 301 Washington Avenue.

Admission: $5 for adults; $4 for seniors and students; $10 for families. Admission is free on Saturday.

Hours: 10 a.m. to 5 p.m., Tuesday through Sunday; closed on Mondays, Jewish holidays, and major holidays (except Christmas).

Phone: (305) 672-5044

When to Go: Any time.

Special Comments: The neighborhood around this former Orthodox synagogue (which predates the Art Deco District a few blocks north) is rapidly changing as developers move in; enjoy the ambience before high-rise condos take over.

Overall Appeal by Age Group:

Pre-school	Grade School	Teens	Young Adults	Over 30	Senior Citizens
★	★★	★★½	★★½	★★½	★★★

Author's Rating: A narrow, yet interesting slice of South Florida history; a beautiful interior that's worth a peek. ★★

How Much Time to Allow: One hour.

Description and Comments This recently restored Art Deco building once served as Miami Beach's first Orthodox synagogue. Today visitors can enjoy nearly 80 stained glass windows, a copper dome, the marble bimah (Torah reading platform), and many Art Deco features such as chandeliers and sconces. Arranged on the slanted floor (a design feature that made it easier for the rabbi to be heard by the congregation) is a collection of temporary exhibits on Jewish life and culture in Florida, as well as nearly 300 years of Jewish history in the Sunshine State. Visitors are sure to find something of interest, and the spacious, light-filled interior is a treat.

Touring Tips For a more meaningful visit, hook up with one of the museum's trained docents (museum guides), who can explain the layout and make a few suggestions on what to see as you browse. Don't miss the 15-minute video that explains the museum's restoration and mission. And look for the window sponsored by notorious gangster Meyer Lansky (it's on the right as you enter the main room). "He was a member of the synagogue," explained my docent, with a smile and a shrug.

Other Things to Do Nearby Drive south and turn right onto Biscayne Street to reach Joe's Stone Crab, the most famous (and crowded) restaurant in South Florida (open mid-October through mid-May). Watch huge freighters and cruise ships on their way to and from the Port of Miami at South Pointe Park. Explore the Art Deco District, which starts above 5th Street, two blocks north.

The Wolfsonian

Type of Attraction: A museum of design dedicated to the art, architecture, design, and cultural history of the period 1885 to 1945. A self-guided tour.

Location: In South Beach; 1001 Washington Avenue.

Admission: $5 for adults; $3.50 for children ages 6–12, seniors, and adult students (with ID). Admission is free on Thursdays from 6 p.m. to 9 p.m.

Hours: 11 a.m. to 6 p.m., Tuesday through Saturday; noon to 5 p.m., Sunday. Open until 9 p.m. on Thursdays (and admission is free). Closed Mondays, the Fourth of July, Thanksgiving, Christmas, and New Year's Days.

Phone: (305) 531-1001

When to Go: Any time.

Special Comments: Park the kids at the beach; the Wolfsonian will bore smaller children silly. Because this place just oozes with European sophistication, to really fit in guys should wear a tweed jacket with leather elbow patches, smoke a pipe, and mutter approvingly in Italian as they move from exhibit to exhibit. Gals may want to opt for the New York "Fashion Nun" look: all black.

Overall Appeal by Age Group:

Pre-school	Grade School	Teens	Young Adults	Over 30	Senior Citizens
—	★	★½	★★	★★★	★★★½

Author's Rating: Design plus art equals Art Deco . . . and who could imagine a more appropriate location for a museum like this than South Beach? A drawback: an off-putting "high-brow" atmosphere. ★★★

How Much Time to Allow: One to two hours.

Description and Comments South Beach is all about surfaces: tanned bodies, thong bikinis, pastel-colored Art Deco hotels, models, and Eurotrash and tourists elbow to elbow on Ocean Drive. At the Wolfsonian, however, visitors get a chance to delve beneath the surfaces and ponder the meanings that lurk within everyday things such as furniture, household items, model trains, posters, and a zillion other objects taken from a collection of more than 70,000 decorative items dating from 1885 to 1945. Major themes in the changing exhibits focus on how design trends function as agents of modernity, how design works as a key element in reform movements, and how design elements are incorporated as vehicles of both advertising and political propaganda. Wear your thinking cap.

Temporary and semi-permanent exhibits are housed in a spiffed-up, former storage building restored to its 1920s, Mediterranean-style elegance. Most of the building is used for storing the collection; the surprisingly small exhibit spaces are located on the fifth, sixth, and seventh floors. Who collected all this stuff? Mitchell Wolfson Jr., an heir to a fortune made in the movie theater business.

Touring Tips Take the elevator up to the seventh-floor exhibit area and work your way down.

Other Things to Do Nearby Great (and not-so-great) restaurants line Washington Street, along with a wide array of shops. Lincoln Road Mall is six blocks north; frenetic Ocean Drive (and the ocean) is two blocks east. Watch out for weaving Rollerbladers.

Zone 2: Miami North

American Police Hall of Fame and Police Museum

Type of Attraction: A collection of law enforcement artifacts and a memorial to more than 6,000 police officers who have died in the line of duty. A self-guided tour.

Location: 3801 Biscayne Boulevard, Miami, at the Julia Tuttle Causeway (I-195).

Admission: $6 for adults, $4 for seniors, $3 for children under age 12, $1 for law enforcement officers, free for family survivors of police officers who died in the line of duty. Free parking.

Hours: 10 a.m. to 5:30 p.m., daily. Closed Christmas Day.

Phone: (305) 573-0070

When to Go: Any time.

Special Comments: Yes, that's a real police cruiser stuck to the museum's outer wall. It makes this one of the easiest attractions to find in Miami.

Overall Appeal by Age Group:

Pre-school	Grade School	Teens	Young Adults	Over 30	Senior Citizens
★	★★★	★★★	★★½	★★	★★½

Author's Rating: The memorial is moving; the museum, bizarre. ★½
How Much Time to Allow: One hour.

Description and Comments The names, ranks, cities, and states of more than 6,000 police officers who died in the line of duty are engraved on 400 tons of white marble in the first-floor memorial. The scene is similar to the Vietnam Memorial in Washington, D.C.: Flowers and mementos left by friends and relatives line the floor beneath the inscriptions. The memorial serves as a graphic reminder that a police officer is killed every 57 hours somewhere in the United States.

Upstairs, 11-year-olds will thrill to a collection of police enforcement artifacts that include a real gas chamber and electric chair ("Old Sparky"), simulated crime scenes that test powers of deduction, and displays of guns and radar units used to detect speeders. Warning: Some of the exhibits are quite gory, such as the post-electrocution photograph of mass murderer Ted Bundy. The folks who put this museum together aren't shy about their support of capital punishment.

Touring Tips Don't miss the lobby picture of a woozy-looking Keith Richards, lead guitarist of the Rolling Stones, along with a zillion other Grade B movie stars and TV personalities who have their mug shots on the wall. Richards is a celebrity supporter of the museum. Go figure.

Other Things to Do Nearby Not a whole lot—surprisingly, the Police Museum is located on the edge of a marginally safe neighborhood. But downtown Miami and Miami Beach are only a few minutes away by car.

Ancient Spanish Monastery

Type of Attraction: The Cloisters of the Monastery of St. Bernard is the oldest building in North America. A self-guided tour.

Location: 16711 W. Dixie Highway, North Miami Beach. From the beach, take the Sunny Isles Causeway, which turns into NE 163rd Street in North Miami Beach; turn right on Dixie Highway and look for the entrance on the right. From I-95, take the NE 167th Street exit east, which leads into NE 163rd Street; then turn left on Dixie Highway.

Admission: $4.50 for adults, $2.50 for seniors, and $1 for children age 12 and under.

Hours: 10 a.m. to 4 p.m., Monday through Saturday; noon to 4 p.m., Sunday.

Phone: (305) 945-1461

When to Go: Any time. Because the Monastery is a popular wedding spot, the grounds are often crowded on Saturday and Sunday afternoons with folks decked out in formal attire.

Special Comments: The former Spanish monastery and the surrounding garden are surprisingly small.

Overall Appeal by Age Group:

Pre-school	Grade School	Teens	Young Adults	Over 30	Senior Citizens
★	★½	★½	★★	★★	★★½

Author's Rating: While the architecture is engaging and the site is an oasis in North Miami, the story of how this monastery found its way to South Florida is a lot more interesting than the building itself. ★★½

How Much Time to Allow: 30 minutes.

Description and Comments Newspaper mogul William Randolph Hearst must have had a stupendous swimming pool in mind when he bought this 12th-century Spanish monastery, and then had it disassembled, boxed, and shipped to New York for eventual transport to his San Simeon estate in California.

Alas, an outbreak of hoof-and-mouth disease in Segovia resulted in the U.S. government's quarantine of the 11,000 crates (because of hay used to pack the stones)—and the boxes moldered in a New York warehouse for 26 years. In 1952, two entrepreneurs with a fervent belief in the future of Florida tourism bought the stones, had the boxes shipped to Florida, and reassembled the monastery on this site over a 19-month period—at a cost of $1.5 million.

Essentially a small courtyard surrounded by a covered walkway built of stone, the monastery boasts everything you expect to find in medieval cloisters: vaulted ceilings, statues, carvings, stained glass windows, and paintings. Yet the old stones look scrubbed and the building, as a result, doesn't feel 850 years old. But what a great place for a wedding.

Touring Tips Don't miss the monastery's one claim to High Art: *La Gracia,* a painting by Spanish master Julio Romero de Torres, which is on display in the monastery's gift shop. It's the twin of another Torres painting, *El Pecado,* which is in the Prado Museum in Madrid, Spain. Sunday mass is at 8 and 10:30 a.m.

Other Things to Do Nearby The new Museum of Contemporary Art in North Miami is nearby; ocean beaches are due east on Route 826, the Sunny Isles Causeway.

Hialeah Park

Type of Attraction: Gorgeous grounds, a racetrack listed on the National Register of Historic Places, and a flock of 400 pink flamingos. A self-guided tour.

Location: 2200 E Fourth Avenue (at 22nd Street) in the north Miami neighborhood of Hialeah. From I-95, take the 79th Street exit west to 4th Street and turn left. Then turn left on 22nd Street; the entrance is on the right. Bear right and park your car near the clubhouse.

Admission: $4.

Hours: 9 a.m. to 5 p.m., Monday through Friday. Call ahead for racing dates. Most weekends feature public events such as flea markets.

Phone: (305) 885-8000

When to Go: Any time. Races, however, are only held three months a year, rotating between spring, fall, and winter.

Special Comments: Bring binoculars; the flamingos are in the track's infield.

Overall Appeal by Age Group:

Pre-school	Grade School	Teens	Young Adults	Over 30	Senior Citizens
★	★½	★★	★★½	★★½	★★★

Author's Rating: Stately, old-world elegance. ★★★

How Much Time to Allow: 30 minutes off-season; half a day during the racing season.

Description and Comments The best way to visit this world-famous thoroughbred racetrack would be to go when the ponies are running. But if you're in town when the ponies are racing at another track, the gorgeous coral clubhouse and stands, along with the flock of pink birds, is worth a stop. Most facilities such as bars and restaurants, however, will be closed.

Touring Tips On quiet mornings during the middle of the week, you've got the whole place to yourself. Behind the clubhouse look for trainers working with race horses. When racing is in progress, Hialeah is a great breakfast stop.

Other Things to Do Nearby Opa-locka, a planned community that fell on hard times but is experiencing a comeback, is north of Hialeah Park and features some outrageous Moorish-style architecture; it's worth a peek, but we don't recommend visiting on foot. For another dose of old Miami, stop by Miami Jai Alai, near the airport.

Historical Museum of South Florida

Type of Attraction: 10,000 years of Florida history on display. A self-guided tour.

Location: 101 West Flagler Street in downtown Miami, in the Metro-Dade Cultural Center. Take the "People Mover" to the Government Center station.

Admission: $5 for adults, $3 for children ages 6–12, free for children under age 6. Combined tickets for the Historical Museum of South Florida and the Miami Art Museum (also located in the Metro-Dade Cultural Center) are $6 per person.

Hours: 10 a.m. to 5 p.m., Monday through Saturday; 10 a.m. to 9 p.m., Thursday; noon to 5 p.m., Sunday.

Phone: (305) 375-1492

When to Go: Any time.

Special Comments: Discounted parking is available at Cultural Center Parking, 50 NW 2nd Avenue and at Metro-Dade County Garage, 140 West Flagler Street. Have your parking ticket validated at the admission desk.

Overall Appeal by Age Group:

Pre-school	Grade School	Teens	Young Adults	Over 30	Senior Citizens
★★	★★★★	★★★½	★★★★	★★★★	★★★★

Author's Rating: A spiffy museum that will entertain and educate both kids and adults. ★★★★

How Much Time to Allow: One to two hours.

Description and Comments With lots of interactive displays (some feature earphones that let you hear jungle sounds, others are big enough to walk through), this sparkling, well-designed museum is a lot of fun. Visitors can discover the Florida that existed before the tourists came—even before people ever set foot in South Florida. The museum also emphasizes the rich cultural diversity of modern Florida's multiethnic population, ranging from Hispanic theater to Jewish heritage.

Touring Tips Kids really like the various colonial-era cannons in the historical exhibits. They'll also like climbing aboard an old 1920s trolley car.

The Indies Company, the museum's gift shop, offers a wide range of items that reflect South Florida and the Caribbean, including a large assortment of old poster reproductions.

Other Things to Do Nearby Couple your visit to the Historical Museum of South Florida with a stop at the Miami Art Museum, across the plaza. If you've never boarded the "People Mover," Miami's automated downtown transportation system, do it now: It's the best 25¢ investment you'll ever make.

Metro-Dade Cultural Center

This downtown conglomeration of attractions consists of the Historical Museum of South Florida (page 192), the Miami Art Museum, and a branch of the Dade County public library.

Miami Art Museum of Miami-Dade County (formerly Center for the Fine Arts)

Type of Attraction: An art gallery that features constantly changing exhibitions of a wide range of art from around the world. A self-guided tour.

Location: 101 West Flagler Street, in the Metro-Dade Cultural Center in downtown Miami. Take the "People Mover" to the Government Center station.

Admission: $5 for adults, $2.50 for seniors and students, free for children ages 6–12. Combined tickets for admission to the Miami Art Museum and the Historical Museum of South Florida are $6 per person. Free on Tuesdays (all day) and on Thursday evenings from 5 p.m. to 9 p.m.

Hours: 10 a.m. to 5 p.m., Tuesday through Friday; noon to 5 p.m., weekends; and till 9 p.m. on Thursday. Closed Monday.

Phone: (305) 375-1700

When to Go: Any time.

Special Comments: Judging from the exhibit of drawings from the British Museum recently on display, the Miami Art Museum is a gallery that emphasizes high-quality art and hosts national touring shows throughout the year. Discounted parking is available at Cultural Center Parking, 50 NW 2nd Avenue and at Metro-Dade County Garage, 140 West Flagler Street. For free parking, validate your parking ticket at the admission desk.

Overall Appeal Comment: Because the museum has no permanent collection and exhibits are constantly changing, it's not possible to rate the gallery by age group.

Author's Rating: Again, it's not possible to rate this museum. But it's a comfortable, large gallery that should be on any art lover's itinerary. The shows are consistently professional and well attended.

How Much Time to Allow: One to two hours.

Description and Comments This is a logical place to visit before or after seeing the Historical Museum of South Florida, located across the plaza. It's a large, airy gallery with exhibits on two floors. Stop at the admission desk to find out what's on display during your visit, or check Friday's edition of the *Miami Herald.*

Other Things to Do Nearby The Miami Art Museum is paired with the Historical Museum of South Florida; Metrorail's "People Mover" makes the rest of downtown Miami easy to get to.

MoCA: Museum of Contemporary Art

Type of Attraction: The only art museum in Miami solely dedicated to modern art. A self-guided tour.

Location: 770 NE 125th Street, North Miami. From Miami Beach, take the Broad Causeway at 96th Street, which becomes NE 125th Street. MoCA is on the left.

Admission: $4 for adults; $2 for seniors and students; free for children under age 12.

Hours: 11 a.m. to 5 p.m., Tuesday through Saturday; noon to 5 p.m., Sunday; closed Monday.

Phone: (305) 893-6211

When to Go: Any time.

Special Comments: All on one level. Docent-led tours are available on weekends.

Overall Appeal by Age Group: Because the gallery changes its exhibits regularly, use these general ratings as a guide.

Pre-school	Grade School	Teens	Young Adults	Over 30	Senior Citizens
★	★	★★	★★★½	★★★½	★★½

Author's Rating: Never a dull moment in Miami's newest museum; a gem. ★★★½

How Much Time to Allow: One hour.

Description and Comments After moving from cramped quarters and undergoing a name change, MoCA is still basically a one-room exhibition hall. But the room's a heck of a lot bigger, allowing MoCA to stage larger shows of cutting-edge, contemporary art. Expect to be flabbergasted (or, at least, amused) by whatever is on display during your visit to Miami. Films, lectures, artists' talks, and excursions are also offered at MoCA.

Touring Tips The gift shop features handcrafted jewelry and one-of-a-kind items.

Other Things to Do Nearby The Museum of Contemporary Art is located in North Miami, infamous for its lack of tourist attractions. The posh shops of Bal Harbour are directly across the Broad Causeway; turn right on NE 123rd Street to get there. One of Miami's best sushi joints is Tani Guchi's Place, a few miles east in a strip shopping center just west of the Broad Causeway (2224 NE 123rd Street; (305) 892-6744). And the Ancient Spanish Monastery is a few miles north in North Miami Beach.

Zone 3: Miami South

The Art Museum at Florida International University, South Campus

Type of Attraction: A small art gallery featuring a wide range of temporary exhibits. A self-guided tour.

Location: SW 107th Avenue and 8th Street, Miami (near the Florida Turnpike).

Admission: Free.

Hours: 10 a.m. to 9 p.m., Monday; 10 a.m. to 4 p.m., Tuesday through Friday; noon to 4 p.m., Saturday. Closed Sunday.

Phone: (305) 348-2890

When to Go: Any time.

Special Comments: Folks with physical disabilities should call the museum five days in advance of their visit if they need special assistance.

Overall Appeal Comment: Because the museum hosts temporary art exhibits and has no permanent collection, it's not possible to rate this attraction by age group.

Author's Rating: Because the gallery has no permanent collection, it's not possible to give it a rating. But it's an attractive, if small, art gallery that's very comfortable for roaming. It has a reputation as a top-notch gallery that brings in high-caliber shows. The exhibit on Latin American folk art on display during our visit was great.

How Much Time to Allow: One hour.

Description and Comments This small but attractive gallery offers a wide range of high-quality exhibits throughout the year. Recent shows included "*Visiones del Pueblo:* The Folk Art of Latin America," paintings and drawings by abstract expressionist Elaine de Kooning, and photography by award-winning Cuban artists. A lecture series, offered free to the public, has included talks by a former chief art critic of the *New York Times* and Latin American novelist and statesman Mario Vargas Llosa.

Touring Tips Before making the drive to West Miami, call ahead or check the Friday edition of the *Miami Herald* to see what's on exhibit.

Other Things to Do Nearby While it's not very close—there's not much else of interest to visitors on the western edge of Miami—drive east on 8th Street to Little Havana for lunch or dinner at Versailles, 3555 SW 8th Street, at SW 37th Avenue (phone (305) 445-7614). Parallel to 8th Street to the south is Coral Way, which leads to Coral Gables and the Miracle Mile.

The Barnacle State Historic Site

Type of Attraction: The oldest home in Dade County (1891); a panoramic view of Biscayne Bay; an oasis of beauty and calm in hectic Coconut Grove. House tours are guided only; tours of the grounds are self-guided.

Location: In Coconut Grove; 3485 Main Highway.

Admission: $1.

Hours: 9 a.m. to 4 p.m., Friday through Sunday; closed Monday through Thursday and Thanksgiving, Christmas, and New Year's Days.

Phone: (305) 448-9445

When to Go: Any time.

Special Comments: Pets are allowed on the grounds but must be kept on a leash.

Overall Appeal by Age Group:

Pre-school	Grade School	Teens	Young Adults	Over 30	Senior Citizens
★	★½	★½	★★	★★	★★½

Author's Rating: A real find for history buffs and folks interested in how the landed gentry lived in South Florida a century ago. It's also a terrific picnic spot with a drop-dead view of Biscayne Bay. ★★

How Much Time to Allow: An hour or so for the building tour; or however long it takes to recharge your batteries after a morning of shopping or people-watching in the Grove.

Description and Comments Early 20th-century yacht designer and wrecker (a person who earns a living by salvaging ships that run aground) Ralph Middleton Munroe first visited South Florida in 1877 and returned in 1886 to purchase 40 acres facing Biscayne Bay. In 1891 he built his home, called the "Barnacle," a one-story structure raised off the ground on wood pilings with a central room octagonal in shape. Today, visitors can tour the unique house filled with nautical touches; the building provides a glimpse of a way of life that no longer exists. Outside, a tropical hardwood "hammock" (or forest) isolates the grounds from busy Main Highway, giving way to a view that attracts neighbors such as Sylvester Stallone and Madonna.

Touring Tips Guided house tours are free and conducted at 10 a.m., 11:30 a.m., 1 p.m., and 2:30 p.m., Friday through Sunday; meet on the porch of the main house. Tours are limited to the first ten people who show up, so try to arrive a few minutes early. Bring a picnic lunch.

Other Things to Do Nearby The Grove is second only to South Beach for world-class people-watching, shopping, and dining. If the Barnacle whetted your appetite for more outdoor splendor on the shores of Biscayne Bay, continue south on Main Highway a few miles to Fairchild Tropical Garden.

Fairchild Tropical Garden

Type of Attraction: Eighty-three beautifully landscaped acres containing plants from tropical regions around the world. Guided and self-guided tours.

Location: 10901 Old Cutler Road, Miami; south of Coconut Grove on Old Cutler Road.

Admission: $8; children under age 13 admitted free. The fee includes a narrated, 30-minute, open-air tram tour of the garden.

Hours: 9:30 a.m. to 4:30 p.m., daily. Closed Christmas Day. The Rainforest Cafe is open 11 a.m. to 2 p.m.; Monday, closed.

Phone: (305) 667-1651

When to Go: Any time, but avoid hot and humid summer afternoons. In the fall, winter, and spring, the late afternoon sun lights the foliage with a rich, red glow. While the park is seldom crowded, fewer people visit during the week than on weekends.

Special Comments: The expanded Garden Shop sells tropical gardening books, plants, and unique gifts. The free tram tour leaves on the hour.

Overall Appeal by Age Group:

Pre-school	Grade School	Teens	Young Adults	Over 30	Senior Citizens
★	★½	★★	★★★	★★★½	★★★★

Author's Rating: This manicured park filled with lush palms and exotic trees and dotted with man-made lakes is a knockout. ★★★★½

How Much Time to Allow: At least two hours; half a day or more for a leisurely exploration.

Description and Comments Fairchild Tropical Garden is the largest tropical botanical garden in the United States; its mission is education, scientific research, and display. The grounds and plant life are stunning, in spite of the beating they took from Hurricane Andrew in 1992. You don't have to be a certified tree hugger to appreciate the beauty and tranquility found here.

Touring Tips After taking the tram tour, go back to areas pointed out by the guide that interest you. For example, Cycad Circle features the same plants that dinosaurs munched 300 million years ago. The 1939 Gate House has been restored and is now a historical museum with permanent exhibits on plant exploration. Sandwiches, drinks, and snacks are available at the snack bar, where you can eat under a huge sapodilla tree (weekends only). If you bring your own food, picnic next door at Matheson Hammock Park.

Other Things to Do Nearby Parrot Jungle is right around the corner; Coconut Grove is loaded with places to eat, drink, and shop. Matheson Hammock Park features a beach, marina, and a terrific view of downtown Miami.

Gold Coast Railroad Museum

Type of Attraction: A museum featuring steam and diesel locomotives, as well as a presidential railroad car. Guided and self-guided tours.

Location: South of Miami near the entrance to Metrozoo. Take the Florida Turnpike Extension to SW 152nd Street and follow signs to Metrozoo.

Admission: $5 for adults; $2 for children ages 3–12.

Hours: 10 a.m. to 3 p.m. daily.

Phone: (305) 253-0063

When to Go: Any time except hot, humid summer afternoons.

Special Comments: Unfortunately, the museum took a direct hit from Hurricane Andrew in 1992. As a result, only a few railroad cars and locomotives were open during our visits. But the owner expects to have a roof over the trains in 1998.

Overall Appeal by Age Group:

Pre-school	Grade School	Teens	Young Adults	Over 30	Senior Citizens
★★★	★★★★	★★	★★½	★★	★★

Author's Rating: A must-see for railroad buffs and kids. ★★½

How Much Time to Allow: One hour.

Description and Comments This complex of Navy blimp hangars destroyed in a 1945 hurricane rose again to become a railroad museum—only to be wiped out by another hurricane in 1992. While the owner is getting things back in shape, visitors can still check out a few railroad cars and take a 15-minute train ride (which leaves on the hour starting at noon).

Touring Tips The Gold Coast Railroad Museum is a nice diversion before or after visiting Metrozoo, which is right next door. It will be a more worthwhile destination after the new building that houses the museum is completed. Call before you visit.

Other Things to Do Nearby Metrozoo, Monkey Jungle, the Weeks Air Museum, and a wide selection of fast-food restaurants are all close.

Lowe Art Museum

Type of Attraction: A diverse art collection ranging from antiquities to Renaissance, traditional, contemporary, and non-Western works. A self-guided tour.

Location: Just off US 1 on the Coral Gables campus of the University of Miami; two blocks north of the University Metrorail Station.

Admission: $5 for adults, $3 for senior citizens and students, free for children under age 12. Slightly higher fees are sometimes charged for special shows.

Hours: 10 a.m. to 5 p.m. Tuesday through Saturday; noon to 5 p.m. Sunday. Closed Monday.

Phone: (305) 284-3535

When to Go: Any time.

Special Comments: The museum recently completed a 10,000-foot expansion.

Overall Appeal by Age Group:

Pre-school	Grade School	Teens	Young Adults	Over 30	Senior Citizens
★	★★	★★½	★★★	★★★½	★★★

Author's Rating: A little bit of everything in bite-sized chunks that don't overwhelm; the best art museum in the Miami area. ★★★★

How Much Time to Allow: At least an hour; if the special exhibitions grab you, figure a half-day.

Description and Comments The oldest visual arts institution in Dade County boasts a collection of 7,000 works of art in its permanent collection, including Baroque art, paintings by Spanish masters such as El Greco, and works by modern artists such as Warhol, Lichtenstein, and Hanson.

The Lowe also features several special exhibitions each year, further varying the kind of art you'll see on any visit. The museum also emphasizes non-Western art, with exhibits of Southwestern Indian art, Latin American art, Guatemalan textiles, and pre-Columbian objects. For art lovers, the Lowe is a real find.

Touring Tips The Lowe Museum of Art is all on one floor, which makes it an easy destination to tour for elderly and disabled folks. The museum store offers unusual gifts, art books, museum publications, and cards for sale.

Other Things to Do Nearby Coconut Grove is a great place for eating, drinking, shopping, and people-watching. The Venetian Pool in Coral Gables is a classy swimming hole; Parrot Jungle and Fairchild Tropical Garden are two of the Miami area's best tourist destinations.

Metrozoo

Type of Attraction: A "new style" zoo that features cageless animals that roam on plots of land surrounded by moats. Guided and self-guided tours.

Location: South of Miami. Take the Florida Turnpike Extension to the SW 152nd Street exit and follow the signs to the entrance.

Admission: $8 for adults and $4 for children ages 3–12.

Hours: 9:30 a.m. to 5:30 p.m., daily; open every day of the year.

Phone: (305) 251-0400 for a recorded message; (305) 251-0401 for more information.

When to Go: With much of its lush, shady foliage ripped out by Hurricane Andrew in 1992, it's imperative that visitors avoid touring the zoo on sweltering summer afternoons. "You'll die here midday in July and August," a zoo employee reports. Come before 10 a.m. or after 3:30 p.m. to beat the worst of the heat. Saturday, predictably enough, is the most crowded day, while Sunday morning is usually a quiet time to see the zoo. Keep in mind, too, that animals are most active early in the morning and late in the day.

Special Comments: At Ecology Theatre in the Children's Zoo, handlers bring out a variety of animals for close-up views. Hedgehogs usually steal the shows, which are free and held at 11 a.m., 1 p.m., and 3 p.m. Kids will love the petting zoo. Chimps and gorillas—the most popular exhibits—are fed at 2 p.m.

Overall Appeal by Age Group:

Pre-school	Grade School	Teens	Young Adults	Over 30	Senior Citizens
★★★★★	★★★★★	★★★★	★★★★	★★★★	★★★★

Author's Rating: It's no surprise that this is rated by experts as one of the best zoos in the world. And no cages mean that people who normally hate zoos may love this one. ★★★★★

How Much Time to Allow: At least two hours—although that's enough time to induce heat stroke on a sweltering summer afternoon.

Description and Comments Metrozoo was clobbered by Hurricane Andrew, and the worst blow was the total destruction of Wings of Asia, Metrozoo's world-class bird exhibit. But don't let that deter you from making a visit. The zoo's monorail service is again making a complete loop of the park, and more than 7,000 trees have been planted since the hurricane.

Touring Tips Take the free Zoofari Monorail, which makes a complete loop of Metrozoo. The round trip takes 20 to 25 minutes. Then either get off at station 1 and begin walking toward station 2 or continue on the train to station 4 (the last stop) and walk back toward the zoo entrance. Along the way you'll pass outdoor exhibits featuring gorillas, chimpanzees, elephants, Himalayan black bears, a white Bengal tiger, and other exotic animals. They're all uncaged—and appear a lot more content than animals behind bars in other zoos. Some exhibits feature "viewing caves" that let you view animals through plate-glass windows on their side of the moat.

Folks who would like to avoid the stairs or long ramps leading to the monorail stations—or who just don't feel like walking—can take a narrated tram tour ($2). You'll also see some behind-the-scenes areas such as the animal hospital.

Keep in mind that while Southern Florida's semitropical climate makes it possible to build a cageless zoo, it also means that visitors are at the mercy of the weather. Try to plan your day accordingly: Metrozoo doesn't issue rain passes.

Other Things to Do Nearby The Gold Coast Railroad Museum is located outside of the entrance of Metrozoo. Other nearby attractions include the Weeks Air Museum and, closer to Miami, Parrot Jungle and the Fairchild Tropical Garden. But if you've done justice to Metrozoo, you'll be too tired for more sight-seeing.

Miami Museum of Science & Space Transit Planetarium

Type of Attraction: A kid-friendly science museum and a planetarium for space cadet wannabes. Self-guided tours.

Location: 3280 South Miami Avenue, Miami, where I-95 merges into US 1.

Admission: $10 for adults, $6 for children ages 3–12, and $8 for students and seniors age 62 and older.

Hours: Museum: 10 a.m. to 6 p.m., daily. Closed Thanksgiving and Christmas Days. Planetarium shows are offered on the hour beginning at 1 p.m. weekdays, 11 a.m. weekends

Phone: (305) 854-4247

When to Go: Weekends are usually more crowded than weekdays. But if you're planning to come during the week, call the day before to find out if any school groups are scheduled for the day you plan to visit: Three bus loads of second graders running amok in the museum can ruin the experience. Otherwise, the museum is rarely crowded unless a new exhibit just opened.

Special Comments: The Wildlife Center offers close-up views of a wide variety of live animals, from huge tortoises to a bald eagle. If you've got small children in your party and Metrozoo isn't on your itinerary, stop here.

Overall Appeal by Age Group:

Pre-school	Grade School	Teens	Young Adults	Over 30	Senior Citizens
★★★★	★★★★	★★	★	★	★

Author's Rating: A high-tech play area for kids. ★

How Much Time to Allow: One to two hours, but you may have to drag younger kids away. Shows in the planetarium last a little longer than a half-hour.

Description and Comments While this science museum will thrill youngsters, older visitors can't help but notice the worn indoor/outdoor carpeting, the exhibits that don't work, and its overall shabby appearance. In fact, the museum looks even more forlorn than on our initial visit three years ago. Overall, it's more like a high-tech playground for kids than a museum.

Touring Tips During the week, come in the afternoon to avoid school groups.

Other Things to Do Nearby Coconut Grove has a huge selection of eateries, drinkeries, and shopping opportunities. The nearby Rickenbacker

Causeway leads to Seaquarium and posh Key Biscayne; Coral Gables and the Miracle Mile are only minutes away. Vizcaya is just across the street. The Lowe Art Museum offers the best collection of art in South Florida.

Parrot Jungle and Gardens

Type of Attraction: A bird sanctuary and botanical gardens that also include trained bird shows, a flock of pink flamingos, and wildlife shows. A self-guided tour.

Location: 11000 SW 57th Avenue (South Red Road), about 11 miles south of downtown Miami. Take I-95 south until it turns into US 1, then turn left on SW 57th Avenue; the entrance is on the right.

Admission: $12.95 for adults, $8.95 for children ages 3–12.

Hours: 9:30 a.m. to 6 p.m., daily.

Phone: (305) 666-7834

When to Go: Weekends are usually very crowded, so try to arrive before 2 p.m. to beat the worst of the crowds. Monday through Wednesday are the least crowded days.

Special Comments: Parrot Jungle is scheduled to move and reopen on 18.6 acres on the north side of Watson Island (the first island on the way to Miami Beach on the MacArthur Causeway) in spring 1999. While that's a more convenient location, it's hard to imagine all this tropical lushness being recreated in a new spot—which is all the more reason to make the trip to South Miami and visit this venerable Miami tourist site in its old digs, which will remain open until the new $26 million park debuts. When you do visit the existing Parrot Jungle, expect to get lost (well, disoriented) as you wander through this lush—but small—tropical paradise.

Overall Appeal by Age Group:

Pre-school	Grade School	Teens	Young Adults	Over 30	Senior Citizens
★★★★★	★★★★★	★★★★½	★★★★	★★★★	★★★★

Author's Rating: What a hoot—or, better yet, screech. Don't miss it. ★★★★½

How Much Time to Allow: Two hours if you want to catch all the shows.

Description and Comments You'll find a lot more than a zillion parrots (actually, about 2,000) at Parrot Jungle. Alligators, gibbons, pink flamingos, tortoises, a children's playground, a petting zoo, and a Miccosukee Indian display are waiting to be discovered in this lush tropical garden. Fortunately, winding paths disperse the crowds that flock to this place throughout its 12 acres. Along the way you'll see more than 1,100 varieties of birds and more than 1,000 types of plants. It's a great park and a real Florida classic.

Touring Tips Don't miss the trained bird show in the Parrot Bowl Amphitheater: macaws and cockatoos ride bikes, drive trucks, and race chariots. Watch trainers work with young birds in the Baby Bird Training Area, and see non-avian Florida wildlife in the Jungle Theater. In the Bird Posing Area get your picture taken with a macaw perched on your head; there's no charge.

Other Things to Do Nearby Fairchild Tropical Garden will restore your sense of tranquility after touring the Parrot Jungle on a crowded day; Coconut Grove features eateries, bars, shops, and great people-watching. The Lowe Art Museum is on the Coral Gables campus of the University of Miami, just off US 1.

Seaquarium

Type of Attraction: A tropical marine aquarium. A self-guided tour.

Location: 4400 Rickenbacker Causeway (on Virginia Key between Key Biscayne and Miami).

Admission: $19.95 plus tax for adults, $15.95 plus tax for children ages 3–9, children under age 3 admitted free. Parking is $3 and the causeway toll is $1.

Hours: 9:30 a.m. to 6 p.m., daily; ticket office closes at 4:30 p.m.

Phone: (305) 361-5705

When to Go: During the high tourist season (Christmas through April), try to arrive at 9:30 a.m. You can catch all of the shows by 1:30 p.m. and miss most of the crowds. Monday is the slowest day of the week; the throngs peak on the weekend.

Special Comments: Kids will love the frolicking dolphins in the Flipper Show. Don't sit too close to the water during the shows or you'll get soaked by a diving dolphin or killer whale.

Overall Appeal by Age Group:

Pre-school	Grade School	Teens	Young Adults	Over 30	Senior Citizens
★★★★★	★★★★★	★★★★	★★★½	★★½	★★

Author's Rating: Very expensive—and a bit worn around the edges. And now you have to pay to park! ★★

How Much Time to Allow: Four hours to see all of the shows; two hours to see one or two shows and catch the exhibits that interest you.

Description and Comments Unquestionably, the hottest attraction at this South Florida tourist mainstay is Lolita, Seaquarium's killer whale. It's an adrenaline rush you don't want to miss when this 20-foot-long behemoth goes airborne—and lands with a splash that drenches the first ten rows of spectators. Plan your visit around the Killer Whale Show, usually offered twice daily. Call ahead for the schedule and plan your visit around the whale show.

Other performances at Seaquarium include the "Flipper" Show, a reef aquarium presentation, the Top Deck Dolphin Show, the Golden Dome Sea Lion Show, and a shark presentation. There's also a rain forest, a sealife touch pool, a wildlife habitat, a crocodile exhibit, and a tropical aquarium to view between shows.

The Seaquarium shows are slick and well orchestrated. But like the disco music played during the performances, this marine-life park struck us as a little worn . . . and outdated. (It's almost 40 years old.) And following the recent dose of consciousness-raising from the hit film *Free Willy* (and its sequels), a lot of folks may feel a twinge of guilt as they watch these magnificent, but captive, animals.

Touring Tips Plan your visit to Seaquarium so that you eat lunch before or after your visit: the food for sale in the aquarium is overpriced. Don't miss a manatee presentation, usually scheduled twice daily: It may be your only opportunity to see these docile, endangered mammals. A staffer talks about the manatees' plight and feeds them. You may also get to see a manatee do a "trick"—roll over on its back for the trainer. Then go see the "Flipper" Show for more action.

Other Things to Do Nearby Key Biscayne has plenty of places to eat and great beaches; back on the mainland, the Miami Museum of Science & Space Transit Planetarium is near the entrance to the Rickenbacker Causeway; Vizcaya, a fabulous estate and gardens, is across from the museum. The Lowe Museum of Art in Coral Gables is an excellent art museum.

Vizcaya Museum and Garden

Type of Attraction: A magnificent 16th-century Italian Renaissance–style villa and formal gardens built by the cofounder of International Harvester. Guided and self-guided tours.

Location: 3251 South Miami Avenue, Miami; near the Rickenbacker Causeway and across from the Miami Museum of Science.

Admission: $10 for adults, $5 for children ages 6–12; free for children age 5 and under.

Hours: 9:30 a.m. to 5 p.m., daily. The ticket booth closes at 4:30 p.m., and the gardens close at 5:30 p.m.

Phone: (305) 250-9133

When to Go: Vizcaya is rarely mobbed. To beat the crowds in the high tourist season (Christmas through April), try to arrive soon after the gates open in the morning.

Special Comments: The mansion is beautifully decorated for the holidays in December.

Overall Appeal by Age Group:

Pre-school	Grade School	Teens	Young Adults	Over 30	Senior Citizens
★	★★	★★½	★★★	★★★½	★★★★

Author's Rating: The mansion: Robber-baron decadence in a stunning setting on Biscayne Bay; so-so art. ★★★ The gardens: fabulous. ★★★★★

How Much Time to Allow: Two hours.

Description and Comments Chicago industrialist James Deering built his winter home on the shores of Biscayne Bay in 1916, an era when the fabulously rich weren't shy about showing off their wealth. Vizcaya's 34 rooms are loaded with period furniture, textiles, sculpture, and paintings from the 15th century through the early 19th century. The effect is that of a great country estate that's been continuously occupied for 400 years.

Most visitors go on a guided tour of the first floor that lasts 45 minutes. (If no tour guides are available, you're given a guidebook and turned loose.) Highlights of the magnificent rooms include a rug that Christopher Columbus stood on, an ornate telephone booth (check out the early example of a dial telephone), and dramatic carved ceilings and patterned marble floors. The house also has some eccentricities: Mr. Deering didn't like doors slamming from the continuous breeze off the bay, so many doors were hung at off-angles so they would close slowly. The breeze is not as much of a problem today: the proliferation of high-rise condos on Biscayne Bay blocks much of the wind.

Touring Tips After the guided tour, explore the second-floor bedrooms on your own. Then stroll the ten-acre formal gardens, which feature spectacular views of Biscayne Bay. The Great Stone Barge in front of Vizcaya's East Facade acts as a breakwater and creates a harbor for small boats.

Other Things to Do Nearby The Miami Museum of Science is across the street; Seaquarium and Key Biscayne are on the other side of the Rickenbacker Causeway; Coconut Grove is the place to go if you're hungry. The Lowe Museum of Art is on the campus of the University of Miami in Coral Gables, just off US 1.

Weeks Air Museum

Type of Attraction: A museum dedicated to the preservation and restoration of aircraft from the beginning of flight through World War II. A self-guided tour.

Location: Kendall-Tamiami Airport in Southwest Miami (on SW 137th Avenue, a few miles northwest of Metrozoo).

Admission: $5.95 for adults, $4.95 for seniors, $3.95 for children ages 4–12; free for children age 3 and under.

Hours: 10 a.m. to 5 p.m., daily.

Phone: (305) 233-5197

When to Go: Any time.

Special Comments: As restoration continues from the clobbering the museum took from Hurricane Andrew in 1992, more aircraft and exhibits will be added. An interesting note: The goal of the museum is to restore most of the planes on display to flying condition.

Overall Appeal by Age Group:

Pre-school	Grade School	Teens	Young Adults	Over 30	Senior Citizens
★	★★★	★★½	★★½	★★½	★★★½

Author's Rating: A small, attractive museum that will appeal to aviation and World War II history buffs—and those old enough to fondly recall the Swing Era. ★★½

How Much Time to Allow: One hour.

Description and Comments The big attractions here are full-sized, mostly World War II–era fighting aircraft that we've all seen in the movies—such as the huge Grumman F6F-3 Hellcat fighter that helped U.S. forces gain air superiority over Japan in the Pacific half a century ago. On the other end of the scale is the P-51 fighter, built for the European theater of war. While surprisingly small compared to the Hellcat, this sleek-looking warbird had the range to go "all the way" in its mission of protecting Allied bombers on their way to targets deep in Europe. Other fascinating airplanes on display include the Tempest (a British fighter bomber with a top speed of 440 mph), an A-26 Invader (a twin-engine bomber; steps leading up to the cockpit let visitors peek inside), and a German Messerschmidt ME-108 fighter.

Touring Tips Don't miss the exhibits on the Tuskegee Airmen, the all-black 99th Fighter squadron that fought with distinction in Africa, Sicily, and Europe. The well-stocked gift shops feature a wide selection of goodies that will appeal to aviation buffs, including model kits of World War II aircraft, prints, T-shirts, goatskin bomber jackets, and aviation-themed postcards.

Other Things to Do Nearby Metrozoo and the Gold Coast Railroad Museum are only minutes away. For something to eat, go out the main entrance of the airport and drive either north or south on SW 137th Avenue for a wide selection of fast-food eateries.

Zone 4: Southern Dade County

Biscayne National Park

Type of Attraction: The nation's largest aquatic park: 181,500 acres of underwater reefs, islands, and the closest coral reef snorkeling to Miami. Guided and self-guided tours.

Location: The Convoy Point Visitor Center, the only part of the park accessible by car, is about 25 miles south of Miami and six miles east of US 1 and Homestead. From the Florida Turnpike Extension take SW 328th Street (North Canal Drive) to the park entrance on the left.

Admission: Free. A park concession offers three-hour glass-bottom-boat tours of the bay and reef. The cost is $19.95 for adults, $17.95 for seniors, and $9.95 for children age 12 and under; the trips leave at 10 a.m. daily. Four-hour snorkeling trips to the reef are $27.50 per person and include all equipment; the boat leaves at 1:30 p.m. daily. Advance reservations for either trip are strongly advised. Canoe rentals are $8 an hour or $22 a half-day; prices include paddles and life jackets.

Hours: The visitor center is open daily, 8:30 a.m. to 5 p.m.

Phone: (305) 230-7275. For reservations for snorkel and boat trips, call (305) 230-1100

When to Go: Any time, weather permitting. While mosquitoes and other biting insects are present year-round, their populations are lowest from January to April. Around holiday weekends, call at least three days in advance for a reservation for a boat tour or diving trip. While reservations usually aren't necessary at other times, call ahead to make sure a boat trip isn't canceled due to a chartered event.

Special Comments: Because the park is almost completely underwater, visitors are at the mercy of the weather; tours and canoe rentals are sometimes canceled in windy conditions. If the air is cold, snorkelers can rent wet suits. Boat schedules change seasonally, so it's always a good idea to call first.

Overall Appeal by Age Group:

Pre-school	Grade School	Teens	Young Adults	Over 30	Senior Citizens
★★	★★★	★★★	★★★½	★★★★	★★★★

Author's Rating: Viewing a coral reef through a face mask or glass-bottomed boat sure beats looking at fish through glass in an aquarium. ★★★★

How Much Time to Allow: Half a day or longer.

Description and Comments Clear blue water, a bright yellow sun, dark green woodlands, coral reefs, and islands combine to create a subtropical paradise only an hour or so from hectic Miami. Unlike most parks, however, Biscayne is dominated by water—and enjoying it requires renting a canoe or taking a boat excursion.

The top attraction for most folks is snorkeling the coral reefs. Brilliantly colored tropical fish such as stoplight parrotfish, finger garlic sponge, goosehead scorpionfish, and peppermint goby populate the shallow-water reefs drenched in sunlight. A reef explorer outfitted in mask, snorkel, flippers, and a life vest can spend hours drifting lazily in the waters above the reefs while watching a procession of astounding marine life.

Touring Tips Call at least a day ahead of time to make reservations for a boat trip. Exploring the reefs is best on calm, sunny days. Unless you're an experienced snorkeler or diver, go on the group trip, which is run by experts who provide plenty of hand-holding for novices. Canoes are available for rent for exploring the mangrove shoreline along the mainland. Fishermen can try their luck for saltwater fish from the jetty; stop at the visitor center for regulations and in Homestead for fishing licenses. The new visitor center is attractive and has a few small displays on bay ecology, local history, and Hurricane Andrew.

Other Things to Do Nearby The Everglades National Park is due west of Homestead. If you haven't had your fill of Florida tourist schlock yet, stop by the Coral Castle, just north of Homestead on US 1. You'll also find a nearly endless selection of fast-food joints along the venerable old highway.

Coral Castle

Type of Attraction: A Latvian eccentric's hand-built, coral-block monument to the fiancée who jilted him. A self-guided tour.

Location: 28655 South Federal Highway (at SW 286th Street)—about 20 miles south of Miami on US 1; 10 miles north of Homestead.

Admission: $7.75 for adults, $6.50 for seniors, $5 for children ages 7–12. Free for children under age 7 (with paying adult).

Hours: 9 a.m. to 6 p.m., daily.

Phone: (305) 248-6344

When to Go: On weekends, arrive by 11 a.m. to beat the crowds.

Special Comments: The Coral Castle shares a trait with the Spanish Monastery in North Miami Beach: its history is more interesting than the attraction.

Overall Appeal by Age Group:

Pre-school	Grade School	Teens	Young Adults	Over 30	Senior Citizens
★	★★	★★	★★½	★★	★★

Author's Rating: Don't waste your time or money on this one. ★

How Much Time to Allow: 30 minutes.

Description and Comments For reasons unknown, Latvian weirdo Edward Leedskalnin (who died in 1951) carved this bizarre monument to "Sweet Sixteen," a girlfriend who jilted him back in the Old Country. He single-handedly cut and moved huge coral blocks using hand tools—a notable feat, but the results are hardly a "castle." It's essentially a courtyard filled with carvings of huge coral chairs, a table that doubles as a bird bath, a fountain, a sundial, and other stone oddities.

Some folks find the structures eerie and amazing—and, no doubt about it, the Coral Castle is genuine Florida kitsch. Our opinion: Unless you're a mechanical engineer fascinated by how this guy moved all this rock around, save yourself some money and skip it.

Touring Tips If you decide to plunk down the cost of admission, don't miss the nine-ton coral gate. It is, the tour brochure says, "Ed's most outstanding achievement." We agree—but it's hardly anything to brag about. The big rock weighs 18,000 pounds and, the brochure continues, "can be moved, using one finger to push it." Right. It took a hearty shove from our 200-pound reporter to budge the hunk of coral.

Other Things to Do Nearby The Fruit & Spice Park and Monkey Jungle are nearby. To the south, Homestead is the jumping-off point to the Everglades and Biscayne National Parks, and the Keys.

Fruit & Spice Park

Type of Attraction: A showcase for the South Florida agricultural community featuring more than 500 varieties of exotic fruits, herbs, spices, and nuts from around the world. A self-guided tour.

Location: 35 miles south of downtown Miami. From US 1, drive west on SW 248th Street (Coconut Palm Drive). The entrance is on the left after SW 187th Avenue (Redland Road).

Admission: $3.50 for adults, $1 for children under age 12.

Hours: 10 a.m. to 5 p.m., daily.

Phone: (305) 247-5727

When to Go: Any time. In January, the Redland Natural Arts Festival features artists, crafts people, and outdoors people who draw big crowds to the park.

Special Comments: The gift shop has a wide and exotic selection of chutneys, pickles, jams, jellies, marinades, and other fruit-related goodies for sale.

Overall Appeal by Age Group:

Pre-school	Grade School	Teens	Young Adults	Over 30	Senior Citizens
★	★½	★	★★	★★½	★★★

Author's Rating: For the horticulturally inclined. ★½

How Much Time to Allow: One hour.

Description and Comments The 30-acre park contains an astounding selection of exotic, fruit-bearing plants—and you're free to sample anything that's hit the ground. (No above-ground harvesting permitted.) The well-manicured grounds also feature picnic tables and rest rooms; cold drinks are sold in the gift shop. It's the only park of its kind in the United States.

Touring Tips Guided tours are offered weekends at 1 p.m. and 3 p.m. Satisfy any hunger pangs *before* visiting the poisonous plant area.

Other Things to Do Nearby Some South Florida classic attractions are within an easy drive: the Coral Castle and Monkey Jungle. For folks looking for fresh fruit and vegetables right off the vine, stop at a "U Pick" field. For a reasonable fee you can pick everything from corn to tomatoes, squash, cucumbers, and strawberries. Most "U Pick" fields are open from November through April.

Monkey Jungle

Type of Attraction: A primate zoo where visitors walk in screened walkways that pass through large "habitats" (actually, larger cages) that feature a wide variety of monkeys. A self-guided tour.

Location: 14805 SW 216th Street (Hainlin Mill Drive), about 20 miles south of Miami. Take the Florida Turnpike Extension to Exit 11 (SW 216th Street) west and drive 3 miles to the entrance on the right.

Admission: $11.50 for adults, $9.50 for seniors, $6 for children ages 4–12; free for children age 3 and under.

Hours: 9:30 a.m. to 5 p.m., daily. Ticket office closes at 4 p.m.

Phone: (305) 235-1611

When to Go: Avoid the hottest times of the day by arriving by 10 a.m. or just before 4 p.m. Crowds are lighter during the week than on weekends.

Special Comments: Don't forget mosquito repellent; visitors are outside the entire time. If it rains, pick up a rain pass at the entrance.

Overall Appeal by Age Group:

Pre-school	Grade School	Teens	Young Adults	Over 30	Senior Citizens
★★★★★	★★★★★	★★★★	★★★	★★★	★★★

Author's Rating: A lot of fun—and it's okay to feed the primates. ★★★½

How Much Time to Allow: One hour; two hours if you want to catch all the shows.

Description and Comments Gibbons, spider monkeys, orangutans, a gorilla, chimpanzees, and more are close at hand as you walk through screened walkways that wind through a tropical forest. While not all the monkeys roam free—a lot of them reside in large cages located along the walkways—many primates can be seen when you pass through the larger jungle habitat. Founded in the 1930s, Monkey Jungle is a slice of pre-Disney Florida that most visitors shouldn't miss.

Touring Tips Bring quarters; monkey food dispensers that resemble bubblegum machines are located along the walkways. Four different shows featuring swimming monkeys, a gorilla, twin chimpanzees, and orangutans start at 10 a.m. and run continuously at 45-minute intervals.

Other Things to Do Nearby Coral Castle, Metrozoo, the Weeks Air Museum, and the Gold Coast Railroad Museum are nearby. For something different—and a little less touristy—stop by the Fruit & Spice Park on SW 248th Street, about five miles away.

Part Eleven

The Everglades

Introduction

If a restless urge hits you to do more than just laze on the beach and vibrate in sync with Miami's caffeine-fueled rhythms, take a day trip to a place that feels like it's a million miles away—the Everglades.

While eyes adjusted to the gaudiness of Miami's beaches and urban landscapes need time to adapt, the Everglades is a unique destination that offers a satisfying contrast to the high-tempo city—and it's not much more than an hour away by car. But be warned: some folks fall in love with this subtly gorgeous, tranquil place and don't want to leave.

It's Not a Swamp

The Everglades ecosystem encompasses a major chunk of South Florida, including the 2,100-square-mile Everglades National Park, the second largest national park (after Yellowstone) in the lower 48 states. To many people who have never been here—or have only driven through—the Everglades may seem to be nothing to get excited about. It looks like just a broad expanse of grass, water, and trees. In other words, just another swamp.

They're wrong. The Everglades is, in fact, the last remaining subtropical wilderness in the continental United States. This huge expanse of water, sawgrass, clumps of trees called "hammocks," and pockets of tropical jungle is also an unparalleled wildlife sanctuary containing an astounding variety of mammals, reptiles, birds, and fish. Our advice: Folks who enjoy the outdoors and thrill to seeing wildlife in its natural environment should put the Everglades on their "A" list during a visit to South Florida.

A trip to the Everglades, while only a brief drive from Miami, entirely removes visitors from the hubbub of daily life in the big city. It's all replaced by the cries of birds, the splash of fish leaping from the water, and the sound

Everglades National Park

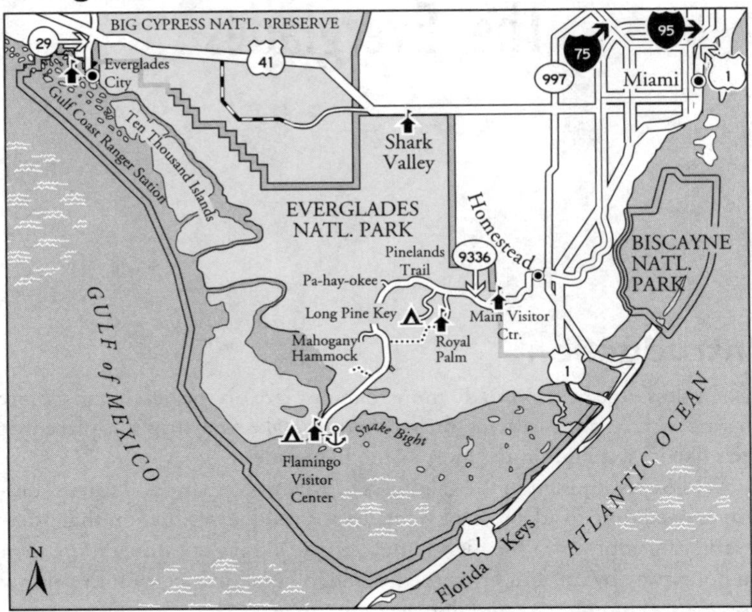

of the wind rippling through the sawgrass. The almost limitless expanses of natural beauty remind us that humans are not really the center of the universe.

A Vast, Slow-Moving River

Admittedly, the Everglades doesn't look like very much when viewed through a car window: seemingly endless expanses of grass and water fade into the distance, with only an occasional clump of trees to break the monotony.

These apparently empty spaces, however, are deceiving: the landscape is teeming with life and activity. The Everglades is a complex, evolving ecosystem that is the result of a unique combination of climate, topography, and vegetation. To experience the Everglades—and to find out what's so special about it—you've got to get out of your car.

To appreciate the Everglades, it helps to understand what's going on here. This huge expanse of grass and water is a vast, slow-moving, shallow river that's flowing over land nearly as flat as a pool table. For eons, the overflow of Lake Okeechobee to the north has moved south slowly over this land into Florida Bay, nourishing millions of acres of sawgrass as the water ebbs and flows.

In her best-selling 1947 book, *The Everglades: River of Grass,* Florida environmentalist Marjory Stoneman Douglas popularized the notion of the Everglades as a vast, flowing river. Douglas, who died in 1998 at the age of 107, continued to write and speak out about preserving this unique ecosystem until the end of her life. She did so because the Everglades is in serious danger of being destroyed.

The Everglades used to encompass everything south of Lake Okeechobee—including Miami—but encroaching civilization has pushed its perimeter back until today the Everglades is only a fraction of its former size. Today's Everglades National Park makes up only about one-seventh of what's left of the Everglades, and it's the only portion of the ecosystem that's federally protected. New initiatives to save this unique ecosystem include $200 million in funds provided by Congress in 1996. But true restoration, experts say, is a long-term goal and will be very expensive. Pick up almost any edition of the *Miami Herald* and you'll find news articles reporting the raging controversies surrounding efforts to protect the remaining—and seriously threatened—portions of this unique environment.

While the Everglades is subtle and doesn't easily give up its charms to short-term visitors, day-trippers can still gain an appreciation of the area and enjoy a rewarding visit—at least during the winter months, when the mosquito population is down; we don't recommend visiting the Everglades April through October, when mosquitoes and other biting insects make a visit unbearable. (But even in winter, apply insect repellent on an Everglades visit.) Another reason to visit in the winter is that you'll see more wildlife. Winter is the dry season, and a vast array of animals and birds congregate near the remaining water.

Where to Go

Shark Valley

From Miami, the closest entrance to Everglades National Park is *Shark Valley,* located on Route 41 (the Tamiami Trail) about 35 miles west of downtown. (Another entrance, the Western Water Gateway at Everglades City on the Gulf Coast, is 80 miles west of Miami and more convenient for visitors traveling from Florida's west coast.) To avoid a seemingly endless procession of traffic lights on SW 8th Street (Route 41 in the city), take Route 836 (the Dolphin Expressway) west to the Florida Turnpike, and go south one exit to Route 41 west. Admission to the park is $10 and is good for a week at this and other park entrances. For more information, call Everglades National Park at (305) 242-7700.

Take the Tram

If a day trip to Shark Valley is your only visit to the Everglades, our advice is to take the two-hour, motorized-tram tour that leaves from the Shark Valley parking lot on the hour from 9 a.m. to 4 p.m. daily in the winter and at 9:30 a.m, 11 a.m., 1 p.m., and 3 p.m. daily in the summer. The cost is $9 for adults, $8.10 for seniors, and $5 for children under age 12. (Try to arrive early; the parking lot is small and this is a popular visitor destination.) Reservations are recommended for tram tours; call (305) 221-8455.

Soon after the open-air tram leaves the visitor center, you'll discover what all the excitement is about as you view an incredible number of birds, alligators resting beside the narrow road, and a beautiful landscape. Well-informed and enthusiastic guides do a good job of explaining the unique topography and pointing out the unusual fauna. The tram stops often to let visitors view and photograph the wildlife and terrain.

The tram follows a 15-mile paved loop road. At the halfway point, visitors disembark at an observation tower for one of the best views in South Florida: a 360-degree, 18-mile panorama of the Everglades. Rest rooms, vending machines, and water fountains are also available at the 20-minute stop.

Rental Bikes and Binoculars

Another option when visiting Shark Valley is to rent a bicycle at the visitor center. Single-speed bikes rent for $4 an hour between 8:30 a.m. and 3 p.m.; bikes must be returned by 4 p.m. And don't forget to bring binoculars when you visit; if you forget, rent a pair at the visitor center.

Airboats

Another highlight of a Shark Valley excursion: taking an *airboat ride.* While the motorized contraptions are illegal inside the national park, small airboat operations found all along Route 41 offer visitors 30-minute rides into the 'Glades. The excursions may not be "ecologically correct"—the boats are big, extremely noisy, and, some say, destructive to the environment—but a ride on one sure is fun.

Most drivers make a stop at a hammock (a small, wooded island) that features a re-creation of an Indian village. Your driver will often try to locate some alligators, usually small specimens two or three feet in length. "They look cute," my driver said as he tossed pieces of bread into the water to attract the critters, "but they've got as many teeth as an adult." We kept our hands inside the boat.

Note: Airboats are so incredibly loud that customers are given wads of cotton to stuff in their ears. You need them. Very small children may be frightened by the noise. The price for a half-hour ride ranges from $7 to $9 per person.

An Indian Village

The Miccosukee Indians are descendants of Seminole Indians who retreated into the Everglades to escape forced resettlement during the 19th century. They lived on hammocks in open-sided "chickees"—thatched-roof huts built from cypress—and hunted and fished the Everglades by canoe. They also learned how to handle alligators.

At the *Miccosukee Indian Village,* on Route 41 a mile or so west of the Shark Valley entrance to Everglades National Park, alligators are the stars of the show—and if this your only opportunity to visit the Everglades, this is your chance to see an alligator do more than snooze in the sun. Alligator wrestling exhibitions are offered at 11 a.m., 12:30 p.m., 1:30 p.m., 3 p.m., and 4:40 p.m.; admission to the attraction is $5 for adults and $3.50 for children ages 4–12. Airboat rides are $7 per person. The hours are 9 a.m. to 4:15 p.m. daily. For more information, call (305) 223-8380.

In addition to seeing a Miccosukee Indian put a live gator through its paces, you'll get a peek at Miccosukee culture and life on a tour of the "village" (a small collection of open-air chickees and alligator pens) and a small museum. Lots of crafts and tacky souvenirs are also offered for sale.

The Royal Palm Visitor Center

Another option for both day-trippers to Everglades National Park and folks who want to spend a few days in the Everglades starts south of Miami near Florida City at the *Royal Palm Visitor Center,* located at the park's main entrance. To get there, take Route 9336 from US 1 at Homestead for 10 miles to the gate; admission is $10 per car and is good for a week.

While this entrance to the park is a longer drive for most folks—more than an hour from downtown Miami in non–rush hour traffic—it's worth the time and effort. The new visitor center (it replaces the one destroyed by Hurricane Andrew) features interactive displays, a small theater, and an enclosed walkway to a "borrow"—a water-filled pit created when coral was excavated. Visitors can pick up free brochures, view educational displays, obtain information on boat tours and canoe rentals, and get a map to the many trails that intersect with the 38-mile main road that leads to Flamingo. While Flamingo is a stretch for day-trippers, the village is the park's largest visitor complex, featuring a motel, a restaurant, a small grocery store, campgrounds, boat tours, a marina, and a visitor center.

Easy Walks

The two-lane road also serves as the jumping-off point for short walking explorations into the Everglades. This end of the park, by the way, is a better destination for folks who prefer walking and exploring on their own over the guided tram tour offered at Shark Valley.

A well-planned day here will quickly reveal much that's fascinating about the Everglades. The nearby *Anhinga Trail* is a half-mile boardwalk that takes visitors through areas teeming with wildlife and shows off the subtle beauty of the region at its best. The adjacent *Gumbo Limbo Trail,* on the other hand, is completely different: the one-third-mile-long asphalt-covered path takes visitors through a dense jungle unique to South Florida.

Other stops visitors should make along the road to Flamingo include the *Pa-hay-okee Overlook, Mahogany Hammock,* featuring the largest stand of mahogany trees in the United States, and a number of ponds that offer views of bird life that may be unequaled anywhere else in the world. All the trails are on boardwalks, so there's no need to worry about wet feet.

Flamingo

The end of the road is the village of *Flamingo,* which offers visitors boat rides on Florida Bay, canoe rentals, birding cruises, backcountry boat excursions, a restaurant, a marina, and the only overnight sleeping facilities in the park (outside of primitive camping). If you've got the time and interest, it's a great place for an extended visit.

Overnight visitors should plan to take a sunset cruise on the *Bald Eagle,* a large pontoon boat that cruises Florida Bay for 90 minutes several times a day. The views of the bay, dense mangrove forests, and the shoreline are spectacular, and the guide narrating our tour offered first-time visitors a few words of wisdom: "A lot of people blast down here from Homestead at 65 miles per hour, get here and ask us, 'What is there to do?' Folks, that's not the way to do it."

His suggestion: "There's a lot of subtle beauty here and you've got to relax to see it. Get away from your car, walk one of the trails or rent a canoe." As the guide spoke, huge flocks of birds were leaving the mainland and flying across the bay through the light of the setting sun to roost on uninhabited keys. His point was made.

The sight-seeing tour of the bay is $10 for adults and $5 for children ages 6–12. Other services visitors can use to explore the Flamingo area include canoe rentals ($22 for a half-day and $32 for a full day) and bicycle rentals ($8 for a half-day and $14 all day).

Rates at the *Flamingo Lodge Marina & Outpost Resort's* comfortable (but not fancy) motel are $98 a night from December 15 to March 31, single or double occupancy (plus 11.5% tax); $66 from May 1 to October 31; $83 from November 1 to December 14 and from April 1 to April 30. Fully equipped cottages and houseboats are also available for rent. Call the lodge at (941) 695-3101 for more information and at (800) 600-3813 to make reservations.

An Alligator Farm

Outside the park entrance near Florida City is another small, private attraction worth a look: the *Everglades Alligator Farm.* More than 3,000 alligators (most of them little guys in "grow out" pens), a collection of snakes and crocodiles (including an eight-and-a-half-foot-long speckled caiman), two mountain lions, two lynxes, and a black bear reside in this minizoo. The farm is located on SW 192nd Avenue; follow the signs out of Florida City.

The two main attractions are a 20-minute alligator show (a handler "wrestles" a gator and answers questions from visitors) and the only airboat rides on this end of the Everglades (no airboats are allowed in the national park). Alligator feedings, alligator shows, and snake shows alternate on the hour. Don't plan to stick around for all three shows, though. This attraction is too small to invest that much time.

The park is open from 9 a.m. to 6 p.m. daily; admission is $12.50 for adults, $6 for children ages 4–12, and free for children age 3 and under, which includes a 30-minute airboat ride. Skip the ride and admission is $7 for adults and $3 for kids. Our advice: Go for the ride. For more information, call the gator farm at (800) 644-9711 or (305) 247-2628.

Part Twelve

The Florida Keys

Introduction to the Keys

Say the words "Florida Keys," and most folks think of black-and-white images of Humphrey Bogart in *Key Largo* weathering a hurricane in an old clapboard house with a nasty Edward G. Robinson. Or maybe they picture a robust Ernest Hemingway imbibing at Sloppy Joe's and penning yet another masterpiece in his study. Others flash on ex-hippies and artists reliving the late '60s in laid-back Key West.

Alas, most of these romantic images come from a never-ending flow of fiction, film, and public-relations hype. Today's reality is that the Keys are a tourist, diving, and sportfishing mecca that draws over a million visitors each year. It's been more than a decade, locals say, since the Keys' earthy, rum-soaked sleaziness was largely pushed aside by restoration, revitalization, and the good intentions of the tourist industry.

The End of the Road

But dig a little deeper into the Keys' mystique and you'll find a hard-to-ignore fact: this is, after all, the end of the road—literally. US 1 stretches for more than 100 miles beyond the tip of mainland South Florida, linking a string of islands that form a natural barrier between the Atlantic Ocean and the Gulf of Mexico that ends up closer to Cuba than to the U.S. mainland.

While the PR copy overstates the romance, intrigue, and hipness to be found in the Keys, there are remnants of an end-of-the-road feel—in Key West, anyway. Here you'll find a sense of escape into the exotic, a feeling that your next step might be the jungles of South America, or the equally exotic world of different attitudes, some of which might not be happily tolerated on the mainland. While the Keys are increasingly touristy and overdeveloped, they still afford a comfortable abode for misfits and dropouts, artists and writers, gays and lesbians, and anyone else not in lock step with the American dream.

A Geographic Overview of the Keys

Physically, the Florida Keys are a 150-mile chain of islands made of fossilized coral rock. In the 18th and 19th centuries, pirates buried treasure here, fortunes were made scavenging sea wrecks on the reef, and smugglers and slave traders plied their trades, finding cover in the lush, dark hardwood hammocks located on the islands.

A few miles offshore lies the jungle of the sea, the coral reef. Thousands of sea plants and animals thrive in and around the coral reef in water anywhere from 10 to 60 feet deep. The cracks and holes in the reef provide protection or homes for all types of marine animals. The variety of life on display makes for a moving kaleidoscope of colors and shapes—and a wonderland for divers and snorkelers. The living, slow-growing reef is very fragile, however, and visitors must be careful not to stand on, sit on, or touch the coral, because it will die. Doing so, by the way, almost always results in a painful scratch.

Early History

Not long after Christopher Columbus set foot in the New World in 1492, Spanish explorers Ponce de Leon and Antonio de Herrera were the first Europeans to sight the Florida Keys, on May 15, 1513. Over the next few centuries, pirates were the only Europeans to visit the string of islands.

Key West was not settled until 1822, and development in the rest of the Keys came even later. Early settlers farmed productive groves of Key limes, tamarind, and breadfruit. In the Lower Keys, pineapple farms flourished, and a large pineapple processing factory supplied canned pineapple to most of the eastern United States.

The real money, however, was in salvaging cargo from ships sunk on nearby reefs—huge fortunes were made. As a result of the efforts of the "wreckers," Key West became the wealthiest city in the early years of the American republic. Later, sponge fishermen developed a thriving market for the high-quality sponges harvested in the waters off Key West. Later, cigar makers from Cuba built factories in the city.

Decades of Boom and Bust

Henry Flagler, the associate of John D. Rockefeller who opened up the east coast of Florida at the end of the 19th century with his railroad, extended his tracks to the Keys in 1905. The Overseas Railroad—also called "Flagler's Folly"—was an incredible engineering feat for its time. The greatest technical achievement was the Seven Mile Bridge, which links Marathon to the Lower Keys. The railroad reached Key West in 1912 and wealthy visitors took the train to vacation here.

The Depression years were bleak in the Keys, and Key West declared bankruptcy in 1934. More bad luck: While Flagler's bridges took everything Mother Nature threw their way, the Labor Day hurricane of 1935 tore up the railroad; the bridges later were adapted for roadways. In 1938, the Overseas Railroad became the Overseas Highway.

The new road opened up hope for the renewal of tourism, but World War II intervened. During the war, the opening of a submarine base in Key West started an economic revival, as boosted by the development of a commercial shrimp industry. Ernest Hemingway and other notable writers and artists called Key West home—at least some of the year—and enhanced its reputation as a mecca for creative types. The most recent, tourist-fueled economic upswing began in the early 1980s—and, judging by the size of the crowds on Duval Street, it shows no signs of letting up.

Why Go to the Florida Keys?

The Florida Keys are the primary vacation destination for about 1.5 million people who visit South Florida each year. Most, but not all, are outdoorsy people who come to enjoy the islands' unique location between two large bodies of water: the Atlantic Ocean and the Gulf of Mexico.

The mingling of these waters results in a fantastic array of marine life—and world-class sportfishing. Some visitors come to dive and snorkel in gin-clear waters and view the only coral reef in the United States. (For more information on diving and snorkeling in the Keys, see Part Seven: Exercise and Recreation, page 149.) Others explore the Keys' unusual and beautiful backcountry that is full of birds and marine life. Finally, Key West is a popular tourist destination that draws over a million visitors each year.

One reason *not* to come to the Keys is to savor miles and miles of gleaming white beaches: There's no naturally occurring sand. It takes waves to make sand, and the offshore reef eliminates the surf action.

Day-Tripping to the Keys

For folks on a visit to Miami who can spare a day or two out of their schedule, the Keys offer a dramatic—and usually appreciated—contrast to the high-octane, overcaffeinated pace of hot, hot, hot Miami. The Upper Keys aren't much more than an hour's drive away from the city. Most folks who take a day trip to the Keys don't get below the Upper Keys; if you only have a day yet *must* visit Key West, we suggest taking a bus tour. See the chapter on specialized tours, page 172, for information on commercial tours to Key West.

When to Visit the Keys

The tourist season in the Florida Keys roughly mirrors that of Miami and the rest of South Florida. The winter season begins in mid-November and ends around Easter; both Christmas and Easter are periods when hotels, motels, restaurants, and other tourist-dependent facilities are jammed.

While the summer months are off-season, keep in mind that the Keys are a popular destination for many South Florida residents seeking relief from the intense heat and humidity; the Keys are typically 10 degrees cooler than Miami and much breezier. As a result, a lot of native Floridians jam US 1 on Friday afternoons and evenings during the summer for a weekend escape; most of them return on the following Sunday evening. Out-of-state visitors should try to avoid the weekend traffic crushes.

The summer months are also increasingly popular with foreign visitors, especially those from Asia and Germany. Increasingly, Key West's popularity as a port of destination on minicruises out of Miami and Fort Lauderdale is resulting in many people returning to the town for a summer vacation.

Summer visitors discover that rooms are cheaper and Key West is less crowded. A note to anglers: While migrating tarpon swim past the Keys April through June, don't expect to find a fishing guide who's available; they're booked at least a year in advance—unless you get lucky and there's a cancellation.

Locals say the best months to visit the Keys are September and October: the weather is warm, crowds are nonexistent and lodging is cheaper.

How to Get More Information Before Your Trip

For additional information on Key West and the Florida Keys, call (800) FLA-KEYS (352-5397). If you're planning on visiting Key West, for example, you can get an accommodations guide listing hotels, motels, bed and breakfasts, rental properties, and real estate agents. All the information is free.

Getting to the Keys

By Plane

While both Key West (at the end of the string of islands) and Marathon (located in the Middle Keys) have small commercial airports, most folks headed to the Keys by air arrive at Miami International Airport, rent a car, and drive to their final destination.

A glance at a map shows why: MIA is located west of Miami near Route 836, a major east-west highway that connects with Florida's Turnpike

Homestead Extension. You can literally be in the Upper Keys within an hour after landing at MIA—if you didn't check any baggage and the line at the rental car agency is short. If your final destination is Key West, figure on about a three-hour drive from the airport, or longer if it's a Friday afternoon.

For folks concerned about Miami's reputation for crime against tourists, we have good news: getting to the Keys from MIA takes you *away* from high-crime areas, not through them. At the rental car agency, get explicit driving directions. Most people will take LeJeune Road south to Route 836 west. After you get on Route 836, it's about six miles to Florida's Turnpike. Take it south to Homestead, another 12 miles or so.

Continuing to the Keys by Car

From the end of Florida's Turnpike at Florida City, *US 1* heads south toward the tip of Florida through stands of tangled mangrove and thick trees; Mile Marker 127, just south of Homestead, counts down to Mile Marker 00 in Key West.

Say good-bye to four-lane expressways: US 1 is a mostly two-lane road as it heads over land and water on its way to Key West. Traffic on the narrow road can be a bear, especially around weekends and holidays, when many South Floridians and tourists head for Key West and other points along the way. During the winter, avoid driving to the Keys on Friday afternoons and evenings, and on Sunday evenings. The traffic is usually horrendous and multihour backups are routine.

And don't think that off-season is any better. That's when Miami residents and other South Floridians descend on the Keys by the thousands to escape the heat and humidity that bakes Miami in the summer. Try to leave on Friday morning and return on Monday to beat the worst of the weekend traffic.

After passing Florida City, you can make a more dramatic entrance to the Keys than ho-hum US 1 by hanging a left onto *Card Sound Road* (Route 905A). You'll miss most of the tourist traffic heading south and the toll bridge over Card Sound offers a great view of undeveloped Key Largo and Florida Bay. Savor the view—farther south on Key Largo, the commercialism is rampant.

Driving South toward Key West: The Upper Keys

After merging back with US 1 (now also called the Overseas Highway), continue south on to *Key Largo.* The name is pure hype: The eponymous, late '40s flick starring Bogart and Robinson wasn't filmed here. The local flacks changed the name of the island from Rock Harbor to Key Largo to cash in on the publicity generated by the movie.

More tenuous links with Tinseltown are on tap at the local Holiday Inn, where the original *African Queen,* the small, steam-powered boat used in the film of the same name starring Bogie and Katharine Hepburn, is on display in the hotel's marina (when it's not on promotional tours). Needless to say, that film wasn't made here either—it was filmed in England and Africa.

Welcome to Suburbia

From US 1, don't expect a whole lot in the way of legendary Keys' ambience. Key Largo is close enough to Homestead and the southern 'burbs of Miami to serve as a bedroom community to the city, and strip malls, restaurants, gas stations, and fast-food joints line the highway. To find anything interesting to see, you've got to get off the island.

Luckily, that's easy to do. *John Pennecamp Coral Reef State Park,* located at Mile Marker 102.5, offers visitors an easy escape to snorkeling, diving, and glass-bottom-boat trips. In addition, a small sandy beach (a rare commodity in the Keys) and a visitor center make this unusual park a worthwhile stop. (See the chapter on sights in the Florida Keys for more information.) The park is also a major draw for the million-plus divers who come to Key Largo each year, making it the "Diving Capital of the U.S."

Another snorkeling option is *Key Largo Undersea Park,* an acre-wide enclosed lagoon where snorkelers can swim with more than 100 marine species. Other attractions include an underwater hotel, a working undersea marine research center, marine archaeology experiments, and an underwater art studio. First-time snorkelers get expert supervision, extensive preswim instruction, and enjoy the placid waters of the inshore lagoon.

The park is open daily from 9 a.m. to 3 p.m.; admission is free and self-guided tours are $10 (which includes use of a mask, snorkel, fins, and life vest). The rate for a family of four is $35. Scuba diving in the lagoon costs $20 for a one-tank dive without equipment, and $40 per person with all equipment. For directions and more information, call (305) 451-2353.

Tavernier is the next town traversed as you continue south on US 1. *Harry Harris Park,* located on the left at Mile Marker 92.5, is a county park offering a sandy beach, a tidal pool, barbecue pits, picnic tables, a playground—and an excuse to pull over and relax.

Past Tavernier is a 20-mile stretch of islands collectively known as Islamorada (pronounced EYE-la-ma-RAHD-a), which touts itself as the "Sportfishing Capital of the World." Indeed, this is big-time deep-sea fishing country, as the many marinas and bait-and-tackle shops along the road attest; folks with other interests should keep driving south. An exception: As with all the Keys, the snorkeling and diving at offshore reefs is excellent. Stop in any dive shop along the highway for more details.

Theatre of the Sea, a fish-and-sea-mammal emporium at Mile Marker 84.5, is the second-oldest marine park in the world. Sea lions, dolphins, glass-bottom-boat tours, saltwater aquariums, and ongoing shows make this a worthwhile stop, especially for kids. See page 248 for more information.

Long Key State Recreational Area, at Mile Marker 68.5, offers canoe rentals, camping, and another excuse to get out of the car, smell the salt air, and unwind. Two nature trails on boardwalks offer views of mangrove forests and tropical hammocks.

The Middle Keys

South of Long Key are the Middle Keys, about halfway to Key West. Views of water on both sides of the highway start to appear and you get the feeling that you're actually off the North American continent and out to sea.

The next town is Marathon, the second-largest community in the Keys; it even has an airport. While the waters offshore are a big draw with the fishing and boating crowd, the town itself doesn't exude a lot of personality.

But there are some worthwhile stops. At the *Dolphin Research Center,* a nonprofit, educational facility located at Mile Marker 59, visitors can spend time with researchers and dolphins; one-hour, guided walking tours are offered four times a day Wednesday through Sunday. Tickets are $12.50 for adults, $10 for seniors age 55 and older, and $7.50 for children ages 4–12. No reservations are required; for more information, call (305) 289-1121.

The Natural History Museum of the Florida Keys at Mile Marker 50.5 is a small museum offering exhibits on the history, geology, and biology of the Keys; there's also a short nature trail and a children's museum. (For more information, see page 246.) For a quick dip, *Sombrero Beach,* off the Overseas Highway at Mile Marker 50, is a family beach on the ocean with a small grassy park and picnic tables.

Next is the *Seven Mile Bridge* connecting Marathon to the Lower Keys, built in the early 1980s at a cost of $45 million. To the right is the original bridge, built by Henry Flagler for his Overseas Railroad in the early years of the twentieth century. The fine structure took all the weather the Keys could throw its way, but the infamous Labor Day hurricane of 1935 destroyed the railroad and the bridge was converted into a highway. Now it's a fishing and jogging pier *par excellence.*

The Lower Keys

Entering the Lower Keys is like stepping back in time; it's easy to imagine that the rest of the Keys, now so commercial, must have looked like this 30 years ago. These islands are heavily wooded, primarily residential, and decidedly noncommercial.

The Lower Keys are where you find *Bahia Honda State Recreation Area,* located at Mile Marker 37 and one of the loveliest spots in the Keys. Attractions in the 300-acre park include a nationally ranked white sand beach, nature trails, plentiful bird life, snorkeling, and diving. It's a popular day-trip destination for Key Westers—or Conchs (pronounced "conks"), as they're called—with a yen for the feel of sand between their toes.

Big Pine Key is home to canine-sized Key deer, an endangered species under federal protection since 1952; the miniature white-tailed deer are only found on Big Pine Key and 16 surrounding keys. *The Key Deer National Wildlife Refuge* is the only wildlife refuge in the Keys accessible without taking a boat ride; your best chances to see the deer are in the early morning, late afternoon, or early evening. Take Key Deer Boulevard to Watson Boulevard to pick up information at the refuge headquarters, open Monday through Friday, 8 a.m. to 5 p.m.

Looe Key National Marine Sanctuary, a five-square-mile area of submerged reef six miles southwest of Big Pine Key, is considered the best reef in the Keys for snorkeling, diving, fishing, and boating. Its gin-clear waters reveal underwater sights such as brain coral, tall coral pillars rising toward the surface, and other interesting formations. To visit the reef, make arrangements at any dive shop.

Key West

As US 1 enters Key West, a sign for the far right lane reads: "Right Lane Go At All Times." Follow these directions and North Roosevelt Boulevard leads to Duval Street and Old Town Key West, full of bars, restaurants, hotels, bed and breakfasts, museums, galleries, blocks of charming old homes, and congested, narrow streets.

If you ignore the sign above and go left as you enter Key West you'll pass Houseboat Row, the Atlantic Ocean, snazzy resorts, Key West International Airport, Southernmost Point, and then Old Town.

Taking an Orientation Tour

If you're a first-time visitor, you might want to get oriented before you drive right into town. Park at the Welcome Center near the intersection of US 1 and North Roosevelt Boulevard and sign up for the next *Conch Tour Train:* an open-air, narrated "trolley"—really an open-air bus—that transports visitors around Key West and gives them an overview of the town.

Is it corny? You bet. The train's "engine" is a diesel-powered truck disguised as a locomotive, and even has a whistle. But the 90-minute tour is fun and informative.

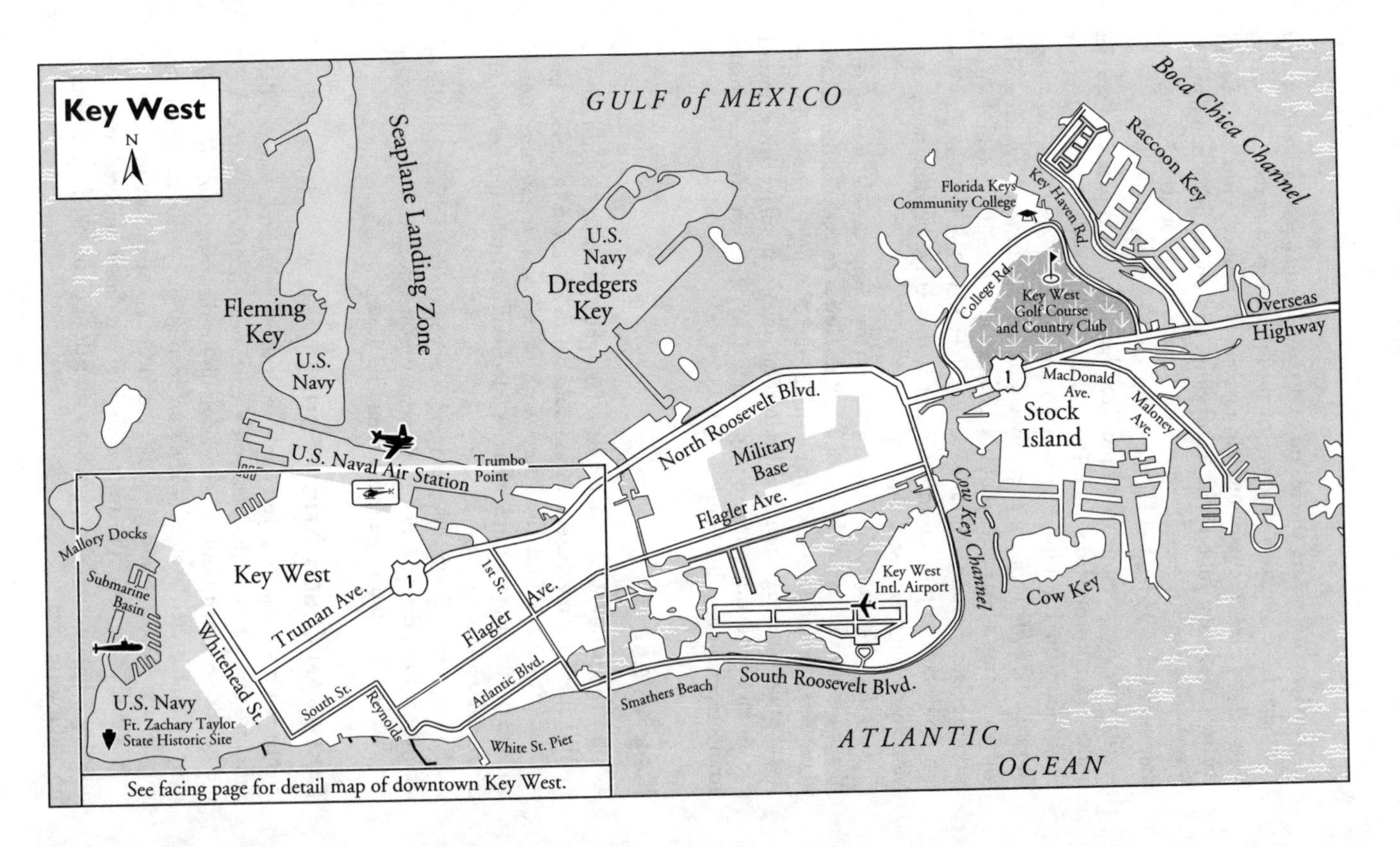
Key West
N
GULF of MEXICO
Seaplane Landing Zone
Fleming Key
U.S. Navy
U.S. Navy Dredgers Key
Boca Chica Channel
Raccoon Key
Florida Keys Community College
Key Haven Rd.
College Rd.
Key West Golf Course and Country Club
Overseas Highway
1
MacDonald Ave.
Maloney Ave.
Stock Island
U.S. Naval Air Station
Trumbo Point
North Roosevelt Blvd.
Military Base
Flagler Ave.
Cow Key Channel
Cow Key
Mallory Docks
Key West
Submarine Basin
Truman Ave.
1st St.
Flagler Ave.
Key West Intl. Airport
Whitehead St.
U.S. Navy
Ft. Zachary Taylor State Historic Site
South St.
Reynolds
Atlantic Blvd.
White St. Pier
Smathers Beach
South Roosevelt Blvd.
ATLANTIC OCEAN
See facing page for detail map of downtown Key West.

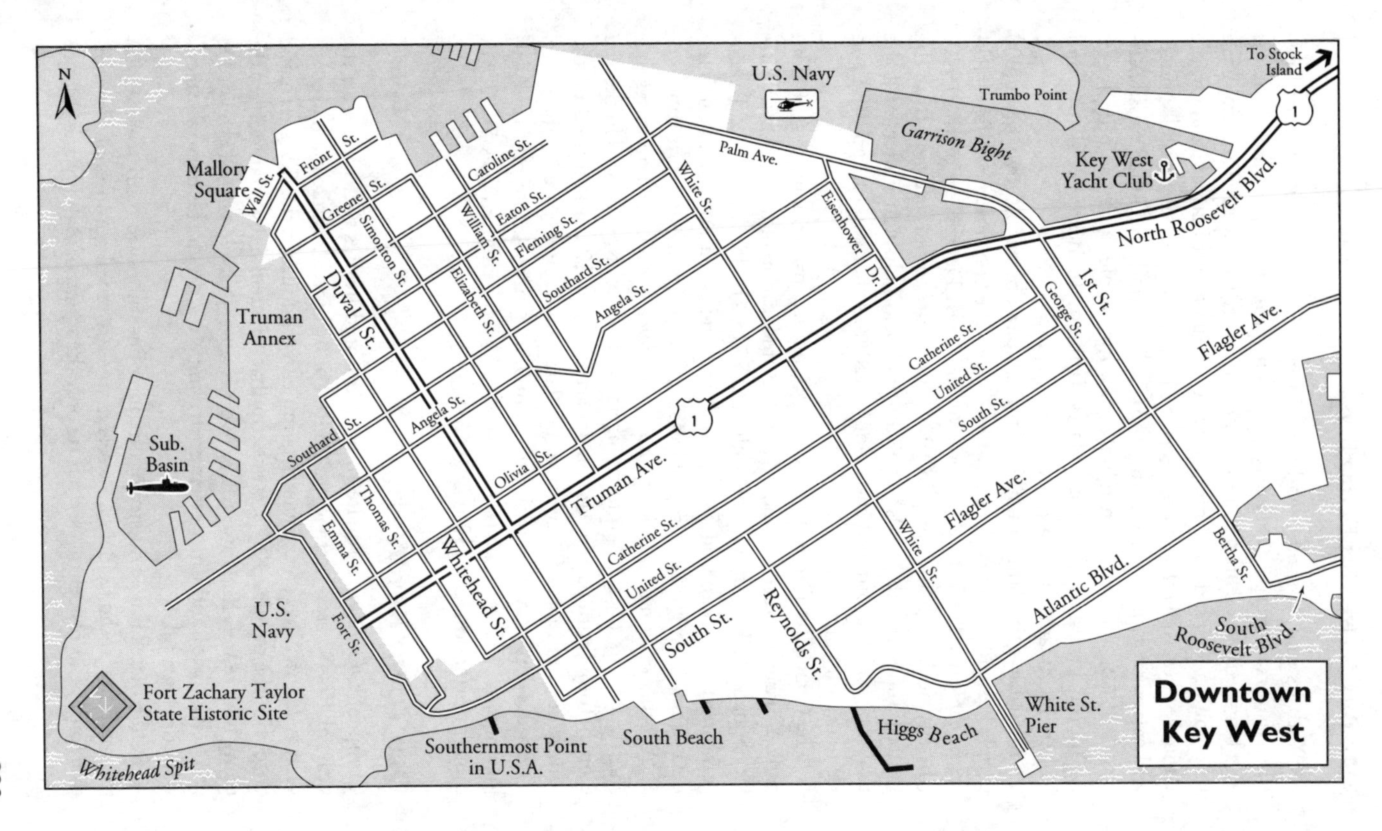
Downtown Key West
To Stock Island
U.S. Navy
Trumbo Point
Garrison Bight
Key West Yacht Club
North Roosevelt Blvd.
Palm Ave.
White St.
Eisenhower Dr.
1st St.
George St.
Flagler Ave.
Mallory Square
Wall St.
Front St.
Greene St.
Caroline St.
Simonton St.
William St.
Eaton St.
Fleming St.
Southard St.
Angela St.
Duval St.
Elizabeth St.
Truman Annex
Catherine St.
United St.
South St.
Angela St.
Southard St.
Olivia St.
Truman Ave.
Sub. Basin
Thomas St.
Emma St.
Whitehead St.
Catherine St.
United St.
Flagler Ave.
White St.
Bertha St.
Atlantic Blvd.
U.S. Navy
Fort St.
South St.
Reynolds St.
South Roosevelt Blvd.
Fort Zachary Taylor State Historic Site
White St. Pier
Higgs Beach
South Beach
Southernmost Point in U.S.A.
Whitehead Spit
N

With its rich, complicated history, Key West can be difficult for first-time visitors to grasp. A ride on the Conch (pronounced "conk," the name of a large, edible shellfish found in the waters off Key West) Tour Train can help you understand why this city was once the wealthiest per capita in the United States, show that it once was the largest producer of natural sponges and cigars, explain its roles during the Civil War and the Cuban missile crisis of 1962, and reveal insights into why people such as John James Audubon, Ernest Hemingway, Harry Truman, Tennessee Williams, and Robert Frost came to identify with Key West.

You'll also gain some insight into the ups and downs this town of 30,000 people has endured over the centuries—from the boom years of the wreckers in the early 1800s to the depths of the Great Depression of the 1930s (the city declared bankruptcy in 1934), to its attempted secession from the United States in the 1980s. The tour will also help you understand the town's physical layout and show you attractions that you can go back and visit later on your own.

The Conch Tour Train leaves every 30 minutes from 9 a.m. to 4:30 p.m. daily. You can board at the Roosevelt Boulevard location or in Old Town's Mallory Square. Tickets are $15 for adults and $7 for children ages 4–12. Passengers can disembark in Old Town, wander around or get lunch, and catch the next "train" 30 minutes later. Call (305) 294-5161 for more information.

Another option for a guided tour is *Old Town Trolley,* open-air buses that shuttle visitors on a 90-minute, narrated tour of Key West. Unlike the Conch Tour Train, passengers can depart at any of 12 marked stops on the tour route and reboard another trolley later; many hotels are on the route. The tours depart every 30 minutes from 9:30 a.m. to 4:30 p.m. from Mallory Square. The tour is $16 for adults and $7 for children ages 5–12. For more information, call (305) 296-6688.

Old Town Key West

Compact *Old Town,* a square mile of restored houses that makes up the heart of Key West, is best viewed on foot or by bicycle. While main avenues such as *Duval Street* are frequently jammed with tourists, the side streets still ooze with the peculiar Key West charm that's made the town famous. As the many bike rental shops attest, Key West is a very bicycle-friendly town. Do yourself a favor and don't attempt driving a car down the narrow streets; walk or ride a bike.

While there's little evidence of anything but unbridled tourist schlock on the main drags, the residential streets frequently reveal glimpses of the anarchic spirit of its residents—even if it's only the sound of Bob Dylan's "Blonde on Blonde" blasting from a hippie crash pad at nine in the morning. And much of the architecture is beautiful, iconoclastic, and fun to look at.

Boom Town

Key West's tolerant spirit has fueled its latest economic revival: the town has become a mecca for gay people. The large population of homosexuals in Key West has given support to restoration efforts, pushed up the price of real estate, and given the town a solid economic boost.

Today's main tourist strip is the once-seedy Duval Street, renovated with well-manicured boutiques, T-shirt shops, bars, T-shirt shops, restaurants, T-shirt shops, galleries, beachwear shops, and other essentials to vacationing tourists. (For God's sake, do your duty and buy a T-shirt!) For folks unfamiliar with the layout of Old Town, Duval Street serves as an anchor as it cuts a swath across the island from the Gulf of Mexico to the Atlantic Ocean.

A Daily Celebration

On the Gulf end of Duval Street is *Mallory Square,* famous for its daily sunset celebration. The "square" is in fact a cramped, old concrete wharf that hosts a mini street festival late each afternoon. During high tourist season (between Christmas and Easter), it's shoulder-to-shoulder along the dock with tourists, cruise ship passengers, and street vendors selling anything from fruit-and-yogurt shakes to "Southernmost" falafels.

Key West–style free entertainment includes a troupe of trained cats (most impressive), a bowling ball juggler, an escape artist, innumerable Dylan clones strumming guitars, and the "Southernmost Bag Piper" (least impressive). You'll have trouble seeing any of this, though, because of the throngs.

For folks expecting a re-creation of Haight-Ashbury during the mid-'60s, Mallory Square is a letdown: no hippies pass joints to toast the setting sun, and no bohemian types pass around a bottle of rum to mark the end of another day. Our feeling is that this famous "ritual" is touristy and overrated . . . at least when the crowds are overpowering.

Cruise Ships

Speaking of crowds: Keep an eye peeled for huge cruise ships docked at the foot of Whitehead Street, near Mallory Square. Not that you'll have any trouble seeing them—the bigger ships tower over the docks and look like they could accommodate the entire population of Key West. The presence of one or more of the big ships could mean even bigger crowds along Duval and Whitehead streets, so try to tour away from the dock area until the ships leave. Restaurants, however, aren't usually affected: many of the cruise passengers return to their ships for meals.

Beyond the Hype

On the Atlantic side of Duval Street—actually, a block over on parallel Whitehead Street—is *Southernmost Point,* another example of Key West hype. A huge buoy perched on land and a placard mark the most southern point in the United States. But, as any schoolchild will readily point out, the land continues south a few yards to the water's edge—the *real* southernmost point. Still, you can't deny the draw of this otherwise undistinguished place: it's usually packed with tourists getting their picture taken in front of the buoy.

Behind the tourist schlock and commercialization, Key West still retains enough of its quixotic past to charm visitors. Our advice: To really enjoy Key West, get off Duval Street, wander its back roads, visit its unique and interesting museums, get a handle on its rich and unusual history. Stop at an outdoor café for a two-hour lunch and hang out in bars that don't have T-shirt shops on the premises (which rules out Sloppy Joe's and Jimmy Buffett's Margaritaville, two very touristy places). Slow the pace, give it a chance, and you'll soon discover Key West's charms.

Outdoor Recreation in Key West and the Keys

If you start to grow a little restless from lounging around bars and restaurants and moseying around museums, remember that Key West is, geographically speaking, in a unique position: between the Atlantic Ocean and the Gulf of Mexico. For outdoor enthusiasts, there's a wealth of things to do and see, including world-class snorkeling and scuba diving, deep-sea fishing, sight fishing, and exploring the Dry Tortugas and Fort Jefferson, a 19th-century coastal fortification 70 miles west of Key West that's only accessible by boat or sea plane.

"We're on the seam of two huge bodies of water and tremendous tidal forces and flows of water wash across the Keys twice daily," explains Captain Jeff Cardenas, a retired fishing guide and owner of the Saltwater Angler, a custom fishing rod, tackle, and outdoors shop in Key West. "The result is wonderful feeding and breeding grounds for aquatic wildlife—and a tremendous water clarity. Key West is where the land runs out and the ocean takes over."

Anglers looking for some recommendations for reputable guides and fishing boat charters available at Key West marinas can stop by the *Saltwater Angler* at 219 Simonton Street and talk to Captain Cardenas, who spent 10 years guiding flats fishermen in the Keys before opening his custom rod shop. He's an expert on the outdoors around Key West and happy to offer advice. The phone number is (305) 294-3248. You'll also find a discussion on the hows, whys, and wheres of South Florida sportfishing in "Deep-Sea Fishing" in Part Seven: Exercise and Recreation, page 153.

Seaplanes of Key West offers full- and half-day flights to Fort Jefferson and the Dry Tortugas that include coolers, ice, sodas, and snorkeling gear—all you need to bring is a towel and a camera. Four-hour trips leave at 8 a.m. and noon daily; prices are $159 for adults, $109 for children ages 7–12, and $80 for children ages 2–6.

The 70-mile flight is 40 minutes each way; the plane flies at low altitude so passengers can view the clear waters, shipwrecks, and marine life. You spend two hours on the island. Full-day trips are $275 for adults, $195 for children ages 7–12, and $140 for children ages 2–6. For reservations, call (800) 950-2359.

Another option for visiting Fort Jefferson and the Dry Tortugas is the *Fort Jefferson Ferry,* which sails out of Lands End Marina (251 Margaret Street in Key West) for full-day excursions. The 100-foot *Yankee Freedom* boasts a large, air-conditioned salon with a chef's galley, a large sundeck, and freshwater showers for swimmers, snorkelers, and divers. The ferry departs on Monday, Wednesday, and Saturday (weather permitting) at 8 a.m. and returns at 6:45 p.m.; it's three hours each way, and visitors can enjoy about four hours on the island (including a complete tour of the fort). The price for the all-day trip is $85 for adults, $75 for seniors age 62 and older, and $50 for children age 16 and under. For schedule and booking information call (800) 634-0939 or (305) 294-7009.

Exploring the Backcountry

Mike Wedeking of *Reflections Nature Tours* in Big Pine Key has guided visitors for seven years on kayak trips to the Keys' backcountry. No experience is necessary to paddle the calm, shallow waters in stable, easy-to-paddle sea kayaks on tours that emphasize seeing wildlife. On the trip you'll view birds, animals, and marine life in Great White Heron Wildlife Refuge and Everglades National Park; snorkeling is another popular option on the tours. Trips are $45 per person and last about four hours; tour times vary. A guide, equipment, instruction, and a light lunch are provided. Big Pine Key is 30 miles from Key West. Reflections is based at Palmer's Place Resort Motel at Mile Marker 28.5. For more information or to make a reservation, call (305) 872-2896.

Boat Tours, Etc.

The *MV Discovery,* a glass-bottom boat with an underwater viewing room that puts you at eye level with marine life, offers trips at 10:30 a.m., 1:30 p.m., and 4 p.m. Tickets for the two-hour trip are $18 for adults and $12 for children (plus tax); kids sail free on the first trip of the day. The ship is located at the Lands End Marina, 251 Margaret Street in Key West. For more information, call (305) 293-0099.

A seemingly limitless number of kiosks and dive shops in Key West offer half-day snorkeling and diving trips to the reef. Shop around for the best price and most convenient departure time. If you have your own gear, you can snorkel right from the beach at Fort Zachary Taylor State Historic Site, located in the Truman Annex at Whitehead and Southard streets in Old Town Key West.

Attractions in Zone 5: The Florida Keys

While most visitors to the Florida Keys are outdoor enthusiasts who come to enjoy a unique, subtropical area between the Gulf of Mexico and the Atlantic Ocean, there's more to do on this string of islands than just fish, dive, snorkel, or explore the backcountry. The Keys, and especially Key West, offer many interesting attractions that are worth the time and effort to visit.

To make it easy to locate visitor attractions in the Keys, we've divided the islands into subzones of Zone 5. (Zones 1 through 4 are in Greater Miami.) Zone 5A is the Upper Keys (Key Largo and Islamorada to Long Key); Zone 5B is the Middle Keys (Conch Key to the Seven Mile Bridge just below Marathon); and Zone 5C is the Lower Keys (Bahia Honda Key to Key West).

Audubon House & Tropical Gardens (Zone 5C)

Type of Attraction: The restored home of an early 19th-century Key West harbor pilot and wrecker. A self-guided tour.

Location: Whitehead and Greene streets in downtown Key West.

Admission: $7.50 for adults; $5 for students; $3.50 for children ages 6–12.

Hours: 9:30 a.m. to 4:45 p.m., daily.

Phone: (305) 294-2116

When to Go: Any time.

Special Comments: You must climb three sets of stairs; the second-floor gallery of Audubon porcelains is air-conditioned.

Overall Appeal by Age Group:

Pre-school	Grade School	Teens	Young Adults	Over 30	Senior Citizens
★	★½	★★	★★½	★★★	★★★½

Author's Rating: A beautifully restored house and gardens. ★★★

How Much Time to Allow: One hour.

Description and Comments Captain George H. Geiger was an early Key West harbor pilot and wrecker who, like many Key West residents, made a fortune salvaging cargo from ships wrecked on the Florida Reef. Captain Geiger and his heirs lived in this house for more than 120 years, but in 1958 the deteriorating structure was slated for demolition. Through the efforts of local conservationists, the house was saved and restored, decorated with exquisite period pieces collected in Europe, and dedicated as a museum commemorating the Key West visits of painter and ornithologist John James Audubon. The restoration of the house inaugurated a movement that saved many historically significant Key West buildings.

Touring Tips Don't miss the children's room on the third floor; two pairs of 19th-century roller skates look like forerunners of in-line skates popular today. Outside, orchid-filled trees evoke the wealthy, cosmopolitan lifestyle of early Key West residents. Check out the duplex outhouse in the corner of the garden.

Other Things to Do Nearby Jessie Porter's Heritage House, the Harry S Truman Little White House, the Wreckers' Museum House, and Mel Fisher's Treasure Exhibit are all within a few blocks.

East Martello Museum (Zone 5C)

Type of Attraction: A Civil War fort converted to an eclectic museum. A self-guided tour.

Location: 3501 South Roosevelt Boulevard, Key West, near the airport.

Admission: $6 for adults; $2 for children ages 7–12.

Hours: 9:30 a.m. to 4 p.m., daily.

Phone: (305) 296-3913

When to Go: Any time.

Special Comments: The climb up the lookout tower requires negotiating a steep spiral staircase.

Overall Appeal by Age Group:

Pre-school	Grade School	Teens	Young Adults	Over 30	Senior Citizens
★★★★	★★★★	★★★½	★★★	★★★	★★★

Author's Rating: A bizarre museum with a little bit of everything. ★★★

How Much Time to Allow: One to two hours.

Description and Comments It might be easier to catalog what you *won't* find here, but we'll give it a try. The low brick ceilings and arches of this old fort house a horse-drawn hearse and wicker casket (circa 1873), ship models, exhibits on Native Americans, Civil War and Spanish American War military artifacts, a hotel safe, "junkyard" art, a deep-sea diver's air suit and a wooden air pump, and a crude raft used by Cubans to escape the Castro regime. Ankle biters can play in the "junior museum"—a tiny house that adults must stoop over to enter—located on the well-manicured grounds. There's also an art museum that features temporary exhibits.

Touring Tips On the way up the spiral staircase leading to the lookout tower, stop to view an exhibit of odd and whimsical "junkyard" art by Stanley Papio.

Other Things to Do Nearby The Atlantic Ocean is directly across Roosevelt Boulevard.

Ernest Hemingway Home & Museum (Zone 5C)

Type of Attraction: The house and gardens of Nobel Prize–winning author Ernest Hemingway. Guided and self-guided tours.

Location: 907 Whitehead Street, Key West.

Admission: $6.50 for adults; $4 for children ages 6–12.

Hours: 9 a.m. to 5 p.m., daily.

Phone: (305) 294-1575

When to Go: In the morning during hot weather; the house isn't air-conditioned.

Special Comments: Hemingway loved cats and about 40 of their alleged descendants (some with six or seven toes per foot) lounge around the one-acre grounds; yet some experts dispute the local legend that says these cats are the descendants of the great writer's pets. Either way, folks not fond of (or allergic to) felines, beware. Visitors must climb two sets of steep stairs on the tour.

Overall Appeal by Age Group:

Pre-school	Grade School	Teens	Young Adults	Over 30	Senior Citizens
★	★★	★★½	★★★	★★★½	★★★★

Author's Rating: An interesting slice of American literary history. ★★★★

How Much Time to Allow: One hour.

Description and Comments Ernest Hemingway owned this Spanish-Colonial house, built in 1870, from 1931 until his death in 1961. In his study in the loft of his pool house he wrote some of his most famous novels and short stories, including *A Farewell to Arms,* "The Snows of Kilimanjaro," and *For Whom the Bell Tolls.* The spacious mansion gives visitors a glimpse into genteel life in the '30s. Much (but not all) of the furniture and memorabilia on display belonged to Hemingway.

Touring Tips Don't skip the optional 30-minute guided tour; the tour leaders are witty, literate, and tell great stories about the writer, whom many critics consider the greatest American author. The 65-foot, saltwater swimming pool was the first built in Key West; part of the cats' water fountain located between the house and the pool is a urinal rescued by the writer from Sloppy Joe's Bar.

Other Things to Do Nearby The Key West Lighthouse Museum is across the street.

Fort Zachary Taylor State Historic Site (Zone 5C)

Type of Attraction: A partially restored Civil War fort and museum; the best beach in Key West. Guided and self-guided tours.

Location: Southard Street (in the Truman Annex), Key West.

Admission: $2.50 for a car with one person; $5 for a car with two people plus 50 cents for each additional person; $1.50 for pedestrians and bicyclists.

Hours: 8 a.m. to sundown, daily.

Phone: (305) 292-6713

When to Go: Any time, but it's elbow to elbow on the beach on weekends.

Special Comments: Free guided tours of the fort are offered at noon and 2 p.m., daily.

Overall Appeal by Age Group:

Pre-school	Grade School	Teens	Young Adults	Over 30	Senior Citizens
★★★★★	★★★★★	★★★★	★★★★	★★★★	★★★★

Author's Rating: A triple hit: a neat fort, interesting history, and a beach you can snorkel from. ★★★★

How Much Time to Allow: Half a day: Allow 30 minutes to an hour to tour the fort, spend the afternoon on the beach, then catch the best view of the sunset in Key West.

Description and Comments For 145 years, Fort Zachary Taylor defended the harbor of Key West. During the Civil War it was one of four Union forts in Confederate territory that never fell into Southern hands. As a result, hundreds of cannons trained on the nearby shipping lanes kept ships bottled up in Key West throughout the Civil War. The workmanship of the exquisite brickwork throughout the fort couldn't be duplicated today.

Touring Tips Don't miss the 30-minute guided tour of the fort, which gives visitors a quick education on the evolution of seacoast fortification through the 19th and 20th centuries. You'll also hear some interesting anecdotes from the park ranger who leads the tour. For example: Many 10-inch cannons were so loud that local merchants demanded a 15-minute warning before practice firing so they could rush home and open their windows; the concussion of the big guns could shatter the glass!

There's also a great view of the Gulf of Mexico from the top of the fort. The ocean beach is made of coral and is great for swimming, snorkeling, and sunbathing; the west side of the park offers anglers a wide variety of saltwater fish (a Florida fishing license is required). Shaded picnic areas, tables, grills, several outdoor showers, and a bathhouse are available to visitors.

Other Things to Do Nearby The Harry S Truman Little White House is on the grounds of the adjacent Truman Annex.

Harry S Truman Little White House Museum (Zone 5C)

Type of Attraction: The restored vacation home of President Harry Truman. A guided tour.

Location: 111 Front Street (one block up Caroline Street through the presidential gates), Key West.

Admission: $7.50 for adults; $3.75 for children age 12 and under.

Hours: 9 a.m. to 5 p.m., daily. Guided tours leave every 15 minutes or so.

Phone: (305) 294-9911

When to Go: Any time.

Special Comments: Visitors must negotiate a set of steep stairs on the tour.

Overall Appeal by Age Group:

Pre-school	Grade School	Teens	Young Adults	Over 30	Senior Citizens
★	★½	★½	★★	★★★	★★★★★

Author's Rating: A nostalgia trip for folks old enough to remember "Give 'Em Hell" Harry. ★★½

How Much Time to Allow: One hour.

Description and Comments President Harry Truman spent 175 vacation days during his presidency (1945–53) at this house in Key West. Today the building is completely redone to posh 1949 standards, although most of the furnishings aren't original. One exception is the custom-made mahogany poker table. The guide tells visitors that while Truman disapproved of gambling in the White House, poker playing with "the boys" was a major form of relaxation for the president when he was vacationing in Key West.

Touring Tips The tour begins with a 10-minute video that evokes the Truman era and primes visitors for the tour. The guides offer interesting tidbits about Truman's personal life when vacationing in Key West. For example, Bess Truman didn't often accompany her husband because she preferred their home in Independence, Missouri. Don't miss the gift shop, which sells aprons inscribed, you guessed it, "If you can't stand the heat, get out of the kitchen."

Other Things to Do Nearby Mel Fisher's Treasure Museum, the Key West Aquarium, and the Audubon House are all close.

Jessie Porter's Heritage House and Robert Frost Cottage (Zone 5C)

Type of Attraction: An 1830s sea captain's home full of literary memorabilia and antique furnishings from the China Trade. A guided tour.

Location: 410 Caroline Street, Key West.

Admission: $6 for adults, $5 for senior citizens, $3 for students, free for children under age 12.

Hours: 10 a.m. to 5 p.m., daily. Closed Christmas Day.

Phone: (305) 296-3573

When to Go: Any time.

Special Comments: Unlike many old Key West homes open to visitors, this residence never needed restoration; it's exactly as its owner left it after her death in 1972.

Overall Appeal by Age Group:

Pre-school	Grade School	Teens	Young Adults	Over 30	Senior Citizens
★	★½	★★	★★★	★★★½	★★★★

Author's Rating: Fascinating stuff; don't miss it. ★★★★½

How Much Time to Allow: 30 minutes.

Description and Comments Jessie Porter, a granddaughter of one of Key West's founders, was a friend to famous writers such as Ernest Hemingway, Tennessee Williams, and Robert Frost. In addition to photos of a few of

America's great literary stars and some original manuscripts, this old house is filled with priceless artifacts, unique furnishings, musical instruments, exquisite silk kimonos . . . the list goes on and on. In the backyard is a small cottage where poet Robert Frost spent many winters. While it's not open to the public, the tour guide plays a tape of Frost reading one of his poems.

Touring Tips Look for the marijuana leaves imprinted in the handmade tiles around the fireplace. The freshwater well outside the front door was used by Native Americans as early as the 12th century.

Other Things to Do Nearby The Audubon House, the Harry S Truman Little White House, and the Wreckers' Museum are all close.

John Pennecamp Coral Reef State Park (Zone 5A)

Type of Attraction: A 178-square-mile underwater park featuring snorkeling tours, scuba diving trips, and glass-bottom-boat trips.

Location: On US 1 at Mile Marker 102.5, Key Largo (about a 90-minute drive south of Miami).

Admission: The entrance fee to the park is $4 per car and 50 cents per person (including the driver, so the minimum cost is $4.50). Snorkeling tours are $25 plus tax for adults and $20 plus tax for children under age 18. Tours leave at 9 a.m., noon, and 3 p.m.

Four-hour guided scuba trips are $37 per person and leave at 9:30 a.m. and 1:30 p.m. Rental of two air tanks for the two one-hour dives is $14.

Four-hour sailing and snorkeling trips on a 38-foot catamaran are $28.95 for adults and $23.95 for children under age 18 and leave at 9 a.m. and 1:30 p.m.

Two-and-a-half-hour glass-bottom-boat tours cost $15 plus tax for adults and $8.50 for children under age 12 and depart at 9:15 a.m., 12:15 p.m., and 3 p.m.

Hours: 8 a.m. to sunset.

Phone: (305) 451-1621

When to Go: Any time, to visit the park. For diving and snorkeling trips to the reef, on weekends during the winter, reservations should be made several weeks in advance; call at least a day ahead of time during the week to reserve a spot.

Special Comments: All trips are subject to weather conditions and a minimum number of paying customers. Only certified divers can go on the scuba trips; anybody who can swim can go on a snorkeling tour. Complete rental and instruction are available for scuba diving. Full certification takes three days and costs $350 (assuming more than one person is in the class; see page 149 for more information on becoming certified); a "resort" course that lets you dive with an instructor or dive master takes a full day and costs $150. For more information on diving courses, call the dive center at (305) 451-6323.

Overall Appeal by Age Group:

Pre-school	Grade School	Teens	Young Adults	Over 30	Senior Citizens
★★★★	★★★★	★★★★	★★★★★	★★★★★	★★★★

Author's Rating: Find out why Key Largo is the dive capital of the United States. ★★★★★

How Much Time to Allow: Half a day or longer.

Description and Comments The 78 miles of living coral reef in this park are only a small portion of one of the most beautiful reef systems in the world. But because it's all underwater, the best way to see it is . . . underwater. Unless you can't swim, we recommend taking the snorkel tour. After the 30-minute boat ride to the reef, it's over the side for up-close views of a fantastic array of aquatic life. The boat crew gives plenty of coaching to novices and a 10-minute minicourse on how to snorkel. The fee includes rental of a mask, flippers, and snorkel. (You get to keep the new snorkel.) All snorkelers must wear inflatable life vests, which are provided.

Touring Tips If swimming with the fishes doesn't appeal or nonswimmers are in your party, take the two-and-a-half-hour, glass-bottom-boat tour. Other facilities in the park include hiking trails, a small swimming beach, an aquarium, canoe rentals, and a visitor center featuring ecological displays on Keys flora and fauna. Good news: The park recently added a new—and larger—bath house with freshwater showers.

Other Things to Do Nearby Theater of the Sea is 18 miles south in Islamorada. Key Largo is very commercial and has plenty of places to eat, sleep, and shop.

Key West Aquarium (Zone 5C)

Type of Attraction: An old-fashioned aquarium featuring sea life from both the Atlantic and the Gulf of Mexico. Guided and self-guided tours.

Location: 1 Whitehead Street, Key West.

Admission: $8 for adults; $4 for children ages 4–12. Children under age 3 admitted free. Tickets are good for two days.

Hours: 10 a.m. to 6 p.m., daily. Guided tours and feedings at 11 a.m., 1 p.m., 3 p.m., and 4:30 p.m.

Phone: (305) 296-2051

When to Go: Any time.

Special Comments: If you're on a short visit to Key West, spend your valuable touring time elsewhere and come back on a later visit.

Overall Appeal by Age Group:

Pre-school	Grade School	Teens	Young Adults	Over 30	Senior Citizens
★★★★★	★★★★	★★★½	★★★	★★½	★★

Author's Rating: Great for the kiddies, but otherwise a bit ho-hum. ★★½

How Much Time to Allow: One hour.

Description and Comments This aquarium is small but comfortable, and will especially please younger children. At the touch tank kids can handle conch, starfish, and crabs. You'll probably never get closer to a shark unless you hook one.

Touring Tips This is a browsing kind of place with long rows of fish tanks at eye level to stroll past. The moray eels are especially creepy, and you'll see many specimens of smaller sharks such as lemon, blacktip, and bonnethead.

Other Things to Do Nearby You're in the heart of downtown Key West: Mel Fisher's Treasure Exhibit, the Audubon House, and Mallory Square are within a few blocks' walk.

Key West Cemetery (Zone 5C)

Type of Attraction: The final resting place of many prominent—and unusual—Key West residents. Guided and self-guided tours.

Location: The main gate is at Margaret and Angela streets, Key West.

Admission: Free.

Hours: 7 a.m. to sunset.

Phone: (305) 292-8170

When to Go: Any time, but avoid the middle of the day in hot weather.

Special Comments: Although all the residents are buried above ground, it's not a ghoulish place.

Overall Appeal by Age Group:

Pre-school	Grade School	Teens	Young Adults	Over 30	Senior Citizens
★	★	★★	★★★	★★★	★★★

Author's Rating: A wacky side of Key West that's managed to avoid the rest of the island's rampant commercialism. ★★★

How Much Time to Allow: One hour, although it could take most of the day to explore the entire 25 acres.

Description and Comments A high water table and tough coral rock explains the unusual burial practices in this corner of paradise—everyone here is "buried" above ground. As a result, the cemetery is filled with coffin-shaped tombs, many of them stacked on top of one another like mortuary condominiums. In addition, pets are often interred next to their owners.

Touring Tips Guided tours depart the main gate Tuesday and Thursday mornings at 9:30 a.m.; the cost is $5 per person. The most inspired headstone inscription in the cemetery may be that of a famous Key West hypochondriac, Mrs. B. P. Roberts: "I told you I was sick."

Other Things to Do Nearby The cemetery is on the edge of Old Town Key West; explore some of the quiet, shaded streets lined with charming houses that range from shacks to Victorian masterpieces. Some are lovingly restored while others look as if they haven't been touched since Hemingway lived here. Look in the yards for concrete cisterns, which were once the chief source of fresh water on the island.

Key West Lighthouse Museum (Zone 5C)

Type of Attraction: An 1848 lighthouse and a museum that tells the story of lighthouses in the Florida Keys. A self-guided tour.

Location: 938 Whitehead Street, Key West.

Admission: $6 for adults; $2 for children ages 6–12.

Hours: 9:30 a.m. to 4:30 p.m., daily. Closed Christmas Day.

Phone: (305) 294-0012

When to Go: Any time.

Special Comments: Folks who aren't in shape or don't like heights should skip the climb to the top of the 90-foot lighthouse.

Overall Appeal by Age Group:

Pre-school	Grade School	Teens	Young Adults	Over 30	Senior Citizens
★★	★★★★	★★★★	★★★★	★★★★	★★★

Author's Rating: A great view and interesting history. ★★★★

How Much Time to Allow: One hour.

Description and Comments Next to doing "12-ounce curls" (drinking beer) at Sloppy Joe's, a climb to the top of the lighthouse is the most rewarding workout in Key West. The 88 steps to the top lead to an impressive view of the Atlantic Ocean, the Gulf of Mexico, and cruise ships docked in the harbor.

Touring Tips The nearby museum (formerly the Keeper's Quarters when this was an operating lighthouse) is small, dark, cool, and filled with fascinating artifacts from the days when the big light atop the tower guided navigators through the treacherous waters outside Key West.

Other Things to Do Nearby Hemingway House is directly across Whitehead Street.

Key West's Shipwreck Historeum (Zone 5C)

Type of Attraction: A replica of an 1856 Key West wreckers warehouse where skits, films, laser technology, and actual artifacts combine to present a picture of 19th-century Key West life and how the wrecking profession influenced the island's society. A self-guided tour.

Location: 1 Whitehead Street at Mallory Square, Key West.

Admission: $8 for adults; $4 for children ages 4–12; free for children under age 4.

Hours: 9:45 a.m. to 4:45 p.m., daily. Shows begin 15 minutes before and after the hour.

Phone: (305) 292-8990

When to Go: Any time.

Special Comments: The Historeum is not wheelchair accessible. You must descend several stairs to where the movie is shown, and the museum tour involves several flights of stairs. The lookout tower provides an incredible view of the historic district and the barrier reef, but requires visitors to climb nine flights of stairs. Those afraid of heights might want to skip this part of the attraction.

Overall Appeal by Age Group:

Pre-school	Grade School	Teens	Young Adults	Over 30	Senior Citizens
★½	★★½	★★★	★★★★	★★★★	★★★★

Author's Rating: Talented actors, interesting history, and impressive booty. ★★★★

How Much Time to Allow: Approximately 45 minutes for the entire tour.

Description and Comments Drift back in time as Asa Tift, a famous, 19th-century Key West wrecker, greets you in his warehouse as a potential crew member. Listen to the story of how Key West became the "richest city in the U.S.A." when the vessel *Isaac Allerton* sank in 1856. A 20-minute video depicts the life of the wreckers and their fight to save lives and precious cargo from ships doomed by the dangerous reefs. Much of the story is told through comments and stories from some of Key West's prominent figures of the time.

Touring Tips The *Isaac Allerton* was the richest shipwreck in our history, and the self-guided museum tour displays a multitude of impressive artifacts—the ship was headed for New Orleans loaded with expensive and precious items intended to decorate the Customs House. Asa Tift seems busy at work in the room where you begin the museum tour, but he will be happy to stop and answer any questions you might have. The actor playing Tift will make it worth your time to stop and chat—our guide was loaded with interesting Key West tidbits. Don't forget about Tift's Wreckers Lookout, which marks the end of the tour. If you're up for the climb, you will be rewarded with a spectacular view.

Other Things to Do Nearby You're in the heart of Mallory Square and only a few blocks' walk from the Aquarium, the Audubon House, and Mel Fisher's Treasure Exhibit.

Mel Fisher's Treasure Exhibit (Zone 5C)

Type of Attraction: A display of treasure recovered from two Spanish galleons sunk off Key West in a 1622 hurricane. A self-guided tour.

Location: 200 Greene Street, Key West.

Admission: $6.50 for adults; $2 for children ages 6–12. AAA and AARP discounts available.

Hours: 9:30 a.m. to 5 p.m., daily. The last video presentation is at 4:30 p.m.

Phone: (305) 294-2633

When to Go: Any time.

Special Comments: Don't expect to find any mention of the raging dispute between Fisher and the government over who owns what. The gift shop is full of tacky stuff like paper pirate hats and eye patches for the kids.

Overall Appeal by Age Group:

Pre-school	Grade School	Teens	Young Adults	Over 30	Senior Citizens
★★★	★★★★	★★★★	★★★½	★★★	★★★½

Author's Rating: Impressive booty, a small exhibit, and plenty of self-promotional schlock. ★★½

How Much Time to Allow: One hour.

Description and Comments Ever dreamed of finding a trove of treasure worth millions? Well, Mel Fisher, the best-known salvager in the Keys, did—and bars of solid silver, a solid gold dinner plate, pieces of eight in a cedar chest, and cannons and sailors' artifacts from the 17th century are among the items on display in this small museum. Exhibits also explain how modern treasure hunters find the ancient wrecks and bring the loot up from the bottom of the sea. Yet the relentless self-promotion and commercialism of this private museum—not to mention its small size—are a letdown.

Touring Tips The *Margarita,* part of a fleet of ships sailing from Havana, Cuba, in 1622 and sunk during a hurricane during its passage to Spain, was discovered in 1980. But it wasn't until 1985, when Fisher located the hull structure and the main cargo of the fleet's flagship *Nuestra Senora de Atocha,* that the bulk of the treasure was found; a 20-minute video tells the story.

Other Things to Do Nearby The Key West Aquarium, the Harry S Truman Little White House, and the Audubon House are all within a few blocks.

Natural History Museum of the Florida Keys (Zone 5B)

Type of Attraction: A child-friendly museum emphasizing the natural history and ecology of the Florida Keys. A self-guided tour.

Location: On US 1 at Mile Marker 50.5, Marathon.

Admission: $7.50 for adults; $6 for seniors; $4 for students; free for children age 6 and under.

Hours: 9 a.m. to 5 p.m., Monday through Saturday; noon to 5 p.m., Sunday.

Phone: (305) 743-9100

When to Go: Any time.

Special Comments: Don't forget mosquito repellent before walking the quarter-mile nature trail.

Overall Appeal by Age Group:

Pre-school	Grade School	Teens	Young Adults	Over 30	Senior Citizens
★★★★	★★★★★	★★★	★★½	★★½	★★½

Author's Rating: A small, spanking-new museum geared for children, who will love it. ★★½

How Much Time to Allow: One to two hours.

Description and Comments A small, new, and tasteful museum with exhibits on ancient Indians, pirates, wreckers, and the railroaders who built the rail line to Key West. Kids will like the re-creation of an underwater cave, as well as the 15,000-gallon saltwater lagoon, and tanks featuring spiny lobsters, an iguana, and a parrot. A separate children's museum features touch tanks that lets kids handle spiny sea urchins and other creatures, and a corner with books and a chair for reading.

Touring Tips The nature trail leads to a rare tropical palm hammock, home to some rare and unusual plants.

Other Things to Do Nearby Seven Mile Bridge, one of the engineering marvels of the world when it was completed in 1910, is a few miles south. Farther south at Mile Marker 37, Bahia Honda State Park offers weary travelers a real sand beach (rare in the Keys), a nature trail, and a respite from the highway.

Ripley's Odditorium

Type of Attraction: A carnival funhouse for youngsters and loony adults featuring exhibits from "Ripley's Believe It or Not." A self-guided tour.

Location: 527 Duval Street, Key West.

Admission: $9.95 plus tax for adults; $6.95 plus tax for children ages 4–10.

Hours: 9 a.m. to 11 p.m.

Phone: (305) 293-9686

When to Go: Any time.

Special Comments: A number of exhibits are right out of a roadside carnival, so be ready for unsettling special effects—both optical and physical—such as wobbly decks and lunging "sharks."

Overall Appeal by Age Group:

Pre-school	Grade School	Teens	Young Adults	Over 30	Senior Citizens
★★	★★★★	★★★★★	★★★	★★	★½

Author's Rating: Tacky, tasteless, and often hilarious. Expensive, too. ★★

How Much Time to Allow: One hour for adults, two to three hours for youngsters.

Description and Comments Is it really Ripley, returned from the dead, who materializes at his desk and invites visitors to explore his museum? Or is it a "hologram" of an actor who looks vaguely like Christopher Walken wearing a smoking jacket? Who cares?

Join in the fun on an exploration of this ridiculous—and funny—"museum." You'll find oddities of questionable authenticity ("shrunken" heads), endlessly repeating film clips of human bizarreness (a guy blowing up a balloon through his eye), grainy film clips with corny narration of New Guinea natives chowing down on grubs and a roast crocodile (gross!), lots of juvenile sex teasers (walk by in one direction, you get a glimpse of a naked lady's backside, but walk by in the other direction and she's gone). It's all corny, seedy, and often quite funny.

Touring Tips Some people—opera lovers and their ilk—might offer this touring advice: Don't. In reality, this is a perfect rainy day kind of place. You don't have to be a kid to enjoy this wacky place, but having one along would certainly increase the fun. And don't ask yourself what any of this has to do with Key West.

Other Things to Do Nearby Buy a T-shirt: Duval Street must offer more T-shirts for sale than any other place in the universe. Knock down a you-know-what at Jimmy Buffett's Margaritaville (across the street) or stretch your legs for a stroll to the Southernmost Point; hang a left as you leave Ripley's. Is the sun low in the sky? Then head for Mallory Square and the sunset celebration; it's to the right.

Theatre of the Sea (Zone 5A)

Type of Attraction: A marine park offering continuous shows featuring sea lions and dolphins, "bottomless" boat rides, snorkeling trips, an aquarium, and opportunities to swim with dolphins.

Location: On US 1 at Mile Marker 84.5 in Islamorada.

Admission: $15.25 for adults; $8.75 for children ages 3–12; free for children under age 3. Group rates are available. Price of admission does not include the Dolphin Swim, boat rides, or snorkeling trips.

Hours: 9:30 a.m. to 4 p.m.

Phone: (305) 664-2431

When to Go: Any time.

Special Comments: If you are interested in taking a dip with the dolphins, call ahead for reservations. Also note that this is your only opportunity to swim at the park.

Overall Appeal by Age Group:

Pre-school	Grade School	Teens	Young Adults	Over 30	Senior Citizens
★★★	★★★½	★★★	★★★	★★★	★★★½

Author's Rating: ★★★

How Much Time to Allow: At least 2½ hours; half a day for a leisurely exploration.

Description and Comments Established in 1946, Theater of the Sea is the world's second-oldest marine park. Here, you can explore the surroundings of the deep in a natural lagoon setting. Activities at the park such as bottomless-boat rides, aquatic shows, and lagoon tours will entertain guests of all ages, as well as educate them about marine life. Children are especially drawn to the

"Touch Tank," where they can pet a shark or kiss a sea lion. Also, children of all ages are invited to take part in the shows.

Touring Tips To escape the crowds and the heat, the best time to go is early in the morning during the week. Show up at 8:30 a.m. for a four-hour snorkeling trip and 13-mile boat cruise. The boat leaves the dock at 9 a.m. daily; the cost is $49.95 for adults and $29.95 for children ages 6–12. Snorkeling equipment is included.

Other Things to Do Nearby The Tiki Bar is right next door. Adults can refresh themselves with a cocktail and a little Calypso music, while the kids play in the pool. Float and jet ski rentals are also available.

PART THIRTEEN

Dining and Restaurants

Dining in Miami*

That Miami and its environs (Dade County) is an "eating out" area is reflected in the number of restaurants it sustains. In Dade County alone there are more than 6,000 restaurants, with upwards of 6,000 more in adjoining Broward and Palm Beach counties. There are more restaurants per resident in Florida than anywhere else in the country.

Most of them are "good"—or else they would not survive the competition—and a surprising number are very good and excellent.

With its diverse population—more than 60 percent of Miami's residents are Hispanic, mixed with sizable Haitian, Jamaican, Indian, and Asian communities—it follows that the eateries are as diverse as the population, making for a lively and exciting restaurant scene.

Because it continues to be an area with a growing population, Miami and South Florida seem to draw a continuing stream of young chefs, many of them graduates of U.S. culinary schools, which have proliferated in this area during the past decade. There's also been a recent influx of chefs from regions of Italy rarely represented here, offering wonderfully sophisticated, yet rustic, countryside cuisine that is a revelation even to those who consider themselves well-versed in Italian cooking.

The most exciting, innovative, and truly native trend in culinary development, however, comes from the young and talented American chefs who are creating a distinct new "Florida" cuisine, sometimes referred to as "Florida-Caribbean" or "New World" cooking. By any name this style of cooking has captured the interest of food writers, not only from around

* Restaurants in the *Unofficial Guide* were profiled by Lucy Cooper, former restaurant critic at the *Miami Herald* for 15 years and author of the cookbook *Southern Entertaining—A New Taste of the South* (Seaside Publishers).

this country, but from other countries as well. These local chefs are combining and adapting the culinary styles of neighboring Caribbean countries with products that are native to the tropics, a fact that has encouraged the growth of numerous specialty farms in South Florida. These small farmers, along with individual local fishermen, bring their harvests directly to the back doors of these young restaurateurs who insist on products so fresh that dewdrops still glisten on them.

Thus, Miami restaurants boast a profusion of exotic foods unique to Florida, such as plantains, papaya, mangoes, hot chili peppers, malanga, yucca, and other exotic fruits and vegetables. In the pages of the dining profiles that follow, the specializations of various restaurants will be evident.

The Business Scene

In the Coral Gables section of Miami, home of some of Miami's finest restaurants, businessmen and women pour into upscale restaurants in a flood. Influenced in part by the Hispanic population, as well as the concentration of businesses here, lunch is often a leisurely affair, designed for conducting business while enjoying fine food. Most restaurants of note are filled during the lunch hours. These restaurants remain busy during the dinner hour, too, catering to a concentration of affluent residents in nearby areas.

Coral Gables restaurateurs, and to a lesser extent those in Coconut Grove, are beneficiaries of the bonanza offered by the influx of Hispanics. As one owner put it, "We get the older crowd during the early hours, then what you might call the regular Americans. Last, usually at ten and later, the Hispanics, late and lively people, begin to arrive. So, particularly on weekends, I'm guaranteed three seatings."

South Beach

For the past five years South Beach's revitalized Art Deco District has been highly publicized and glorified around the world—with some justification. It is indeed glitzy, strange, and bizarre, bursting with locals and internationals in indescribable fashions. In addition to the familiar faces of movie stars, models, photographers, celebrities, and wannabes abound.

Along this strip called South Beach, restaurants pop up and disappear faster than the quick tropical showers. A hot new bar or restaurant will draw the trendies one week, only to be stone cold dead the next. On weekends the sight-seer can scarcely make his or her way through the throngs of sidewalk diners. Most South Beach restaurants have outdoor terraces or porches, placing tables and chairs on the sidewalk for the overflow. This is a "see and be seen" street, much like the Via Veneto of Rome in the '60s, if a bit seedier.

Parking on the beach is difficult day and night. Even if you find a space near the restaurant of your choice, a valet parking attendant is apt to rush up before you leave the car, informing you that it will cost you $10 and sometimes $15 for the privilege. Prices vary. Sometimes you are asked to pay $6 if you don't mind that your car will be parked some four blocks away. Sometimes the charge is $8. For privileged parking at beachside, you might be asked for $10 or more.

There may be free parking available if you look hard enough, but chances are that the space you find will be at least several blocks away.

Be forewarned that nearly every restaurant on the beach, or Ocean Drive, adds a 15–18 percent gratuity to your bill. If you are ignorant of this practice and add another 15 percent, don't expect to be informed of your error. The "new" South Beach suffers a bit from growing pains, so the newcomer must bear with it and be on the lookout. The sounds and sights, however, are worth the price of admission.

Ethnic Dining

Because of its ethnic diversity and appeal to world tourism, Miami harbors a wide variety of restaurants, including a plethora of Cuban restaurants, many of them in what is called "Little Havana" in Zone 3 or Miami South. Most are dedicated to serving traditional Cuban food, with rice and black beans, plantains, and yucca almost always accompanying the entrees. Additionally, however, there is an emerging number of "new" Cuban restaurants offering new and often lighter twists on the traditional. Foremost among them are Victor's and Yuca restaurants.

Perhaps the most popular, and some of the best, of the ethnic restaurants are Italian. Both in Coral Gables and on South Beach, good Italian restaurants abound. Among the best are Osteria del Teatro and Tuscan Steak in South Beach, La Bussola, Claudius, Giacosa, Caffe Baci, and Caffe Abbracci in Coral Gables. In North Miami there's Il Tulipano, arguably the best Italian restaurant in Dade county.

Among other ethnic groups represented are French, Thai, Indian, Greek, Middle Eastern, Japanese, Vietnamese, and Chinese. Several Chinese restaurants in the area specialize in dim sum, including the prominent and elaborate Tropical Chinese Restaurant. Peruvian, Argentinean, Mexican, Brazilian, and Nicaraguan restaurants also are to be found, though in lesser numbers.

Both the Hispanic and American populations of Miami are partial to steak and other red meats. European tourists, long aware of the high quality of American beef, seek out steak houses so they can see for themselves. There has been, in fact, such a resurgence of interest in steak houses that one must often wait in line for a table. Among the classier and more expensive of these is The Palm, beloved by the rich and sometimes famous.

Steak notwithstanding, the question most often asked by tourists of concierges is, "Can you give me the name of a good seafood restaurant?" Quite natural, since Miami floats like an island between the Gulf waters and the ocean. Although there are one or two outstanding specialty seafood restaurants, such as Joe's Stone Crab, restaurants like Mark's Las Olas in Ft. Lauderdale, Chef Allen's, and Il Tulipano in North Miami usually have their fish delivered to the kitchen door on a daily basis, ensuring impeccable freshness. All restaurants in South Florida like to say they specialize in fish and seafood and many actually do. The tourist will find no lack of restaurants that serve local fish in tropical South Florida.

It's O.K. to Be Casual

There has been, during the past decade, a decided trend toward informality in restaurant decor, service style, and dress requirements. Most tourists, winter residents, and even locals come to this tropical area to relax and do not relish dressing formally. Therefore the dress code is lenient. Less than a handful of restaurants require a jacket.

Some lovely restaurants that offer formal, professional service and fine wines remain and continue to be popular. One of them is La Paloma, a Swiss-American restaurant on Biscayne Boulevard. It features ornate surroundings, top-notch service, and generally modest prices. Even so, a jacket is not required.

Outdoor Dining

Strangely enough, there was little outdoor dining in Miami and South Florida until the '80s. There were waterfront restaurants that offered dining on the porch or terrace, but as the natives mumbled, "Only tourists would go out in that hot sun."

All that has changed since the local lifestyle became more and more informal. Everyone, it seems, including residents, now wants to eat outdoors, humidity notwithstanding. Many new restaurants are built to offer outdoor dining, and older restaurants are scrambling to do the same.

Except for the cafeterialike counters in the food courts of shopping malls, there are few cafeterias in Miami. Perhaps this is because there are too many low-priced options in chain operations such as The Olive Garden, Shoneys, and others.

Pizza parlors are as popular here as they are in all parts of America. Today, however, in the New American restaurants where young chefs reign, you'll find a variety of pizzas, many of them stylishly accomplished.

Breakfast

Usually tourists eat breakfast in their hotels and are not searching for breakfast spots. There are a few places, however, that draw both locals and tourists on a continuing basis.

On South Beach, the News Cafe attracts more people than there are seating spaces. The Rascal House, on North Miami Beach, has been the most steadily popular and busy restaurant through the years. It is a landmark worth visiting if you like deli-style food. Some of the better and more interesting breakfast spots to pop up lately are in recently renovated hotels such as the Raleigh, Delano, and Astor, all in South Beach.

In Ft. Lauderdale, it's Lester's Diner for everyone from truck drivers to the area's movers and shakers, who may appear as early as 3 a.m. Breakfast here is strictly hash house–style and wonderful.

Then, of course, there are the bagel houses. Among the most popular in Dade County are The Bagel Emporium in Coral Gables and Bagels & Co. in North Miami on Biscayne Boulevard.

Landmark Restaurants

There are few true landmark restaurants in South Florida, perhaps because of its youth, and because some places, on their way to becoming legends, simply closed their doors.

Perhaps the best-known legend in the Miami area is Joe's Stone Crab on South Beach, which opened some 80 years ago, when Miami was in its infancy. It attracts both local residents and tourists, hundreds of them daily. The restaurant is closed during the summer months.

Its single attraction is stone crabs, a delicious shellfish available in surrounding waters, and one sold in nearly every other restaurant in South Florida during the season. Somehow, they seem to taste better at Joe's, maybe because of all the celebrities here. Beginning in the days of J. Edgar Hoover and Walter Winchell, and continuing the tradition today with movie stars, sports figures, and power brokers, sooner or later, everyone goes to Joe's Stone Crab.

Equally phenomenal is the Rascal House, a deli-style restaurant that opened in the 1950s and, it is said, feeds some 5,000 people a day during the season. This is easy to believe when you view the long lines forever waiting to get in. Surprisingly, the waits are never long. The restaurant is a model of efficiency; its waitresses are remarkably good and in a half-hour you'll be munching on the gratis pickles and beets.

Hotel Dining

At the turn of the century, Miami hotels harbored some of its best restaurants. This all changed in the '50s and '60s as many hotels, particularly those catering to tourists, downgraded their restaurants to what resembled fast-food outlets. But this downward trend was reversed in the late '70s and early '80s, when the focus on good and exciting food became prominent again. Many hotels scrambled to open fine restaurants once more, hiring talented chefs to run their kitchens. The best of these today are the Blue Door at the Delano Hotel; the Inter-Continental; and the Don Shula Hotel and Golf Resort in Miami Lakes, where the Shula name and reliable food are the attraction.

Except in the case of South Beach, hotel dining rooms meet with limited success in attracting local residents. In South Beach, however, most of the restaurants profiled in this guide are attached to the small hotels that line that area. In many cases, the restaurants are operated independently of the hotel management, and are frequented by the thousands who roam the streets of South Beach regularly. The quality of the restaurants has little or nothing to do with the quality of the hotels.

This situation may be changing, however, as several newly renovated hotels enter the picture. Among these are the Astor and the much-hyped Tides Hotel.

Good, and Getting Better

Because of the importance of tourism, Miami has always offered many good restaurants. But until very recently, its culinary scene was never considered in the same league with San Francisco, New Orleans, and New York.

In the past five or six years, however, Florida chefs have emerged as among the most touted in the country. There has developed what might be called the "hybrid Florida-Caribbean," or "New World" cuisine, due largely to the tremendous influx of Cubans and other Hispanics to the area and the availability of their exotic products, flavors, and spices, traces of which now can be found in most Miami restaurants—including Italian and French.

Pioneers in the development of this new and richly flavorful cuisine are Mark Militello of Mark's Las Olas, Allen Susser of Chef Allen's, and Robbin Haas of Red Square. The essence of their Caribbean-inspired cooking, dedicated to using the freshest products, has fanned out to influence young chefs in restaurants throughout South Florida. These chefs in turn have influenced other ethnic chefs to follow suit, thus improving the quality of independent restaurants throughout the area.

The restaurants described here are among the best in the various cuisine categories. Some are not necessarily great, but are considered the best in their category. Most of the restaurants listed in this guide are frequented by local residents as well as tourists. In the sweltering summer, tourism dies in South Florida, and unless restaurants attract a substantial local trade, they too die. Thus you can be sure the restaurants listed are not just "tourist traps."

Florida restaurants in the '90s are emerging as among the most exciting in the country, mainly because of the innovative new Florida cuisine and its offshoots, and partly because of the fierce competition here that tends to improve service.

Altogether, though there remains a good percentage of mediocre restaurants, the dining in Miami has never been more diverse and exciting. During this past year, the improvement has been dramatic.

The Restaurants

Our Favorite Restaurants of Miami and the Keys: Explaining the Ratings

We have developed detailed profiles for the restaurants we think are the best in town. Each profile features an easily scanned heading that allows you, in just a second, to check out the restaurant's name, cuisine, star rating, cost, quality rating, and value rating.

Star Rating The star rating is an overall rating that evaluates the entire dining experience, including style, service, and ambience, in addition to the taste, presentation, and quality of the food. Five stars is the highest rating possible, meaning the place has the best of everything. Four-star restaurants are exceptional and three-star restaurants are well above average. Two-star restaurants are good. One star is given to average restaurants that demonstrate an unusual capability in some area of specialization, for example, an otherwise forgettable place that has great barbecued chicken.

Cost To the right of the star rating is an expense category giving the general price range for a complete meal. A complete meal for our purposes consists of an entree with vegetable or side dish, and choice of soup or salad. Appetizers, desserts, drinks, and tips are excluded. Categories and related prices are listed below.

Inexpensive	$14 or less per person
Moderate	$15 to $30 per person
Expensive	Over $30 per person

Quality Rating On the far right of each heading appears a number and a letter. The number is a food quality rating based on a scale of 0 to 100, with 100 being the best rating attainable. The quality rating is based expressly on the taste, freshness of ingredients, preparation, presentation, and creativity of food served. There is no consideration of price. If you are a person who wants the best food available and cost is not an issue, you need look no further than the quality ratings.

Value Rating If, on the other hand, you are looking for both quality and value, then you should check the value rating, expressed in letters. The value ratings are defined as follows:

A	Exceptional value, a real bargain
B	Good value
C	Fair value, you get exactly what you pay for
D	Somewhat overpriced
F	Significantly overpriced

Location Just below the heading is a designation for geographic zone. This will give you a general idea of where the restaurant described is located. For ease of use, we divide Miami and environs into five geographic zones:

Zone 1.	Miami Beach
Zone 2.	Miami North
Zone 3.	Miami South
Zone 4.	Southern Dade County
Zone 5.	The Florida Keys

If you are staying in Miami Beach and intend to walk or take a cab to dinner, you may want to choose a restaurant from among those located in Zone 1. If you have a car, you might include restaurants from contiguous zones in your consideration. (See pages 8–14 for detailed zone maps.)

Payment We've listed the type of payment accepted at each restaurant using the following code:

AMEX	American Express (Optima)
CB	Carte Blanche
DISC	Discover
DC	Diners Club
MC	MasterCard
VISA	VISA

Who's Included Because restaurants are opening and closing all the time in Miami, we have tried to confine our list to establishments with a proven track record over a fairly long period of time. Very new restaurants (and older restaurants under new management) are listed but not profiled. Those newer or changed establishments that demonstrate staying power and consistency will be profiled in subsequent editions. Also, the list is highly selective. If we leave out a particular place it does not necessarily mean that restaurant is not good, but only that it was not ranked among the best in its genre. Detailed profiles of each restaurant follow in alphabetical order at the end of this chapter.

The Best Miami Area Restaurants

Name	Star Rating	Price Rating	Quality Rating	Value Rating	Zone
American					
JADA	★★★★½	Mod/Exp	92	B	3
Red Square	★★★★	Expensive	90	B	1
The Forge/Jimmy'z at Cuba Club	★★★½	Expensive	92	B	1
Shula's Steak House	★★★½	Mod/Exp	90	C	2
Joe Allen	★★★	Moderate	84	C	1
Louie's Backyard	★★★	Mod/Exp	84	C	5
Prezzo	★★★	Moderate	84	A	2,3
Cafe Tu Tu Tango	★★★	Inexpensive	82	A	3
Kaleidoscope	★★★	Moderate	82	C	3
Rascal House	★★½	Moderate	78	B	1
Ziggy's Conch Restaurant	★★½	Moderate	77	C	5
News Cafe	★★	Inexpensive	70	C	1
Austrian					
Mozart Stube	★★★	Moderate	84	B	3
Chinese					
Chrysanthemum	★★★	Moderate	84	B	1
Continental					
La Paloma	★★★½	Moderate	89	A	2
Marker 88	★★★	Moderate	80	B	5
Cuban					
Victor's Cafe	★★★★	Mod/Exp	93	B	3
Yuca	★★★★	Expensive	90	B	1
Lario's on the Beach	★★½	Inexpensive	78	B	1
Versailles	★★	Inexpensive	70	B	3
Florida-Caribbean					
Astor Place	★★★½	Mod/Exp	90	A	1
Bagatelle	★★★	Moderate	80	C	5
French					
Blue Door at Delano	★★★★	Expensive	92	B	1

The Best Miami Area Restaurants (continued)					
Name	Star Rating	Price Rating	Quality Rating	Value Rating	Zone
French (continued)					
The Restaurant on Little Palm Island	★★★	Mod/Exp	84	C	5
Cafe des Artistes	★★★	Moderate	83	B	5
Indian					
Darbar	★★★	Moderate	83	D	3
International					
Tantra	★★★	Expensive	78	C	1
Irish					
John Martin's	★★★	Moderate	83	C	3
Italian					
Tuscan Steak	★★★★	Expensive	96	B	1
Osteria del Teatro	★★★★	Moderate	94	B	1
Il Tulipano	★★★★	Mod/Exp	92	B	2
Caffe Abbracci	★★★½	Mod/Exp	90	C	3
Claudius	★★★½	Mod/Exp	90	B	3
Giacosa	★★★½	Mod/Exp	89	B	3
La Bussola	★★★½	Mod/Exp	88	B	3
Caffe Baci	★★★	Moderate	88	B	3
Caffe Milano	★★½	Moderate	78	D	1
Japanese					
Tani Guchi's Place	★★★	Moderate	83	B	2
New American					
Nemo	★★★½	Moderate	92	B	1
Ocean Terrace Grill, Cheeca Lodge	★★★	Moderate	82	B	5
New Florida					
Chef Allen's	★★★★★	Mod/Exp	98	B	2
Mark's Las Olas	★★★★½	Mod/Exp	94	A	
The Ocean View	★★★½	Moderate	89	B	5
Pier House Restaurant	★★★½	Mod/Exp	88	B	5
Gus' Grille	★★★½	Moderate	86	B	5

The Best Miami Area Restaurants (continued)

Name	Star Rating	Price Rating	Quality Rating	Value Rating	Zone
New World					
Norman's	★★★★½	Mod/Exp	98	B	3
Pacific Rim					
Pacific Time	★★★★	Moderate	90	C	1
Pan Asian					
China Grill	★★★★	Expensive	94	B	1
Russian					
Red Square	★★★★	Expensive	90	B	1
Seafood					
Joe's Stone Crab Restaurant	★★★	Mod/Exp	88	C	1
Spanish					
Casa Juancho	★★★½	Moderate	89	B	3
Cafe Barcelona	★★★	Moderate	84	B	3
Steak					
Tuscan Steak	★★★★	Expensive	96	B	1
Morton's of Chicago	★★★★	Expensive	92	B	3
Smith & Wollensky	★★★	Expensive	85	C	1
Miami Palm Restaurant	★★★	Expensive	84	D	1
Christy's	★★★	Moderate	83	B	3
Swiss/Continental					
La Paloma	★★★½	Moderate	89	A	2
Thai					
Ruen Thai	★★★	Moderate	84	B	1
BangkokBangkok II	★★	Inexp/Mod	75	D	3

More Recommendations

Here are a few quick recommendations for special interest groups:

The Best Bagels

Bagels & Company 11064 Biscayne Boulevard, Miami, 892-2435

Bagel Emporium 1238 South Dixie Highway, Coral Gables, 666-7417

Bagel Factory 1427 Alton Road, Miami Beach, 674-1577

The Best Bakeries

Andalusia 248 Andalusia Avenue, Coral Gables, 445-8696

Biga 1080 Alton Road, Miami Beach, 535-1008

JoAnna's Marketplace 8247 South Dixie Highway, Miami, 661-5777

Lorenzo's American-Italian Supermarket and Pastry Shop 16385 West Dixie Highway, North Miami Beach, 945-6381

The Best Bar and Snacks

Cafe Tu Tu Tango CocoWalk, 3015 Grand Avenue, Coconut Grove, 529-2222

Casa Juancho 2436 SW 8th Street, Miami, 642-2452

Red Square 411 Washington Avenue, Miami Beach, 672-0200

Victor's Cafe 2340 SW 32nd Avenue, Miami, 445-1313

The Best Breakfast

La Carreta multiple locations, 444-7501

Royal Canadian Pancake House 1216 Washington Avenue, 604-9983

Versailles 3555 SW 8th Street, Miami, 445-7614

The Best Burgers

Beverly Hills Cafe 1559 Sunset Drive, Coral Gables, 666-6618

Fuddruckers 3444 Main Highway, Coconut Grove, 442-8164

Hard Rock Cafe 401 Biscayne Boulevard, 377-3110

The Best Burgers (continued)

Joe Allen 1787 Purdy Avenue, Miami Beach, 531-7007

Johnny Rockets multiple locations

The Best Coffee

Chef Allen's 19088 NE 29th Avenue, North Miami Beach, 935-2900

Victor's Cafe 2340 SW 32nd Avenue, Miami, 445-1313

Yuca 501 Lincoln Road, Miami Beach, 532-YUCA

The Best Decor

The Forge 432 41st Street, Miami Beach, 538-8533

La Paloma 10999 Biscayne Boulevard, North Miami, 891-0505

South Beach Brasserie 910 Lincoln Road, Miami Beach, 534-5511

Tuscan Steak 433 Washington Avenue, Miami Beach, 534-2233

Victor's Cafe 2340 SW 32nd Avenue, Miami, 445-1313

The Best Delis

Deli Lane Cafe 7230 SW 59th Avenue, Miami, 665-0606

Epicure Market 1656 Alton Road, Miami Beach, 672-1861

JoAnna's Marketplace 8247 South Dixie Highway, Miami, 661-5777

Lorenzo's American-Italian Supermarket and Pastry Shop 16385 West Dixie Highway, North Miami Beach, 945-6381

Rascal House 17190 Collins Avenue, North Miami Beach, 947-4581

Scotties 3117 Bird Avenue, Coconut Grove, 443-5257

The Best Desserts

China Grill 404 Washington Avenue, Miami Beach, 534-2211

Flemings: A Taste of Denmark 8511 SW 136th Street, Miami, 232-6444

Nemo 100 Collins Avenue, Miami Beach, 532-4550

The Best Late Night Service

Cafe Tu Tu Tango CocoWalk, 3015 Grand Avenue, Coconut Grove, 529-2222

Casa Juancho 2436 SW 8th Street, Miami, 642-2452

News Cafe 800 Ocean Drive, South Miami Beach, 538-6397

Victor's Cafe 2340 SW 32nd Avenue, Miami, 445-1313

The Best Pizzas

Bugatti 2504 Ponce de Leon Boulevard, Coral Gables, 441-2545

Cafe Tu Tu Tango Cocowalk, 3015 Grand Avenue, Coconut Grove, 529-2222

Prezzo Loehman's Fashion Island, 18831 Biscayne Boulevard, North Miami, 933-9004

The Best Raw Bars

Fish 18841 Biscayne Boulevard, North Miami, 932-5022

Monty's Stone Crab 2550 S. Bayshore Drive, Coconut Grove, 858-1431

Rusty Pelican 3201 Rickenbacker Causeway, Key Biscayne, 361-3818

The Best Rest Rooms

Blue Door Delano, 1685 Collins Avenue, Miami Beach, 672-2000

China Grill 404 Washington Avenue, Miami Beach, 534-2211

Tuscan Steak 433 Washington Avenue, Miami Beach, 534-2233

The Best Salad Bars

Chart House 51 Chart House Drive, Coconut Grove, 856-9741

Porcao 801 Brickell Bay Drive, Miami, 373-2777

The Best Steaks

Christy's 3101 Ponce de Leon Boulevard, Coral Gables, 446-1400

The Forge 432 41st Street, Miami Beach, 538-8533

The Best Steaks (continued)

Morton's 1200 Brickell Avenue, Miami, 400-9990

The Palm 9650 E. Bay Harbor Drive, Bay Harbor Island, 868-7256

Smith & Wollensky 1 Washington Avenue, Miami Beach, 673-2800

Tuscan Steak 431 Washington Avenue, Miami Beach, 534-2233

The Best Sunday Brunches

Biltmore Hotel 1200 Anastasia Avenue, Coral Gables, 445-1926

Dining Galleries Fontainebleau Hotel, 4441 Collins Avenue, Miami Beach, 538-2000

Joe Allen 1787 Purdy Avenue, Miami Beach, 531-7007

Porcao 801 Brickell Bay Drive, Miami, 373-2777

Yuca 501 Lincoln Road, Miami Beach, 532-YUCA

The Best Sushi Bars

Kampai Waterways Shopping Center, 3575 NE 207th Street, North Miami Beach, 931-6410

Shibui 10141 SW 72nd Street, Kendall, 274-5578

Toni's Sushi Bar 1208 Washington Avenue, Miami Beach, 673-9368

The Best Views

Louie's Backyard 700 Waddell Avenue, Key West, 294-1061

Monty's on the Beach Miami Beach Marina, 300 Alton Road, Miami Beach, 673-3444

Smith & Wollensky 1 Washington Avenue in South Pointe Park, Miami Beach, 673-2800

Sunday's on the Bay Crandon Marina, 5420 Crandon Boulevard, Key Biscayne, 361-6777

ASTOR PLACE

Florida-Caribbean	★★★½	Moderate/Expensive	QUALITY 90
			VALUE A

956 Washington Avenue (Astor Hotel)
(305) 672-7217 Miami Beach Zone 1

Customers: Young residents, tourists, businesspeople
Reservations: Accepted
When to go: Early
Entrée range: $13.95–21.95
Payment: AMEX, VISA, MC, DC
Service rating: ★★★
Friendliness rating: ★★★
Parking: Valet
Bar: Full service
Wine selection: Good
Dress: Casual
Disabled access: Good

Breakfast: Every day, 7:30–11:30 a.m.
Brunch: Sunday, noon–2 p.m., gospel brunch with Maryel Epps.
Lunch: Every day, 11:30 a.m.–2:30 p.m.; limited menu, 2:30–6 p.m.
Dinner: Sunday–Thursday, 6 p.m.–midnight; Friday and Saturday, 6 p.m.–1 a.m.

Setting & atmosphere: In yet another handsomely designed restaurant, Dennis Max makes his second debut in South Beach. Located in the lower lobby of the beautifully refurbished Astor Hotel, the 144-seat bistro focuses on a slanted glass skylight above an indoor-outdoor atrium and is highlighted by cuisine murals on the upper walls and designer floor lamps with red shades casting a glow throughout the several rooms.

House specialties: Appetizers: crab and shrimp cakes, boniato, starfruit salsa, and lobster emulsion; wild mushroom pancake "shortstack" drizzled with balsamic syrup. Entrees: herb-scented rotisserie chicken, smashed red bliss potatoes, and roasted vegetable ragout; corn-crusted yellowtail snapper, lemon boniato mash, roasted corn sauce, smoked pepper relish; grilled ancho-rubbed pork chops, jalapeño jack cheese "arepa," campfire white bean stew.

Other recommendations: Mainplate salad of sushi salad, ginger-seared scallops, curried tuna, bok choy, wasabi, and orange sesame vinaigrette.

Summary & comments: Executive chef Johnny Vinczencz explains his cuisine style as an intertwining of Southwestern and Latin cooking, using ingredients from various local and ethnic cultures—what he likes to call Caribbean Cowboy cuisine. The results are both richly flavorful and artistic in presentation.

BAGATELLE

Florida-Caribbean	★★★	Moderate	QUALITY 80	VALUE C

115 Duval Street, Key West
(305) 296-6609 Florida Keys Zone 5

Customers: Tourists, locals
Reservations: Accepted
When to go: Any time
Entrée range: $15.95–23.95
Payment: VISA, AMEX, MC, DC
Service rating: ★★★
Friendliness rating: ★★★
Parking: Nearby lots
Bar: Full service
Wine selection: Good
Dress: Casual
Disabled access: Adequate

Lunch: Every day, 11:30 a.m.–3 p.m.; light menu, 3–4 p.m.
Dinner: Every day, 5:30–10 p.m.

Setting & atmosphere: Built by a sea captain in 1884, this restaurant is considered a prime example of Key West architecture, a truly historic Key West house. Renovated in 1974, it offers expansive verandas, charming wicker furniture, and interesting island food. Its straightforward Keys fare, attractively presented, has made Bagatelle an enduring and popular tourist attraction.

House specialties: Among the appetizers: conch ceviche marinated with lime juice, cilantro, and Scotch bonnet peppers; escargot Martinique in puff pastry with mushrooms and shallots in brandy crème sauce; hearts of palm salad with avocado and fresh vegetables in balsamic vinaigrette. Among the entrees: grilled jumbo shrimp with garlic herb butter over pasta; pan-fried snapper Rangoon with fresh tropical fruits in butter rum sauce; macadamia-crusted fish sautéed with mango butter sauce; Jamaican chicken sautéed with papaya, banana, and curry.

Other recommendations: Seared rare tuna rolled in black peppercorns and served with garlic, soy, and sesame sauce; Bahamian conch steak sautéed in lime butter sauce; Keys pasta with shrimp, lobster, sautéed fish, fresh herbs, and mushrooms in rich cream sauce; grilled tenderloin of pork marinated in garlic, ginger, and soy.

Summary & comments: This choice house in Old Town Key West is classic revival in style and has had a rich history of owners. Dining on the verandas alone is a nostalgic regress into a historic past.

BANGKOKBANGKOK II

Thai	★★	Inexpensive/Moderate	QUALITY 75
			VALUE D

157 Giralda Avenue, Coral Gables
(305) 444-2397 Miami South Zone 3

Customers: Locals, businesspeople, tourists
Reservations: Accepted
When to go: Early
Entrée range: $8.95–17.95
Payment: VISA, AMEX, MC
Service rating: ★★★
Friendliness rating: ★★
Parking: On street
Bar: Wine and beer
Wine selection: Adequate
Dress: Casual, business
Disabled access: Good

Lunch: Monday–Saturday, 11:30 a.m.–5 p.m.
Dinner: Monday–Thursday, 5–10:30 p.m.; Friday and Saturday, 5–11 p.m.; Sunday, 5–10 p.m.

Setting & atmosphere: A typical Thai setting of several rooms with wood walls, carved hangings, figurines, fans, and parasols on walls. Waitresses dressed in colorful, long dresses give quick service, though the food is average.

House specialties: Among the appetizers: tom yum goong soup with shrimp in lemony broth; slices of beef tenderloin with shallots, toasted chilis, and lime; spring rolls; pork on a grill. Among the entrees: pad thai; roasted and fried crispy duck with cucumbers, onions, green peppers, carrots, pineapple, and sweet and sour sauce; shrimp red curry; grilled tiger prawns with sweet and sour tamarind sauce; steamed and fried whole fish with fiery chili sauce.

Other recommendations: Vegetable curry; shrimp sautéed with garlic and ground pepper in sherry sauce; barbecued baby back ribs with special fried rice.

Summary & comments: Inexpensive lunch specials are served with a spring roll and soup or salad, as well as a generous serving of steamed rice. Most entrees are modestly priced too, though one can leave somewhat disappointed.

BLUE DOOR AT DELANO

Tropical French	★★★★	Expensive	QUALITY 92
			VALUE B

1685 Collins Avenue (Delano Hotel)
(305) 674-6400 Miami Beach Zone 1

Customers: Young locals, tourists, celebrities
Reservations: Accepted
When to go: Any time
Entrée range: $19–34
Payment: AMEX, VISA, MC, DC,
Service rating: ★★★★
Friendliness rating: ★★★
Parking: Valet
Bar: Full service
Wine selection: Good
Dress: Casual
Disabled access: Good

Breakfast: Every day, 7–11 a.m.
Lunch: Every day, 11:30 a.m.–3 p.m.; all-day menu until 7 p.m.
Dinner: Every day, 7 p.m.–midnight

Setting & atmosphere: In the relatively new, well-hyped, all-white Delano, a walk through the long lobby where white, gauzy draperies define interesting seating alcoves with chinchilla throws covering uniquely fashioned chaises brings the diner to the all-white restaurant. Even the table flowers are white lilies. An extensive outdoor dining terrace and pool area leads all the way to the beach. Presentations are beautifully artistic. The name "Blue Door" was chosen as a symbol of the blue door, surrounded by shrubbery, that opens from the street to the hotel area. This is the only other visible color.

House specialties: Thon-Thon, black and blue tuna with marinated daikon in lime juice; pan-seared foie gras with jicama, kumquats, and starfruit in sweet and sour sauce; big raviole, jumbo ravioli filled with taro mousseline and white truffle oil; loup cajou, Chilean sea bass in a brown butter sauce with cashew nuts, garlic, lime, and fresh herbs, served with fresh hearts of palm; dourade acacia, crisp fillet of red snapper with eggplant confit in honey and sherry vinegar; boeuf au manioc, filet of beef in a cabernet sauce with yucca biscuits and mache salad.

Other recommendations: Salade pourpre, salad of red endives, radicchio, lola rosa, red oak leaves, shrimp, smoked salmon, foie gras, purple potatoes, peanuts, and shaved parmesan cheese; Saumon epice, fillet of salmon on toasted angel hair pasta with tomatoes, black olives, basil, and spicy aioli.

Summary & comments: This is a setting one must see to believe. It is a magnet to celebrities, but thanks to the prompt and friendly wait staff, dining here can be surprisingly down to earth.

CAFE BARCELONA

Spanish	★★★	Moderate	QUALITY 84
			VALUE B

160 Giralda Avenue, Coral Gables
(305) 448-0912 Miami South Zone 3

Customers: Businesspeople, locals, internationals
Reservations: Recommended on weekends
When to go: Early or late
Entrée range: $14–26
Payment: VISA, AMEX, MC
Service rating: ★★★
Friendliness rating: ★★★
Parking: Nearby lot, valet
Bar: Wine and beer
Wine selection: Good
Dress: Casual, business
Disabled access: Good

Lunch: Monday–Friday, 11 a.m.–4 p.m.
Dinner: Every day, 6–11 p.m.

Setting & atmosphere: Specializing in Spanish-Catalonian cuisine, Barcelona brings authentic dishes, different in style from the more prevalant Cuban-Spanish dishes found in many Hispanic restaurants. Its orange-gold terra-cotta walls, with scrolled gold border, and flowered tablecloths topped with green mats offer a warm, inviting atmosphere. Owner Jose Manso is a former proprietor of a Barcelona restaurant.

House specialties: Along with good country bread and a crock of ripe olives, there are many interesting choices. Among the appetizers: sautéed spinach with raisins and pine nuts; zucchini stuffed with ground beef, raisins, and pine nuts on rosemary-seasoned tomato sauce; scrambled eggs with shrimp and asparagus tips. Among the entrees: arroz con camarones (rice with shrimp), Costa Brava-style; sea bass baked in sea salt; codfish with garlic confit; grilled lamb and shrimp brochette; braised duck legs with poached pears in pear sauce.

Other recommendations: Oven-baked goat cheese on tarragon-scented tomato sauce; grouper served in a clay pot with seafood sauce; flat Spanish potato omelette.

Entertainment & amenities: Player piano.

Summary & comments: Catalan cooking is believed to be the best and most sophisticated in Spain. Owner Jose Manzo brings a particularly interesting style of cuisine to an area rich with Hispanic tradition.

CAFE DES ARTISTES

French/Caribbean	★★★	Moderate	QUALITY 83 / VALUE B

1007 Simonton Street, Key West
(305) 294-7100 Florida Keys Zone 5

Customers: Tourists, internationals, locals
Reservations: Accepted
When to go: Any time
Entrée range: $23.95–29.95
Payment: VISA, AMEX, MC
Service rating: ★★★
Friendliness rating: ★★★
Parking: Nearby
Bar: Full service
Wine selection: Good
Dress: Casual
Disabled access: Good

Dinner: Every day, 6–11 p.m.

Setting & atmosphere: Housed in an old hotel very much in keeping with Key West's architectural style, Cafe des Artistes's interior is therefore a pleasant surprise, for it is fashionably French. Cool, linen-covered walls and tablecloths against dark woods, a profusion of flowers and French music in the background, and walls covered with paintings by Key West artists set a romantic tone somewhat unique to the Keys. The second-story dining deck, however, is a contrast, offering an open, casual atmosphere and simpler, less expensive fare.

House specialties: Among the appetizers: terrine of grilled eggplant with tomato and citrus vinaigrette; terrine of duck liver with port and truffles with lentil vinaigrette; grilled shrimp in pumpkin broth with extra virgin olive oil and Reggiano; rustic tart of onion, smoked bacon, blended goat cheese, and pickled red cabbage. Among the entrees: yellowtail sautéed with shrimp and scallops in lemon butter; lobster flambéed in cognac with shrimp in saffron butter, mango, and basil; herb and garlic roast sirloin of milk-fed veal in roasted shallot sauce with portobello mushrooms; roast half-duckling with fresh raspberry sauce.

Other recommendations: Carpaccio of sliced filet mignon with braised leeks and pecorino in white truffle vinaigrette; sautéed Hudson Valley foie gras on croissant with honey thyme sauce and caramelized apple.

Summary & comments: This restaurant, said to have been built by one of the Al Capone gang in 1934, offers an opportunity, rare in the Keys, to dine elegantly on French food that, due to the influence of its surroundings, contains interesting Caribbean nuances.

CAFE TU TU TANGO

American	★★★	Inexpensive	QUALITY 82 / VALUE A

3015 Grand Avenue, Coconut Grove
(305) 529-2222 Miami South Zone 3

Customers: Young locals, tourists, internationals
Reservations: Not accepted
When to go: Any time
Entrée range: $2.95–8.95
Payment: VISA, AMEX, MC
Service rating: ★★★
Friendliness rating: ★★★
Parking: Mall lot
Bar: Full service
Wine selection: Satisfactory
Dress: Casual
Disabled access: Satisfactory

Lunch & dinner: Sunday–Wednesday, 11:30 a.m.–midnight; Thursday, 11:30 a.m.–1 a.m.; Friday and Saturday, 11:30 a.m.–2 a.m.

Setting & atmosphere: An attractive and entertaining replica of an artist's loft in Spain, Tu Tu Tango is as appealing in atmosphere as in the food. The attention to authentic detail extends even to the tables, where there are brush pots holding the tableware.

House specialties: The menu here offers more creative grazing dishes than entrees. It is intended that the diner order a pizza here, a ham and crabmeat croquette there. Among the many choices are white bean chili with smoked chicken, roasted corn, and Gruyère cheese; onion and potato frittata; ginger snapper served on sesame pasta with soy ginger glaze; duck and spinach empanadas; grilled shrimp wrapped in Italian bacon with garbanzo bean sauce.

Other recommendations: Sliced calzone with ratatouille, herbed ricotta, mozzarella artichokes, and tomatoes; baby back ribs with spiced barbecue sauce; red curry chicken sautéed with red onion, red pepper, and peanuts in red curry coconut cream sauce.

Entertainment & amenities: Spontaneous entertainment with singers, dancers, and others performing at will.

Summary & comments: This is a lively, attractive restaurant, its style unique, its dishes interesting. Planned as a casual stopping-off place where one can simply order one dish or spend hours choosing several dishes throughout the afternoon or evening.

CAFFE ABBRACCI

Italian	★★★½	Moderate/Expensive	QUALITY 90
			VALUE C

318 Aragon Avenue, Coral Gables
(305) 441-0700 Miami South Zone 3

Customers: Businesspeople, locals, tourists, internationals
Reservations: Accepted
When to go: Early
Entrée range: $12.50–23
Payment: VISA, AMEX, MC, DC
Service rating: ★★★★
Friendliness rating: ★★★★
Parking: Street
Bar: Full service
Wine selection: Good
Dress: Casual, business to elegant
Disabled access: Good

Lunch: Monday–Friday, 11:30 a.m.–3 p.m.
Dinner: Sunday–Thursday, 6–11 p.m.; Friday and Saturday, 6 p.m.–midnight

Setting & atmosphere: In a Renaissance setting of burnt gold walls with contrasting dark woods and vaulted ceiling, *Abbracci,* which translated means "hugs" (as evidenced in all the wall paintings), greets everyone with an abundance of warmth and embraces. The restaurant attracts an urban crowd of lawyers, politicians, bankers, and social types. A lounge with reflective mirrors and inviting bar eases the waiting and beckons the sated diner to sip a soothing after-dinner cappuccino or espresso.

House specialties: Among the appetizers: cold orange and coriander-marinated shrimp with white beans and tonnato sauce; a melt of mozzarella cheese topped with sautéed porcini mushrooms and white wine, garlic, and caper sauce; gnocchi al gorgonzola. Among the entrees: pounded veal chop grilled and crowned with marinated fresh tomatoes, radicchio, and arugula; grilled baby lamb chops with fresh herbs, dried cherries, and vin santo sauce; grilled medallions of beef tenderloin with marsala, goose liver, and orange sauce.

Other recommendations: Goat cheese wrapped in radicchio, grilled, and served on grilled peppers and endive; risotto with fresh asparagus and parmesan cheese; farfalle pasta with olive oil, garlic, diced tomatoes, and mixed grilled vegetables.

Summary & comments: Owner Nino Pernetti, a seasoned restaurateur, creates an atmosphere of warm, urban sophistication that seems to ensure a busy and enduring lunch and dinner crowd.

CAFFE BACI

Italian	★★★	Moderate	QUALITY 88
			VALUE B

2522 Ponce de Leon Boulevard, Coral Gables
(305) 442-0600 Miami South Zone 3

Customers: Locals, businesspeople, tourists, internationals
Reservations: Accepted
When to go: Early
Entrée range: $14–23.50
Payment: VISA, AMEX, MC, DC
Service rating: ★★★
Friendliness rating: ★★★
Parking: Valet
Bar: Wine and beer
Wine selection: Very good
Dress: Casual, business
Disabled access: Good

Lunch: Monday–Friday, noon–3 p.m.
Dinner: Sunday–Thursday, 6:30–11 p.m.; Friday and Saturday, 6:30–11:30 p.m.

Setting & atmosphere: Set in a long, narrow structure whose gold vaulted ceiling, peach colored walls, and enormous flower arrangements add drama and a casual Italian style, Baci is a warm and friendly restaurant, where the cooking is primarily that found in the Abruzzo region of Italy. It is a region said to produce the best cooks in Europe. The cuisine is rooted in ancient regional lore, with a fresh, at-the-moment approach to cooking.

House specialties: Among the appetizers: salmon and yellowtail carpaccio with juniper berries and crushed peppercorns on arugula and radicchio salad; crisp fried shrimp and calamari with piquant marinara sauce; grilled jumbo portobello mushrooms on salad greens. Among the entrees: tagliatelle pasta with porcini mushrooms; risotto alla marinara with seafood; lamb chops roasted with red wine, truffles, and rosemary; crisp veal chop Milanese sautéed in virgin olive oil; grilled Norwegian salmon with yellow pepper puree and pink peppercorns.

Other recommendations: Bufala mozzarella on sliced ripened tomatoes with basil leaves and olive oil; shrimp and scallops sautéed in mustard cream sauce and cognac.

Summary & comments: Owner Federica Rossi, herself from Abruzzo, has researched the root cooking of the region, and with Chef Mimmo Giuliani, brings to the area a fresh, bright, and unique style of Italian cooking, steeped in the traditions of her region.

CAFFE MILANO

Italian	★★½	Moderate	QUALITY 78
			VALUE D

850 Ocean Drive
(305) 532-0707 — Miami Beach Zone 1

Customers: Locals, tourists, internationals
Reservations: Accepted
When to go: Early or late
Entrée range: $15–50
Payment: VISA, AMEX, MC, DC
Service rating: ★★★
Friendliness rating: ★★★
Parking: Valet
Bar: Full service
Wine selection: Good
Dress: Casual, semiformal in the evenings
Disabled access: Good

Lunch: Every day, noon–5 p.m.
Dinner: Sunday–Thursday, 6 p.m.–midnight; Friday and Saturday, 6 p.m.–1 a.m.

Setting & atmosphere: Owned by Roberto Bearz from Milan, Italy, this restaurant, set in trendy South Beach, offers both indoor and outdoor dining. Wall murals and paintings by Colombian artist Valentino Cortacar are amusing and Picassolike in character, in tune with the casual and offbeat nature of the area.

House specialties: Bearz and staff offer a range of dishes typical of the Milan region of Italy. Among the appetizers: bresaola (air-dried beef) with radicchio; platter of Italian cold meats; warm goat cheese, watercress, and fennel salad; pasta e fagioli; carpaccio of beef with artichokes and parmesan cheese. Among the entrees: House-made tortelloni stuffed with ricotta, spinach, rum, and cinnamon, with porcini mushroom and meat sauce; veal T-bone chop Milanese with tomato and arugula; grilled filet mignon with roast potatoes and arugula vinaigrette; grilled swordfish with romaine lettuce and artichokes.

Other recommendations: Carpaccio of swordfish with olive oil, black pepper, and rosemary; gnocchi with gorgonzola sauce; risotto with porcini mushrooms.

Summary & comments: Frantically busy on weekends both indoors and out, this restaurant, nonetheless, gives prompt, if casual, service, with most dishes containing a mix of vinaigrette-tossed greens.

CASA JUANCHO

Spanish	★★★½	Moderate	QUALITY 89
			VALUE B

2436 SW 8th Street
(305) 642-2452 Miami South Zone 3

Customers: Hispanic locals, businessmen, internationals
Reservations: Accepted
When to go: Early
Entrée range: $10.95–26.95
Payment: VISA, AMEX, MC, DC
Service rating: ★★★★
Friendliness rating: ★★★
Parking: Valet
Bar: Full service
Wine selection: Good
Dress: Casual, business
Disabled access: Good

Lunch & dinner: Sunday–Thursday, noon–midnight; Friday and Saturday, noon–1 a.m.

Setting & atmosphere: A popular Spanish-style dining spot for active members of the Hispanic community. The structure is richly *español*—Spanish tiles, brick walls, columns, dark woods and beams, and shadowy lighting. The open grills, hanging hams, peppers, garlic, and other foods are strongly reminiscent of Spain.

House specialties: The food is authentically Spanish and well prepared, with some items imported from Spain on a regular basis. Among the appetizers: Spanish roast peppers stuffed with codfish mousse; baby eels in spicy garlic sauce; white Astoria fava beans and baby clams in light marinara sauce; mixed seafood vinaigrette; garlic soup Castillian-style. Among the entrees: chilled whole two-pound Florida lobster with two salsas; grilled snapper fillet over flaming oak logs splashed with fiery garlic and vinegar sauce; codfish sautéed in garlic and Spanish pimento tomato sauce; rabbit cured in sherry and baked with thyme and creamy brown sauce; grilled beef tenderloin pork chop, Spanish sausage, and baby lamb chop.

Other recommendations: Crisp roast suckling pig; arroz a la Castellana with rice, chicken, veal, pork, ham, rabbit, sausage, and chick peas; vegetarian paella with artichokes, asparagus, green beans, garbanzo, lima beans, roast peppers, and sweet peas.

Entertainment & amenities: Live music nightly.

Summary & comments: Hispanics generally are late diners—thus the mood at night is festive, and the various rooms are crowded. One sees a wonderful slice of Hispanic life.

CHEF ALLEN'S

New Florida/Caribbean	★★★★★	Moderate/Expensive	QUALITY 98
			VALUE B

19088 NE 29th Avenue
(305) 935-2900 Miami North Zone 2

Customers: Locals, tourists, internationals
Reservations: Accepted
When to go: Early
Entrée range: $21.95–29.95
Payment: VISA, AMEX, MC, DC
Service rating: ★★★★
Friendliness rating: ★★★★
Parking: Adjoining lot
Bar: Full service
Wine selection: Very good
Dress: Informal, business
Disabled access: Good

Dinner: Sunday–Friday, 6–10:30 p.m.; Saturday, 6–11 p.m.

Setting & atmosphere: Operating in a stylish, contemporary setting, Chef Allen is one of the finest interpreters of America's bold new cuisine, embellishing his dishes with Florida-Caribbean tastes, flavors, and ingredients. A curved ceiling outlined in pink neon accents the creamy pastels of the rooms, all looking into the glassed-in kitchen. Bright, modern paintings stand out against light-colored walls. The menu changes daily and offers endless surprises.

House specialties: A degustation menu of four courses and wines for $52. Appetizers: tuna tartare with Sevruga caviar and vine-ripe "bloody mary" vinaigrette; Bahamian lobster and crab cakes with tropical fruit chutney; rock shrimp hash with roast corn, crisp boniato, and mango ketchup; grilled Florida calamari with warm green lentils and balsamic syrup. Entrees: grilled line-caught cobia with citrus couscous and scallop-mango salsa; pan-seared pompano with smoked onion and sweet potato hash with cilantro tomato broth; yucca-encrusted mangrove snapper with blood orange mojo and moros rice; Tribeca veal chop with double mustard, wild mushroom risotto, and ginger-glazed calabaza.

Other recommendations: Fire-blasted shrimp with vanilla, cinnamon, and papaya-apricot salsa; crisp young duck with wild rice pancake, stuffed poblano pepper, and cranberry ketchup; grilled Caribbean bouillabaisse with grouper, swordfish, snapper, and pink shrimp. The chocolate pistachio soufflé is a must.

Summary & comments: Chef Allen, French- and LeCirque-trained, emerges as one of the finest and most respected chefs in South Florida.

Honors & awards: Among many other awards, Chef Allen's was inducted into the Hall of Fame by the National Restaurant Association in 1993.

CHINA GRILL

Pan Asian	★★★★	Expensive	QUALITY 94
			VALUE B

404 Washington Avenue
(305) 534-2211 Miami Beach Zone 1

Customers: Locals, businesspeople, tourists
Reservations: Accepted, necessary
When to go: Early
Entrée range: $18.50–29
Payment: AMEX, VISA, MC, DC
Service rating: ★★★
Friendliness rating: ★★★
Parking: Valet
Bar: Full service
Wine selection: Good
Dress: Casual to dressy
Disabled access: Good

Lunch: Monday–Friday, 11:45 a.m.–5 p.m.
Dinner: Sunday–Thursday, 6 p.m.–midnight; Friday and Saturday, 6 p.m.–1 a.m.

Setting & atmosphere: In a spectacular, landmark building of glass, onyx, and limestone, China Grill is an equally dramatic setting of sweeping, multilevel space that includes an indoor/outdoor café and sushi/satay bar, several dining areas, and an intimate champagne, sake, and vodka bar. Under the same ownership as the New York China Grill, the 200-seat restaurant is plush, with many enormous, mushroom-shaped gold chandeliers hanging from the ceiling, gold and green tones on the walls and ceilings, and an open kitchen.

House specialties: Among the appetizers: carrot and potato pancakes with ginger cream and caviar; lamb or broccoli rabe dumplings; Peking duckling salad. Among the entrees: Australian organic free-range lamb with quinoa salad and mandarin orange sauce; wasabi-crusted grouper with citrus-potato pancake in red wine miso sauce; Japanese panko-crusted veal chop with summer greens.

Other recommendations: Beijing oysters; wild mushroom profusion pasta with sake-Madeira cream sauce; oriental antipasto.

Summary & comments: The food is delicious and as extraordinarily beautiful as the setting. Though prices are not inexpensive, portions are enormous and can be shared. A fixed-price lunch menu of under $20 will render more food than you can consume. There's a separate VIP area for celebrities and stars, with gold-threaded draperies that may be drawn for privacy. Ordinary folk seem equally welcome. Executive Chef Ephraim Kadish likes to call his cuisine "world cuisine" with Asian flavors and techniques.

CHRISTY'S

Steak House	★★★	Moderate	QUALITY 83
			VALUE B

3101 Ponce de Leon Boulevard, Coral Gables
(305) 446-1400 Miami South Zone 3

Customers: Locals, tourists, internationals
Reservations: Accepted
When to go: Early
Entrée range: $18–25.50
Payment: VISA, AMEX, MC, DC
Service rating: ★★★
Friendliness rating: ★★★
Parking: Nearby lot
Bar: Full service
Wine selection: Good
Dress: Casual, business
Disabled access: Good

Lunch: Monday–Friday, 11:30 a.m.–4 p.m.
Dinner: Monday–Thursday, 4–11:30 p.m.; Friday, 4 p.m.–midnight; Saturday, 5 p.m.–midnight; Sunday, 5–11:30 p.m.

Setting & atmosphere: You are probably due for a wait. Diners line up nightly, sipping the proprietor's gratis wine in a convivial atmosphere. One of the most popular restaurants in the Miami area, Christy's specializes in steaks—big, aged, corn-fed Midwestern ones—in a clublike ambience. Most diners are repeat customers, loyal to the owner who knows most of them by name. The menu is simple and straightforward, the food fresh and well prepared.

House specialties: Among the appetizers: prosciutto and melon; basket of potato skins; zucchini Milanese. Among the entrees: Ten- and 14-ounce steaks; large and small prime ribs of beef; chateaubriand for two; roast duck; broiled lamb chops. All dinners are served with a large Caesar salad and baked potato.

Other recommendations: Double-broiled veal chop; two-pound lobster; steak tartare.

Summary & comments: Nearly 15 years old, this restaurant is legendary in the Miami area. Owner Michael Namour keeps his menu simple and consistent, a formula that has brought him amazing success.

CHRYSANTHEMUM

Chinese	★★★	Moderate	QUALITY 84 / VALUE B

1248 Washington Avenue
(305) 531-5656 Miami Beach Zone 1

Customers: Locals, tourists, internationals
Reservations: Recommended on weekends
When to go: Early
Entrée range: $10–19
Payment: VISA, AMEX, MC, DC
Service rating: ★★★
Friendliness rating: ★★
Parking: Valet
Bar: Full service
Wine selection: Adequate
Dress: Casual, business
Disabled access: Good

Dinner: Sunday–Thursday, 6–11 p.m.; Friday and Saturday, 6 p.m.–midnight

Setting & atmosphere: This is a spacious restaurant featuring Chinese artwork and lovely flower arrangements. Black tablecloths with contrasting white napkins, black chairs cushioned in gray print, soft pink lighting, hanging Chinese lanterns, and a mirrored far wall combine to induce a pleasant kind of leisure. Exceptional food and an efficient staff make this one of the better Chinese restaurants in the area.

House specialties: Among the appetizers: crispy frog legs with Szechuan spices; seared tuna with Chinese salad; aromatic duck with spring onions and cucumbers in pancakes. Among the entrees: whole deep-fried fish in braised chili and cayenne sauce; sautéed jumbo shrimp Szechuan-style sizzled with shallots in sweet and spicy sauce; roasted Peking duck with cucumbers, scallions, and Hoisin sauce in pancakes.

Other recommendations: Five-flavored boned spareribs; soft, homemade Peking-style noodles with mixed vegetables, chicken, or seafood; crispy orange beef with spicy orange glaze; filet mignon sizzled in Mandarin sauce.

Summary & comments: This outstanding restaurant harbors a Hong Kong kitchen staff, known to produce sophisticated Chinese food that is fragrant and beautiful to behold.

CLAUDIUS (CLAVDIVS)

Italian	★★★½	Moderate/Expensive	QUALITY 90 / VALUE B

2626 Ponce de Leon Blvd, Coral Gables
(305) 445-2626 Miami South Zone 3

Customers: Locals, businesspeople
Reservations: Accepted
When to go: Any time
Entrée range: $17–$29
Payment: VISA, MC, AMEX
Service rating: ★★★
Friendliness rating: ★★★
Parking: Valet and self
Bar: Full service
Wine selection: Good
Dress: Business
Disabled access: Yes

Lunch: Monday–Friday, noon–3 p.m.
Dinner: Daily, 6 p.m.–midnight

Setting & atmosphere: Owned and managed by seasoned restaurateur Claudio Giordano, this is a place to unwind and enjoy innovative Italian World Cuisine. A sleek piano bar welcomes diners before entering the majestic "Roman Empire"–designed dining room. Aside from the traditional Italian offerings, their new World Cuisine combines Oriental, Caribbean, and South American influences with Italian cooking. A stark interior features large Roman columns and assorted textures of marble and stone, creating a luminous, cavernous ambience.

House specialties: Caprese salad; tricolore salad; prosciutto di Parma with watercress salad; Picky Toe crab cake served with mustard sauce; homemade veal mousse ravioli with sage butter sauce; tortelli di zucca or homemade tortelli stuffed with pumpkin and light port wine sauce; homemade pansotti with fresh herbs and tomato coulis; saffron and rock shrimp ravioli with Aurora sauce; pan-roasted double-cut veal chop; pan-seared duck foie gras with parmesan risotto, vidalia onion puree, and caramelized cipollini onions.

Other recommendations: Marinated thin beef or salmon slices with virgin olive oil; homemade fettuccini with Florida lobster in light lobster sauce; baby rack of lamb with a green peppercorn mustard sauce; grilled salmon fillet over Israeli toasted couscous.

Entertainment & amenities: Jazz and live Latin dance music (call for schedule).

Summary & comments: With an impressive but tacky exterior, Claudius interiors are sophisticated and elegant. One of the new places to open in the restaurant-crowded Coral Gables, this one has the potential to become a local institution.

DARBAR

Indian	★★★	Moderate	QUALITY 83 / VALUE D

276 Alhambra Circle, Coral Gables
(305) 448-9691 Miami South Zone 3

Customers: Indian residents, tourists, locals
Reservations: Accepted
When to go: Any time
Entrée range: $8.50–15.95
Payment: VISA, AMEX, MC, DC
Service rating: ★★★
Friendliness rating: ★★
Parking: On street
Bar: Wine and beer
Wine selection: Adequate
Dress: Casual, business
Disabled access: Good

Lunch: Monday–Saturday, 11:30 a.m.–2:30 p.m.
Dinner: Monday–Sunday, 6–10:30 p.m.

Setting & atmosphere: Pleasant, symmetrical setting with high ceiling, lots of twinkling lights, and a mix of banquettes and tables. Look out for suggested à la carte add-ons. They mount up quickly.

House specialties: Among the appetizers: puffed, stuffed breads, including vegetable samosa, onion bhajee, keema nan with minced lamb stuffing, and paratha stuffed with potatoes and garden peas; mulligatawny soup. Among the entrees: lamb curry with green peppers, or cooked with yogurt and cream; shrimp curry with leaf spinach; chicken, lamb, or shrimp biryani, cooked with basmati rice with boiled egg, tomato, nuts, and raisins; mixed tandoori platter.

Other recommendations: Chicken madras with onions, garlic, ginger, and capsicum; chicken makhani, barbecued in tomato and butter sauce.

Summary & comments: The setting is attractive and upscale, and the stuffed breads are exceptional.

THE FORGE/JIMMY'Z AT CUBA CLUB

American	★★★½	Expensive	QUALITY 92 / VALUE B

432 41st Street, Miami Beach
(305)-534-4536 Miami Beach Zone 1

Customers: Locals, tourists
Reservations: Accepted
When to go: Any time
Entrée range: $19.95–$69.95
Payment: VISA, MC, AMEX, DISC
Service rating: ★★★★

(The Forge/Jimmy'z at Cuba Club)

Friendliness rating: ★★★
Parking: Valet
Bar: Full service
Wine selection: Outstanding
Dress: Business attire/casual elegant
Disabled access: Yes

Dinner: Every day, Sunday–Thursday, 6–11 p.m.; Friday and Saturday, 6 p.m.–midnight.

Setting & atmosphere: One of the most luxurious restaurants in the city, The Forge is an institution of fine dining. With the opening of Jimmy'z at Cuba Club, a cigar club, restaurant, and disco, The Forge expands to attracts all nightlife owls. Works of art and one of the best wine lists in the country make dinning at the Forge and the adjacent Jimmy'z a most complete experience. Join the party on Wednesday nights, when The Forge and Jimmy'z become the most frequented and fun spot in the city. Chef Kal is the genius who creates the high volume and extensive menu.

House specialties: Chilled jumbo shrimp; shrimp marlin; petrossian smoked salmon; yellowfin tuna tartare; The Forge's chopped salad; The Forge's "Super Steak," voted the #1 steak in America by *Wine Spectator* Magazine; prime rib; snapper cashew; duck cassis; rack of lamb; chocolate soufflé.

Other recommendations: Escargots; beluga caviar; caesar salad; glamourous chicken; salmon fa-tuche; venison; filet mignon

Entertainment & amenities: Wednesday night Forge Party with Roberto Costa, DJ. Theme parties at Jimmy'z by Regine; Tuesday night Jazz at Jimmy'z.

Summary & comments: The Forge is one of Miami's most complete and reliable dinning experiences.

GIACOSA

Italian ★★★½ Moderate/Expensive

QUALITY	VALUE
89	B

394 Giralda Avenue, Coral Gables
(305) 445-5858 Miami South Zone 3

Customers: Locals, businesspeople, tourists
Reservations: Accepted
When to go: Early
Entrée range: $13.95–28.95
Payment: VISA, AMEX, MC, DC
Service rating: ★★★
Friendliness rating: ★★★
Parking: Valet and lot
Bar: Full service
Wine selection: Good
Dress: Casual, business to elegant
Disabled access: Good

(Giacosa)

Lunch: Monday–Friday, noon–3 p.m.
Dinner: Monday–Friday, 6–11 p.m.; Friday and Saturday, 6 p.m.–midnight; Sunday, 6–10:30 p.m.

Setting & atmosphere: Light and airy tropical colors, cushioned period chairs, intricate drapery arrangements over filmy curtains, and patterned throw rugs speak of an earlier period in Coral Gables history. A blend of deep and pale green walls are a soft complement to crisp white tablecloths. In this inviting environment, owner/chef Alfredo Alvarez re-creates classical dishes from each region of Italy and gives them his own innovative touch.

House specialties: Along with daily specials, the following appetizers are available: roast onion stuffed with shrimp; radicchio-wrapped goat cheese on cucumbers in raspberry sauce; carpaccio of fresh fish in lemon sauce; steamed mussels with saffron and fresh tomatoes. Among the entrees: trenette with roast red peppers and bacon; seafood risotto Mediterranean-style; grilled veal chop with roasted garlic and herb butter; roast rack of lamb with truffles; grilled prawns with risotto.

Other recommendations: Scallop-filled tortelli with thyme cream sauce; Italian gravlax with fennel; salt-layered grilled whole fish; seafood Livornese, peasant-style; tournedos Rossini with goose liver and truffles.

Summary & comments: This attractive restaurant is noted for its friendly atmosphere and accommodating attitude, as well as its innovative regional Italian dishes. The menu changes regularly.

Honors & awards: *South Florida* magazine Critic's award 1993 for best Italian restaurant in Coral Gables.

GUS' GRILLE

New Florida	★★★½	Moderate	QUALITY 86 / VALUE B

103800 Overseas Highway (Key Largo Bay Beach Resort), Key Largo
(305) 453-0066 Florida Keys Zone 5

Customers: Tourists, internationals
Reservations: Accepted
When to go: Any time
Entrée range: $14.50–21.50
Payment: VISA, AMEX, MC, DC, DISC
Service rating: ★★★★

Friendliness rating: ★★★★
Parking: Valet
Bar: Full service
Wine selection: Very good
Dress: Casual, business
Disabled access: Good

(Gus' Grille)

Breakfast: Every day, 7:30–11:30 a.m.
Lunch: Every day, 11:30 a.m.–4:30 p.m.
Dinner: Every day, 4:30–11 p.m.

Setting & atmosphere: Gus' offers one of the most attractive and colorful nautical settings in the Keys, and some of the best food. Speckled pink, green, and pale terra-cotta tiles cover the floors, and tropical shades of pinks, mauves, emerald greens, and lavenders are repeated in the banquettes, wall decorations, and tables. A second-floor extension is somewhat more formal in decor, and dress expectations are a bit higher.

House specialties: Among the appetizers: Bahamian conch chowder; lump crab cake; chicken chili quesadilla. Among the entrees: paella with saffron risotto; pecan-crusted yellowtail snapper, pan-sautéed with Frangelica reduction and potatoes; Florida spiny lobster sautéed with saffron cream, tomato confit, olive pesto, and goat cheese mashed potatoes; certified Angus New York strip steak with black peppercorn crust.

Other recommendations: Spinach and feta in phyllo with dill cucumber yogurt sauce and calamata olives; calzone with wild mushrooms, roasted peppers, spinach, ricotta, and goat cheese; linguine with Florida lobster tail, spinach, tomato concasse, garlic cream, and basil; braised veal shank with wild mushroom sauce, caramelized root vegetables, and white beans.

Summary & comments: This resort was built immediately after Hurricane Andrew, and is one of the loveliest in the Upper Keys. The restaurant focuses on Caribbean-style cooking, using the abundance of fresh fish available there.

IL TULIPANO

Italian ★★★★ Moderate/Expensive

QUALITY	VALUE
92	B

11052 Biscayne Boulevard
(305) 893-4811 Miami North Zone 2

Customers: Businesspeople, locals, tourists, celebrities
Reservations: Accepted
When to go: Early
Entrée range: $15–28
Payment: VISA, AMEX, MC, DC
Service rating: ★★★★
Friendliness rating: ★★★★
Parking: Valet
Bar: Full service
Wine selection: Exceptional
Dress: Business, casual
Disabled access: Good

Dinner: Monday–Thursday, 6–11 p.m.; Friday and Saturday, 6 p.m.–midnight; Sunday, closed.

Setting & atmosphere: Located in an 80-year-old Art Deco building with double oak doors handcarved with the tulip motif, Il Tulipano is small and impeccably appointed with crisp linens, fine china, vignettes of Italian art, and a fresh tulip at every table. It is home to an affluent dining-out crowd accustomed to unabashed pampering.

House specialties: Large, tricolored roasted peppers bathed in olive oil and balsamic vinegar; cloudlike agnolotti impannate; risotto verde with baby asparagus spears; enormous Mediterranean red prawns with olive oil, garlic, and thyme; veal cutlet Valdostana with prosciutto, fontina cheese, and fresh tomato sauce.

Other recommendations: Fresh mozzarella with red beefsteak tomatoes and basil, dribbled with black pepper and olive oil; grilled swordfish with rosemary garlic sauce; herb and wine-poached baby octopus on vine-ripened tomatoes and wheels of polenta.

Summary & comments: Now owned and managed by seasoned restaurateur Ron Wayne, Il Tulipano runs better then ever. In keeping with the style of the previous owner, Filipo Il Grande, Ron's personality has brought a new and different level of friendliness. Very well-trained staff give their best as the kitchen produces homemade Italian cuisine. The prices are expensive, but consistently worth every penny.

Honors & awards: *Wine Spectator* Best of Award of Excellence; DiRona award for one of the most distinguished restaurants in America.

JADA

Regional American ★★★★½ Moderate/Expensive

QUALITY	VALUE
92	B

5837 Sunset Drive, Downtown South Miami
(305) 665-4190 Miami South Zone 3

Customers: Locals
Reservations: Accepted
When to go: Early
Entrée range: $16–30
Payment: VISA, MC, AMEX
Service rating: ★★★
Friendliness rating: ★★★★
Parking: Self parking and ample all around
Bar: Wine and beer
Wine selection: Very good
Dress: Casual
Disabled access: Yes

Dinner: Every day; Sunday–Thursday, 5:30–10 p.m.; Friday and Saturday, 5:30–11 p.m.

Setting & atmosphere: A young team, David Gordon and chef Jake Klein, have created one of the best neighborhood restaurants anyone can imagine. A sleek and cozy decor is serves as just a prelude to some of the most inventive and delicious foods prepared in town. A great deal of love, care, and personal attention goes into JADA. Filled to capacity since its opening, diners are treated to straightforward preparations and are invited to try ingredients they normally wouldn't. The public and critics are raving about this place; you will too.

House specialties: Roasted portobello arepa; tuna sashimi with spinach salad; salmon tartare with wasabi Scotch bonnet vinaigrette; shiitake and goat cheese ravioli with carrot ginger nage; Vietnamese-style beef and noodle soup; jackfruit barbecued duck and beer-battered onion rings; Thai chicken with lemon grass and eggplant puree; red cooked lamb shank over garlic mashed potatoes.

Other recommendations: Grilled Hoisin game hen and sweet potato mash; coriander-rubbed veal chop with Cuban pumpkin risotto; day-boat black grouper; Szechuan peppercorn-seared tuna, warm truffled sweet potato salad.

Summary & comments: One of the most welcome additions to the South Miami dining scene, this high-end neighborhood dining spot makes its own mark with chef Jake Klein at the helm of the kitchen.

JOE ALLEN

American	★★★	Moderate	QUALITY 84	VALUE A

1787 Purdy Avenue, Miami Beach
(305) 531-7007 — Miami Beach Zone 1

Customers: Locals, tourists
Reservations: Accepted
When to go: Any time
Entree range: $10–20
Payment: VISA, MC
Service rating: ★★★
Friendliness rating: ★★★★
Parking: Ample metered parking
Bar: Full service
Wine selection: Satisfactory
Dress: Casual
Disabled access: Good

Lunch: Weekdays, noon–4 p.m.; Sunday and Saturday brunch, noon–4 p.m.

Dinner: Daily 4 p.m.–midnight; bar open until 2 a.m., Friday and Saturday

Setting & atmosphere: Legendary restaurateur Joe Allen, owner and operator of a string of successful namesake establishments, including the original location in the heart of New York's theater district, brings his signature style of informal dining to South Florida. Seafoam-colored walls are adorned by metallic figurines, riding invisible waves on multicolored surfboards. Wall-mounted silver fans spin noiselessly as diners sit on comfortable, old-time restaurant chairs, refinished in a light copper automotive paint. The industrial-looking bar is reminiscent of Key West. Very friendly and courteous staff offer the most attentive service imaginable.

House specialties: Appetizers include gazpacho Andaluzas with spicy croutons; arugula salad with grilled portobello mushrooms, roasted red peppers and gorgonzola dressing. Sandwiches include great hamburgers with french fries; roast turkey on country bread with smoked mozzarella and calf's liver pâté. Pizzas include the traditional Margherita and five more. Entrees include grilled New York sirloin steak with french fries; sautéed calf's liver with mashed potatoes and sautéed spinach; meatloaf with mashed potatoes; oven-roasted chicken breast stuffed with shrimp, served with portobello mushrooms, asparagus, and shrimp sauce.

Other recommendations: Grilled rainbow trout with grilled zucchini and arugula salad; linguini putanesca; no-fat vegetable stew with chicken or pasta.

Summary & comments: The price and value are great, the service is as friendly as it gets. This new addition to the Miami Beach dining scene is hard to find, but once there, one is sure to come back over and over again.

JOE'S STONE CRAB RESTAURANT

Seafood ★★★ Moderate/Expensive

QUALITY
88
VALUE
C

227 Biscayne Street
(305) 673-0365 Miami Beach Zone 1

Customers: Tourists from around the world, locals
Reservations: Not accepted
When to go: Early
Entrée range: $4.50–32
Payment: VISA, AMEX, MC, DC
Service rating: ★★★
Friendliness rating: ★★★
Parking: Valet
Bar: Full service
Wine selection: Adequate
Dress: Casual
Disabled access: Good

Lunch: Tuesday–Saturday, 11:30 a.m.–2 p.m.
Dinner: Sunday–Thursday, 5–10 p.m.; Friday and Saturday, 5–11 p.m.

Setting & atmosphere: This may be South Florida's most popular and famous restaurant. Its purpose: to serve stone crab in season, from mid-October to mid-May. Simple and utilitarian, it serves as many as 1,500 per day, as it has for 80 years. Service is good, efficient, and no-nonsense in style. Unless you visit for lunch or an early dinner, you can expect a wait.

House specialties: Though other restaurants serve stone crabs, none seem to taste quite like those at Joe's. Nearly essential accompaniments are the generous plates of hash browns and coleslaw. A popular side dish specialty is creamed spinach. Fried soft-shell crabs; blue crab cakes; sautéed fillet of sole; ginger salmon.

Other recommendations: Fried or grilled pompano, swordfish, or grouper; New York sirloin or broiled lamb chops for non-fish eaters; Maine lobster is the most expensive entree, costing as much as $32. Prices usually no higher than $24.95.

Summary & comments: This restaurant is a legend, popular with locals, and a must for tourists. Always busy, a bit noisy, it is an exciting experience. Owned and operated by the original owner's granddaughter, Joan Sawitz Bass, Joe's luster never diminishes.

Honors & awards: Holiday and Golden Spoon Awards and dozens more.

JOHN MARTIN'S

Irish ★★★ Moderate

QUALITY	VALUE
83	C

253 Miracle Mile, Coral Gables
(305) 445-3777 Miami South Zone 3

Customers: Locals, internationals, tourists, nostalgic Irishmen
Reservations: Accepted
When to go: Early
Entrée range: $7–17
Payment: VISA, AMEX, MC, DC
Service rating: ★★★★
Friendliness rating: ★★★★
Parking: In nearby lot
Bar: Full service
Wine selection: Adequate
Dress: Casual, business
Disabled access: Good

Open: Monday–Thursday, 11:30 a.m.–midnight; Friday and Saturday, 11:30 a.m.–1 a.m.; Sunday, 11:30 a.m.–10:30 p.m.

Setting & atmosphere: The charm of Irish owners John Clarke (chef) and Martin Lynch (manager) and the Irish staff here is seductive. Combining both a pub on one side and a lovely Waterford Room on the other, they have enjoyed considerable popularity for more than a decade. From the Irish soda bread to the Irish smoked salmon, the restaurant strives to remain ethnically on track.

House specialties: Among the appetizers: smoked salmon with homemade brown soda bread; spinach salad with aged Roquefort and warm bacon dressing; Irish potato soup with chopped bacon, fresh cream, and scallions. Among the entrees: shepherd's pie; fresh herb and potato-stuffed chicken breast wrapped in bacon; Gaelic steak flamed in a whiskey mushroom sauce; roast duckling with port and raspberry sauce.

Other recommendations: Grilled shrimp with mustard sauce; pan-fried Dover sole meunière; Irish stew.

Entertainment & amenities: Irish music and sing-alongs several nights each week.

Summary & comments: Friends since childhood, Lynch and Clarke professionally trained in England, noted the need for Irish representation in the Gables, and apparently were right. The restaurant enjoys a singular kind of popularity.

KALEIDOSCOPE

American	★★★	Moderate	QUALITY 82 / VALUE C

3112 Commodore Plaza, Coconut Grove
(305) 446-5010 — Miami South Zone 3

Customers: Businesspeople, tourists, locals
Reservations: Accepted
When to go: Early
Entrée range: $8.95–16.95
Payment: VISA, AMEX, MC, DC
Service rating: ★★★
Friendliness rating: ★★★
Parking: Street
Bar: Full service
Wine selection: Good
Dress: Casual
Disabled access: Good

Brunch: Sunday, 11 a.m.–3 p.m.
Lunch: Monday–Saturday, 11:30 a.m.–3 p.m.
Dinner: Monday–Thursday, 6–11 p.m.; Friday and Saturday, 6 p.m.–midnight; Sunday, 5:30–10:30 p.m.

Setting & atmosphere: Here you'll find a delightful, bright tropical setting long popular with locals in the Coconut Grove area. A charming terrace looks out on the street below, and a wine bar is a busy meeting spot for diners.

House specialties: Among the appetizers: Bahamian seafood griddle cakes with crisp fried leeks and spicy sweet and sour coulis; grilled Cajun-spiced gulf prawns; bruschetta with tomato, fresh basil, and roasted garlic. Among the entrees: penne with Jamaican-spiced roasted chicken and grilled yams, broccoli, capers, tomatoes, and fresh herbs; roasted medallions of black grouper in spicy herb crust with grilled vegetables and garlic mashed potatoes, Key lime beurre blanc; cassoulet of duck, andouille sausage, bacon, and white beans.

Other recommendations: Grilled radicchio stuffed with goat cheese and walnuts in raspberry vinaigrette; sesame-crusted seared yellowfin tuna with baby bok choy and oriental wild rice; crisp roasted duck with Indian harvest wild rice, orange chutney, rum glaze, and green peppercorns.

Summary & comments: The setting, with its special flair, continues to draw diners through the years, and the food, now in the hands of a young and innovative chef, draws equal interest.

LA BUSSOLA

Italian ★★★½ Moderate/Expensive

QUALITY	VALUE
88	B

264 Giralda Avenue, Coral Gables
(305) 445-8783 Miami South Zone 3

Customers: Businesspeople, internationals, tourists, locals
Reservations: Accepted
When to go: Early
Entrée range: $17.95–29
Payment: VISA, AMEX, MC, DC
Service rating: ★★★★
Friendliness rating: ★★★
Parking: Nearby lot, street, valet for dinner
Bar: Full service
Wine selection: Excellent
Dress: Casual, business
Disabled access: Good

Lunch: Monday–Friday, noon–3 p.m.
Dinner: Sunday–Thursday, 6–11 p.m.; Friday and Saturday, 6–11:30 p.m.

Setting & atmosphere: Created by Kiril Anatkov, an architect-artist, La Bussola's interior is a stunning work of art. Murals depicting ancient scenes and costumes, gold-flecked columns, and gossamer draperies serving as room dividers set a tone of elegance and grace in this restaurant. Owner Elizabeth Giordano is acknowledged to operate one of the finest Italian restaurants in the Miami area.

(La Bussola)

House specialties: Among the appetizers: julienne of roasted peppers with grilled jumbo shrimp; broiled jumbo sea scallops with orange sauce and mint-marinated artichokes; mixed grill of wild mushrooms, wilted spinach, and roasted pine nuts. Among the entrees: spinach and cheese ravioli with fresh thyme and white truffle sauce; mushroom-crusted baked red snapper with thyme Chardonnay sauce; grilled veal chop with sun-dried tomatoes and rosemary potatoes.

Other recommendations: Bistecca alla fiorentina with herbs and olive oil; rare venison chops with wild cherry sauce, polenta, raisins, and pine nuts; grilled rare tuna with herbs and yellow and red beefsteak tomatoes.

Summary & comments: This stunning restaurant is lively and busy both at lunch and dinner, yet service remains impeccable and caring. It exemplifies high-style Italian cooking.

Honors & awards: American Academy of Restaurant Sciences Top 10 in the country award.

LA PALOMA

Continental/Swiss ★★★½ Moderate

QUALITY	VALUE
89	A

10999 Biscayne Boulevard
(305) 891-0505 Miami North Zone 2

Customers: Locals, tourists, winter residents
Reservations: Accepted
When to go: Early or late
Entrée range: $12.95–25.95
Payment: VISA, AMEX, MC, DC
Service rating: ★★★★
Friendliness rating: ★★★★
Parking: Valet
Bar: Full service
Wine selection: Good
Dress: Casual, business
Disabled access: Good

Lunch: Monday–Friday, 11:30 a.m.–3 p.m.
Dinner: Every day, 5 p.m.–midnight.

Setting & atmosphere: La Paloma is all about the way things were. A plush Victorian setting with tapestried Victorian chairs, elaborate washed taffeta green draperies against deep green walls, and mirrored inserts, shimmering chandeliers, and impeccable white linens transport the diner to the salons of "The Age of Innocence." Dresden figurines and fine china glitter in ornate breakfronts, and fresh roses grace every table.

House specialties: The menu is rich with many ageless classics. Among the appetizers: oysters Rockefeller; coquille St. Jacques; escargot Bourguignonne;

bisque de homard. Among the entrees: chicken Kiev; duckling with orange sauce; steak au poivre; jumbo grilled veal chop with wild mushrooms; fillet of sole with capers, lemon, scallions, and fresh tomato dice; Wiener schnitzel. Entrees are accompanied by house salad and a mix of vegetables.

Other recommendations: Grilled rack of lamb à la diable; bouillabaisse; fettuccini with jumbo shrimp and saffron sauce; poached salmon with tarragon sauce.

Entertainment & amenities: Pianist.

Summary & comments: This restaurant never wavers from offering its version of Swiss food, which includes the influences of French, Italian, and German cuisine. It brings a determinedly elegant and gracious touch to the dining process with its ornate setting, well-prepared dishes, and the kind of professional service rarely found today. It can provoke a nostalgic longing for the way things ought to be.

LARIO'S ON THE BEACH

Cuban	★★½	Inexpensive	QUALITY 78	VALUE B

820 Ocean Drive
(305) 532-9577 — Miami Beach Zone 1

Customers: Locals, tourists, internationals
Reservations: Not accepted
When to go: Early
Entrée range: $5.95–13.95
Payment: VISA, AMEX, MC, DC
Service rating: ★★★
Friendliness rating: ★★★
Parking: Valet
Bar: Full service
Wine selection: Fair
Dress: Casual
Disabled access: Good

Lunch & dinner: Sunday–Thursday, 11:30 a.m.–midnight; Friday and Saturday, 11:30 a.m.–2 a.m.

Setting & atmosphere: Gloria Estefan looms mightily as an attraction, though chances of seeing her here are rare. She and her husband own the building, but the Lario family owns the biggest part of the restaurant. A combination of Art Deco and utilitarian, the decor consists of simple wooden tables and chairs, surrounded by burnt-gold walls. Simulated blue skies peek through cutouts in the curved ceiling.

House specialties: The food here is traditional Cuban, served straightforwardly and without frills. Among the appetizers: Basque-style tortilla (flat, filled omelette); tamal platter; ceviche; stuffed plantains. Among the entrees:

Cuban steak palomilla; roast pork loin, Cuban-style; picadillo à la Cubana; deep-fried chicken chunks; arroz con pollo; shrimp or lobster creole.

Other recommendations: Cuban sandwich; yucca, boiled or sautéed; ham hocks with potatoes; stuffed chicken breast; zarzuela de mariscos for two; paella Valenciana for two.

Entertainment & amenities: Live entertainment, Fridays through Sundays.

Summary & comments: A bustling, informal, Cuban-style bistro where dropping in and lingering leisurely at any time of day is permissible. The same dishes are available at lunch and dinner, accommodating the Cuban style of eating substantially at lunchtime. Newcomers should try such dishes as yucca, plantains, black beans, and croquettes stuffed in various ways to savor a taste of traditional Cuba.

LOUIE'S BACKYARD

American ★★★ Moderate/Expensive

QUALITY	VALUE
84	C

700 Waddell Street, Key West
(305) 294-1061 Florida Keys Zone 5

Customers: Tourists, locals, internationals
Reservations: Accepted
When to go: Early
Entrée range: $25–29.50
Payment: VISA, AMEX, MC, DC
Service rating: ★★★
Friendliness rating: ★★★
Parking: Alongside restaurant
Bar: Full service
Wine selection: Good
Dress: Casual
Disabled access: Good

Brunch: Sunday, 11:30 a.m.–3 p.m.
Lunch: Monday–Saturday, 11:30 a.m.–3 p.m.
Dinner: Every day, 6–10:30 p.m.

Setting & atmosphere: Nestled among a profusion of tropical foliage, flowering bougainvillea, and hibiscus, the restaurant looks out on a dockside dining deck that sits on the sandy beach. A series of docklike porches and patios rise to permit unencumbered views of the Gulf waters. Built in the early 1900s and formerly a private residence, Louie's Backyard was renovated more than ten years ago and now ranks as one of the Keys' most popular restaurants.

House specialties: Among the appetizers: crisp fried cracked conch with red pepper jelly and pickled ginger slaw; Bahamian conch chowder with bird pepper hot sauce salad; pan-seared shrimp and chorizo with whiskey corn cream and corn muffins. Among the entrees: pan-cooked Atlantic salmon with sweet soy, wakame salad, shiitake mushrooms, and spinach; grilled tamarind-glazed Key West shrimp, roasted yam barbecue sauce, and cayenne-dusted plantain chips; grilled black angus steak with Rioja wine sauce, mashed potatoes, and roasted red onion-corn relish; rare-roasted New Zealand venison loin with Madeira, sun-dried cherry sauce, and spinach and feta strudel.

Other recommendations: Grouper with Thai peanut sauce, stir-fry of grilled shrimp, and chorizo; free-range chicken breast with oyster-tasso gumbo and fettuccini.

Summary & comments: This is a popular, attractive restaurant that typifies the laid-back Key West character. Though it sits in the middle of the town, it seems a reclusive and relaxing hideaway.

MARK'S LAS OLAS

New Florida	★★★★½	Moderate/Expensive	QUALITY 94 / VALUE A

1032 E. Las Olas Boulevard, Ft. Lauderdale
(954) 463-1000

Customers: Young businesspeople; tourists, locals
Reservations: Accepted
When to go: Early
Entrée range: $17–26
Payment: AMEX, VISA, MC, DC
Service rating: ★★★
Friendliness rating: ★★★
Parking: Valet
Bar: Full service
Wine selection: Very good
Dress: Casual
Disabled access: Good

Lunch: Monday–Friday, 11:30 a.m.–2:30 p.m.
Dinner: Monday–Thursday, 6–10:30 p.m.; Friday and Saturday, 5:30–11:30 p.m.; Sunday, 5:30–10:30 p.m.

Setting & atmosphere: Because of his fame and high standing in South Florida, Mark Militello opened in Ft. Lauderdale in the wake of a publicity blitz. His restaurant is beautiful, modern, glitzy, and noisy with the sound of voices from the crowds both at the tables and at the bar. A bevy of young chefs work wonders in the long, open kitchen. A large, wood-burning rotisserie was installed because Militello believes it maximizes the flavor and healthful quality of meats. The only problem here is getting a table.

House specialties: Among the appetizers: crispy potato-goat cheese tart, fresh herbs, and dried tomatoes; semolina-dusted risotto cake with herb salad and tomato coulis; cured ham-wrapped rabbit loin with collard greens and black-eyed peas. Entrees: white duck with mango-honey glaze and charcoaled vegetable and sweet potato–vanilla bean puree; pan-seared pompano with pumpkin-scented rice and charred pineapple rum salsa; grilled marinated veal chop with Tuscan white beans, fresh herb salad, and zinfandel sauce.

Other recommendations: Saffron linguine with gulf shrimp, seared tomatoes, arugula, roasted chilis, olives, and capers; pizza of red bliss potatoes, crispy pancetta, rosemary, onion confit, and gorgonzola cheese; fresh cracked conch with black bean–mango salsa and vanilla-rum butter sauce.

Summary & comments: Now with only one restaurant location open, chef Militello concentrates 100 percent of his time and efforts in Ft. Lauderdale. He is a chef of endless creativity who has achieved national acclaim. He grows much of his own produce and requires vendors to deliver the day's fresh products to his door. A well-trained staff makes the dining experience one of the best in South Florida

MARKER 88

Continental/Caribbean ★★★ Moderate

QUALITY
80
VALUE
B

Overseas Highway US 1, Mile Marker 88, Islamorada
(305) 852-9315
(305) 852-5503
Florida Keys Zone 5

Customers: Tourists, locals, fishermen, celebrities
Reservations: Accepted
When to go: Early
Entrée range: $16.95–28.95
Payment: VISA, AMEX, MC, DC, CB, DISC
Service rating: ★★★
Friendliness rating: ★★★
Parking: Alongside building
Bar: Full service
Wine selection: Very good
Dress: Casual
Disabled access: Good

Dinner: Tuesday–Sunday, 5–11 p.m.; Monday, closed.

Setting & atmosphere: Located in a rustic, weathered building, Marker 88 has been a major culinary player ever since chef/owner Andr Mueller left Ziggy's Conch Restaurant to open his own eatery. His is a lushly tropical setting with a profusion of native plants, nautical artifacts, and treasures rescued from local waters.

House specialties: Among the appetizers: conch ceviche with red onions and sweet-and-sour sauce; oysters Moscow topped with caviar and creamy horseradish; Cuban black bean soup. Among the entrees: conch steak; yellowtail, snapper, grouper, dolphin, or pompano prepared many ways, including fried, sautéed meunière, broiled, poached, grilled, Grenoblaise, and blackened; shrimp Milanesa with angel hair pasta; Apalachicola soft-shell crabs fried, meunière, or with garlic butter; veal Wiener schnitzel.

Other recommendations: Florida lobster imperial; Everglades frog legs fried or meunière with garlic butter or Provençale sauce; steamed seafood platter for two; steak au poivre.

Summary & comments: Almost every famous person who has visited the Keys has also visited Marker 88, which overlooks the Florida Bay. An interesting mix of dishes, from conch fritters to such longtime French classics as rack of lamb Provençale, is available here in an area free of urban clutter.

Honors & awards: *Florida Trend's* Best Restaurant in the Keys award; *South Florida Magazine* Reader's Choice Award for five years.

MIAMI PALM RESTAURANT

Steak ★★★ Expensive

QUALITY 84

VALUE D

9650 E. Bay Harbor Drive, Bay Harbor Island
(305) 868-7256 Miami Beach Zone 1

Customers: Businesspeople, tourists, internationals, locals
Reservations: Accepted
When to go: Early
Entrée range: $19.50–30; lobster, market price
Payment: VISA, AMEX, MC, DC

Service rating: ★★★
Friendliness rating: ★★
Parking: Valet
Bar: Full service
Wine selection: Good
Dress: Informal, business
Disabled access: Good

Dinner: Every day, 5–10:30 p.m.

Setting & atmosphere: This is the Miami version of the famous New York Palm, a noted steak house. The style here is upscale saloon. Even the waiters with their offhand, less-than-friendly attitudes are part of the "act," typical in certain New York saloons. A long, highly visible bar, wood floors, and numerous pictures and caricatures of old-time stars and celebrities add an air of authenticity to the saloon concept.

House specialties: The Palm is a steak house, specializing in big prime steaks. Another specialty is the lobster, never less than four pounds. Among the appetizers are clams oreganata, crabmeat cocktail, and pasta of the day. Among the entrees: veal Milanese and sautéed shrimp. Side dishes, all of them à la carte, are excellent and enough for two. Among them are french fried onions, creamed spinach, hash browns, and cottage fries.

Other recommendations: Prime ribs of beef; crisp broiled chicken; sliced beefsteak tomato; sliced sweet onion salad.

Summary & comments: This is a restaurant to visit when you have an irresistible urge for a big steak or lobster, with no concern for cost.

MORTON'S OF CHICAGO

American/Steakhouse ★★★★ Expensive

QUALITY	VALUE
92	B

1200 Brickell Avenue, Miami
(305) 400-9990 Miami South Zone 3

Customers: Business people, locals, tourists
Reservations: Accepted
When to go: Early
Entrée range: $17.95–29.95
Payment: VISA, MC, AMEX
Service rating: ★★★★1/2
Friendliness rating: ★★★★1/2
Parking: Valet
Bar: Full service
Wine selection: Excellent
Dress: Business attire
Disabled access: Yes

Lunch: Monday–Friday, 11:30 a.m.–2:30 p.m.
Dinner: Monday–Saturday. 5:30–11 p.m.; Sunday, 5–10 p.m.

Setting & atmosphere: A private men's club–like ambience features dark woods, leather booths, and white linen tables. Walls are highlighted with serigraphs by artists LeRoy Neiman and photographs of local and national celebrities. Service is among the best in town and the food is so straightforward, there is no room for mistakes. Great wine selections are perfect match for the USDA prime aged meats. This is one of 38 Morton's locations nationwide.

House specialties: All of it is USDA prime aged grain-fed steaks; smoked Pacific salmon; fresh lump crabmeat cocktail; sautéed wild mushrooms; double filet mignon with béarnaise sauce; porterhouse steak; New York strip steak; domestic rib lamb chops; broiled Block Island swordfish steak; special fed, farm-raised salmon; whole Maine lobster; sautéed fresh spinach and mushrooms.

Other recommendations: Ribeye steak; Sicilian veal chop; lemon oregano chicken; shrimp Alexander with sauce beurre blanc; steamed fresh asparagus.

Summary & comments: This is one of the most reliable and best steak houses to open in the Miami area. A simple, clublike decor makes one feel very much at home. Service is some of the best in town, if not the best.

MOZART STUBE

Austrian	★★★	Moderate	QUALITY 84
			VALUE B

325 Alcazar Avenue, Coral Gables
(305) 446-1600 Miami South Zone 3

Customers: Locals, tourists, internationals
Reservations: Accepted
When to go: Early
Entrée range: $14–21
Payment: VISA, AMEX, MC, DC
Service rating: ★★★★
Friendliness rating: ★★★★
Parking: Street
Bar: Wine and beer
Wine selection: Adequate
Dress: Casual, business
Disabled access: Good

Lunch: Monday–Friday, 11:30 a.m.–3 p.m.
Dinner: Every day, 5:30–11 p.m.

Setting & atmosphere: A small, convivial beer garden where the food is authentic, delicious, and plentiful. Distinguished by coarse wood walls on one side, its ledge lined with Germanic artifacts and mirrors on the other, plaid tablecloths, and wine racks above the bar, Mozart Stube serves long, chilled glasses of draft beer in a noisy atmosphere where good times are part of the fare.

House specialties: Among the appetizers: liver-dumpling soup; herring in sour cream; sausage salad with herb mayonnaise. Among the entrees: wurst plate of bratwurst, knockwurst, sausage loaf, and weiswurst; roast pork with bread dumpling and sauerkraut; Wiener schnitzel with roasted potatoes and salad; sauerbraten of beef pot roast with dumpling and red cabbage.

Other recommendations: Spiced beef and potato soup; shrimp and lobster meat in puff pastry; roasted veal or pork shank to order; rainbow trout sautéed in a lemon butter sauce.

Summary & comments: For an afternoon or evening of relaxed fun and truly good and homey Austrian fare, there is no finer restaurant than Mozart Stube.

NEMO

New American	★★★½	Moderate	QUALITY 92
			VALUE B

100 Collins Avenue
(305) 532-4550 — Miami Beach Zone 1

Customers: Young locals, tourists, area businessmen
Reservations: Accepted
When to go: Early
Entrée range: $13–19
Payment: AMEX, VISA, MC, DC
Service rating: ★★★
Friendliness rating: ★★★
Parking: Valet
Bar: Full service
Wine selection: Very good
Dress: Casual
Disabled access: Good

Brunch: Sunday, noon–4 p.m.
Lunch: Monday–Friday, noon–3 p.m.
Dinner: Monday–Saturday, 7 p.m.–midnight; Sunday, 6–11 p.m.

Setting & atmosphere: A restaurant that dares to be different even for South Beach, Nemo's is conspicuously copper toned, with an abundance of pounded copper in the bar and the free-form bar chairs. Copper lighting fixtures are pocked with jewels, reflecting the artistry of chef Michael Schwartz, also a jewelry designer. The menus too are a simulation of the pounded copper decor, and the wait staff, dressed in jeans, wear Schwartz-designed jewelry. In this highly unusual setting the food is seriously very good.

House specialties: Among the appetizers: polenta fries (a must); garlic- and ginger-cured salmon rolls with tobiko caviar and wasabi mayo; crispy prawns with spicy salsa cruda and mesclun greens. Among the entrees: sautéed mahimahi with sautéed asparagus and orange-basil citronette; spicy pork loin with caramelized onions and papaya relish; grilled swordfish with ragout of white beans, tomato, and broccoli rabe.

Other recommendations: Sizzling calamari salad with romaine hearts, roasted peppers, and Caesar dressing; curried lentil stew with sweet caramelized onions and wilted greens.

Summary & comments: Chef Michael Schwartz, once a chef at Wolfgang Puck's Chinois and a partner of New York restaurateur Myles Chevitz, applies a fusion of culinary techniques to his cooking in an unusual and pleasant atmosphere that can best be described as "South Beach casual."

NEWS CAFE

American	★★	Inexpensive	QUALITY 70 / VALUE C

800 Ocean Drive
(305) 531-0392
(305) 538-6397

Miami Beach Zone 1

Customers: Locals, tourists, show business people
Reservations: Not accepted
When to go: Any time
Entrée range: $5.25–10
Payment: VISA, AMEX, MC
Service rating: ★★★
Friendliness rating: ★★
Parking: Valet
Bar: Full service
Wine selection: Fair
Dress: Casual
Disabled access: Good

Open: 24 hours.

Setting & atmosphere: This restaurant is the most popular on the beach, busy indoors and out, morning to night. The decor is basic, with wood booths, benches, and plastic chairs. The atmosphere, not the setting, is important. Sports news flashes continually, and magazines and newspapers from major cities are available near the bar, where the action is frenzied, the feeling offbeat. People-watching the colorful and diverse crowd is the major draw here—everyone visits sooner or later.

House specialties: The menu is geared more to snack dishes than dinner entrees. Among the appetizers: bruschetta; steak tartare; bagels with cream cheese, tomato, onion, and Nova; Caesar salad; cold gazpacho. Among the entrees: pasta with fresh tomato, basil, and grilled chicken; pasta with olive oil, basil, and garlic; knockwurst with sauerkraut; steak and fries; Vienna schnitzel.

Other recommendations: Roast pork sandwich; grilled hamburger; cold vegetable pasta; quiche Lorraine; fruit salad; breaded chicken cutlet plate.

Summary & comments: People do not come here to "dine," but rather to satisfy basic hunger needs while watching the action. Have a salad and sandwich, relax, and watch what makes South Beach the most talked about and amusing section of the Miami area. A 15 percent gratuity is added automatically to your bill, as is the case in nearly every South Beach restaurant.

NORMAN'S

New World	★★★★½	Moderate/Expensive	QUALITY 98 / VALUE B

21 Almeria Avenue, Coral Gables
(305) 446-6767 Miami South Zone 3

Customers: Locals, business leaders, tourists
Reservations: Accepted
When to go: Early
Entrée range: $18.50–28.50
Payment: AMEX, VISA, MC, DC
Service rating: ★★★★
Friendliness rating: ★★★★
Parking: Valet
Bar: Full service
Wine selection: Very good
Dress: Casual, business
Disabled access: Good

Lunch: Monday–Friday, noon–2 p.m.
Dinner: Monday–Thursday, 6–10:30 p.m.; Friday and Saturday, 6–11 p.m.; Sunday, closed.

Setting & atmosphere: Open and airy, with a second-floor loft reserved for smokers and private parties, Norman's is a treasure of Mediterranean touches. Its recycled green marble bar, diamond-shaped inlaid floors, richly upholstered chairs and banquettes, and a modern kitchen with two wood-burning ovens is a setting befitting chef Norman Van Aken's inventive New World Cuisine.

House specialties: The following are representative samples from a menu that changes daily. Appetizers: jerked chicken skewer on pigeon pea salsa; bacalao fritters with ancho–black olive aioli; yucca-stuffed shrimp with sour orange mojo, greens, and tartar salsa. Entrees: rum- and pepper-painted grouper on mango-habanero mojo with boniato-plantain mash en poblano; palomilla strip steak au poivre with cabrales crema, blistered bell peppers, stacked sweet tater torta, and West Indian pumpkin.

Other recommendations: Signature dish of foie gras wafers on Cuban breads "shortstack" with exotic fruits caramel.

Summary & comments: Norman Van Aken is considered one of the country's finest and most inventive chefs, the forerunner in the development of Florida's New World cuisine. Often called a Picasso in the kitchen, he sets a stylish, sophisticated, and unique tone with both his cuisine and restaurant setting.

Honors & awards: Doctor of Culinary Arts, honoris causa from Johnson & Wales University; James Beard Award.

OCEAN TERRACE GRILL

New American/Caribbean	★★★	Moderate	QUALITY 89	VALUE B

Overseas Highway US 1, Mile Marker 82
(Cheeca Lodge), Islamorada
(305) 664-4651 Florida Keys Zone 5

Customers: Tourists, locals
Reservations: Accepted
When to go: Any time
Entrée range: $11–23.50
Payment: VISA, AMEX, MC, DC
Service rating: ★★★
Friendliness rating: ★★★
Parking: Valet
Bar: Full service
Wine selection: Good
Dress: Casual
Disabled access: Good

Breakfast: Every day, 7–11 a.m.
Lunch: Every day, 11 a.m.–5 p.m.
Dinner: Every day, 5–10 p.m.

Setting & atmosphere: The Grill offers a lovely, open setting, tropical in style, with a vaulted ceiling, skylights, comfortable rattan chairs, and wooden checkerboard tables. It invites a leisurely, informal dining experience, with well-prepared, interesting food in a highly contemporary Keys style.

House specialties: Among the appetizers: seafood fritters with key lime garlic aioli and tomato sauce; snapper fingers and yucca puffs with spicy tartar and soy mango dipping sauces; quesadilla of fresh mozzarella, spinach, tomato, and pesto sauce. Among the entrees: grilled rum-glazed snapper with plantain–sweet potato mash and mango chutney; roasted fresh leg of lamb with grilled sweet onions and potatoes; seafood platter of local fish, scallops, shrimp, crab cakes, rice, grilled vegetables, and garlic toast for two.

Other recommendations: Corn and crab chowder; sautéed shrimp with tomato sauce, whipped potatoes, onions, and peppers; local dolphin fish sandwich, jerked with grilled onions and cheese.

Summary & comments: This grill, and a more formal dining room called Atlantic's Edge, which is open only at night, are inhabited primarily by the hotel guests, although fishermen and many drivers to the Keys are lured daily by the interesting food and relaxing ambience.

THE OCEAN VIEW

New Florida/Caribbean	★★★½	Moderate	QUALITY 82
			VALUE B

1435 Simonton Street (Reach Resort), Key West
(305) 296-5000 Florida Keys Zone 5

Customers: Tourists, locals
Reservations: Accepted
When to go: Any time
Entrée range: $15.95–29.95
Payment: VISA, AMEX, MC, DC
Service rating: ★★★★
Friendliness rating: ★★★★
Parking: Valet
Bar: Full service
Wine selection: Good
Dress: Casual
Disabled access: Good

Breakfast: Sunday–Friday, 7–11 a.m.; Saturday and Sunday, 7 a.m.–noon.
Lunch: Sunday–Friday, 11 a.m.–2 p.m.; Saturday and Sunday, noon–2 p.m.
Dinner: Sunday–Thursday, 6–10 p.m.; Friday and Saturday, 6–11 p.m.

Setting & atmosphere: In the Mediterranean-style setting of the dining room with its peach-stucco architecture, the diner can view the sunset far into the distance. An open deck offers outdoor dining on cool nights when gentle Gulf breezes and native music are a soothing magnet and an invitation to leisurely island dining.

House specialties: Among the appetizers: mushrooms in a crock with wine-garlic cheese sauce; smoked scallops with mustard sauce, garlic mayonnaise, and garlic bread; conch fritters. Among the entrees: grilled chicken breast with grilled pineapple, mango, and papaya sauce; grilled mahimahi with roasted peppers and mango salsa; grilled or blackened fresh tuna with papaya and mango relish.

Other recommendations: Beefsteak tomato salad with buffalo mozzarella and basil balsamic vinaigrette; filet mignon with sauce béarnaise; barbecued shrimp with Jamaican jerk seasoning and rum barbecue sauce.

Entertainment & amenities: Caribbean music.

Summary & comments: This lovely retreat offers a nearly perfect getaway setting. Even the breakfast fare is exceptional, with choices like frittata of vegetables and parmesan cheese, a breakfast quesadilla of scrambled eggs, monterey jack cheese, and green chilis, and buttermilk-pecan pancakes, to name a few.

OSTERIA DEL TEATRO

Italian	★★★★	Moderate	QUALITY 94 / VALUE B

1443 Washington Avenue
(305) 538-7850 Miami Beach Zone 1

Customers: Locals, internationals, tourists
Reservations: Accepted
When to go: Early
Entrée range: $14–28
Payment: VISA, AMEX, MC
Service rating: ★★★★
Friendliness rating: ★★★★
Parking: Valet
Bar: Wine and beer
Wine selection: Good
Dress: Casual, business
Disabled access: Good

Dinner: Sunday and Monday, Wednesday and Thursday, 6–11 p.m.; Friday and Saturday, 6 p.m.–midnight; Tuesday, closed.

Setting & atmosphere: Located in the Art Deco District of South Beach, Osteria is small and intimate, casually sophisticated, and one of the best Italian restaurants in South Florida. Large windows look out on a constantly intriguing street scene; its interior is simple but impeccably set with white tablecloths and napkins against dark woods and soft lights. Its charming host/owner, considered one of the finest managers in the area, greets his diners with open friendliness, while partner/chef Antonio Tettamanzi performs in the kitchen to consistently rave reviews.

House specialties: Among the appetizers: crespelle (thin spinach crêpes stuffed with ricotta and spinach au gratin); grilled fresh wild mushrooms marinated in olive oil, garlic, and marjoram on arugula salad; pappardelle sautéed with crabmeat and scallops in fresh tomato cream with vodka. Among the entrees: poached stuffed salmon with crabmeat and shrimp served on citrus sauce; grilled tuna loin with shiitake mushroom and rosemary sauce; pan-seared poissin served with diced Italian pancetta and marinated eggplant.

Other recommendations: Risotto with imported porcini mushrooms, truffle butter, and herbs; linguine sautéed with jumbo shrimp, roasted peppers, capers, black olives, fresh tomato, and herbs in a tangy garlic-olive sauce.

Summary & comments: A stable, high-style standout in an area where restaurants come and go with dizzying regularity. This owner combo provides fine dining in a lively and friendly atmosphere.

PACIFIC TIME

Pacific Rim	★★★★	Moderate	QUALITY 90
			VALUE C

915 Lincoln Road
(305) 534-5979 Miami Beach Zone 1

Customers: Locals, tourists, internationals
Reservations: Accepted
When to go: Early
Entrée range: $10–30
Payment: VISA, AMEX, MC, DC
Service rating: ★★★
Friendliness rating: ★★★
Parking: Adjoining lot
Bar: Full service
Wine selection: Very good
Dress: Casual
Disabled access: Good

Lunch: Monday–Friday, 11:30 a.m.–2:30 p.m.
Dinner: Sunday–Thursday, 6–11 p.m.; Friday and Saturday, 6 p.m.–midnight.

Setting & atmosphere: Owner Jonathan Eismann came to this pleasant, pastel-toned setting by way of Manhattan's China Grill. He combines his Oriental skills with the tastes of the Caribbean with fascinating results and artistic presentations.

House specialties: Appetizers: grilled giant squid with local Asian greens and hot-and-sour vinaigrette; pan-seared Hudson Valley foie gras with California port, red, and plum wines over organic Asian greens; warm curried Royal Miyagi oysters with chili puree and marinated cucumber. Among the entrees: wok-sautéed local yellowfin tuna with sushi bar flavors, roasted sesame rice, avocado, and fresh Malpeque oyster sauce; whole ginger-stuffed Florida yellowtail snapper tempura with steamed ribbon vegetables and sizzling fish dipping sauce; one duck two flavors—one hot, one cold—with fresh plums and mandarin duck salad, pea sprouts in duck oil.

Other recommendations: Miso-rubbed chicken salad with crisp spinach, sugar snaps, and tomato-infused olive oil; sweet saké-roasted sea bass with warm tomato vinaigrette, Shanghai vinegar, and Pacific spiced potato crisps; shiitake-grilled certified Angus beef with Indochine spices, shiitake mushrooms, bok choy, sugar snaps, sweet saké, and baked Idaho fingerling potatoes.

Summary & comments: Eismann brings a bright new concept to the Miami area, combining Pacific and Caribbean products and techniques that produce unique textures and tastes. He offers a fixed-price three-course menu during the first hour. There's also a nice range of dessert wines available by the glass and bottle.

PIER HOUSE RESTAURANT

New Florida/Caribbean	★★★½	Moderate/Expensive	QUALITY 88
			VALUE B

One Duval Street (Pier House Hotel), Key West
(305) 296-4600 Florida Keys Zone 5

Customers: Tourists, winter residents, celebrities
Reservations: Accepted
When to go: Any time
Entrée range: $25–33
Payment: VISA, AMEX, MC, DC, DISC
Service rating: ★★★★
Friendliness rating: ★★★★
Parking: Adjoining lot
Bar: Full service
Wine selection: Very good
Dress: Casual
Disabled access: Good

Brunch: Sunday, 11 a.m.–2 p.m.
Dinner: Every day, 5–10:30 p.m.

Setting & atmosphere: Located in Key West's most famous hotel, the Pier House Restaurant is one of the area's best. A soothing setting accomplished in soft tropical tones and an extensive outdoor dining patio overlooking the water invite leisurely dining. Its outdoor Havana Sunset Deck draws both natives and visitors to come by and watch the sunset while munching hors d'oeuvres and drinking cocktails, a happening that has become a ritual in Key West.

House specialties: Among the appetizers: sautéed Gulf shrimp with olives, tomato, lemon oil, mustard, and basil; conch eggrolls with vegetable slaw and hot mustard sauce; terrine of salmon and scallops with tomato crème fraiche coulis. Among the entrees: breast of chicken with roasted corn cakes, sautéed spinach and ginger lemon sauce; pan-seared grouper with baby leeks confit; baked Florida lobster with marinated plantains and vegetables; grilled veal chops with portobello mushrooms and rosemary and sage demi-glaze.

Other recommendations: Lobster salad with avocado, grapefruit, and spicy papaya dressing; Pier House bouillabaisse with fresh snapper, lobster, prawns, scallops, mussels, and clams in Spanish saffron mirepoix and rouille croutons; yellowtail snapper sautéed with avocado and papaya.

Summary & comments: Stylish and popular, the restaurant and its Havana dock are a hub of activity and conviviality, particularly during the winter season.

PREZZO

American	★★★	Moderate	QUALITY 84 / VALUE A

18831 Biscayne Boulevard (Loehmann's Fashion Island), Aventura
(305) 933-9004 Miami North Zone 2

8888 SW 136th Street
(305) 234-1010 Miami South Zone 3

Customers: Young and middle-aged locals, tourists, shoppers
Reservations: Accepted for parties of 5 or more
When to go: Early
Entrée range: $8.95–18.95
Payment: VISA, AMEX, MC, DC, DISC, CB

Service rating: ★★★
Friendliness rating: ★★★
Parking: Valet
Bar: Full service
Wine selection: Adequate
Dress: Casual, business
Disabled access: Good

Lunch: Monday–Friday, 11:30 a.m.–3 p.m.; Saturday and Sunday, noon–3 p.m.
Dinner: Sunday–Thursday, 5:30–10:30 p.m.; Friday and Saturday, 5:30–11:30 p.m.

Setting & atmosphere: These are two of four Prezzos owned by noted restaurateur Dennis Max and partner Bert Rappaport. Two others are in Palm Beach County. Rusticity, openness, high ceilings, and a mix of booths, banquettes, and tables distinguish each restaurant. A young, somewhat inexperienced, but willing wait staff is part of the Prezzo image.

House specialties: Among the appetizers: pizzas baked in wood-burning ovens; baked eggplant rolls with mozzarella, pomodoro, and sourdough crostini. Among the entrees: tricolored spaghettini with shrimp, spicy sun-dried tomato cream sauce, and sugar snap peas; potato-crusted chicken breast filled with smoked mozzarella, sautéed spinach, and rosemary sherry sauce; oak-grilled aged NY strip steak, baked potato fries, gorgonzola butter, crispy walnuts, and barolo wine sauce; baked veal meatloaf with onion confit, mashed potatoes, steamed vegetables, and cabernet wine–wild mushroom sauce.

Summary & comments: One of the pleasant aspects of choosing to eat at Prezzo is that one may simply order a pizza, or any other single item on the menu, without embarrassment. What seems to be a growing chain operation is, so far, surprisingly individualized and high in quality and style.

RASCAL HOUSE

American-Deli	★★½	Moderate	QUALITY 78
			VALUE B

17190 Collins Avenue
(305) 947-4581 Miami Beach Zone 1

Customers: Young to very old locals, tourists from around the world, celebrities
Reservations: Not accepted
When to go: Always crowded
Entrée range: $4.95–14.65
Payment: Cash only
Service rating: ★★★★
Friendliness rating: ★★★
Parking: Free in rear
Bar: Full service
Wine selection: Adequate
Dress: Casual
Disabled access: Good

Open: Sunday–Friday, 7 a.m.–12:45 a.m.; Saturday, 7 a.m.–1:45 a.m.

Setting & atmosphere: This landmark restaurant-deli was opened in 1954 by Wolfie Cohen and has been arguably the busiest restaurant in South Florida ever since, serving an average of 5,000 customers daily. People wait in line for tables, counter space, and take-out orders, but the lines move quickly and service is fast and efficient. A typical deli atmosphere with banquettes, booths, and tables, where bowls of pickles, beets, and cole slaw are on the table for immediate picking. A basket of fresh deli rolls arrives immediately, and a bakery alongside is easily available for purchasing bread and pastries to take home.

House specialties: Everything on the menu is available from opening to closing time. The popular items here, after the breakfast hour, are a range of deli sandwiches and platters. There are some 15 dinner entrees, including roast brisket of beef with potato pancakes, boiled beef flanken with trimmings, whole chicken en pot with trimmings, and stuffed cabbage with mashed potatoes.

Other recommendations: Brisket of beef, Romanian pastrami, corned beef, and sliced turkey sandwiches; smoked salmon salad platter; Floridian health platter of fruits and cottage cheese; mile-high lemon pie.

Summary & comments: The Rascal House is noisy, friendly, and always busy. It offers a great experience in Miami Beach life, but is not for calorie counters.

Honors & awards: Numerous awards for best deli in South Florida.

RED SQUARE

American/Russian	★★★★	Expensive	QUALITY 90 / VALUE B

411 Washington Avenue, Miami Beach
(305) 672-0200 Miami Beach Zone 1

Customers: Locals, tourists
Reservations: Accepted
When to go: Early
Entrée range: $14–35
Payment: VISA, MC, AMEX
Service rating: ★★★
Friendliness rating: ★★★★
Parking: Valet
Bar: Full service
Wine selection: Adequate
Dress: Casual/dressy
Disabled access: Yes

Dinner: Sunday–Thursday 7 p.m.–3 a.m.; Friday and Saturday, 7 p.m.–5 a.m.

Setting & atmosphere: Another one of China Grill Management's highly sophisticated but comfortable concepts, Red Square is intimate, plush, and very red. Russian-themed in principle, this is where people meet after work for chilled vodka and caviar. But perhaps the best reason to go to this fun, elegant restaurant/lounge is to savor dinner prepared by the culinary wizardry of chef Robbin Haas.

House specialties: Chilled Maine lobster martini; escargots; mussels meunière; Siberian nachos; filet mignon Roquefort; bouillabaisse; turkey and shiitake mushroom meatoaf; filet stroganoff.

Other recommendations: Caviar with George Blanc potato cakes; cappuccino of wild mushroom soup; crab cakes; Georgian fried chicken with crushed red bliss potatoes and red beans; "sexed-up" salmon on sticky rice with Chinese black bean broth.

Entertainment & amenities: Wednesday night jazz, DJ dancing nightly.

Summary & comments: Known for its bar and lounge atmosphere, Red Square serves some of the best food in town. Still a secret for some, those who have discovered the passionate culinary soul of chef Haas come back weekend after weekend. The bar is bubbly and the good-looking crowds seem to be always celebrating.

THE RESTAURANT ON LITTLE PALM ISLAND

French/Caribbean	★★★	Moderate/Expensive	QUALITY
			84
			VALUE
			C

Overseas Highway US 1, Mile Marker 28.5, Little Torch Key
(305) 872-2551 Florida Keys Zone 5

Customers: Businesspeople, tourists, celebrities
Reservations: Required
When to go: Any time
Entrée range: $25–32
Payment: VISA, AMEX, MC, DC
Service rating: ★★★
Friendliness rating: ★★★
Parking: At reception area
Bar: Full service
Wine selection: Good
Dress: Casual
Disabled access: Adequate

Breakfast: Every day, 7:30–10 a.m.
Brunch: Sunday, 11:30 a.m.–2:30 p.m.
Lunch: Every day, 11:30 a.m.–2:30 p.m.
Dinner: Every day, 6:30–10 p.m.

Setting & atmosphere: Located on a hidden island, a 30-mile drive from Key West and a 20-minute boat ride provided by the management, the resort's restaurant building sits amid a profusion of tropical plants. A former fishing camp built along turquoise waters, it is elegantly rustic and romantic.

House specialties: Among the appetizers: chili pepper-glazed roasted pork loin with melon salsa and fried leeks; duck confit salad with French green beans, sun-dried tomato, and foie gras sausage drizzled with walnut oil; grilled fresh duck foie gras on baby lettuces and wildflowers with fig confit. Among the entrees: Maine lobster steamed with baby vegetables and emulsified turnip cream sauce; pan-seared yellowtail snapper on red onion compote with saffron coriander sauce; grilled tuna loin with green asparagus salad, prosciutto, and chive-olive oil vinaigrette; grilled veal chop with romaine étouffé and tomato compote with truffled jus.

Other recommendations: Calabaza cream soup with wild rice and smoked bacon crème fraiche; grilled antelope loin with manchego cheese polenta and baby vegetables with cabernet, shallot, port wine, and wild berries reduction. Key lime bavarois with Indian apple, kiwi fruit, and raspberry coulis is exceptional.

Summary & comments: This site has long been an exclusive retreat for the rich and famous, including an occasional president. There are luxury suites and bungalows as well as other amenities.

RUEN THAI

Thai	★★★	Moderate	QUALITY 84 / VALUE B

947 Washington Avenue
(305) 534-1504 Miami Beach Zone 1

Customers: Young locals, tourists, internationals
Reservations: Accepted
When to go: Early
Entrée range: $7.95–20.95
Payment: VISA, AMEX, MC, DC, DISC
Service rating: ★★★
Friendliness rating: ★★★
Parking: Valet
Bar: Wine and beer
Wine selection: Adequate
Dress: Casual
Disabled access: Good

Dinner: Sunday–Thursday, 5:30 p.m.–midnight; Friday and Saturday, 5:30 p.m.–1 a.m.

Setting & atmosphere: The crafts of Thailand are evident in the carved woods, the intricate inlaid carvings under glass tabletops, and in the wall hangings. Waiters dressed in red and green satin tunics bring spots of bright color to an otherwise dark interior. A fairly extensive menu offers a good and interesting range of Thai dishes and the staff is willing and able to explain the contents of each dish.

House specialties: Among the appetizers: shrimp in a blanket; beef or chicken satay; jumping squid; the famous mee grob; tearing tiger, grilled beef with shallots, toasted chilis, and lemon dressing. Among the entrees: shrimp curry; pad thai; lobster sautéed with chili paste, onion, red pepper, scallions, and ginger; whole fried red snapper with garlic sauce and pepper; shrimp basil with whole basil leaves and hot chili; pork or beef ginger; chicken curry.

Other recommendations: Vegetarian pad thai; duck curry with Thai curry sauce, cashews, pineapple, carrots, celery, and sweet peas; grouper curry.

Summary & comments: This is one of the more popular Thai restaurants on South Beach, where service is consistent, and the food spicy and fresh tasting.

SHULA'S STEAK HOUSE

American	★★★½	Moderate/Expensive	QUALITY 90
			VALUE C

7601 Miami Lakes Drive (Shula's Hotel and Golf Resort), Miami Lakes
(305) 820-8102 Miami North Zone 2

Customers: Sports fans, locals, tourists, internationals
Reservations: Recommended
When to go: Early
Entrée range: $15.95–58
Payment: VISA, AMEX, MC, DC
Service rating: ★★★★
Friendliness rating: ★★★
Parking: Valet, nearby lot
Bar: Full service
Wine selection: Good
Dress: Casual, business
Disabled access: Good

Breakfast: Monday–Friday, 7–11 a.m.; open every day, January–March.
Lunch: Monday–Friday, 11:30 a.m.–2:30 p.m.
Dinner: Monday–Saturday, 6–11 p.m.; Sunday, 6–10 p.m.

Setting & atmosphere: A rich, comfortable setting of dark woods, sports artifacts, and large photos of the Miami Dolphins in action. The steaks are the best. This is a great place to stop before or after games at Pro Player Stadium. Though there are additional items, red meat is the object here. Dinner prices are à la carte.

House specialties: 16- and 20-ounce New York sirloin; 12-ounce filet mignon; 24-ounce porterhouse; 28-ounce prime rib; 3-pound Maine lobster; chicken and lobster Oscar with fresh tomato-basil hollandaise; knife and fork sandwich of angus burger with Shula's potato salad; penne pasta with sautéed shrimp, fresh spinach, roasted peppers, and shiitake mushrooms in light broth with peasant crumbs.

Other recommendations: If you dare, try the 48-ounce porterhouse and become immortalized on a wall plaque of heroic eaters; rack of lamb; filet mignon salad with herb butter and pink peppercorns on seasoned potato pancake.

Summary & comments: The name Don Shula carries with it the guarantee of high standards and quality. His restaurant lives up to his reputation.

SMITH & WOLLENSKY

American/Steak House	★★★	Expensive	QUALITY 85
			VALUE C

1 Washington Avenue in South Pointe Park, Miami Beach
(305) 673-2800 Miami Beach Zone 1

Customers: Businesspeople, locals, tourists
Reservations: Accepted
When to go: Early
Entrée range: $18.50–34
Payment: VISA, MC, AMEX
Service rating: ★★1/2
Friendliness rating: ★★★
Parking: Valet
Bar: Full service
Wine selection: Excellent
Dress: Casual
Disabled access: Yes

Lunch and dinner: Every day, noon–midnight.

Setting & atmosphere: After an extensive expansion program, and $8.5 million later, restaurateur Alan Stillman has transformed a structure located directly on the channel (Government Cut) from the Port of Miami into a large replica of the New York Smith & Wollensky. With warm woods throughout and primitive American folk art everywhere, this place exudes casual comfort and masculine elegance. Almost every table has a view of the water and the restaurant's temperature-controlled aging room assure diners in South Florida the same quality of prime beef aging that made the New York restaurant known all over the world.

House specialties: Crackling pork shank with firecracker apple sauce; angry lobster; filet mignon; sirloin steak; prime rib; lamb chops.

Other recommendations: Thin-crust pizza; lobster cocktail; mustard-crusted tuna; veal NY/Milan; veal chops; creamed spinach; hash browns.

Summary & comments: Named "the quintessential New York steakhouse" by *Gourmet Magazine,* it's fame for serving prime and temperature-controlled aged beef, this first branch of Smith & Wollensky outside of the Big Apple has received mixed reviews by critics and the public. The quality of the beef is great, but the service and ability of the kitchen to dish out food promptly leaves some diners waiting longer than others. The wine list is one of the best and most user-friendly in town.

TANI GUCHI'S PLACE

Japanese	★★★	Moderate	QUALITY 83 / VALUE B

2224 NE 123rd Street (San Souci Plaza East)
(305) 892-6744 Miami North Zone 2

Customers: Locals, tourists, celebrities
Reservations: Accepted
When to go: Early
Entrée range: $8.95–32
Payment: VISA, AMEX, MC, DISC
Service rating: ★★★
Friendliness rating: ★★★★
Parking: Adjoining lot
Bar: Wine and beer
Wine selection: Simple
Dress: Casual
Disabled access: Good

Lunch: Monday–Friday, 11:45 a.m.–2:30 p.m.
Dinner: Monday–Thursday, 6–11 p.m.; Friday and Saturday, 6 p.m.–midnight; Sunday, 5–10 p.m.

Setting & atmosphere: A simple, Japanese-style setting on two floors, where the atmosphere is pleasantly noisy and friendly. While proprietor Terry Tani Guchi performs in the kitchen, his partner and wife, Carol, exudes warmth and hospitality in the dining areas, happy to give advice on the many exotic dishes on the menu. This is one of the more authentic restaurants, where the menu goes beyond the usual sushis and teriyakis.

House specialties: Among the appetizers: fresh seaweed cooked with aged tofu, onions, and carrots; fish tempura with marinated vegetables; grilled eggplant with peanut miso sauce; crunchy spicy sesame seaweed salad. Among the entrees: sashimi-sushi combination; vegetarian platter; grilled teriyaki New York strip steak with house salad and sautéed vegetables; katsuo, cutlet with homemade bread crumbs over sautéed vegetables and cutlet sauce.

Other recommendations: Conch salad; eel inside outside roll; snow crab and caviar roll with avocado and cucumber; tempura dinner; pan-fried soft noodles with lobster.

Summary & comments: Proprietor Carol, who, with her husband, has operated other area restaurants successfully, manages to engage even the most reluctant customer in the excitement of trying "new" and strange-seeming dishes. Her enthusiasm brings flocks of health-conscious diners to her restaurant.

TANTRA

International	★★★	Expensive	QUALITY 78 / VALUE C

1445 Pennsylvania Avenue, Miami Beach
(305) 672-4765 Miami Beach Zone 1

Customers: Young locals, tourists
Reservations: Accepted
When to go: Any time
Entrée range: $17–44
Payment: VISA, MC, AMEX
Service rating: ★★
Friendliness rating: ★★★
Parking: Self
Bar: Full service
Wine selection: Adequate
Dress: Club casual
Disabled access: Yes

Dinner: Tuesday–Sunday, 7 p.m–midnight. Late menu available until 3 a.m.

Setting & atmosphere: Based on the ancient Indian spiritual philosophy, Tantra is an intimate restaurant and lounge created to awaken all of the senses. A visual sanctuary, the experience begins when one steps into the entrance to be welcomed by a softly lit marble waterfall. In the Rhada room fresh grass paves your way to sunken cushions, and pillows lie beneath a fiber-optic star-filled sky. Ultrasuede banquettes and silk curtains line the perimeter of the dining room. Feeling more like a lounge than a restaurant, Tantra attracts diners for its provocative cuisine. Chef Michael Jacobs, who previously worked at Picholine in New York and Tatou in Beverly Hills, has created an international menu incorporating the flavors of India, North Africa, and Asia.

House specialties: The Tantra plate, a mixed appetizer with sensual offerings such as juicy oysters on the half shell, white Central American prawns, and chilled pepper-crusted tuna; pungent Aphrodite leaves; salmon tartar napoleon with nori seaweed and lemon wasabi cream; savory goat cheese parcels; rustic Maine lobster salad; Moroccan rubbed lamb; Tantra filet, an aged, bone-in tenderloin of beef with truffle-whipped potatoes and saké cream sauce; Frenched wild boar double-cut rib chop with roasted garlic polenta; whole roasted fish.

Other recommendations: Duck pyramid quesadilla-style; housemade dumplings, your choice from a selection; grilled roasted Maine lobster; rosemary- and honey-glazed Florida snapper with jicama and watercress salad.

Summary & comments: A "must visit" place, at least once. Great for events and celebrations or for a fun evening on the town.

TUSCAN STEAK

Italian Steakhouse	★★★★	Expensive	QUALITY 96
			VALUE B

433 Washington Avenue
(305) 534-2233 — Miami Beach Zone 1

Customers: Young residents, businesspeople, tourists
Reservations: Accepted
When to go: Early
Entrée range: $19–34
Payment: VISA, MC, AMEX
Service rating: ★★★★
Friendliness rating: ★★★★
Parking: Valet
Bar: Full service
Wine selection: Excellent
Dress: Casual
Disabled access: Good

Dinner: Sunday–Thursday 6 p.m.–midnight; Friday and Saturday from 6 p.m.–1 a.m.

Setting & atmosphere: Following the same success formula as China Grill, this new endeavor from the China Grill Management Group, debuts in Miami Beach with expansion plans already in the works. The sophisticated interiors in warm, dark wood tones set the stage for this family-style Florentine grill that serves large portions of Tuscan cuisine with Florida accents. A spectacular, 20-item antipasto bar serves diners assorted trays of vegetables, salads, grains, and seafood, all plated to order. A menu divided in three courses features great appetizers, pastas, and entrees, all meant to be shared.

House specialties: White truffle garlic bread; assorted antipasto from the antipasto bar; crab potato rissoles; gnocchi gorgonzola; three-mushroom risotto with Alba white truffle oil; filet mignon gorgonzola with Barolo sauce; and Tuscan Steak's famous Florentine T-bone steak with roasted garlic puree.

Other recommendations: Whole grilled Tuscan-style country chicken with sage; grilled whole yellowtail snapper with braised garlic, thyme, and lime essence; sautéed calf's liver with pancetta, cipollini onions, and a fried egg; amaretto-infused mashed sweet potatoes

Summary & comments: This is one of the most consistent new restaurants in town, where service is always a pleasure and the food is a real down-to-earth delight. A place to take large groups to share the huge portions, and still have enough to take home in a doggy bag.

VERSAILLES

Cuban	★★	Inexpensive	VAL...
			B

3555 SW Eighth Street
(305) 445-7614 Miami South Zone 3

Customers: Local Hispanics, tourists
Reservations: Not accepted, except for large parties
When to go: Early
Entrée range: $4–15.95
Payment: VISA, AMEX, MC, DC, DISC

Service rating: ★★★
Friendliness rating: ★★
Parking: Nearby lot
Bar: Full service
Wine selection: Sufficient
Dress: Casual
Disabled access: Good

Breakfast: Monday–Friday, 8–11:30 a.m.; Saturday, 8 a.m.–noon; Sunday, 9 a.m.–noon.

Lunch & dinner: Monday–Thursday, 11:30 a.m.–2 a.m.; Friday, 11:30 a.m.–3:30 a.m.; Saturday, noon–4:30 a.m.; Sunday, noon–2 a.m.

Setting & atmosphere: This very Latin restaurant could be a transplant from Cuba. Its bakery and counter entrance are abuzz with conversation, sandwich eating, and Cuban coffee sipping. Green walls interspersed with mirrors, a succession of French windows, and tiled floors give the main dining room an open and utilitarian feel. Its menu of traditional Cuban food, uncluttered and unadorned, and its famous Cuban sandwiches are a continual draw. Same menu for lunch and dinner.

House specialties: Here you will find all the typical Cuban dishes. Among the appetizers: ham croquettes; tamals; black bean soup; ceviche; potato or plantain tortilla (flat omelette). Among the entrees: palomilla steak with french fries or plantains, white rice, and black beans; picadillo with white rice, black beans, and plantains; roast pork; fried pork chunks; whole deep-fried snapper with french fries and salad; paella Valencia; zarzuela seafood casserole.

Other recommendations: Cuban sandwich; ropa vieja, shredded beef in creole sauce with rice, black beans, and plantains; beef steak Milanesa; boliche, Cuban-style pot roast with ham and sausage stuffing.

Summary & comments: This is one of the most enduring and most popular restaurants in the Hispanic section of Miami. For a down-to-earth taste of transplanted Cuban life, there is no better example than Versailles.

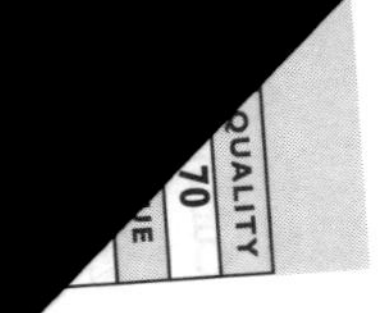

VICTOR'S CAFE

★★★★ Moderate/Expensive

QUALITY
93
VALUE
B

ue

Miami South Zone 3

s,
businesspeople, internationals
Reservations: Accepted
When to go: Early
Entrée range: $12.95–29.95
Payment: VISA, AMEX, MC, DC
Service rating: ★★★★
Friendliness rating: ★★★★
Parking: Valet
Bar: Full service
Wine selection: Good
Dress: Informal, business
Disabled access: Good

Lunch & dinner: Sunday–Thursday, noon–midnight; Friday and Saturday, noon–1 a.m.

Setting & atmosphere: Located in a Cuban-style colonial mansion built by owners Victor del Corral, who opened the first Cuban restaurant in New York, and daughter, Sonia, who manages the Miami restaurant, Victor's Cafe is one of the most popular, innovative, and authentic of Miami's Cuban restaurants. Built around a sky-lighted, atrium-like main dining room, the restaurant attracts Miami's famous and powerful.

House specialties: Victor's offers a blend of traditional and contemporary Cuban and Caribbean dishes. Among the appetizers: lobster-filled cassava empanadas; plantain gourds filled with spicy shrimp and peanut creole hash; french-fried cassava (yucca) fingers. Among the entrees: green plantain-crusted red snapper with avocado-tomatillo sauce; spiny lobster in hot creole sauce; fresh pork in cumin-scented marinade, with yucca in garlic sauce.

Other recommendations: Black bean potage scented with bay leaf, cumin, and oregano; roasted poblano pepper, stuffed with salt cod fricassee, with boniata and cheese sauce; roast pork hash with raisins, olives, and almonds.

Entertainment & amenities: Piano bar; live trio Tuesday to Sunday.

Summary & comments: Nearly seven years old, Victor's has become an important part of upscale Cuban life. For a serious and intriguing taste of regional Cuban food, the Miami diner can do no better.

Honors & awards: *South Florida Magazine* Best Restaurant award.

YUCA

Cuban	★★★★	Expensive	QUALITY 90	VALUE B

501 Lincoln Road
(305) 532-YUCA   Miami Beach Zone 1

Customers: Internationals, Hispanic and other residents, tourists
Reservations: Accepted
When to go: Early
Entrée range: $18–30
Payment: VISA, AMEX, MC, DC
Service rating: ★★★★
Friendliness rating: ★★★
Parking: Valet on weekends
Bar: Full service
Wine selection: Good
Dress: Business, casual
Disabled access: Good

Lunch: Monday–Saturday, noon–4 p.m.
Dinner: Monday–Thursday, 4–11 p.m.; Friday and Saturday, 4 p.m.–midnight; Sunday, 5–11 p.m.

Setting & atmosphere: Located on one end of the popular Lincoln Road Mall, this Yuca (the original Coral Gables location is closed) is a comfortable space decorated with great sophistication. A beautiful mosaic at the entrance to the bar and waiting area, simple columns with twisted-iron and glass, gold- and copper-stained concrete floors, and art by Latin American artists give warmth to the restaurant. Upstairs, a clublike space serves as the stage for Albita, the most talked-about Cuban singing sensation. The food is as innovative as it gets, with deep roots in both Cuban and Latin America cuisines.

House specialties: Among the appetizers: sweet plantain stuffed with dried, cured beef; three-bean terrine served with hearts of palm, avocado, goat cheese, orange mojito, and garlic bread. Among the entrees: green plantain linguine primavera in sofrito sauce; barbecued baby back ribs brushed with spicy guava sauce; grilled palomilla veal chop with moros black bean rice, chayote slaw, and onion essence; plantain-coated dolphin with tamarind tartar sauce.

Other recommendations: Corn tamale filled with conch, with olives, spicy jalapeño, and criollo cheese pesto; twice-cooked pork with boniata puree, black bean broth, stuffed cachucha peppers, and jalapeño vinegar.

Entertainment & amenities: Music weekends.

Summary & comments: This restaurant receives national acclaim from food writers for its elegant take on traditional Cuban food in a light and airy setting. Each dish is a unique experience.

ZIGGY'S CONCH RESTAURANT

American	★★½	Moderate	QUALITY 77 / VALUE C

Overseas Highway US 1, Mile Marker 83, Islamorada
(305) 664-3391 Florida Keys Zone 5

Customers: Tourists, locals
Reservations: Accepted
When to go: Early, weeknights
Entrée range: $11–25
Payment: VISA, AMEX, MC, DISC
Service rating: ★★★
Friendliness rating: ★★
Parking: Alongside building
Bar: Full service
Wine selection: Adequate
Dress: Casual
Disabled access: Good

Dinner: Every day, 5:30–10:30 p.m.

Setting & atmosphere: Open since 1962, Ziggy's is a popular stopping-off restaurant for Key West–bound drivers and visiting fishermen. One must usually wait at the long bar, particularly on weekends, for a table. The undistinguished decor is typical of Keys restaurants, where the food is everything. A standing menu—its emphasis on Florida Keys seafood—is augmented daily by a list of popular specials, all explained orally.

House specialties: Among the appetizers: conch chowder; raw conch salad marinated in lime juice with peppers and onions; conch fritters; cracked conch; oysters prepared five ways. Among the entrees: any native fish prepared fried, broiled, meunière, amandine, or Lorenzo, baked with crabmeat stuffing, lemon butter, and béarnaise sauce; Grenoblais, with capers, lemon sections, and lemon butter; lobster imperial; fried shrimp; fried oysters; grilled farm-raised striped bass on malanga pancake and crisp vinegar vegetable slaw; Florida lobster curry; grilled strip steak.

Other recommendations: Clams casino; grilled or fried dolphin sandwich on Cuban roll with spicy napa slaw; seafood pasta; sautéed snapper on couscous salad with lemon grass, coconut, papaya, and scallions.

Summary & comments: The original chef at Ziggy's was French, a fact that continues to be reflected in the menu. The present executive chef has been there 27 years and continues the French touches. Fresh, native fish, however, is the attraction here.

Appendix
Hotel Information Chart

Hotel	Room Rating	Zone	Street Address
Airport Regency Hotel	★★★	2	1000 NW LeJeune Road Miami, FL 33126
Alexander Hotel	★★★★½	1	5225 Collins Avenue Miami Beach, FL 33140
The Artist House	★★★★	5	534 Eaton Street Key West, FL 33040
Atlantic Shores Motel	★★½	5	510 South Street Key West, FL 33040
Avalon Hotel	★★★	1	700 Ocean Drive Miami Beach, FL 33139
Banyon Resort	★★★½	5	323 Whitehead Street Key West, FL 33040
Bayside Key West Resort	★★★★	5	3444 N. Roosevelt Boulevard Key West, FL 33040
Beach Plaza Hotel	★★	1	1401 Collins Avenue Miami Beach, FL 33139
Beachcomber	★★½	1	1340 Collins Avenue Miami Beach, FL 33139
Beacon Hotel	★★½	1	720 Ocean Drive Miami Beach, FL 33139
Best Western Beach Resort	★★★	1	4333 Collins Avenue Miami Beach, FL 33140
Best Western Hibiscus Motel	★★★	5	1313 Simonton Street Key West, FL 33040
Best Western Key Ambassador	★★★	5	3755 S. Roosevelt Boulevard Key West, FL 33040
Best Western Marina Park	★★★	3	340 Biscayne Boulevard Miami, FL 33132
Best Western Miami Airport Inn	★★★	2	1550 NW LeJeune Road Miami, FL 33126
Best Western Suites at Key Largo	★★★½	5	201 Ocean Drive Key Largo, FL 33037
Best Western Surf Vista	★★½	1	18001 Collins Avenue Sunny Isles, FL 33160
Betsy Ross Hotel	★★½	1	1440 Ocean Drive Miami Beach, FL 33139
Biltmore Hotel	★★★★½	3	1200 Anastasia Avenue Coral Gables, FL 33134

Local Phone	Toll-Free Res. Line	Fax	Rack Rate	No. of Rooms	On-Site Dining	Pool
(305) 441-1600	(800) 367-1039	(305) 443-0766	$$$+	176	✔	✔
(305) 865-6500	(800) 727-1926	(305) 341-6553	$$$$ $$$$	279	✔	✔
(305) 296-3977	(800) 582-7882	(305) 296-3210	$$$$–	6		
(305) 296-2491	(800) 526-3559	(305) 294-2753	$$$ $$$+	72	✔	✔
(305) 538-0133	(800) 933-3306	(305) 534-0258	$$$$–	106	✔	
(305) 296-7786	(800) 225-0639	(305) 294-1107	$$$$$	38	✔	✔
(305) 296-7593	(800) 888-3233	(305) 294-5246	$$$$–	64	✔	✔
(305) 531-6421	(800) 395-9940	(305) 534-0341	$$+	55		
(305) 531-3755	(888) 305-4683	(305) 673-8609	$$$	28	✔	
(305) 674-8200	(800) 649-7075	(305) 674-8976	$$$$+	81	✔	
(305) 532-3311	(800) 832-8332	(305) 531-5296	$$$+	250	✔	✔
(305) 296-6711	(800) 972-5100	(305) 293-9243	$$$ $$+	61		✔
(305) 296-3500	(800) 432-4315	(305) 296-9961	$$$–	100	✔	✔
(305) 371-4400	(800) 526-5655	(305) 372-2862	$$$+	199	✔	✔
(305) 871-2345	(800) 528-1234	(305) 871-2811	$$+	208	✔	✔
(305) 451-5081	(800) 462-6079	(305) 451-4173	$$$ $$–	40		✔
(305) 932-1800	(800) 992-4SUN	(305) 935-5575	$$$–	119	✔	✔
(305) 531-3934	(800) 755-4601	(305) 531-5282	$$$$–	80		✔
(305) 445-1926	(800) 228-3000	(305) 913-3159	$$$$ $$$$	279	✔	✔

Hotel	Room Rating	Zone	Street Address
Blue Marlin Motel	★★½	5	1320 Simonton Street Key West, FL 33040
Blue Moon Hotel	★★★★	1	944 Collins Avenue Miami Beach, FL 33139
Boulevard Hotel Art Deco	★★½	1	740 Ocean Drive Miami Beach, FL 33139
Breezy Palms Resort	★★★	5	80015 Overseas Highway Islamorada, FL 33036
Brigham Gardens	★★★½	1	1411 Collins Avenue Miami Beach, FL 33139
Budgetel Inn Airport	★★½	2	3501 NW LeJeune Road Miami, FL 33142
Cardozo on the Beach	★★★★	1	1300 Ocean Drive Miami Beach, FL 33139
Carlton Hotel	★★	1	1433 Collins Avenue Miami Beach, FL 33139
Casa Grande Suite Hotel	★★★★★	1	834 Ocean Drive Miami Beach, FL 33139
Cavalier Hotel	★★★½	1	1320 Ocean Drive Miami Beach, FL 33139
Cheeca Lodge	★★★★	5	Mile Marker 82, Old Overseas Highway Islamorada, FL 33036
Chesapeake Resort	★★★	5	83409 Overseas Highway Islamorada, FL 33036
Club Hotel & Suites by Doubletree	★★★½	3	100 SE Fourth Street Miami, FL 33131
Club Hotel by Doubletree	★★★½	2	1101 NW 57th Avenue Miami, FL 33126
Colony Hotel	★★½	1	736 Ocean Drive Miami Beach, FL 33139
Comfort Inn Airport	★★½	2	5125 NW 36th Street Miami Springs, FL 33166
Comfort Inn and Suites Airport	★★★	2	5301 NW 36th Street Miami Springs, FL 33166
Comfort Inn Hotel	★★½	1	6261 Collins Avenue Miami Beach, FL 33140
Comfort Inn Key West	★★½	5	3824 N. Roosevelt Boulevard Key West, FL 33040

Local Phone	Toll-Free Res. Line	Fax	Rack Rate	No. of Rooms	On-Site Dining	Pool
(305) 294-2585	(800) 523-1698	(305) 296-1209	$$$$+	61		✔
(305) 673-2262	(800) 724-1623	(305) 534-5399	$$$ $$–	54	✔	✔
(305) 532-0376	na	(305) 674-8179	$$$$–	35	✔	
(305) 664-2361	na	(305) 664-2572	$$	39		✔
(305) 531-1331	na	(305) 538-9898	$$$–	19		
(305) 871-1777	(800) 4-BUDGET	(305) 871-8080	$$	153		✔
(305) 535-6500	(800) 782-6500	(305) 532-3563	$$$$	44	✔	
(305) 538-5741	(800) 7-CARLTON	(305) 534-6855	$$+	67		✔
(305) 672-7003	(800) 688-7678	(305) 673-3669	$$$$ $$$–	34	✔	
(305) 534-2136	(800) 688-7678	(305) 531-5543	$$$$	44		
(305) 664-4651	(800) 327-2888	(305) 664-2893	$$$$ $$$$–	203	✔	✔
(305) 664-4662	(800) 338-3395	(305) 664-8595	$$$$	65		✔
(305) 374-5100	(800) 222-TREE	(305) 381-9826	$$+	134	✔	✔
(305) 266-0000	(800) 444-CLUB	(305) 266-9179	$$$$–	266	✔	✔
(305) 673-0088	(800) 226-5660	(305) 532-0762	$$$$+	50		
(305) 887-2153	(800) 228-5150	(305) 887-3559	$$+	110		
(305) 871-6000	(800) 228-5150	(305) 871-5944	$$$–	267	✔	✔
(305) 868-1200	(800) 228-5150	(305) 868-3003	$$+	150		✔
(305) 294-3773	(800) 228-5150	(305) 294-5739	$$$$$	100		✔

Hotel	Room Rating	Zone	Street Address
Courtyard Airport	★★★½	2	3929 NW 79th Avenue Miami, FL 33166
Crown Hotel	★★½	1	4041 Collins Avenue Miami Beach, FL 33140
David William Hotel	★★★★	3	700 Biltmore Way Coral Gables, FL 33134
Days Inn Art Deco	★★★	1	100 21st Street Miami Beach, FL 33139
Days Inn Key West	★★½	5	3852 N. Roosevelt Boulevard Key West, FL 33040
Days Inn North Beach	★★	1	7450 Ocean Terrace Miami Beach, FL 33141
Days Inn Oceanside	★★★	1	4299 Collins Avenue Miami Beach, FL 33140
Dezerland Surfside Beach Hotel	★★½	1	8701 Collins Avenue Miami Beach, FL 33154
Di Lido Beach Resort	★★★	1	1669 Collins Avenue Miami Beach, FL 33139
Don Shula's Hotel & Golf Club	★★★★	2	15255 Bull Run Road Miami Lakes, FL 33014
Doral Golf Resort & Spa	★★★★	2	4400 NW 87th Avenue Miami, FL 33178
Dorchester	★★½	1	1850 Collins Avenue Miami Beach, FL 33139
Doubletree at Coconut Grove	★★★★	3	2649 S. Bayshore Drive Coconut Grove, FL 33133
Doubletree Grand Hotel	★★★★	3	1717 N. Bayshore Drive Miami, FL 33132
Duval House	★★★½	5	815 Duval Street Key West, FL 33040
Eaton Lodge	★★★½	5	511 Eaton Street Key West, FL 33040
Eaton Manor Guesthouse	★★★	5	1024 Eaton Street Key West, FL 33040
Econo Lodge Resort Key West	★★½	5	3820 N. Roosevelt Boulevard Key West, FL 33040
Eden Roc Hotel	★★★★	1	4525 Collins Avenue Miami Beach, FL 33140

Local Phone	Toll-Free Res. Line	Fax	Rack Rate	No. of Rooms	On-Site Dining	Pool
(305) 477-8118	(800) 228-9290	(305) 599-9363	$$$+	145		✔
(305) 531-5771	(800) 541-6874	(305) 673-1612	$$+	256	✔	✔
(305) 445-7821	(800) 757-8073	(305) 913-1933	$$$ $$–	104	✔	✔
(305) 538-6631	(800) 329-7466	(305) 674-0954	$$+	172	✔	✔
(305) 294-3742	(800) 224-5051	(305) 296-7260	$$$ $$$–	133		✔
(305) 866-1631	(800) 329-7466	(305) 868-4617	$$$$–	93		✔
(305) 673-1513	(800) 356-3017	(305) 538-0727	$$$–	139	✔	✔
(305) 865-6661	(800) 331-9346	(305) 866-2630	$$$ $$$–	225	✔	✔
(305) 538-0811	(800) 327-6105	(305) 672-5148	$$+	334	✔	✔
(305) 821-1150	(800) 24-SHULA	(305) 820-8190	$$$ $$$–	300	✔	✔
(305) 592-2000	(800) 71-DORAL	(305) 591-6630	$$$$ $$$+	699	✔	✔
(305) 534-6971	(800) 327-4739	(305) 673-1006	$$$+	94		✔
(305) 858-2500	(800) 222-TREE	(305) 858-5776	$$$$ $$$+	192	✔	✔
(305) 372-0313	(800) 222-TREE	(305) 372-9455	$$$$+	152	✔	✔
(305) 294-1666	(800) 22-DUVAL	(305) 292-1710	$$$ $$–	29		✔
(305) 292-2170	(800) 294-2170	(305) 292-4018	$$$$+	16		✔
(305) 294-9870	(800) 305-9870	(305) 294-1544	$$$+	23		
(305) 294-5511	(800) 553-2666	(305) 296-1939	$$$ $$–	145	✔	✔
(305) 531-0000	(800) 327-8337	(305) 674-5555	$$$$ $$$–	350	✔	✔

Hotel	Room Rating	Zone	Street Address
Edison Hotel	★½	1	960 Ocean Drive Miami Beach, FL 33139
Embassy Suites	★★★★	2	3974 NW S. River Drive Miami, FL 33142
Essex House Hotel	★★★	1	1001 Collins Avenue Miami Beach, FL 33139
Everglades Hotel	★★	3	244 Biscayne Boulevard Miami, FL 33132
Fairfield Inn Key West	★★½	5	2400 N. Roosevelt Boulevard Key West, FL 33040
Faro Blanco Marine Resort	★★★	5	1996 Overseas Highway Marathon, FL 33050
Fontainebleau Hilton Resort & Spa	★★★★	1	4441 Collins Avenue Miami Beach, FL 33140
The Gardens Hotel	★★★★½	5	526 Angela Street Key West, FL 33040
Governor Hotel	★★★	1	435 21st Street Miami Beach, FL 33139
Grand Bay Hotel	★★★★½	3	2669 S. Bayshore Drive Coconut Grove, FL 33133
Grove Isle Club and Resort	★★★★★	3	4 Grove Isle Drive Coconut Grove, FL 33133
Hampton Inn Downtown	★★½	3	2500 Brickell Avenue Miami, FL 33129
Hampton Inn Key West	★★½	5	2801 N. Roosevelt Boulevard Key West, FL 33040
Heron House	★★★★	5	512 Simonton Street Key West, FL 33040
Holiday Inn Airport	★★½	2	1111 S. Royal Poinciana Boulevard Miami Springs, FL 33166
Holiday Inn Beachside	★★★	5	3841 N. Roosevelt Boulevard Key West, FL 33040
Holiday Inn Coral Gables	★★½	3	2051 LeJeune Road Coral Gables, FL 33134
Holiday Inn Downtown	★★★	3	200 SE 2nd Avenue Miami, FL 33131
Holiday Inn Key Largo	★★½	5	99701 Overseas Highway Key Largo, FL 33037

Local Phone	Toll-Free Res. Line	Fax	Rack Rate	No. of Rooms	On-Site Dining	Pool
(305) 531-2744	(800) 766-6016	(305) 672-4153	$$$$+	62		✔
(305) 634-5000	(800) 772-3787	(305) 635-9499	$$$$ $$$+	360	✔	✔
(305) 534-2700	(800) 553-7739	(305) 532-3827	$$$$ $$$$–	81		
(305) 379-5461	(800) 327-5700	(305) 577-8390	$$$–	371	✔	✔
(305) 296-5700	(800) 228-2800	(305) 292-9840	$$$$+	132		✔
(305) 743-9018	(800) 759-3276	(305) 743-2918	$$+	126	✔	✔
(305) 538-2000	(800) HILTONS	(305) 673-5351	$$$$$ $$$$–	1206	✔	✔
(305) 294-2661	(800) 526-2664	(305) 292-1007	$$$ $$$+	17		✔
(305) 532-2100	(800) 542-0444	(305) 532-9139	$$+	126	✔	✔
(305) 858-9600	(800) 327-2788	(305) 859-2026	$$$$ $$$+	258	✔	✔
(305) 858-8300	(800) 88-GROVE	(305) 858-5908	$$$$ $$$$+	49	✔	✔
(305) 854-2070	(800) HAMPTON	(305) 854-2070	$$+	69		✔
(305) 294-2917	(800) HAMPTON	(305) 296-0221	$$$	159		✔
(305) 294-9227	(800) 294-1644	(305) 294-5692	$$$$–	23		✔
(305) 885-1941	(800) HOLIDAY	(305) 884-1881	$$$+	217	✔	✔
(305) 294-2571	(800) 292-7706	(305) 296-5659	$$$$–	222	✔	✔
(305) 443-2301	(800) HOLIDAY	(305) 446-6827	$$$$	168	✔	✔
(305) 374-3000	(800) HOLIDAY	(305) 374-5897	$$$+	258	✔	✔
(305) 451-2121	(800) THE-KEYS	(305) 451-5592	$$$$+	132	✔	✔

Hotel	Room Rating	Zone	Street Address
Holiday Inn La Concha	★★★½	5	430 Duval Street Key West, FL 33040
Holiday Inn Marathon	★★★	5	13201 Overseas Highway Marathon, FL 33050
Holiday Inn Select LeJeune Center	★★★	2	950 NW LeJeune Road Miami, FL 33126
Hotel Astor	★★★★½	1	956 Washington Avenue Miami Beach, FL 33139
Hotel Delano	★★★★½	1	1685 Collins Avenue Miami Beach, FL 33139
Hotel Impala	★★★★	1	1228 Collins Avenue Miami Beach, FL 33139
Hotel Intercontinental	★★★★½	3	100 Chopin Plaza Miami, FL 33131
Hotel Place St. Michel	★★★★	3	162 Alcazar Avenue Coral Gables, FL 33134
Hotel Sofitel	★★★★½	2	5800 Blue Lagoon Drive Miami, FL 33126
Howard Johnson Airport West	★★½	2	7330 NW 36th Street Miami, FL 33166
Howard Johnson Miami Airport	★★½	2	1850 NW LeJeune Road Miami, FL 33126
Howard Johnson Motor Lodge	★★½	5	3031 N. Roosevelt Boulevard Key West, FL 33040
Howard Johnson Port of Miami	★★★	3	1100 Biscayne Boulevard Miami, FL 33132
Howard Johnson Resort Key Largo	★★★	5	102 Overseas Highway Key Largo, FL 33037
Hyatt Key West Resort & Marina	★★★★	5	601 Front Street Key West, FL 33040
Hyatt Regency Coral Gables	★★★★½	3	50 Alhambra Plaza Coral Gables, FL 33134
Hyatt Regency Miami	★★★★	3	400 SE Second Avenue Miami, FL 33132
Indian Creek Hotel	★★★½	1	2727 Indian Creek Drive Miami Beach, FL 33140
Island City House Hotel	★★★★	5	411 William Street Key West, FL 33040

Local Phone	Toll-Free Res. Line	Fax	Rack Rate	No. of Rooms	On-Site Dining	Pool
(305) 296-2991	(800) 745-2191	(305) 294-3283	$$$$ $$$–	160	✔	✔
(305) 289-0222	(800) 224-5053	(305) 743-5460	$$$+	116	✔	✔
(305) 446-9000	(800) 465-4329	441-0725	$$$$+	304	✔	✔
(305) 531-8081	(800) 270-4981	(305) 531-3193	$$$$$	42	✔	✔
(305) 672-2000	(800) 555-5001	(305) 674-6499	$$$$$ $$$$+	208	✔	✔
(305) 673-2021	(800) 646-7252	(305) 673-5984	$$$ $$–	17		
(305) 577-1000	(800) 327-0200	(305) 577-0384	$$$ $$+	644	✔	✔
(305) 444-1666	(800) 848-4683	(305) 529-0074	$$$$+	27	✔	
(305) 264-4888	(800) 258-4888	(305) 266-7161	$$$ $$+	281	✔	✔
(305) 592-5440	(800) 446-4656	(305) 477-8155	$$+	120		✔
(305) 871-4350	(800) 446-4656	(305) 871-6810	$$$–	244	✔	✔
(305) 296-6595	(800) 654-2000	(305) 296-8351	$$$+	64	✔	✔
(305) 358-3080	(800) 654-2000	(305) 358-8631	$$+	115	✔	✔
(305) 451-1400	(800) 947-7320	(305) 451-3953	$$$ $$–	100	✔	✔
(305) 296-9900	(800) 554-9288	(305) 292-1038	$$$$ $$$$–	120	✔	✔
(305) 441-1234	(800) 233-1234	(305) 441-0520	$$$$ $$$$–	242	✔	✔
(305) 358-1234	(800) 233-1234	(305) 358-0529	$$$$$	615	✔	✔
(305) 531-2727	(800) 491-2772	(305) 531-5651	$$$$–	61		✔
(305) 294-5702	(800) 634-8230	(305) 294-1289	$$$ $$–	24		✔

Hotel	Room Rating	Zone	Street Address
Islander Motel	★★	5	Overseas Highway Mile Marker 82.1 Islamorada, FL 33036
Kent Hotel	★★★½	1	1131 Collins Avenue Miami Beach, FL 33139
Key Lodge Motel	★★	5	1004-1 Duval Street Key West, FL 33040
La Mer Hotel	★★★★	5	506 South Street Key West, FL 33040
La Quinta Miami Airport	★★½	2	7401 NW 36th Street Miami, FL 33166
La Te Da	★★★½	5	1125 Duval Street Key West, FL 33040
Leslie Hotel	★★★	1	1244 Ocean Drive Miami Beach, FL 33139
Lily Guesthouse	★★★½	1	835 Collins Avenue Miami Beach, FL 33139
LTI Seville Beach Hotel	★★★	1	2901 Collins Avenue Miami Beach, FL 33140
Majestic Hotel	★★★	1	660 Ocean Drive Miami Beach, FL 33139
Marina Del Mar Resort	★★½	5	527 Caribbean Drive Key Largo, FL 33037
Marlin	★★★★★	1	1200 Collins Avenue Miami Beach, FL 33139
Marriott Biscayne Bay	★★★★	3	1633 N. Bayshore Drive Miami, FL 33132
Marriott Key Largo Bay Beach Resort	★★★★	5	103800 Overseas Highway Key Largo, FL 33037
Marriott's Casa Marina Resort	★★★★	5	1500 Reynolds Street Key West, FL 33040
Marriott's Reach Resort	★★★★	5	1435 Simonton Street Key West, FL 33040
Marseilles Hotel	★★★	1	1741 Collins Avenue Miami Beach, FL 33139
Mayfair House Hotel	★★★★★	3	3000 Florida Avenue Coconut Grove, FL 33133
Mermaid Guest House	★★★	1	909 Collins Avenue Miami Beach, FL 33139

Local Phone	Toll-Free Res. Line	Fax	Rack Rate	No. of Rooms	On-Site Dining	Pool
(305) 664-2031	na	(305) 664-5503	$$+	114		✔
(305) 604-5000	(800) 688-7678	(305) 531-0720	$$$$–	53		✔
(305) 296-9915	(800) 458-1296	na	$$$$–	23		✔
(305) 296-5611	(800) 354-4455	(305) 294-8272	$$$ $$–	11		✔
(305) 599-9902	(800) 531-5900	(305) 594-0552	$$+	165		✔
(305) 296-6706	(800) 528-3320	(305) 296-0438	$$–	16	✔	✔
(305) 534-2135	(800) 688-7678	(305) 672-2881	$$$$$	40	✔	
(305) 535-9900	na	(305) 535-0077	$$$$–	18		
(305) 532-2511	(800) 327-1641	(305) 673-1592	$$$$	318	✔	✔
(305) 538-0133	(800) 933-3306	(305) 534-0258	$$$+	106	✔	
(305) 451-4107	(800) 451-3483	(305) 451-1891	$$$+	76	✔	✔
(305) 673-8770	(800) 688-7678	(305) 672-2881	$$$$ $$$$–	12	✔	
(305) 374-3900	(800) 228-9290	(305) 375-0597	$$$ $$–	603	✔	✔
(305) 453-0000	(800) 932-9332	(305) 453-0093	$$$ $$+	149	✔	✔
(305) 296-3535	(800) 626-0777	(305) 296-3008	$$$$ $$$–	311	✔	✔
(305) 296-5000	(800) 626-0777	(305) 296-3008	$$$$ $$$–	149	✔	✔
(305) 538-5711	(800) 327-4739	(305) 673-1006	$$$+	112	✔	✔
(305) 441-0000	(800) 433-4555	(305) 447-9173	$$$ $$$+	179	✔	✔
(305) 538-5324	na	(305) 538-2822	$$$–	10		

Hotel	Room Rating	Zone	Street Address
Miami Airport Courtyard South	★★★½	2	1201 NW LeJeune Road Miami, FL 33126
Miami Airport Fairfield Inn South	★★½	2	1201 NW LeJeune Road Miami, FL 33126
Miami Airport Hilton & Towers	★★★★	2	5101 Blue Lagoon Drive Miami, FL 33126
Miami Airport Marriott	★★★½	2	1201 NW LeJeune Road Miami, FL 33126
Miami Beach Ocean Resort	★★★½	1	3025 Collins Avenue Miami Beach, FL 33140
Nancy's William Street Guest House	★★½	5	329 William Street Key West, FL 33040
National Hotel	★★★	1	1677 Collins Avenue Miami Beach, FL 33139
Newport Beachside Crowne Plaza Resort	★★★½	1	16701 Collins Avenue Miami Beach, FL 33160
Ocean Front Hotel	★★★★½	1	1230 Ocean Drive Miami Beach, FL 33139
Ocean Key House Suite Resort & Marina	★★★★	5	Zero Duval Street Key West, FL 33040
Omni Colonnade Hotel	★★★★½	3	180 Aragon Avenue Coral Gables, FL 33134
Paradise Inn	★★	1	8520 Harding Avenue Miami Beach, FL 33141
Park Central Imperial Hotels	★★★	1	640 Ocean Drive Miami Beach, FL 33139
Pelican Cove Resort	★★½	5	84457 Overseas Highway Islamorada, FL 33036
Penguin Hotel	★★½	1	1418 Ocean Drive Miami Beach, FL 33139
Pier House	★★★½	5	One Duval Street Key West, FL 33040
Popp's Motel	★★	5	95500 Overseas Highway Key Largo, FL 33037
Princess Ann Hotel	★★	1	920 Collins Avenue Miami Beach, FL 33139
Quality Inn Key West	★★★	5	3850 N. Roosevelt Boulevard Key West, Fl 33040

Local Phone	Toll-Free Res. Line	Fax	Rack Rate	No. of Rooms	On-Site Dining	Pool
(305) 642-8200	(800) 228-9290	(305) 644-1168	$$$+	126		✔
(305) 643-0055	(800) 228-9290	(305) 649-3997	$$+	282	✔	✔
(305) 262-1000	(800) HILTONS	(305) 267-0038	$$$ $$$–	500	✔	✔
(305) 649-5000	(800) 228-9290	(305) 642-3369	$$$$	365	✔	✔
(305) 534-0505	(800) 550-0505	(305) 534-0515	$$$ $$–	245	✔	✔
(305) 744-7207	(800) 71-NANCY	(305) 296-1740	$$$$+	6		✔
(305) 532-2311	(800) 327-8370	(305) 534-1426	$$$ $$$+	154	✔	✔
(305) 949-1300	(800) 327-5476	(305) 947-5873	$$$ $$–	355	✔	✔
(305) 672-2579	(800) 783-1725	(305) 672-7665	$$$ $$+	27	✔	
(305) 296-7701	(800) 328-9815	(305) 292-7685	$$$$$ $$$$–	95	✔	✔
(305) 441-2600	(800) 843-6664	(305) 445-3929	$$$ $$$+	157	✔	✔
(305) 865-6216	(800) 683-3311	(305) 865-9028	$+	96		✔
(305) 538-1611	(800) 727-5236	(305) 534-3408	$$$$	128	✔	✔
(305) 664-4435	(800) 445-4690	(305) 664-5134	$$$ $$–	63	✔	✔
(305) 534-9334	(800) 235-3296	(305) 672-6240	$$$	44	✔	
(305) 296-4600	(800) 327-8340	(305) 296-9085	$$$$$ $$$$–	142	✔	✔
(305) 852-5201	na	(305) 852-5200	$$+	9		
(305) 534-2196	na	na	$$+	45		
(305) 294-6681	(800) 533-5024	(305) 294-5618	$$$$–	148	✔	✔

Hotel	Room Rating	Zone	Street Address
Radisson Mart Plaza	★★★★	2	7111 NW 72nd Avenue Miami, FL 33126
Raleigh Hotel	★★	1	1775 Collins Avenue Miami Beach, FL 33139
Ramada Inn Key West	★★½	5	3420 N. Roosevelt Boulevard Key West, FL 33040
Ramada Limited Resort & Marina	★★★	5	99751 Overseas Highway Key Largo, FL 33037
Red Roof Inn Airport	★★½	2	3401 NW LeJeune Road Miami, FL 33142
Riande Continental	★★★½	1	1825 Collins Avenue Miami Beach, FL 33139
Riande Continental Miami Bayside	★★★	3	146 Biscayne Boulevard Miami, FL 33132
Ritz Plaza Hotel	★★★	1	1701 Collins Avenue Miami Beach, FL 33139
RIU Pan American Ocean Resort	★★★½	1	17875 Collins Avenue Sunny Isles, FL 33160
Santa Maria Motel	★★½	5	1401 Simonton Street Key West, FL 33040
Sea View Hotel	★★★★	1	9909 Collins Avenue Bal Harbour, FL 33154
Seascape	★★★½	5	1075 75th Street Marathon, FL 33050
Shelborne Beach Hotel	★★★½	1	1801 Collins Avenue Miami Beach, FL 33139
Sheraton Bal Harbour Resort	★★★★	1	9701 Collins Avenue Bal Harbour, FL 33154
Sheraton Biscayne Bay	★★★½	3	495 Brickell Avenue Miami, FL 33131
Sheraton Gateway	★★★½	2	3900 NW 21st Street Miami, FL 33142
Sheraton Suites Key West	★★★★	5	2001 S. Roosevelt Boulevard Key West, FL 33040
Sol Miami Beach Hotel	★★½	1	3925 Collins Avenue Miami Beach, FL 33140
Sonesta Beach Resort	★★★½	3	350 Ocean Drive Key Biscayne, FL 33149

Local Phone	Toll-Free Res. Line	Fax	Rack Rate	No. of Rooms	On-Site Dining	Pool
(305) 261-3800	(800) 333-3333	(305) 261-7665	$$$ $$$–	334	✔	✔
(305) 534-6300	(800) 848-1775	(305) 538-8140	$$$ $$$+	107	✔	✔
(305) 294-5541	(800) 228-2828	(305) 294-7932	$$$$	104	✔	✔
(305) 451-3939	(800) THE KEYS	(305) 453-0222	$$$$	90		✔
(305) 871-4221	(800) RED ROOF	(305) 871-3933	$$$–	155		✔
(305) 531-3503	(800) RIANDE-1	(305) 531-2803	$$$$–	260	✔	✔
(305) 358-4555	(800) RIANDE-1	(305) 532-7689	$$$+	250	✔	
(305) 534-3500	(800) 522-6400	(305) 531-6928	$$$ $$$+	132	✔	✔
(305) 932-1100	(800) 327-5678	(305) 604-3326	$$$ $$–	148	✔	✔
(305) 296-5678	(800) 821-5397	(305) 294-0010	$$$–	51		✔
(305) 866-4441	(800) 447-1010	(305) 866-1898	$$$ $$$–	200	✔	✔
(305) 743-6455	(800) 332-SEAS	(305) 743-8469	$$$+	10		✔
(305) 531-1271	(800) 327-8757	(305) 531-2206	$$$ $$$–	280	✔	✔
(305) 865-7511	(800) 999-9898	(305) 864-2601	$$$$ $$$$–	644	✔	✔
(305) 373-6000	(800) 284-2000	(305) 374-6619	$$$$$	598	✔	✔
(305) 871-3800	(800) 933-1100	(305) 871-0954	$$$ $$–	408	✔	✔
(305) 292-9800	(800) 452-3224	(305) 294-6009	$$$$$ $$$$$–	180	✔	✔
(305) 531-3534	(800) 531-3534	(305) 531-1765	$$$$–	268	✔	✔
(305) 361-2021	(800) SONESTA	(305) 365-2082	$$$$ $$$$+	295	✔	✔

Hotel	Room Rating	Zone	Street Address
South Beach Oceanfront Motel	★★½	5	508 South Street Key West, FL 33040
South Beach Resort	★★½	1	2201 Collins Avenue Miami Beach, FL 33139
Southernmost Motel in the USA	★★½	5	1319 Duval Street Key West, FL 33040
Tudor Hotel	★★★	1	1111 Collins Avenue Miami Beach, FL 33139
Waldorf Towers Hotel	★★★	1	860 Ocean Drive Miami Beach, FL 33139
Wellesley Inns Airport West	★★★	2	8436 NW 36th Street Miami, FL 33166
Westin Beach Resort Key Largo	★★★½	5	97000 S. Overseas Highway Key Largo, FL 33037
Westin Resort Miami Beach	★★★★½	1	4833 Collins Avenue Miami Beach, FL 33140
Winterhaven Hotel	★★	1	1400 Ocean Drive Miami Beach, FL 33139
Wyndham Miami	★★★★	3	1601 Biscayne Boulevard Miami, FL 33132

Local Phone	Toll-Free Res. Line	Fax	Rack Rate	No. of Rooms	On-Site Dining	Pool
(305) 296-5611	(800) 354-4455	(305) 294-8272	$$$$+	47		✔
(305) 534-1511	(800) 356-6902	(305) 532-0854	$$$$	354	✔	✔
(305) 296-6577	(800) 354-4455	(305) 294-8272	$$$ $$–	127	✔	✔
(305) 534-2934	(800) 843-2934	(305) 531-1874	$$$+	120	✔	
(305) 531-7684	(800) 933-2322	(305) 672-6836	$$$+	45	✔	
(305) 592-4799	(800) 444-8888	(305) 471-8461	$$$–	106		✔
(305) 852-5553	(800) 539-5724	(305) 852-5198	$$$$$ $$$$$–	200	✔	✔
(305) 532-3600	(800) WESTIN-1	(305) 532-2334	$$$$ $$$–	423	✔	✔
(305) 531-5571	(800) 395-2322	(305) 538-3337	$$$+	64	✔	
(305) 374-0000	(800) 332-0232	(305) 374-0020	$$$$ $$$+	528	✔	✔

Index

1998 *Unofficial Guide* Reader Survey

If you would like to express your opinion about Miami or this guidebook, complete the following survey and mail it to:

> 1998 *Unofficial Guide* Reader Survey
> PO Box 43059
> Birmingham AL 35243

Inclusive dates of your visit: ______________________________

Members of your party:	Person 1	Person 2	Person 3	Person 4	Person 5
Gender:	M F	M F	M F	M F	M F
Age:					

How many times have you been to Miami? ______________

On your most recent trip, where did you stay? ______________

Concerning your accommodations, on a scale of 100 as best and 0 as worst, how would you rate:

The quality of your room? ____ The value of your room? ____
The quietness of your room? ____ Check-in/check-out efficiency? ____
Shuttle service to the parks? ____ Swimming pool facilities? ____

Did you rent a car? ____________ From whom? ______________

Concerning your rental car, on a scale of 100 as best and 0 as worst, how would you rate:

Pick-up processing efficiency? ___ Return processing efficiency? ___
Condition of the car? ___ Cleanliness of the car? ___
Airport shuttle efficiency? ___

Concerning your dining experiences:

Including fast-food, estimate your meals in restaurants per day? ________
Approximately how much did your party spend on meals per day? ______
Favorite restaurants in Miami: ______________________

____

Did you buy this guide before leaving? ☐ while on your trip? ☐

How did you hear about this guide? (check all that apply)

Loaned or recommended by a friend ☐ Radio or TV ☐
Newspaper or magazine ☐ Bookstore salesperson ☐
Just picked it out on my own ☐ Library ☐
Internet ☐

1998 *Unofficial Guide* Reader Survey (continued)

What other guidebooks did you use on this trip? ____________________

____

____

____

On a scale of 100 as best and 0 as worst, how would you rate them?

____

____

____

Using the same scale, how would you rate *The Unofficial Guide(s)?*

____

Are *Unofficial Guides* readily available at bookstores in your area? __________

Have you used other *Unofficial Guides?* ____________________

Which one(s)? ____________________

____

____

____

____

____

Comments about your Miami trip or *The Unofficial Guide(s):*

____

____

____

____

____

____

____

____

____

____

____

____

____

____

____